On Animation
The Director's Perspective
VOLUME 1

On Animation
The Director's Perspective
VOLUME 1

Editor
Ron Diamond

Interviewers
Bill Kroyer and Tom Sito

Associate Editors
James Brusuelas and Tom Knott

CRC Press
Taylor & Francis Group
Boca Raton London New York

CRC Press is an imprint of the
Taylor & Francis Group, an **informa** business

Associate Editors: James Brusuelas and Tom Knott
Cover design by Alan Bodner (bodnerart.com)

CRC Press
Taylor & Francis Group
6000 Broken Sound Parkway NW, Suite 300
Boca Raton, FL 33487-2742

International Standard Book Number-13: 978-1-138-06653-3 (Paperback)
978-1-138-06707-3 (Hardback)

Library of Congress Cataloging-in-Publication Data

Names: Sito, Tom, 1956- interviewer. | Kroyer, Bill, interviewer. | Diamond, Ron, editor.
Title: On animation : the director's perspective / Ron Diamond.
Description: Boca Raton, FL : CRC Press, Taylor & Francis Group, 2019-
Identifiers: LCCN 2017014453| ISBN 9781138067073 (v. 1 : hardback : alk. paper) | ISBN 9781138066533 (v. 1 : pbk. : alk. paper) | ISBN 9781138066564 (v. 2) | ISBN 1138066567 (v. 2)
Subjects: LCSH: Animation (Cinematography) | Animators--Interviews.
Classification: LCC TR897.5 .O5 2019 | DDC 777/.7--dc23
LC record available at https://lccn.loc.gov/2017014453

Visit the Taylor & Francis Web site at
http://www.taylorandfrancis.com

and the CRC Press Web site at
http://www.crcpress.com

For Lisa, Sara, and Anna

CONTENTS

FOREWORD

My love affair with animation started around 1962 not with a movie in a theater, but with an album on a record player. It was a 78 RPM of "Cinderella," with songs and story. I carried it around our house on a small portable turntable and listened to "Bibbidi-Bobbidi-Boo," "A Dream Is a Wish Your Heart Makes," the entire soundtrack really, ad nauseam.

Such is the magic of animated films. The great ones (and there are so many great ones) become so powerfully ingrained in our culture that a little girl can fall hopelessly in love with animation just by listening to the music.

I'm sure that, on more than one occasion, my parents were tempted to break that scratchy record, but instead they let my love affair deepen. I am forever grateful they were so tolerant because, improbably enough, 30 years later animation would become my career … and my passion.

In 1992, I began work as the producer of *Toy Story*. At the time, I had only worked in live action and had just come off of *Dances with Wolves* and *The Addams Family*. Live action and animation are very different expressions of the film art form (I describe it as the difference between a sprint and a marathon), but at the center of both is the director.

And now, as I start development on my eighth animated feature, I think about the creative team that will collaborate on that film, and I am excited to meet the person who will be the director.

The directors featured in this collection of interviews are masters of the art. Each has a different way of working and brings something entirely unique to the mix. Each has a specialty, whether it is traditional animation, computer animation, or stop-motion. Using imagery, words, and music, they have taken audiences on imaginative journeys to amazing worlds inhabited by unforgettable characters, and created some of the most beloved family entertainment of all time. We and our children, and even our children's children, have watched and re-watched these outstanding pieces of storytelling.

I consider myself very fortunate to know them all and have worked with most. We've been through it all together; the hard work, the long hours, the good days and bad days, the redo, the notes, and ultimately the anxiety-inducing opening weekend.

Thanks to this book, you'll get to know them as well. Bill Kroyer and Tom Sito have spent several years asking questions about how these animation directors got started, how their life experiences influenced their work, what is their process, how do they maintain their vision and still collaborate with their team, what are their biggest challenges, and what brings them joy.

I know that after you spend some time with these incredible individuals, you will have a greater appreciation for the role of the animation director in conjuring up the extraordinary magic of an animated film.

Bonnie Arnold
Producer
DreamWorks Animation

ACKNOWLEDGMENTS

Coming up with the idea for this book was the easy part; making it happen took the combined efforts and enthusiasm of many people over many years. For starters, if it weren't for Ed Catmull, former President of Walt Disney Animation Studios and Pixar Animation Studios, this book would have not have been possible. When I reached out to Ed and told him about the idea, he immediately expressed interest and gave the book his blessing. This opened the doors to meet with the directors who were currently working at Disney, and allowed us to license many critical images, since so many of the directors in the book at one time or another worked at what many referred to as "Disney's." From the beginning to the end, the next most essential person was my friend of over 30 years, animation and VR producer, recruiter, and former director of the Ottawa International Animation Festival, Tom Knott. Tom oversaw the lion's share of the image selection, clearances, and communication with the directors and the studios. Without Tom's significant support and diligent work, this book would not exist.

I'd like to thank Bill Kroyer and Tom Sito for their tireless devotion in researching and interviewing the directors, and for welcoming me as I'd chime in with questions of my own during the interviews. And for their participation, candor, and honesty in sharing their experiences and expertise and giving us a glimpse into their inner worlds, the directors themselves (in the order they appear in the book): John Musker, Ron Clements, John Lasseter, Andrew Stanton, Brenda Chapman, Nick Park, Tomm Moore, Chris Wedge, Roger Allers, Chris Buck, Tim Johnson, Bill Plympton, Brad Bird, Henry Selick, Don Bluth, Pete Docter, Chris Sanders, Dean DeBlois, Vicky Jenson, Rob Minkoff, Jennifer Yuh Nelson, Carlos Saldanha, and Kevin Lima.

Special thanks to our tireless editors James Brusuelas, Jon Hofferman, and Carol Frank, to Bonnie Arnold for a fantastic Foreword, and to Alan Bodner for beautiful cover designs.

Early in the process, we were supported greatly by Dan Sarto, co-founder and COO of AWN, Inc., editors Bill Desowitz and Rick DeMott, and interim coordinator Aria Stewart.

Sincere thanks to all of the studio contacts who facilitated the interviews and the clearance of images: Chris Wiggum, Margaret Adamic, Maxine Raley, Gregory Coleman, Wendy Lefkon, Heather Feng-Yanu, Michelle Moretta, Victoria Manley, Marguerite Enright, Leigh Anna MacFadden, Christine Freeman, Debby Coleman, Kiera McAuliffe, Alex Ambrose, Mary Walsh, Fox Carney, Michael Buckhoff, Dave Bossert, Victoria Thornbery, Jerry Rees, Jessica Roberts, Katie Smith, Julia Reeves, Shelley Gorelik, Melanie Bartlett, Casie Nguyen,

Andy Bandit, Lucy Manos, Brook Worley, Laura Baltzer, Patrick Skelly, Jerry Schmitz, Richard Hamilton, David Hail, Beverly Moyer, Michael Garcia, Chase Schultz, Daniel Chun, David Hall, Cathleen Girdner, Kim Kline, Lillian Ritchie, Justin Melillo, Waiolo Shannon, Robbin Kelley, Shanna Robalino, Noreen Ong, Gary Goldman, Kip Goldman, Gabrielle Ruffle, Angie Last, Deborah Rouse, Heather Koopmans, Megan Bradford, Rosemary Colliver, Jenniphur Ryan, Mark Shapiro, Yael Gabbay, Owen Miller, Lorne Mitchell, Julie Heath, Jacklyn Pomales, Margarita Diaz, Andy Jeyes, Roni Lubliner, and Desiree Meade.

A massive thanks to the Acme Filmworks studio crew and the interns for their dedication and support: George Khair, Misty Myers, Diane Schlactus, Masha Evans, Kaitlyn Cavanagh, Josephine Moss, Tara Beyhm, Kelsey Peterson, Hae-Joon Lee, Amy Lee, Christian Kemabia, Helen Shi, Kerin Amit, Nolan Nissle, Dhanesh Jameson, and Molly Tomecek.

And, last but not least, thanks to Lisa Frank, Sara Diamond, Anna Diamond, Mark Diamond, Debi Perluss, Isaac Diamond, Dan Sarto, Debbie Sarto, Becky Sarto, and Nikki Sarto for unbridled support, love, and encouragement.

Tom Knott also offers personal thanks to Will Ryan, Shannon Tindle, and Ann Knott.

Ron Diamond
Executive Producer

EDITORS

Ron Diamond founded ACME Filmworks in 1990 to create commercials, shorts, and long-form animated projects with more than 50 notable international animation artist storytellers. In addition to producing over 1600 commercials, Ron produced the TV Series *Drew Carey's Green Screen Show* for the WB Network and *Drawn from Memory* for PBS' American Playhouse. He is a recognized expert on international animation and lectures at schools and animation festivals worldwide. He curates specialty animation programs for festivals. Since 1998, he curates *The Animation Show of Shows*, a feature length movie comprising new notable international animated shorts; presents them at the major animation studios, tech companies, game companies, animation schools, and animation festivals; and releases them for the general public. He co-founded the Animation World Network (AWN.com) in 1996.

Bill Kroyer is an Oscar-nominated director of animation and computer graphics commercials, short films, movie titles, and theatrical films. Trained in classic hand-drawn animation at the Disney studio, Bill was one of the first animators to make the leap to computer animation as computer image choreographer on Disney's ground-breaking 1982 feature *TRON*. He pioneered the technique of combining hand-drawn animation with computer animation on projects such as his theatrical animated feature film *FernGully: The Last Rainforest* and his short film *Technological Threat*. As senior animation director at Rhythm & Hues Studios, he directed animation on scores of commercials and many feature films, including *Cats and Dogs*, *Garfield*, and *Scooby Doo*. Bill served as co-chair of the Science and Technology Council of the Academy of Motion Picture Arts and Sciences and is a governor of the Academy's Short Films and Feature Animation branch. He is a tenured professor and is director of digital arts at the Dodge College of Film and Media Arts at Chapman University in Orange, California. In 2017, Bill and his wife Sue received the prestigious June Foray Award from the International Animation Society (ASIFA) for significant contributions to the art and industry of animation.

Tom Sito is an animator, animation historian, and professor of animation at the University of Southern California, Los Angeles. His movie credits include Walt Disney's *Beauty and the Beast* (1991), *Who Framed Roger Rabbit* (1988), *The Little Mermaid* (1989), *Aladdin* (1992), *The Lion King* (1994), *Pocahontas* (1995), and *DreamWorks' Shrek* (2001), and *Osmosis Jones* (2001). He has worked on television series such as the *Super Friends* (1978) and *He-Man and the Masters of the Universe* (1983). He is president emeritus of the Animation Guild, Local 839 Hollywood and on the Board of Governors of the Motion Picture Academy of Arts & Sciences. He received the June Foray Award in 2011 and the Dusty Outstanding Alumni Award in 2016. He is the author of several books: *Drawing the Line: The Untold Story of the Animation Unions from Bosko to Bart Simpson* (University of Kentucky Press, 2006), *Timing for Animation,* 2nd Edition (CRC Press/A Focal Press Book, 2009) *Moving Innovation: A History of Computer Animation* (MIT Press, 2013), and *Eat, Drink, Animate: An Animators Cookbook* (CRC Press, 2019). In 2014, he was featured in the PBS American Experience documentary *Walt Disney*.

INTRODUCTION

Animation. Not a day goes by that I don't think about it. Animated images dance through my head: memories of favorite films, snippets of past projects, abstract shapes, and evocative faces. While I work in animation, I don't believe I'm alone in this obsession. For vast numbers of people throughout the world, animation is a singularly rich art form, encompassing some of the most profound and pleasurable cinematic moments we have experienced.

As with all forms of artistic expression, each creation is measured by the success of its realization. However, in animation, the road to a finished product is especially daunting, and the challenges facing an animation director must be met with an especially high degree of resourcefulness, insight, and endurance. In feature animation production, a director must collaborate with multiple teams of highly skilled artists, storytellers, engineers, composers, lyricists, musicians, and producers in an immensely labor-intensive undertaking. To carry forward a personal vision in a process that can take 5 to 7 years, sometimes even longer, requires extraordinary persistence, tenacity, and commitment.

The demands on a director, or in some cases a two-director team, frequently include an in-depth knowledge of fine art, literature, theater, animation, and cinema history, as well as highly refined skills in communication, writing, humor, stagecraft, performance, design, painting, draftsmanship, visual effects, music, camera, lighting, and editing. They must also have the ability to helm a nine-figure production employing the skills of dozens—if not hundreds—of experts and to draw out of them the best they have to offer. And, on top of all that, they must tell a great and beautiful story that appeals to a large and diverse audience.

They must be able to defend their ideas and to challenge them as well, to construct a formidable production plan, and also be ready to tear it down and rethink it if the story isn't working or the characters aren't just right. This is what it takes to be an animated feature film director—as well as to be able to retain a sense of humor, to keep working when exhausted, and to meet crazy deadlines imposed by others or, worse yet, by oneself.

This book is about the blood, sweat, and tears of the craft of animation direction at the most complex levels—but it's also about inspiration and faith in oneself. I believe that by learning more about these artists' personal histories—what grabbed them, often at a very early age—and compelled them to follow the path of animation, we can acquire a deeper understanding of their art and find greater enjoyment in their artistic creations.

For this book, we followed a few basic guidelines. The first was that, to be included, a director had to have directed at least two animated feature films. Apart from providing a baseline qualification (since, unfortunately, we couldn't include everyone), the idea was also to explore what it was like to direct a feature for the first time and how that experience differed from successive directing experiences. We were very interested in this learning process, and we hope you'll find it as fascinating as we did.

In addition, we wanted the directors to speak freely, to be unbridled in the telling of their experiences. We then worked with them to edit the work down to convey an honest and revealing story that clearly leads us through their journeys.

Finally, it was decided that fellow feature film directors should conduct the interviews, since who is better suited to ask informed questions and discuss the ins and outs and nuts and bolts of animation? This turned out to be an inspired idea; our two interviewers, Bill Kroyer and Tom Sito, were exemplary in drawing out the directors and in producing remarkably insightful discussions that have the pleasant familiarity of colleagues talking to colleagues.

I have been fortunate to have known several of these directors since their college days and others along the path and have stayed in touch with them throughout their careers. Their unmistakable glimmer of greatness was visible early on, and we are all the beneficiaries of their brilliance as they went on to direct some of the greatest animated features of our time. These interviews reveal commonalities of the collective experiences of some of our finest contemporary minds, and the lessons they learned. This is not just a book about approaches to animation production but also a primer on how to live a life filled with art, passion, giving, friendship, love, and contentment.

I am truly pleased to present this collection of 23 interviews in two volumes for you to enjoy. As for those directors who couldn't be included, we look forward to publishing future volumes in which we can get to know them and their stories as well.

Ron Diamond
Executive Producer

1
John Musker Interview

John Musker, © Walt Disney Co.
Courtesy: Everett Collection

You will not meet a more unassuming guy than John Musker. In his ubiquitous hooded sweatshirt, you would never guess he is one of the industry's most successful and acclaimed directors. We've known each other since we met in the old Disney training program, where we shared the infamous "Rat's Nest" (described in this interview). His "steel-trap memory," as I call it, allows him to remember things about my life that even I don't recall. It also makes for a fascinating reminiscence, as you will see.

That memory and razor-sharp observation skills bring a unique depth to his films, and have made him one of the industry's most feared caricaturists. In fact, his astounding output of hilarious, on-the-nose drawings caused the creation of The Walt Disney Studios' annual caricature show, now a three-decade-long tradition.

John doesn't just know stories, facts, and personalities. He knows art. He has a remarkable personal collection of prints, drawings, and posters, and it is that understanding of why they are wonderful that enriches his film design. He found a perfect partner in Ron Clements, and that duo have rightfully been acknowledged as having saved the fading medium of animated features with *The Little Mermaid*, the film that launched the second "golden age."

John is a solid midwestern kind of guy, and maybe that is why so many people in animation keep in touch with him, seek his advice, share insights, and look to him during tough times. For all his spectacular screen accomplishments, the small, personal film he drew all by himself to memorialize the passing of his good friend Joe Ranft is considered by most of us to be one of the most poignant works of animation art ever done.

We interviewed John in the "Hat Building" at The Walt Disney Studios.

Bill Kroyer

Bill: What started this affair with animation?

John: The Disney features I saw as a kid: *Sleeping Beauty, Pinocchio, One Hundred And One Dalmatians,* and the *Mickey Mouse Club* affected me very powerfully. They were seductive. They were fascinating to me. Certainly, I saw a lot of animation on television that also had a strong effect. I was a card-carrying member of the Huckleberry Hound Fan Club. I think I still have that membership card. I could give you the secret handshake, but then I'd have to kill you! I also got a huge dose of Warner Brothers cartoons on WGN TV in Chicago. Thank you, Ray Rayner and Garfield Goose.

Bill: When did you first realize that you might be involved in animation?

John: Weirdly enough, I think it was about the age of seven. I read Diane Disney Miller's biography of Walt Disney, her father. I don't know why. I was just really interested in animation, and I remember borrowing that book from the library. I was a middle-class blue-collar kid from Chicago. So I never owned any books. The local library also had Bob Thomas's book,

The Art of Animation, which was basically a promotional book for *Sleeping Beauty*. But it told how you do animation, and it was like a book of spells to me, a gateway into a secret world.

Bill: You checked that out of a public library at the ripe age of seven?

John: I did. I would have loved to own it. Years later, at CalArts, I saw my classmate John Lasseter with his own personal copy! Then I looked closer and saw "Whittier Public Library" on the spine. Wait a minute …

Bill: Did you keep it too?

John: No. I had to give it back. But I would check it out and give it back, check it out and give it back, and … that book was a revelation. Animation was an actual profession. It could be my job. As a kid I used to always draw, so I thought I would go to work for Walt Disney someday. That was at age seven or eight! I remember being very sad when Walt Disney died. I was only 13, and I really believed that I would work with the man one day, not just for the brand name. My interests did change over time, though. I used to write my future occupations on a paper taped to my bedroom door. I had an odd list of things, and they appeared there concurrently: submarine captain, private detective, priest, animator, astronaut. Most of these interests grew out of books I was reading. And, of course, this was the sixties. I methodically clipped all the articles out of the *Chicago Daily News* I could find on the space program. I was just fascinated by the adventures of folks like John Glenn and Alan Shepard.

Bill: Did you ever think of doing your own animation in grade school or high school?

John: In high school, I considered doing my own animated film. I think I had the Preston Blair book, and over one summer I was going to try to make an actual film. I even built myself a desk, as instructed by Preston Blair. Around the same time, I also discovered Zagreb Film, the Yugoslavian animation studio. I saw a huge Zagreb retrospective at the Chicago Film Festival.

Bill: You saw them on the big screen?

John: Yes, I did. I took the bus downtown and saw them at some big theatre. There were many short films by great director-animators like Grgic and Vukotic; every director had "ic" at the end of their name. I really loved those films. So the film that I was designing was very much influenced by them. It was a Zagreb-esque short. I don't remember the story exactly, but I think there was a guy playing a violin, a robot guy with roller skate shoes, and a girl. The guy with the violin is trying to impress the pretty girl. It was all pantomime. Over the course of the short, the guy can't make any headway with the girl, but sees how she is smitten with this roller skating robot. So he starts lopping off body parts and trading them with the robot who gives him the equivalent mechanical parts. He ultimately replaces everything and looks just like the robot, replacing his head last. But the irony is that the girl doesn't bite. She ultimately goes off with the robot, who now looks just like the guy did originally, while our schmuck hero is now stuck being a mechanical man.

Bill: How did you end up at Northwestern?

John: I went to Loyola Academy, a Jesuit high school, where I was strongly recommended, some might say forced, to study Latin, Greek, and Chinese. I was in the honors program. I didn't have a choice! And I'm Catholic—I'm used to following orders. Actually, I enjoyed learning Greek and Chinese. There was a fairly influential priest at my high school who told us we should explore the humanities broadly in college and not zero in on a profession right away. I thought that sounded right. There were no electives in my Catholic high school, certainly no art classes. I had to enroll at the Art Institute in Chicago for a summer. I was the cartoonist on my high school paper, "The Prep." I did caricatures of the faculty and fellow students. When high school was coming to an end, exploring the humanities was still stuck in my brain. I thought I would major in English and force myself to read the great books. I thought that would give me a broad background to work with. I still felt I was going to end up drawing somewhere. And in those days you couldn't really study animation in school. So, I went to Northwestern in the fall of 1971 to get this "humanities" education. In a way, my plan worked. I was, in fact, forced to read the greats: *The Great Gatsby*, Nabokov, Chaucer, Spenser, *The Decameron*, Dostoevsky, Conrad, Shakespeare, Dickens, Hemingway, etc. I also took art history classes, which I really enjoyed and got a lot out of.

Bill: You had no film instruction?

John: No, except for a film history class at Northwestern taught by Peter Wollen. I got to see *Potemkin*, *Citizen Kane*, and Godard, the classics. It was basically a film retrospective, and you had to write papers. In fact, the one I wrote about *Citizen Kane* seemed to impress Professor Wollen enough that he asked if I planned on going into film. In some way this encouraged me.

Bill: Did you do any drawing at Northwestern?

John: One art class. The school paper, *The Daily Northwestern*, already had an editorial cartoonist, so I didn't initially draw for it like I had my high school paper. But then, after about a year, the business manager of the *Daily*, Mark Freund, whom I had known in high school, approached me and said their cartoonist just retired (graduated). I had seen this fellow's cartoons—what was his name …? Oh yeah … Bill Kroyer was his name. Yeah, it was you! Of course, I said yes to drawing the cartoons. I think I was paid the massive sum of 25 dollars per week.

Bill: How does this lead to CalArts?

John: A few things happened. I heard Richard Williams, the great Canadian-British animator-director, speak very passionately about animation at a retrospective of his films at the Chicago Film Festival around 1972. And then there was a big "celebration" of animation at Northwestern itself in about 1973. I heard Chuck Jones speak at this event, and he showed a variety of his Warners cartoons that I hadn't really seen in years: *What's Opera, Doc?*, *One Froggy Evening*, *Feed the Kitty*. Great, great films. I was just amazed all over again. Chuck made animation sound like an actual career. More importantly, he impressed on me that you could still learn things even at a ripe old age. That sounded appealing to me. Then I read Christopher Finch's *The Art Of Walt Disney*, where he actually identified animators by name and described what characters they had done. He also mentioned a new training program for young animators. I immediately wrote to Disney and learned that I needed to put together a portfolio, which wasn't easy. I had to get drawings of animals. Now, of course, I was never around animals. I'm an Irish guy who grew up in a house with no animals 'cause my mother had terrible allergies (don't all the Irish?). So I went to the Lincoln Park Zoo in the dead of winter and drew the monkeys that were somehow enduring the Chicago cold. Those Chicago monkeys are tough. Me, not so much. Then I had an epiphany. I went to the Field Museum of Natural History, where they have the dioramas of all the animals. Bingo! They were not moving, they were very steady, and they were not in the bitter cold! Much easier to draw. Then I sent the portfolio off to Disney and I waited a few weeks. I was cautiously hopeful, but, unfortunately, got a "Dear John" rejection letter. They said my animal drawings were "stiff." Well of course! Those animals weren't just stiff, they were *stuffed*! They couldn't be stiffer! In a way, it was a compliment. I drew them exactly the way I saw them. That's when I had my first real "What do I do now?" moment. Then, oddly, I received another letter the following week.

Bill: From Disney?

John: Yeah, it was weird. Evidently, they thought I might have been confused, that maybe I meant to send the portfolio to CalArts. I had never heard of CalArts! Now, I had sworn never to go to graduate school. I was afraid of becoming a permanent student. I was terrified I would end up hiding from the real world in the safer world of academia. But I got over that angst, thinking that if I wanted to get into animation, this might somehow get me there, even if it seemed I was starting my college career all over. (I wasn't getting a master's; they had no such graduate degree in "character animation.") So I sent exactly the same portfolio to CalArts, and I got accepted! And it wasn't cheap. Ironically, my family visited California that summer on vacation while I had to remain home, earning money working at a hotel in order to help pay my schooling. They saw CalArts before I ever did. I arrived never having seen the school.

Bill: So you just went to California all by yourself?

John: All by my lonesome.

Bill: Did you even know how to get to the campus?

John: CalArts sent a van to pick people up at the airport. And in the van was a guy of slightly indeterminate gender, which was sort of eye-opening for me. California at this time was a completely different culture from Chicago. But over the course of the next few weeks, I got more comfortable with this new world. I met my fellow classmates, which included John Lasseter, Brad Bird, Doug Lefler, Jerry Rees, Bruce Morris, Darrell Van Citters, and Nancy Beiman, among others. Many of them knew more about animation than I did. Some of them had prior studio experience and could even recognize a certain animator by their style. They could pick out Milt Kahl's scenes or Freddie Moore's. This was pretty amazing to me, who had barely learned who these "greats" of Disney animation were. This was the very first year of CalArts "Character Animation" program (1975). Jack Hannah, a veteran director at Disney who had done Donald Duck and Chip and Dale shorts, ran the Character Animation program back then and also taught animation. Given that Jack spent the best years of his career directing, his "teaching" had more to do with gags and "business," the province of a story man and director, and little to do with the actual techniques of animating a character, bringing it to life convincingly. Elmer Plummer, who was a wonderful Millard Sheets–like watercolorist, who at Disney in the golden age had storyboarded the mushroom dance in *The Nutcracker Suite* in *Fantasia* and the roustabouts erecting the tent in the rain in *Dumbo*—he also Taught at Chouinards—was our figure-drawing teacher. Bill Moore, who had also taught at Chouinards, was our design professor. He was acerbic tough, and funny too. He was also the strongest and most influential teacher in the program. T. Hee, former Disney and UPA [United Productions of America] designer and director of rather portly frame, was by then something of an aging, rail-thin hippie. He taught caricature. And Ken O'Connor, great "layout man" from Disney who did brilliant staging in films like *Snow White*, *Fantasia*, *Cinderella*, *Peter Pan*, *Alice in Wonderland*, and many others, taught us layout, perspective, and staging. But my fellow classmates, Brad, John, Darrell, Jerry, Nancy, et al., they were so talented and knowledgeable about animation. In many ways, they were my teachers as well.

John Musker accepting the Elmer Award at Cal Arts.
Photo: Harry Sabin.

Bill: With a group like that, I would guess that you learned as much from them as you did the instructors.

John: Absolutely. We were a very collaborative group. Lots of give and take. If you asked me what the "model" for the Pixar studio was, I would say it was based on CalArts and the collegial atmosphere that we cultivated there.

Bill: You guys did a film in your first year, right?

John: Yes, I did a film. Although "film" is a bit misleading. It was more of a short test of pencil animation, just a string of a few cuts or "scenes," as we call shots in animation. At the end of the school year, unbeknownst to us, the Disney review board decided to pay a visit. So we put our figure drawings on display, we put up our design projects, we previewed our animation, and we even had wine and cheese. But it was all pencil tests, little scenes with no dialogue. I did two or three different scenes. One was a girl walking into a bar, kind of a pre–Jessica Rabbit, Lauren Bacall–esque noir girl. She slinks across a bar, spins on her heel, and sits down. In close-up, she takes a drag on a cigarette, blows smoke, and shoots a casual look in the direction of a burly bartender. That was it.

Bill: What did the Disney people say?

John: They liked it. Maybe because it involved drinking (a pastime occasionally embraced by some in the animation industry). They offered me a job based on that test. I was somewhat stunned. Of course, I was the same guy they had rejected a year before, but I wasn't about to point that out to them. It was so much to digest that I wasn't sure about jumping in right away. The thought of being instantly absorbed into the Disney and California landscape was scary. I still thought of myself as a Chicago guy, and my family was back there. But Disney was accommodating and proposed that I just work for a shorter summer stint and then return to school. They said I could work with Eric Larson, one of Disney's legendary "nine old men," the core group of animators who went all the way back to *Snow White*. Eric now mentored neophyte animators in the training program. I would work with him as an intern for six or eight weeks during the summer. I thought that was a better plan. I would learn what I could from Eric and then go back and finish another year of school. It also gave me more time to adjust and grow up, to warm up to the idea that I might have a life and a future in California. I still needed to break that bond with Chicago. So that summer I worked with Eric Larson. It was there that I met Betsy Baytos, a vivacious, young animation trainee, who also danced in the eccentric styles of the 1920s and was charmingly kooky. Eric was extremely helpful. He was a patient and revelatory mentor. He talked to me about concepts like arcs and staging. He was very big on clarity and action analysis rooted in the personality and the physicality of the character you were animating. He drew over your animation and showed how much stronger you could make it.

Bill: After your internship was over, you went back and finished school.

John: Well, I returned to school with the idea I'd apply what I learned from Eric that next year, get used to living in California, and then go to work for Disney full time after that. It was a fun year. I made another "film," a six-minute short that had a Chicago feel to it. There were a couple of greaser guys and this girl, who was actually a caricature of Betsy Baytos. She was the girl in the middle of this triangle, the one the guys are competing for. It was a bunch of gags, lots of fast timing, and very cartoony. Fortunately, I lucked out again. Disney liked it. Out of that second year, five people from the program were hired by Disney: Brad Bird, Jerry Rees, Henry Selick, Doug Lefler, and me. That was the summer of '77. In fact, I started at Disney the same week *Star Wars* opened. I hadn't heard of *Star Wars*. But everyone was going to see it. So I tagged along and waited in line at the Chinese Theatre with my new, similarly young and nerdy, fellow Disney animation brethren. That was the start of my Disney career.

Bill: So now you are in the training program with Eric …

John: I am in the training program. We were in a room next to Eric. I think there were four or five of us in that room. It was you, me, Brad, Henry, and Arland Barron, I believe. We were working on pencil tests with Eric. The first test I did for Eric, however, didn't go well at all. The review board didn't like it. I think they were on the verge of kicking me out.

Bill: You had to do what I did—a test in four weeks, right?

John: Right. You had to do a test and you had to get approved in order to continue. They may have let you in the door, but you had to prove you were capable of doing the job. You probably don't remember my test.

Bill: It was a big woman …

John: No, that was later. This was the skinny Sherlock Holmes–ish stork and a little hyper owl sidekick. Overall, it was rather scribbly and loose, so it didn't go well with the review board. Eric came back into the room with a long face, telling me that I needed to slow down and refine my scenes. On my next test, I did this Stromboli-esque guy again, still loosely drawn, but more tied down than the last one. It went over much better. Frank and Ollie called me in for a chat afterward, and told me what they thought worked well and what was less successful. It was amazing how supportive they were. I was really flying high that day.

Bill: But wasn't there another problem right after that test? I recall that they threw a tough challenge at us right away.

John: Yes, there was another test. The studio was desperate to get cleanup help on *Pete's Dragon*. There was a test to see who could do the carefully painstaking drawing that "cleanup" artists did, the final drawing of the characters before they are put in color.

Bill:	That's right.
John:	Yeah? Well you passed! Henry passed. He was and is an exceptional draftsman. Only those who had explicit control in their drawing passed that test. Brad Bird and I both flunked. People actually thought we "threw" the test to avoid doing cleanup! Not so. We we're really trying! But Brad's work came off scratchy, and mine wobbly. We just weren't good at the tight drawing necessary for cleanup. I think my lack of experience was still rearing its head. I still didn't even know how to do a really solid in-between.
Bill:	You did survive, though.
John:	I did. But there was still trouble ahead. There was conflict over who was going to direct *The Small One*. This was an animated Christmas featurette that was being readied as a training ground for the new animators that would prepare them for more complex work on upcoming features like *The Black Cauldron*. Eric Larson was set to direct it. But Don Bluth didn't like the "cartoony" direction that Eric was embracing. Don felt that for Disney animation to regain its former glory, he was the studios' best and only chance to revive its past. He should shape the new talent. Don argued his case to management who agreed. And suddenly, beloved Eric was no longer directing, and Don Bluth was! To make matters worse, Glen Keane's original designs for the piece—round, simple, animatable, and old school cartoony—were also removed. His designs were replaced by John Pomeroy's. John's work was more angular, rooted more in seventies' Disney than in the "rounder" forties' style that Glen and Eric were pursuing. So a schism began right there, between Don Bluth and some of the CalArts folk like Brad, Jerry, and myself. Eric was a direct connection to the classic Disney films we loved. And he taught us all. In our minds, he didn't deserve this demotion. So we went to work on *Small One*, but we were not happy campers. We were asked around this time to animate a ten-foot (about six seconds) scene that showed a character and an emotion, kind of an audition to see who would be made an "animating assistant" on *Small One*. Typically, I wound up going way over and did a scene about three times the length they asked. This was during the height of Farrah Fawcett mania. I did this test of a fat girl in a mirror with big, fluffy, Farrah Fawcett hair. She has the Farrah Fawcett smile, and she is tossing her long, blow-dried mane around coquettishly. But then she stops, takes a long look at her image, and sadly pulls her Farrah wig off. With her short hair revealed, she sinks down forlornly into her chair. Although it was way over length, they liked it well enough to promote me to "animating assistant," and I started to work officially on *Small One*. I was assigned to work with Cliff Nordberg, whose work was fairly broad and funny. He had worked on the cartoonier characters in the features with people like Ward Kimball, John Sibley, and Woolie Reitherman.
Bill:	He was a real veteran.
John:	I learned a lot from Cliff. I still feel like I really learned animation from you, the CalArts gang, and Eric Larson. But a lot came from Cliff, who was sort of my mentor. Cliff was an intuitive animator, a guy who went by his gut feeling. He didn't ponder a

character's soul. He was concerned with a character's physicality. If he was a heavy guy, then his weight would suggest the way he moved. Cliff would sort of act it out and draw as he went along. He would discuss things he had learned from Ward Kimball, the great animator of Jiminy Cricket, the crows in *Dumbo*, Lucifer the cat, and Jose Carioca. For example, Cliff told me that Ward said an animator must "look for the funny picture." That's a very simple way of saying that if there's a funny tableau in the scene, make sure you allow the audience to see that drawing. It must have enough time on it, be clearly staged, and there should be no distracting movements that might take away the impact of that "funny drawing." Working with Cliff was fun and instructive, but none of us CalArtians were too thrilled with *The Small One*, which was pretty far from our own tastes. We weren't fond of the designs, the animation, the staging, and the lack of creative input we had. Coming from the collaborative atmosphere of CalArts, this system seemed dictatorial and draconian and a far cry from the perhaps "rose-colored glasses" versions of the early days of Disney that we had heard about. Don had been in the business far longer than any of us. And he had complete confidence in his vision, his skills in story, animation, direction, and production values. So, not unexpectedly, Don didn't feel it was the place for the "new kids on the block" to be giving suggestions to a seasoned veteran.

Bill: **Is this when the mini-revolt occurred?**

John: Well, there was kind of a mini-rebellion. Don had his devoted followers, but a number of people were unhappy. That's when you, Bill, who was animating on *The Fox and the Hound*, tried to intervene on our behalf. It was not well received, and essentially disregarded. You suggested we take our case to Ron Miller, but we didn't see that as a realistic possibility.

Bill: **I went to Ron Miller to get him involved, not so much to subvert Don. But I think Don, when he found out what was going on …**

John: … was very unhappy. He came right downstairs to our bullpen office in D wing to settle things. We vented. It was at that meeting that he dubbed our room a "Rat's Nest" of innuendo. We took that name on happily. Henceforward, our room was the Rat's Nest, and Brad, Jerry, Bill, Henry, Dan Haskett, and me were the "Rats." Andy Gaskill was so amused at this he even designed a cool logo for us that we proudly displayed on our door (and which I have to this day).

Bill: **I remember that you talked more than all of us put together in that meeting. I think we were all kind of freaked! Don was a very aggressive guy.**

John: Don told us that Disney had always been a place with a strict hierarchy, with firm divisions between the established animators and newcomers. As recent hires with little experience, we were clearly in the group that should venture no opinions on the film.

Additionally, Don did not care for my animation or Brad Bird's either. So it made for a tense atmosphere. A group picture was taken at this time of the crew on *Small One*, including Don. I think I still have it. Lots of undercurrents in that picture!

Bill: **After that you were a staff animator on *The Fox and the Hound*.**

John: I was. And that movie had a tense atmosphere all its own. Woolie Reitherman was the producer on it but really was riding roughshod over Art Stevens, almost Woolie's contemporary, who was supposed to be directing. Frankly, Woolie had some ideas that were in questionable taste and rather far afield from the basic storyline. In Woolie's scenario, there was a sequence involving Charo, the blonde bombshell wife of Xavier Cougat. He cast her as the voice of a sexy flamingo. Woolie even shot live-action footage of Charo on the back lot, dancing in a bright pink leotard and sweating under the roasting, noonday Burbank sun! Oh to see that footage now! Anyway, I continued to work with Cliff Nordberg on the characters of Dinky and Boomer, a cartoony woodpecker and sparrow, the comic relief in the picture. For the most part, the storyline and sensibilities of *Fox and the Hound* weren't especially engaging to me. So during that time, I put much more of my creative focus toward courting this beautiful librarian Gale Warren, who worked down the hall in the studio library.

Bill: **But weren't your scenes used extensively in that movie?**

John: I did a pretty fair amount of animation. I did a lot of scenes containing the trio: Dinky, Boomer, and Big Mama. Director Ted Berman didn't always like my approach. There was a scene where the trio of characters were huddled conspiratorially, and then shot a sympathetic look at the little fox below them. I had them do it relatively in unison, partly because it seemed more entertaining that way. Ted felt it was too "Three Stooges" and had me stagger the timings on the looks to avoid any comic effect, which I did. And voilà, whatever faint comedy that once was there vanished instantly!

Bill: **Did anything change for you after that?**

John: The big thing that happened was that Don Bluth left. On September 13, his birthday, 1979, he left to do his own feature and took a handful of creative people with him. The studio was terrified. How would we finish *Fox and the Hound* without those folks? But ironically, because of this exodus, the studio needed animators to do the scenes Don and John had left behind, scenes involving the human characters, the Hunter and the Widow. Walt Stanchfield, a key cleanup artist and teacher, had seen some of my human drawings in the annual caricature show and liked them. So I was drafted to do a number of those scenes.

Bill: **Did you do any directing on *The Fox and the Hound*?**

John: No, I didn't. That came with *The Black Cauldron*. Tom Wilhite was an executive in the live-action end of Disney at the time. He was interested in giving young talent an arena to work in. He had gotten to know people like John Lasseter, Tim Burton, and myself and was looking for ways to get our voices into the films being made at the time. Tom was aware that *The Fox and the Hound* hadn't connected with some of the younger animators' sensibilities. He was concerned with bridging the gap between the senior leadership and the younger CalArts guys. Tom thought a younger director should join the veterans already in place, and after discussions with a number of people, approached me to fill that role. Now at that time, the job of lead animator was still the artistic zenith. Directors were thought of as just a necessary evil. I think I got drafted because I was a good listener, I was reasonably intelligent, and my animation wasn't regarded that highly. Losing me from the animation ranks was not thought of as a serious loss. So Tom convinced Ron I should be made a director to get a young voice in the room. Ron Miller called me up to his office, Walt's old one, and said, "How would you like to be a director?" My response was just very mealymouthed, in the extreme. I was interested, but I felt uncomfortable admitting any ambition, I think. Growing up in the Midwest, you don't toot your own horn. You never toot your own horn. So my reaction was not at all a ringing yes and probably not very reassuring to Ron. But after I left and pondered a bit, I thought, "I should have spoken more forcefully. I should take this role on. I can help get a younger point of view into these films. I can help people be heard." I would be their advocate. I wanted people like Tim Burton and other people whose ideas I thought were cool to get a chance to see them on the screen. And maybe I could even do a good job at directing a film and telling a story. So I went back to Ron Miller and said that although my initial reaction was muted, I would very much like to be a director on *Black Cauldron*. So I became a director, but unfortunately, one that was imposed on the rest of the multi-director team already in place on *Black Cauldron*: Art Stevens, Rick Rich, and Ted Berman (who had just directed *Fox and Hound*). They didn't want me on that team. Art Stevens called me a "junior" director. I mentioned this to Wilhite, who promptly told me that I was a director, not a junior anything. Art and the others were steamed. These guys had to wait decades for their shot and here's this young punk getting this break at the age of 27. But the decision ultimately rested with Tom and Ron Miller, and they wanted me in. After my appointment, John Lasseter had an interesting idea. He thought I hould get Tim Burton to help design the characters in *Black Cauldron*. John asked me if I had seen Tim's sketchbooks. I knew Tim from CalArts, I knew his film, but I had never seen his sketchbooks. So I called Tim in and he showed them to me. Wow! hey were amazing, brilliant, imaginative, fun, and uniquely Tim's. He had wonderful drawings of attenuated dogs, dark-eyed girls, fantastic sketches of the people he saw lined up for the midnight showings of the *Rocky Horror Picture Show*. I showed these to Joe Hale, the new producer Tom Wilhite had installed on *Cauldron*, a veteran of Ward Kimball's unit who had worked amiably with Henry Selick on a live-action project. Joe was senior enough to not alarm Ron Miller. He could work with the veterans at the studio, but seemed open to collaborating with the young talent. Joe loved Tim's drawings, and Tim was put on the picture to explore the characters and its world. Tim had a lot of great ideas. His gwythaints, the nasty flying army of the villainous Horned King, were drawn with heads that were hands, grasping and scary. Tim had a variety of ideas for the Horned King himself. One had him madly consulting his advisors, hand puppets who "spoke" to him. He had an idea that as the Horned King got angry, his horns began to gnarl and grow, twisting and angrily thrusting from his bony head. His version of the heroine Eilonwy had big black eyes and was a precursor of Sally in *Nightmare Before Christmas*. Joe initially loved these drawings. Sadly, however, the other directors didn't. It wasn't long before we heard people saying, "This isn't Disney." On top of that, there were big arguments concerning

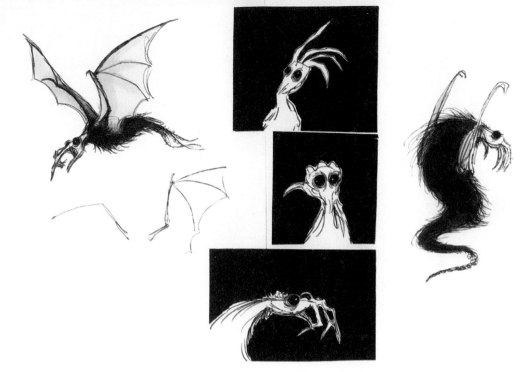

Character designs, Tim Burton, *The Black Cauldron*, 1985 © Disney.

the story. The story artists wanted to keep more of the tone of the books, and the directors were scattered, but seemed to wanted to make it a routine action adventure with little eccentricity. The emotion in the books seemed to have disappeared. At the time, I myself was storyboarding sequences that were not moving forward at all because the other directors didn't like them. Although I was called a director, I wasn't really directing anything.

Bill: **You were boarding by yourself?**

John: Some by myself and some with Randy Cartwright. Our storyboards were not well received by the other directors, especially Art Stevens. Basically, Art Stevens didn't want me on the picture. I was pushing the Tim designs or at least a cartoonier approach. There were now two camps, and poor Joe, the producer who was supposed to make this all work, was conflicted. So he went to Ron Miller and told him to choose: Did he want to do something more stylized à la Tim, or something more traditionally Disney? According to Joe, Ron said, "Why would I not want to do a traditional Disney film? Right now, a rerelease of *Lady and the Tramp* is doing great over in Europe. Why would I want to change that?" I was upset. I felt that Joe had oversimplified the argument. I thought the designs the other directors were pushing were not "classic" Disney, but were thin and unappealing imitations. I thought Tim's designs could be made dimensional enough so they still moved in a dimensional space. But Ron's statements ended that. Tim's work was discarded at that point and other drawings, which to me were dull, were now the accepted models. I was not happy. My attempt to be a voice for the disenfranchised was a failure. Every day I thought I would just quit. If you look at the model sheets from that time, the ones I had to approve with the other directors, you'll see big signatures: Art Stevens, Rick Rich, Ted Berman. I, however, would write my name in the smallest possible script as a pathetic act of political protest.

Bill: **But you directed it …**

John: No, I never really got a chance. My boards were mothballed. I got a credit on *Black Cauldron*: "Additional material by" or "Stuff we threw out by." The experience I did get, which helped in terms of learning to direct, pertained to story meetings and auditions of potential voice actors. I especially remember the auditions. Meeting Jonathan Winters was the single funniest day I ever had at the Disney studio. But auditions back then weren't conducted like they are now, where you run through people every ten minutes and then do callbacks. Back then, auditions could go on for hours. For example, I was there for Gary Burghoff's audition for Gurgi, the growly creature that attaches himself to Taran, the hero of *Cauldron*. Gary, better known as Radar in TV's MASH, tried variations literally for hours. These were initially encouraged by Ted Berman, who told him they had no idea what the character should sound like. After three hours of endless fumbling around, they couldn't get Gary out of the studio and Ted practically threw him out.

Bill: **With all that animosity in the studio, how did you move on to direct Basil of Baker Street, or I should say** *The Great Mouse Detective***?**

John: At this point, Ron Clements had shown the book *Basil of Baker Street*, about a mouse Sherlock Holmes, to Joe Hale, and he liked it as a possible feature. It was decided that the malcontents on *Black Cauldron* should leave *Black Cauldron* to the other directors and form a small unit to work on *Basil*. Thus, Ron Clements, who was unhappy over the way the story of *Cauldron* was being adapted, was assigned to *Basil* along with me as director and veterans Pete Young, Vance Gerry, and writer Steve Hulett. And Ron Miller himself was going to personally produce it. This was Ron's way of mentoring us I think. As I tried to shape the tone of the movie, I wanted to do more than put a mouse in a deerstalker cap. My tastes in British comedy at the time were heavily influenced by *Monty Python* and also *The Goon Show* (British absurdist radio satire with Peter Sellers and Spike Milligan that the Pythons themselves had grown up on). And that was part of what colored my initial version of Basil. Basil was very "John Cleese." He was manic (and depressive), abrupt, smart, and lacked social graces. Instead of the violin, he played the tuba, a mouse-sized tuba. The homely Dr. Dawson was kind of an unwitting ladies' man. The opening of the film was a *Citizen Kane* parody where the story was told in flashback by a wheelchair-bound Dawson, now residing in a home for shell-shocked veterans of the Afghan war. It was boarded by the great Joe Ranft, who gave it many of his idiosyncratically funny and heartfelt touches. After about six months, we finally showed it to Ron Miller. We had sequences on storyboards, nothing on reels. Ron absolutely hated it! He thought it was too "out there."

Bill: So you made the wrong choice?

John: Yeah, once again. He basically said, "Start over." For me, that was difficult. I didn't want to do that. I wanted out. But I backed off and let it move in a more traditional Disney direction. Vance Gerry did wonderful work bringing more charm and warmth to the story, the look, and the characters. That was Ron Miller's ultimate criticism of my version: "This is Disney! Where's the warmth?" He had a point. My version lacked that. Joe Ranft did a classic drawing based on Ron Miller's reaction where Ron looks sort of like Frankenstein and roars, "WHERE'S THE GODDAMN WARMTH?" I still have that drawing, 30 years later, pinned up in my room. It's a good reminder. In the final film of *Basil*, I was able to still inject some of the edge that I thought was in Doyle's own writing of Holmes, some of the Cleesian persona I thought amusing, but the film was tempered by the warmth

Dave Michener, Burny Mattinson, John Musker, and Vincent Price—Recording session for *The Great Mouse Detective*, 1986 © Disney.

Vance added. At this same time, Brad Bird, who had a falling out of his own a few years before and had exited the studio, was developing with Jerry Rees an animated feature based on Will Eisner's classic noir detective strip, *The Spirit*. I loved *The Spirit*, had envisioned making a version of it myself one day. In my spare time, I helped Brad get the project going, as did Glen Keane and others. I did animation, storyboarded a couple of long sequences, and was ready to jump ship and relocate to northern California with Brad and Jerry if it got funding. Word of this got back to management. Burny Mattinson was elevated to codirector partly because of my lack of firm commitment to seeing *Basil* through.

Bill: **Then the sudden appearance of Eisner …**

John: Sudden is right. But first, there were the threats of a takeover of Disney. Ron Miller was ousted and Michael Eisner and Frank Wells were brought in. And Roy Disney, who had earlier left Disney unhappy with Ron Miller's direction of the studio, orchestrated Michael's hire and returned to Disney himself. But we wondered, does anybody realize Ron Miller was actually producing *Basil* and now we are producer-less? We were like kids in a classroom who were the only ones that knew the teacher was never coming back. It was strange. For a moment, there was no supervision, no leader to look to. We were all in limbo. Shortly thereafter, we learned that we actually had to pitch the movie to Michael Eisner. Although we had been working on it for three years, it was very possible that it might get shelved in the wink of an eye.

Bill: **Three years?**

John: Three years in boards … I think we had a few reels. Ron was very distracted by the takeover attempts, and we were moving in slow motion. So we pitched *Basil* on beat boards to Michael Eisner, and he says, "OK, I see you got the comedy and the adventure. But what's going to make us cry? You need something to make us cry." He starts talking in a way that I never heard Ron Miller talk. He then calls in Jeffrey Katzenberg, and we show him everything that we have. This is our first meeting with him. Jeffrey looks at our bar room sequence, one where a plaintive woman mouse sings a Victorian ditty that gets a bit bawdy. Jeffrey's response: "Why can't we have Michael Jackson do a song for it?" We were totally thrown. Michael Jackson? Victorian England? It was then we realized that we were not in Kansas anymore.

Bill: **Thinking outside the box.**

John: There was no box. In hindsight, Jeffrey's thought was not so wacky. It was risky in a kind of cool way (although hiring the biggest pop star on the planet to do a song isn't entirely daring), but it was another universe than the Disney we had been working for. So they greenlit the movie, but cut the budget in half and gave us half the time. We had to knock a year off production and do the movie for ten million dollars, which was a tight squeeze budget-wise even then. Our roles also got shuffled around. Burny Mattinson was now producing the film, and Ron and Dave Michener became codirectors. I wasn't the sole director anymore. I answered to Burny now. It wasn't necessarily an ideal situation for me. Fortunately, Burny was very supportive, collaborative, and generous all in all. He was open to ideas, and had some fun ideas of his own that sent the movie off in a better direction. And in the meantime, Brad never did get *The Spirit* off the ground.

Bill: Is this when you and Ron began to work together as a team?

John: I think our teamwork was forged on *Black Cauldron*, as it were, ironically enough. We discovered we shared much of the same tastes in storytelling and writing. This was further amplified as we collaborated on *Basil*. I had always known Ron as an animator. He was a low-key guy with a good head on his shoulders. During the Bluth days, as much as Don tried to entice him, or anyone else for that matter, he was the guy that said, "Don't drink the Kool-Aid." No matter what, he would question something if it didn't look or feel right. And on *Black Cauldron*, we learned that we had similar ideas about how to adapt a book into a film and how to take a character from the page to the big screen.

Bill: But you ended up finishing *The Great Mouse Detective*.

John: We did. To us, though, it was always *Basil of Baker Street*. That's what we called it.

Bill: And it did OK at the box office, right?

John: Well … it got really good reviews. The studio was excited. But both Jeffrey Katzenberg and Michael Eisner were disappointed with how much money it made. People liked it. It was Glen Keane's first chance to really design and develop a character, which he did with the villain Ratigan. It was a step in the right direction, especially after *Black Cauldron*.

Bill: And it set you on track to helm *The Little Mermaid*.

John: It did. Ron was the one that pitched *The Little Mermaid*. He found the original Anderson story in a book of fairy tales he read in a bookstore in North Hollywood, the Paperback Shack. He was in search of ideas for features to pitch at a "Gong Show," a meeting with Jeffrey and Michael designed to unearth new ideas for films, a vehicle they had used at Paramount. Upon reading *Mermaid*, Ron loved the story's visual qualities. In terms of animation, it had great potential, and he wondered, "Why has this never been made into a film?" Then he got to the tragic ending, and said, "Now I know." Ron wrote a two-page outline of his version. After some delay, Michael and Jeffrey liked it enough to put it into development as a feature. It ultimately languished, waiting for Michael Cristofer, a fine actor and writer of *Witches of Eastwick* and writer-director of *Gia*, and a person whose tastes ran toward the dark side, to write *Little Mermaid*. He never quite got going on it, so Ron asked me if

I would be interested in writing it with him, the two of us having collaborated amicably on *Basil* and *Cauldron*, if he could get Peter Schneider, who really ran feature animation for Jeffrey and Roy, to agree. Ron's pitch to Peter was we're here, we're cheap, we're rarin' to go, whaddya got to lose? Peter said OK.

Bill: **You and Ron went on to direct the movie, but you also acted as a producer. How did that happen?**

John: Howard Ashman, the amazing lyricist and playwright, was being courted by Disney. Of all the projects Disney had in development, he was interested in *Little Mermaid*. He came on to the project as both lyricist and producer. Because he was new to the ways of animation, Peter made me a coproducer with Howard so we could balance out his lack of experience in animation, and not get outvoted by Howard in the process. In those days, Ron was very shy and didn't talk a whole lot. (That has completely changed in the current day. You can't get him to shut up. It's amazing what a little therapy and a loving wife will do!) Because I was the more vocal of the two of us back then, I think they drew my name out of a hat to be coproducer with Howard.

Bill: **How did you and Ron divide the creative process?**

John: When we write, we first work out an outline or a treatment together. When we begin to write the script, I would begin first, improvising scenes in longhand. I would do multiple versions of the same scene, exploring different dialogue approaches and business to put over the ideas. Ron would then take these pages and edit and rewrite, sometimes inventing entirely new versions of the beats, other times just paring down what I had written. This played to Ron's strong suit, as he is great with story structure, whereas I am a little freer with dialogue and character bits. Ron would then take the pages and fashion a script. And he would never show me anything until he was done. Only then would I learn what he used and what he didn't.

Bill: **Is that still how it works?**

John: To this day, that's how we write scripts. Then in production we do many things together: reviewing all storyboards, story reels in editorial, recording sessions, reviewing all initial animation and character designs. As the film moves further ahead, the film is divided into sequences, some of which he has final say over, others which I do.

Bill: **Are there certain types of scenes that you prefer to work on?**

John: I tend to do the action and comedy set pieces. Ron tends to do the more sensitive and warmer sequences. We also split up the songs, since some are bigger production numbers and some are more intimate. Earlier in our career, some of the choices of which sequences each did were determined by reels. Ron and I each had a Moviola in our offices, and in effect, I did certain reels and he did others. Now in the digital age, that is not a factor. We have always kibitzed on one another's sequences, used each other as sounding boards. In the "sweatboxing," or approval process, we see everything each other is working on and can weigh in on it.

Bill: How do you see your talents, strengths, and weaknesses in relation to Ron? And has that relationship evolved?

John: I am more liberal, and he is more conservative. And that can be good and bad, obviously. Ron used to be characterized as a bulldog, and I would say he's still a bulldog. He is certainly a story bulldog! He is not inclined to tear apart structures. He's always concerned if you change something, you may have to deal with an unexpected ripple effect. I'm a little more off the cuff, "Well just try it! Let's see what happens." I would say that's part of our dynamic. I say, "Go ahead and remove it." Ron says, "No! It's there for a reason." There's a push–pull that can be good. Ron is good at protecting the story. He's good at trying to make sure that the acting is sincere and clear. I sometimes overcomplicate things. He brings me back into focus.

Bill: I think you're more vocal about the visual style.

John: I am.

Bill: You're such a student of art and artists.

John: Ron is very well read and self-taught. But he came straight to Disney out of high school, practically, and never had the opportunity to take the art history, film, and literature courses that I was able to. So I have a bit broader range in that respect, maybe. So yes, Ron is at times more of a meat-and-potatoes guy (and I love meat and potatoes!). But he knows what he likes and what he doesn't. And he has a good intuition about that.

Bill: When you two start the process, it's about the whole story, right?

John: Yes, definitely.

Bill: You're not starting with an idea for the parts …

John: Right, it starts with story. Then we come to visuals. But we're very collaborative and we get a lot out of the visual development process. A lot of ideas are generated there and then incorporated into the story. On this last movie, *The Princess and the Frog*, we had a sequence where our heroine was singing about this restaurant that she wants to own. Sue Nichols, a wonderful visual development artist, brought in beautiful "Deco" drawings by Aaron Douglas, a member of the Harlem Renaissance whose work she knew well. She suggested that our heroine's restaurant fantasy would look great in his style. Ron and I had not known Aaron Douglas's work, but we loved what Sue showed us, and we embraced her idea. It turned out really well.

Visual development, Sue Nichols, *The Princess and the Frog*, 2009 © Disney.

Bill: What have you brought personally, as a director, to your films? How would somebody know it's a John film?

John: It's probably a bad thing to admit, but I think there are artists and there are craftsmen. Honestly, I think I lean a little bit more toward the craftsman than the artist. I'm an entertainer. I guess I bring a sense of humor to the material. I try to find something that will surprise the audience, some kind of twist. I try to find and magnify what seems compelling about the story and the characters that drive it. The material needs to be unique. It needs to feel different. I like stories that exploit the medium of animation, stories that can be especially convincing in this medium. Of course, with the ongoing advances in the digital world, it's harder to separate animation and live action; live action relies heavily on digitally created worlds, characters, and effects. Even between Ron and I, I would say I'm more off-center. Not in all cases, but most of the time. With my predilection for comedy, forties filmmaking, and theatre, I would say I'm a caricaturist. That's a part of animation that I just love, the stripping away of inessential things and magnifying others. Even as a kid, I think that's why animation seemed more real than live action: the caricature. You get to the heart of things. You sharpen and throw into relief relatable and hopefully engaging characters for your audience to react to, to invest in emotionally. This is, I would say, animation's primal quality. And our best films certainly work on an emotional level.

It's not just purely about humor. As a director, I believe I contribute to that emotional layer. It's like Randy Newman said, "Scratch a cynic and you'll find a sentimentalist underneath." On the surface I'm more cynical and breezy. Underneath, I'm just mush! I think it's important for films to connect with the audience emotionally. The movies that are going to last the longest are those that get you emotionally involved. My goal is not only to entertain you, but to get you emotionally invested in these characters.

Bill: **With all this consistent collaboration, what would be an example of something that's all yours?**

John: Well, the caricatures I draw reflect a point of view that's all mine. I also made this three-minute film piece for Joe Ranft's funeral, a tribute to a great friend and an exceptional talent and human being who died too young. I drew and edited the whole piece. I was encouraged to post it on YouTube on Joe's subsequent birthday, which I did. People can track that down to maybe get a little feeling for what Joe was like, and what he meant to me and the people around him. It pleased me that the people who knew and loved Joe could see him in that little film. In general, it pleases me when something you labor over seems to resonate with an audience. They see themselves in it and connect to the emotions.

Bill: **I think you've succeeded. *Mermaid*, for example, was such a success. The audience just kept coming back to see it.**

John: Yeah. I don't think Michael Eisner initially saw animation as something that could be financially successful. *Black Cauldron*, which was their intro to Disney features, had cost a lot of money and not done well. I think Michael was quoted in one of the early press pieces as saying Disney needed to continue making animated films because of Disney's legacy, but they weren't expected to make money. When someone remarked how expensive an animated film was to produce, I think he was actually quoted as saying, "These are expensive to make, but we have to do it. It's sort of our thing. It's our obligation almost." I don't think Eisner initially saw animation as a big source of revenue. He just wanted it to break even. Jeffrey, who had not grown up around animation at all, saw it, I think, as a challenge to make it financially successful. Although *Basil* wasn't particularly successful financially (so much so that a disappointed Jeffrey told us he thought the ticket prices for animated films might have to be raised to make them profitable), Spielberg and Don Bluth produced *An American Tail*, and it did better at the box office. It was very much made for a family audience. Even I went to see it on opening night, but it was sold out! I couldn't believe it. Ultimately, its success helped us convince Jeffrey to put more production value into *The Little Mermaid*. *Mermaid* was definitely a surprise, even for Jeffrey. It expanded the traditional audience for animated films. It even became a kind of date movie for teens and adults. Of course, there was *Roger Rabbit* too, which came out before *Mermaid*. But Howard and Alan's music for *Mermaid* was so infectious, smart, and fun that animation became kind of cool. And that gave us momentum. It moved the production of new animated films forward. Obviously, not everything hinged upon the success of *Mermaid*. But *Rescuers Down Under* and

Beauty and the Beast were in development in various stages, and the success of our movie gave momentum to them and other upcoming projects (as well as increasing expectations for them, both creatively and financially). As *Mermaid* was winding down, but before it was released, the studio actually wanted Ron and I to take over *Beauty and the Beast* from the original director, Dick Purdum. He was a talented British-based animator who had been saddled with an early draft of the script that Jeffrey loved. He was told not to change a word. When Jeffrey disliked the reels that emerged from the "perfect" script, there was an emergency confab in Florida during the *Mermaid* press junket. It was there that Howard pitched his version of the story, which handled the characters and the tone (as well as plot elements) considerably differently. He pitched the villain Gaston being a hunter rather than a fop, and his Belle was an imaginative, independent lover of books out of step with her provincial neighbors. He thought the mute, enchanted household objects, which had once been human servants, should not only speak, but should sing and dance. And new directors Kirk Wise and Gary Trousedale and their great story team of Roger Allers, Brenda Chapman, Chris Sanders, et al., brought their own ideas to the project and brought it all to spectacular life (and we had nothing to do with it!).

Bill: **So you were surprised at how successful Mermaid was.**

John: Yes. We had had very successful previews before it was released, but had no real idea how it would do. We liked it. We hoped others would too. I remember going into Peter's office before the movie came out and he told me that, "Steven Spielberg says it's going to make 100 million dollars." I didn't even know Spielberg had seen it. It did well overseas too. And the home video release was an utter surprise. It was Bill Mechanic's decision to release it closer to the theatrical window, about six months later. Roy Disney objected. Even we objected. We thought that would kill theatrical rereleases. But Bill insisted that there was a burgeoning market for home video. And he was right. Many more people saw it on home video, and saw it over and over as children (and adults) replayed it often.

Bill: **After *Mermaid*, did the studio offer you a bunch of projects?**

John: Yeah. They offered us a choice of three movies: *Swan Lake*; *King of the Jungle*, which was some cockamamie thing about lions in Africa (who'd wanna see that?); and *Aladdin*. Howard Ashman had actually pitched *Aladdin* to the studio, and it was part of his deal. We liked Howard, and we really liked *Aladdin*. So we said yes to that. At that time, not even Robin Williams was involved. He was going to be in *FernGully*.

Bill: **It was the first animated voice he did.**

John: We thought of Robin for *Aladdin* before we heard he was doing a voice in *FernGully*. We also knew *FernGully* was going to come out before our movie. Our use of Robin in *Aladdin* seemed so different than what he would do in *FernGully* (playing a bat, and fortunately one who didn't shape-shift like we wanted him to) that we continued to pursue the idea. We were certainly influenced by *Back to Neverland*, in which Jerry Rees and Robin do this kind of a *Duck Amuck* thing, the Chuck Jones's Daffy cartoon where he's constantly transforming as he is redrawn by an unseen hand. Robin changed his voice and persona with such ease. It just seemed ideal for animation. We could make these vocal morphs into a shape-shifting, visual treat. Jeffrey, on the other hand, wasn't so convinced in the beginning that Robin would work. Jeffrey, I believe, envisioned the Genie as a powerful imposing godlike figure. That was definitely not Robin. So Eric Goldberg made an animation test using one of Robin's comedy albums. The comic subject was schizophrenia, so Robin was doing all kinds of voices. Once Jeffrey saw that, he got it and decided to pursue Robin. When Robin finally did come in to look at boards and talk about the movie, he seemed very interested. Still, there were some lingering issues that caused a few problems. At one point, Jeffrey even asked who our second choice for the role was. We had to explain that there wasn't a second choice. I think Robin's pay was a lot less than what he received for live-action films. And I think he had issues with his image and voice being used in the fast-food marketing campaign associated with the movie. I just don't think Robin was ever entirely happy with his contract, even though he loved working on the film, and had enormous fun collaborating with us, Ted Elliott and Terry Rossio our writers, and animator Eric Goldberg. To make matters worse, his movie *Toys* came out at the same time as *Aladdin*. He was paid a lot for that movie, and maybe he even had a piece of that film. But it didn't do well. Then there's *Aladdin*, which is making a huge profit, but for which Robin was paid considerably less. In fact, as he was promoting *Toys* on the talk show circuit, they would always ask him about our movie. He would talk about it, but I think he was grinding his teeth a little bit (because his deal was that he wouldn't be promoting Aladdin).

Bill: **How did *Aladdin's* success change things for you and Ron?**

John: When Disney came wanting to extend our contracts in the wake of *Mermaid*'s success, Maureen Donley, who was our associate producer on *Mermaid*, suggested we talk to Melanie Cook. She was Tim Burton's lawyer. She is a powerhouse. She played in the big leagues. She got us a far better deal than we had in the old system. And again, they wanted a multipicture deal. We were signed up for two movies or seven years, whichever came first. Animation was booming, so they wanted to keep people around. Still, there was a lot of back-and-forth negotiation, and a lot of bluffing! We asked for certain things (like only one picture) that studio management balked at. They broke off negotiations, convinced that, like many others they'd seen before, success had gone to our heads and we would go nuts and ask for impossible things. In the meantime, Ron and I are reading magazines, having been told not to do anything because we weren't under contract. In the end, I think management was surprised that we were willing to compromise and that we weren't totally nuts. We did get a much better deal than we had on *Mermaid*, and it was the groundwork for a number of films we did after. Although we made *Mermaid* on a budget, and they paid us almost nothing to make it, the profit from the merchandising and the video release, etc., went into the billions of dollars.

Bill: You two were responsible for bringing Eric Goldberg to the studio, right?

John: Right. We had always admired the work he was doing in London. Charlie Fink, who was in development at that time, knew that Eric was putting out feelers. I think the burden of running his own studio in London was getting to him. He was clearly looking for an opportunity to come here. Because the studio was working on more than one movie at a time, it was always difficult to pull lead animators away from a movie to work on developing another. And since we were trying to develop *Aladdin*, we had permission to look outside the studio for talent. That's when Charlie told us that Eric was interested in coming to the States and settling down. We had always envisioned the Genie's various personae being kind of cartoony, and Eric was a brilliant comedic animator and draftsman. He was central to creating the Genie. He was involved in picking voice takes, etc. Initially, when it came to Robin's references, like Arnold Schwarzenegger, William Buckley, and Jack Nicholson, we didn't want the Genie to actually transform into them, just suggest them. But Eric pushed us to stretch the rules for comic effect, and to really caricature those specific people. He also pushed the idea of Al Hirschfeld's elegant calligraphic caricature style as being a natural fit for an Arabian film, cueing off the beautiful calligraphy found in Arabic. Anyway, we had written the script with Robin in mind and had written in different personae for Robin to become. He performed the script as written several times. Then he did his improv pass, gradually embroidering more and more. He worked incredibly

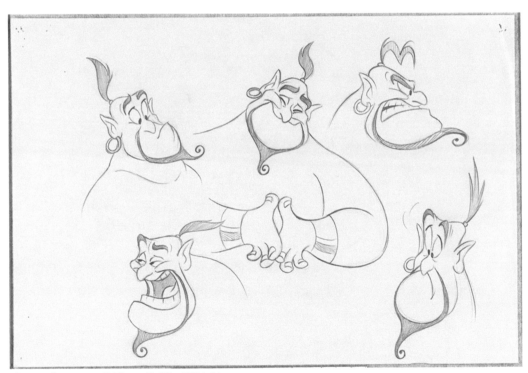

Character designs, Eric Goldberg, *Aladdin*, 1992 © Disney.

hard and did so many "takes" that we had a mountain of material to sift through. We had all of it transcribed. For each scene, we would extract the best content and stitch it together like a ransom note. Eric was very involved in that process, and found many nuggets and had visual ideas of how to exploit them.

Bill: **When you were learning how to write screenplays, did you ever use any formulaic rules or models?**

John: I don't really take any of that into account. I honestly don't even know what the technical terms mean half of the time. Ron is largely responsible for adding structure. When we started I was such a novice. I wasn't even familiar with the basic three-act structure of a screenplay! I thought that was just for plays. Howard also helped, since he came from a playwriting background. His point of view was very much that of a playwright. So I developed some of my writing and scene construction process by working with him. It was all hands-on and learn as you go. And it showed sometimes. On *Mermaid*, Michael Eisner, after viewing story reels, wrote a note that he felt pinpointed a major problem: "At the beginning of the movie the crab is the king's ally and he is hostile towards Ariel. But then later in the movie he is supporting Ariel." He couldn't see a logical transition from one point to the next. Michael then said, "Fix it or there's no movie." Michael could often be too black and white in his approach. But it was a legitimate point. Howard Ashman actually did the rewriting, and it was really fun to see the way he addressed that prob- lem. He wrote the scene in which Ariel washes up on shore and persuades the reluctant crab to help her just by her des- perate expression. The crab's soliloquy as he sits in Ariel's hand and goes from antag- onist to helpmate was written by Howard (edited a bit by us). Howard was also instru- mental in working out the end of the film. We had been struggling with various ways of ending *Mermaid*. How would Ariel get legs once again? Peter Schneider pointed out that we had been telling a father– daughter story from the beginning. He felt that Ariel should get her legs not as a fairy

John Musker and Ron Clements, 1992 © Disney.

tale reward for some noble act (as she had in earlier drafts), but because they are given to her by her father, a visual and dramatic way of showing he was finally letting her go. He was absolutely right. The best idea that ever came from an executive. Additionally, Howard had objected to endings that he thought were off point. He thought the king being motivated to grant Ariel legs because Eric had redeemed himself (which is what we had in earlier screenings) was wrong. He felt that ending only worked if we were telling a story about prejudice. But our ending should involve an overprotective father finally letting his daughter be independent. So Howard wrote that great scene where the father indirectly lets his daughter go. He says to the crab, "She really does love him, doesn't she, Sebastian?" The crab's response, "It's like I always say. Children have to be free to lead their own lives." And then Howard's line from Triton: "I guess there's only one problem left … how much I'm going to miss her." I loved the way Howard was able to get the subtext so clear and yet be indirect about it. The audience has to put it together. I learned a lot from Howard. Working on *Mermaid* was my screenwriting class. And I learned from Ted Elliott and Terry Rossio who wrote on *Aladdin* as well.

Bill: **What was one of the toughest moments in making *Aladdin*?**

John: We had a screening for *Aladdin*, the famous Black Friday screening. Ninety minutes of story reels, our first pass. On *Basil*, Jeffrey had shut the reels off after ten minutes when he wasn't engaged and refused to watch the rest until we had a more compelling opening. These reels of *Aladdin* he watched in their entirety. At the end, his only comment was, "That's a lotta movie," and off he went. Ron and I lunched at El Torito, a little uncertain what to make of Jeffrey's reaction, but cautiously thinking the screening seemed to go OK. After lunch we went to see Don Ernst who was our producer. "Any further word from Jeffrey?" we asked. "He hated it!" Don replied. What!? When we asked Jeffrey later why he hadn't shut off the projector as he had on *Basil*, he said, "I got too much respect for you guys to do that. But I gotta tell ya, I was so bored I spent the entire screening working on the guest list for my wife's surprise party!" So on Good Friday, even though the studio was closed, we came in to meet with Jeffrey. He said, "Listen guys, Steven Spielberg just made *Empire of the Sun*. The script, however, didn't work. He went out, he shot it, edited it together. And guess what? It still didn't work! But had anybody told him the script didn't work? No! Because he is Steven Spielberg. Guys, I'm here to tell you, and I think of you as the Steven Spielbergs of animation, you just made *Empire of the Sun*."

Bill: **Did you have to make major changes?**

John: There were significant differences. Aladdin had a mother in that first version. And Aladdin himself was a little bit younger and more of a quick-talking con man. Jeffrey immediately said the mom had to go. As a character, she was apparently a "zero" in his words. Jeffrey said, and I quote, "86 the mom." And the younger Aladdin was too skinny and not enough of a hero type. When I saw *How to Train Your Dragon*, that kid was a bit like the Aladdin that Jeffrey had rejected. Maybe Jeffrey has mellowed in his old age! But back on *Aladdin*, Jeffrey only wanted a Tom Cruise type of hero. That was basically what he pushed for. And he didn't want Aladdin to have a mother to answer to. Jasmine also changed quite a bit. She became much more active. Jeffrey felt our original Jasmine was overshadowing Aladdin because he was too wimpy: "Guys! They don't fit! She's Julia Roberts … and he's Opie!" In the rewrite, Ted and Terry pushed the *Roman Holiday* idea of the Princess going out into her kingdom in disguise. They stressed her feeling of confinement, something that gave her and Aladdin some common ground. These changes were good for the movie. But we also lost some great songs that Howard Ashman wrote. One was "Proud of Your Boy," a song he sung to his mother, only now he had no mother, and hence no song. There was also a villain song that was very personal for Howard. It was called "Humiliate the Boy." It was a fun villain song, sung by Jafar. It's this comically dark song in which Jafar takes Aladdin, who looks like Prince Ali, and exposes him as a fraud by removing his hair and transforming his body into a weakened state. Howard wrote it while he was dying of AIDS. His body was slowly giving out. He was losing his voice. He was going blind. This song was a comment on the physical indignities that Aladdin went through as Jafar stripped away his Prince Ali disguise, but it certainly seemed like Howard's comic cry of anguish at the indignities his sickness had brought upon him. When we first told Howard we were going to do *Aladdin* as our next film and wanted to revive the songs he had written for it, but which had fallen away as Jeffrey pushed other storylines, he was very happy. But he revealed to us in a phone call that he was indeed suffering from the AIDS virus. He was back home in New York and wanted to warn us that his physical appearance had deteriorated (but that he was fine mentally). He told us to talk to his friend and assistant, Nancy Parent, who would fill in the gaps. She told us he was HIV positive, and he had known for a while. When Howard could no longer travel, we would visit him at this home in New York. It was a lovely house that his partner had built for them. It was hard to see his mind still active, yet his body just giving out. Howard was only 40, yet moved like a 70-year-old. It was heartbreaking. Ultimately, Tim Rice picked up for Howard and wrote "A Whole New World" with Alan, a song that had never gotten past the talking phase with Howard. "Friend Like Me," the Genie's song, was part of Howard's original score, and we didn't change a lyric from Howard's draft.

Bill: **The Genie gets so much attention, but the animation for the magic carpet was even more amazing.**

John: Randy Cartwright animated the carpet. It was the first time, I think, that we used texture mapping. Neither Ron nor I is particularly technologically adept, but we were trying to stretch the boundaries, just like we did on *Great Mouse Detective*. If someone had an idea how to use technology in a cool way, we were open to trying. On *Great Mouse*, it was Mike Peraza and Phil Nibbelink who kept saying, "Wouldn't it be cool if …," which led to the interior of Big Ben being done on the computer. On *Mermaid*, Tina Price pushed us to make Eric's ship a CG [computer graphics] model (which it is only in that first scene coming out of the fog). Tina was also involved in "roto-ing" Randy's hand-drawn animation of the carpet and warping the intricately patterned carpet texture to fit the acting and movements that Randy created. Still, we had to sell this to Jeffrey. We loved getting this intricate pattern on the carpet, but according to the accountants, it was going to cost a lot of money to do this. Jeffrey was incredulous: "I'm paying all that dough for a bunch of squiggles?" He didn't get it. But we fought for it and he gave in. I was very happy about that victory. Randy really "was" the carpet, or vice versa. I remember Randy acting out the scene as the carpet sadly slumps away after Aladdin dismisses it in the cave. I still see Randy doing it when I watch the carpet do that in the movie.

Bill: **Let's move forward and talk about *Treasure Planet*.**

John: After *Aladdin*, we wanted to do *Treasure Planet*, an idea Ron had also written a brief outline for, way back at that first Gong Show. It was a reimagining of Robert Louis Stevenson's

Character design, John Musker, *Aladdin*, 1992 © Disney.

Treasure Island in a science fiction setting. But we had a tough time selling Jeffrey on the idea. He was focused on the female-driven, epic stories, like *Mulan* and *Pocahontas*. *Beauty and the Beast* was nominated for best picture, and I think he became obsessed with that. Even to this day, with his work at DreamWorks, he has always sought to push animation beyond the juvenile market. He wanted to expand the audience. At DreamWorks, he created this crazy mantra, "Disney makes films for the child in all of us. We make films for the adult in every child." I think Lewis Carroll was involved in developing that mission statement. Anyway, *Treasure Planet* didn't fit the mode of films Jeffrey was planning. Ours was a "boys' movie." It was not a musical. It was an action-adventure story. He wasn't interested. *Treasure Planet* wasn't on his radar at all. So there we were, with a big group having lunch with Jeffrey at the foreign press junket for *Aladdin*, which was held at Euro Disney. Jeffrey was waxing enthusiastically about all the great projects in development: *Aida*, *Mulan*, *Lion King*, *Pocahontas*, etc. He never mentioned *Treasure Planet*, although we had been trying to sell him on it for some time. And so we arranged to meet him for dinner and confront him about his disinterest in our pet project, as well as a few other things. We needed to see where we stood.

We discussed our future over dinner in the "New York" steakhouse in the park there. Basically, we were in development hell, and Jeffrey didn't seem interested. Jeffrey suggested a whole new approach for our science fiction story: "What if you took *Romeo and Juliet* as your template and do that in space?" Well, Ron sort of blew up. But I should describe the scene first. There were some journalists at the restaurant, and Jeffrey wanted them to have the full Euro Disney experience. So he filled the place full of mimes and Cirque du Soleil type of characters, the walk-arounds for that park at the time. This was Ron's

Treasure Planet, 2002. © 2002 Disney.

audience as he let loose, "Jeffrey! Every movie doesn't have to be Romeo and Juliet! You're doing this in *Pocahontas* and every other movie in development! They're all live action-y and I wouldn't want to make any of them!" Jeffrey responded in kind: "Well, you're not making them. We just have to find one that you will make!" So the exchanges were flying until Jeffrey's phone rang. After he went off to take the phone call, I said to Ron, "You are doing good. Keep going." I was completely encouraging him. When Jeffrey came back, these Cirque du Soleil characters came over with the food. The whole scene was like a Fellini movie. There is this rather heated, very real conversation going on, and the mimes are still performing. One was even patting Jeffrey on the head!

Bill: Goodfellas …

John: Yeah, it was like Cirque du Soleil meets *Goodfellas*. It was the most surreal dinner. But things did cool down. Jeffrey eventually admitted that the studio was indeed making nothing but romances and musicals centered on a female protagonist. When he came back and talked with Tom Schumacher, who was in charge of development at that time, suddenly there was interest in "boy" movies. And so *Treasure Planet* was resurrected. We had to pitch it all over again. We still had to convince Jeffrey, Roy, and Michael. In the end, we were told that we could make *Treasure Planet* as our "next" movie, but something else had to come first. So we looked at a bunch of

Hercules, 1997. © 1997 Disney.

projects in development. *Hercules* was an idea that animator Joe Haidar had pitched at one of the Gong Shows. We liked it. It seemed like a fun project. So we plucked it off the list. Ron and I immediately saw this as a kind of a sports hero movie, with elements of *Superman* and *Damn Yankees*. This would be our comic book movie. Hercules is half man and half god. He has earthly parents and an otherworldly father. He's stuck in between. And there was also a romantic comedy element (which *Superman* had as well). We were very influenced by *Lady Eve*, the Preston Sturges movie: the handsome, but slightly dim leading man and the sharp woman. She's the cynical girl that falls in love. Our writing was definitely an homage to Preston Sturges.

Bill: Now, we know Ron doesn't have any sisters, but you have some …

John: Yeah, I have five sarcastic, wisecracking sisters. I would say they certainly influenced my writing. And it was fun to write a cynical character, especially in relation to Hercules. He's this beacon. He's a rock everyone collides with and changes as a result. He's like Pollyanna and Mr. Deeds. His idealism ultimately wins out. He changes Meg, our cynical girl. He changes Phil. The character Hades, you know, was originally written with Jack Nicholson in mind. It was similar to when we wrote *Aladdin* with Robin as the Genie. Michael Eisner, who was eager to help fill the void now that Jeffrey was gone, said, "I can get Jack to meet with you." This was truly a fun day at the studio. At that time, Jack's daughter was about three years old and he brought her along. She was dressed as Snow White. We obviously wanted Jack, so we brought in all the *Snow White* merchandise. That's when he said, "You know, I'm the same age as *Snow White*. And I was the last guy at MGM [Metro-Goldwyn-Mayer]. Me and Fred Quimby." It's true, he was born in '37, and he was a cel washer at MGM. Jack Nicholson actually worked in animation until they shut the studio down! So we talked about the movie *Greece* and Alma Tadema paintings, which is something Jack is well versed in. In the end, I remember him transporting all this merchandise we gave him to his car. It was a cool, windy day. When he came back inside, his hair was sticking up and he was still wearing his sunglasses. He hoisted the remaining bags, gave us a devilish Jack grin, shrugged, and said, "Merry Christmas!" It was just *so* Jack! We really wanted him to be Hades. But the studio couldn't cut a deal. Jack wanted a back-end deal, like he had on *Batman*. The studio wouldn't go for it. Years later, at the Venice Film Festival, an Italian journalist asked, "Mr. Nicholson! You were going to be Hades at one time … What happened?" Jack said, "They don't pay any money, and they try to get at you through your kids" [*laughs*].

Bill: Oh! He said that?

John: Yeah, he said that. But it was mainly a money issue.

Bill: Hercules was a hit, and so you got your chance to make *Treasure Planet*.

John: In the wake of Jeffrey leaving to start DreamWorks, management was looking for any and all means to keep people from defecting. They knew that *Treasure Planet* was a project Ron and I were passionate about getting made. And so, surprise, surprise, management was our biggest supporter in getting *Treasure Planet* off the ground. We knew what was going on. Jeffrey's departure and the launching of DreamWorks suddenly gave people in the studio a lot of leverage. A bidding war began. And lo and behold, everybody's salary went up! After all, Jeffrey was not shy about trying to hire people away. He went straight down the list. We even met with him and Steven Spielberg. But Jeffrey had no interest in hearing our ideas.

He had a whole passel of his and Steven's that he wanted to pursue. That was not all that enticing to us. At the end of the meeting, I remember suggesting a few talented people around town they might want to pursue, including Brad Bird.

Bill: **That's because of *Family Dog*.**

John: Ironic because Brad himself was such a fan of Spielberg. Steven had wanted to turn *Family Dog*, the wonderful *Amazing Stories* half hour that Brad had written and directed and which Steven had produced, into a series. Brad didn't think it would work and resisted all the way. They made it, and it didn't work as well.

Bill: **So was *Treasure Planet* your first movie without Jeffrey?**

John: No. Actually, *Hercules* was. Jeffrey read a script we had written, but he left before we really got too far on *Hercules*. Honestly, making movies without Howard or Jeffrey was a transition that we felt. The new management was trying to play Jeffrey's role, and yet not be Jeffrey in some ways by encouraging some un-Jeffrey-like experimentation. For example, on Hercules we wanted to use British caricaturist Gerald Scarfe as a stylist. They encouraged this, something at the time that I don't believe Jeffrey would have supported. Hercules was always running longer than we were budgeted for. We got it down to length by a lot of nips and tucks that, in hindsight, may have hurt the emotion of the movie and gave it an overall rushed quality. Brad Bird picked up on this when he saw the finished film. He thought we should have taken some whole sequence out rather than racing through scenes at the expense of emotional involvement. I think he was right. We did have longer versions of the movie that carried more emotional weight.

Bill: **Where do you think *Treasure Planet* went wrong?**

John: Peter and Tom never warmed up to the movie, even when it was in development before Jeffrey left. The action-adventure and science fiction elements were certainly not their cup of tea. Again, this wasn't a musical. Tom didn't seem to like our ambiguous Long John Silver character, who was always on the fence between a good guy and bad guy. In the meantime, Tom really wanted us to do a sequel to *Roger Rabbit*. He wanted us to do anything but *Treasure Planet*. So he kept putting stuff in front of us, and we kept saying, "No. We want to make this picture." And we did. Then when we screened our first preview, the audience was nothing but mothers and daughters. Where were all the boys? What do we even have in this movie that they are going to like and connect with? It didn't go over well. Ron was wary of structural changes to the film, but I wanted to figure out how improve things. So we reordered things and started moving sequences around in an attempt to get the audience more involved with our protagonist's story. I think we improved it, but I'm not sure Ron would agree. Regardless, when it opened, few came. The audience either never heard of it or found what they saw advertised to be something they had no interest in seeing. I like the movie. But it didn't find an audience. Pirates were a tough sell too in those days. It took Johnny Depp (and Ted, Terry, Gore, and Bruckheimer) to make pirates cool again.

Bill: Do you think there was a logic problem?

John: There may have been a logic problem. The breathing in space? It was a concept we liked, having this retro universe. Overall, the world we created and the characters therein just didn't grab the audience. The reviews were actually good. But the opening box office was disappointing. Even worse, Michael Eisner was then engaged in a very heated disagreement with Roy Disney on the corporate level. And it seemed that a failure Michael could pin on Roy Disney might have been advantageous for him. He could then go to the stockholders and say, "Roy Disney is the guy that liked this movie. He carried it through production." Our movie was essentially written off after opening weekend.

Bill: Regardless, Glen Keane's animation in *Treasure Planet* is exceptional.

John: Glen's work on Silver was a unique hybrid of hand-drawn and CG. And it was an attempt to create a complex, morally conflicted character. There was also some wonderful voice acting by a great cast, not to mention animation by terrific animators like John Ripa, who did Jim; Ken Duncan, who did Captain Amelia; and Sergio Pablos's Doppler. Visually, in terms of art direction, effects, etc., I believe it was one of our strongest films. But certainly Tom and Jeffrey can say, "I told you so!" It failed to excite much interest at the box office.

Bill: How did this affect your relationship with the studio?

John: Michael Eisner no longer cared if we were exclusive to Disney. Instead, he paid us a token salary and allowed us to pitch ideas elsewhere, if he passed on them. Which in fact he did. We heard later from Peter that Michael had thought our ideas were awful (ouch!). We were sort of struggling. We even got an agent to pitch ideas around town. And being a part of the world of filmmaking outside of Disney was an eye-opener. We soon realized how spoiled we were at Disney. It was much harder to get things off the ground in Hollywood. And they typecast us too. We were the animation guys. We tried very hard to stress that we could make live action. But I remember taking scripts and storyboarding sequences for pitches. I don't think the live-action producers we were talking to understood what the heck I was talking about with those storyboards. It was both a fun and difficult time.

Bill: How long did this go on for?

John: For about two and a half years. Then we got involved with *Rapunzel*. It was Glen Keane's project, and he enlisted our help with the story. We wrote a treatment on that which Michael Eisner rejected because he thought it wasn't enough like

Character design, John Musker, *The Princess and the Frog*, 2009 © Disney.

DreamWorks or Pixar, both of which at this time were doing better than Disney. He told us, "Think *Shrek*! Think Pixar!" We were taken off the movie. More pitching "outside" followed. We were briefly involved with a Hitchcockian animated feature at Disney entitled *Fraidy Cat*, but David Stainton, who was now running the department for Eisner, didn't like our reels and let our contract lapse. We were now outside Disney after almost 30 years. It didn't feel that bad in a way, because Disney had so curdled under the last years of Michael and David Stainton that it didn't seem like we were leaving Disney behind. It had already left. We were about to sign with another studio when we touched base with John Lasseter at Pixar. In years past, John had floated the idea of Ron and me doing a movie at Pixar, but the move up north seemed too disruptive for my family. Because of the negotiations at the time between Disney and Pixar, John wasn't allowed to talk about details of Pixar's future. He just told us don't sign with anybody else! So we informed our lawyer and agent to cease discussions with this other venture. We soon read about Disney's purchase of Pixar. Word eventually got to us that John would love us to come back and do a film for Disney! John had been shown projects in development at Disney and saw one entitled *The Frog Princess*. Pixar also had a film loosely based on the *Frog Prince* fairy tale that had stalled a bit. John and Ed Catmull suggested we take a look at *Frog Princess* as a possible next project.

Bill: Had you been aware *Frog Princess* was in development?

John: Yeah. We knew it had been in development while we were in our "struggling" period. We'd actually read a treatment on it that we liked by Greg Erb and Jason Oremland, but we were in such an awkward position with the studio. There were younger directors coming up, and I think we were seen as these old-school idiots. We mentioned our interest in *Frog Princess* to Pam Coates, who was in charge of development at that point for David Stainton, but she said, in effect, David doesn't want you near that one. Variants on *the Frog Prince* had been explored for years at Disney. Eric Goldberg had a pre-*Shrek* parody version. Rob Minkoff had also developed a take on it. The original Pixar version was pitched by Ralph Eggleston, who set it in gangland Chicago in the thirties. Ralph's originally from New Orleans, and the Pixar version moved to that arena. What we read of Pixar's version by that point centered on a spoiled musician who has lost his mojo and rediscovers it in New Orleans. After going through all the treatments written both at Disney and at Pixar, and there was some good stuff in many of them, we thought it should be set in the twenties in New Orleans and feature an African American heroine. We also thought it should be a musical. So we pitched it to John as a hand-drawn film with Randy Newman doing the music. John loved Randy and had no complaints about the 2D concept. I think he felt that the story and the characters of the movie were more critical than whether it was hand-drawn or CG. But John loved hand-drawn animation and was happy to let us work in that medium. In our pitch, we had drawings of the characters we wanted, most of which remained throughout the movie's development process: our heroine, a handsome prince who came to New Orleans from afar to hear jazz, the voodoo villain and voodoo fairy godmother, a lovesick firefly (courtesy of a treatment by Dean Wellins and Chris Ure), and a jazz-loving alligator. But John said, "Before you write anything, you have to go to New Orleans. You have to experience it firsthand." New Orleans, it turned out, was John's favorite city in America. We later heard it was Walt Disney's also. We went down to New Orleans and tried to soak it all in before we developed the story any further. Neither Ron nor I had been to New Orleans previously, and our first visit took place eight months after Hurricane Katrina. Some of the city looked like a war zone. But the French Quarter was largely unaffected because it was on higher ground. Anyway, we met some truly unique characters on that trip. Colleen Salley was this 75-year-old woman that had taught at the University. She was a storyteller, very much in an oral tradition sense. At the Jazz Festival, she would tell children these folktales in a Cajun dialect. We got to know her very well, and she showed us all around the city. Then we met Ava Kay Jones, who was a voodoo priestess. She talked to us about the deeper beliefs beneath voodoo and took us to voodoo emporiums and to the grave of Marie Laveau. We toured the bayou with a Cajun guide named Reggie who was a great, colorful, funny guy. He was missing a few teeth and summoned gators with marshmallows. Reggie told us you could tell the good tour guides from the bad by how many fingers they have left. Of course Reggie had all of his. And sure enough we did see a tour guide with a large bandage on

The Princess and the Frog, 2009. © 2009 Disney.

his hand! Reggie was so entertaining we couldn't help but graft some of him onto our Cajun firefly Ray. Anyway, it was a fantastically fruitful trip. The Jazz Festival alone was worth it. There was such good music from zydeco to gospel, to African drums, Dixieland swing, and second-line brass bands. And the food! We hadn't realized New Orleans is a city obsessed with food! We came back with tons of material that found its way into *The Princess and the Frog*.

Bill: **Hadn't the hand-drawn animation department been gutted by this time?**

John: Yes. There was nothing there. Chris Hibler, who is the grandson of Winston Hibler, a classic story guy that worked with Disney on various things, was now in charge of operations. Fortunately, when he was told to gut everything, he disobeyed accountants and secretly stashed away enough animation desks to do a film. It was like a fairy tale, like *Sleeping Beauty*, where they had to burn all the spinning wheels. "In the deepest, darkest forests of Glendale, in an enchanted warehouse, there by the grace of one brave man, defying the orders of a wicked villain, a magical cache of light boxes still glowed!" We had to get an entirely new production pipeline going. We had to hire back animators. Moreover, we knew this was going to be unapologetically a 2D movie, sort of in a retro way. So the focus was never on using stuff like Deep Canvas, a newer CG-based system for tracking paint strokes. This was going to be a hand-drawn 2D musical.

Bill: How different was it, working under John Lasseter?

John: It was totally different than working for the executives we had in the past. John could draw. John could animate. He was a director, a visual storyteller, a filmmaker! He brought new steps to the process from Pixar, which in some cases dated back to his experiences working at ILM [Industrial Light & Magic]. On dailies, for example, he insisted that every animator should see everyone else's scenes. Everyone had the chance to offer constructive criticism. John thought our workbooks, our drawn blueprints for our staging and cutting, should be turned into "animatics" that blocked out all camera moves in real time and in continuity (before scenes were animated). This animatic process added an extra step to the pipeline, but gave us a truer blueprint of the final staging, cutting, and camera movement. It became our bible in a way. It was always something to go back to and consult. And it was a great guide for the character animators, effects animators, and the layout team. John is a filmmaker, and he brought that sensitivity to his new role. He'd been in the trenches and developed a strong sense of story and how to communicate with an audience. Like Jeffrey, he had good instincts and went with his gut. He didn't have a research team telling him what to think. Ultimately, you have to make the movie for yourself, because you are the audience. Yes, you take notes from preview audiences and your colleagues in the studio, but in the end, the film still has to communicate with you on a personal level. John knows this stuff, and that made him a good sounding board on this film.

Bill: What has life been like after *The Princess and the Frog*?

John: Certainly, the studio has enjoyed great successes with *Tangled*, *Wreck-It Ralph*, and *Paperman*, the wonderful CG–hand-drawn hybrid short that John Kahrs made and incidentally was the first Disney short to win the Oscar® in 41 years, and of course the record-breaking *Frozen*. There are a number of exciting projects in development here by a variety of eager directors. And the studio as a whole is full of a lot of young people bursting with talent and energy, the same "youthful exuberance" that my old CalArts teacher Elmer Plummer saw in Brad Bird back in the day. That bodes well. John Lasseter's enthusiasm and drive to make every project work on every level has had a transformative effect here. Ron and I have a project in development, a feature that we're very excited about, although it's too early to discuss publicly. I still harbor dreams of, in my spare time, doing some little hand-drawn animated shorts where I animate the whole film myself. I have had a number of these that have been brewing for years. I hope I can knuckle down enough to finally make one. Then at long last, maybe I can actually answer your earlier question: What does a "John" film look like?

Bill: **Moana is your first all-CG film. How did you adapt to directing a CG film?**

John: Because *Moana* was our first all CG film, there was a learning curve for Ron and I. We were helped with this transition by Steve Goldberg, the VFX supervisor for *Frozen* and a talented CG artist, whom we worked with as far back as *Aladdin* where he helped bring the Tiger's head/Cave of Wonders to life. Steve led us through a series of tutorials where he explained how the CG pipeline differed from the hand drawn one. How some solo jobs were now split among two people. For example, in hand drawn, we had a single head of layout who was responsible for the staging and cutting of the film as well as the value structure of the shots and the drawing of the rough and finished layouts. In CG at Disney at least, that job has been split between two people, where there is one person in charge of the staging and cutting, and another person involved with the lighting of the scenes.

In broad terms, we saw and learned how there was more prep time up front in CG building and refining assets before production. In hand drawn, if we wanted to explore the animation of a character, in some ways, all we needed was a design drawing of a character, some paper, and a pencil (and a talented animator, of course) and we were off and running. In CG, before we would explore the animation, a character would have to be "built" in the round, "rigged" so that we could move it, and possibly even have some work done on simulations of the movements of cloth and hair.

Brad Bird, as he made the transition from his hand-drawn feature *Iron Giant* to the CG world of *The Incredibles*, told me a funny story how the supervisors on the latter film were fairly comfortable with scenes where entire city blocks would be reduced to rubble, but they begged Brad not to have characters grab one another by their shirts, the believable pliability of fabric and the complexity of such interaction with characters, at that point the more difficult task.

The CG process we encountered on *Moana* also seemed more of a zigzag pattern with multiple "along the way" iterations of shots as opposed to the more linear production pipeline of hand drawn, where a shot or "scene" as we called it would proceed from a storyboard drawing to a rough layout, to ruff animation, clean-up, effects animation, and color in a fairly linear fashion. Thus, when viewing scenes in dailies on *Moana*, it often was unclear to us at a glance what was "finished" and what was not. So, we would view a shot and ask, "Is that the final sky?" and we would be told, "Ignore the sky, it's temporary." And we would say, "But those trees, those are the real trees?" and they would respond, "No, those are place-holders. Forget about the trees." And then our eyes might fix on a few rocks in the foreground and we'd say confidently, "So we should ignore those rocks, too." And they'd respond, "Noooo … those *are* the real rocks." And we would laugh and throw up our hands.

We were also startled by the brevity of the production schedule, for animation particularly. The bulk of *Moana* was animated in about 7 months, with the last half of the movie animated in the final two or three. In hand drawn, we would have spent more like double that amount of time. We did have about 90 character animators on *Moana*, which is more than we would have in hand drawn, but the ability in CG to do iterations and make changes while not reinventing scenes wholly from scratch, perhaps that speed things up.

Overall, it was fun to do things like a living ocean in CG, and all the textures of our costuming, with elements that were grass or bark derived. We also got to experience this new world of "tech anim" or "technical animation," where they brought the hair and the cloth to life. They did an amazing job designing simulations for that, and controls to animate over top of those, and to "lie" to the true physics to get clear and lyrical statements in the hair and cloth. The end result of both the effects work and the hair movement and design made our jaws drop when we saw the finished work! They were and are a new benchmark for those disciplines.

Finally, the experience of working with many talented artists in all phases of production whom we had never worked with before, many of them quite young, and some of whom were weaned on our earlier features like Little Mermaid and Aladdin, was exhilarating for both us and them.

Bill: **If you could go back in time what advice you give yourself about directing your first feature?**

John: If I could go back in time to *Great Mouse Detective*, the first feature I directed on really (I don't think I can count *Black Cauldron* …) and advise myself about it, I'd caution myself to remember that the audience has a lot of material to absorb about characters, their problems, the world they live in, and the rules by which that world operates, in a very short amount of time. So extra care must be spent to make sure all that information gets communicated clearly and entertainingly. At times, the younger "me" might try, like younger animators sometimes do, to put too much into too little time, thus making it harder for the audience to jump aboard. I'd also remind myself to leave breathing room so there is a variety of pace, let some things should play out more slowly to give contrast in the film, which helps keep the audience engaged. And I'd remind myself how lucky I am to be doing this.

2
Ron Clements Interview

Ron Clements, © Walt Disney Co.
Courtesy: Everett Collection

Somebody once explained President Eisenhower's appeal by exclaiming, "He came from the heart of America." That pretty much applies to Ron Clements, too. He is the first to admit, proudly, that his midwestern roots gave him a sense of what the average audience member wanted to see.

But don't make the mistake of thinking this mild-mannered Iowan is a middle-of-the-road type. As you will read, he is tenacious about his art and his principles. Once in the Disney caricature show, a fellow animator submitted the photo of a bulldog (unretouched) and simply labeled it "Ron Clements." It was accepted!

He was hired at Disney without attending any art school. He just had a gift for animating. When I started at Disney in 1977, everyone talked about Ron's Cruella De Vil pencil test. Even the old guys couldn't believe a kid from Iowa—let alone a kid who had never trained at Disney—could animate like that.

complement to the reserved, acerbic wit of John Musker. Together, they directed more Disney animated feature films than any other team has done, or is likely to do.

We interviewed Ron in the "Hat Building" at The Walt Disney Studios.

Bill Kroyer

Bill: This book is all about animation directors, their background, and their path to directing major animated features. We're also interested in your style, your creative process. What was the first moment that you thought about animation as a job?

Ron: I was nine years old, saw *Pinnochio* for the very first time, and was blown away by it. I knew something about what animators did and how they made a film. I thought that one day I would like to work in animation, and maybe even work at Disney.

Bill: Was there anyone in Iowa at the time with similar interests, or someone that could help you move in that direction?

Ron: No, not at all. I never met anyone with the same interests until I came to California. I felt very isolated in Iowa. I was also a big comic book fan, so I had that as well. I was going back and forth on whether I would work in animation or comics. I designed characters. I planned animated films. I tried to write scripts. I drew my own comic books. I came up with new ideas for superheroes. I guess I was a nerd or a geek. But I didn't know anyone in Sioux City with the same interests.

Bill: From nine years old until college, how did you manage to stick with it?

Ron: I had all these films planned, but couldn't shoot anything. So, in the eighth grade I saved up my paper route money and bought a Super 8 camera with single-frame capacity. I actually rigged it up and shot some animation. That kept me going for a while. Then when I was 15, I got a part-time job at a TV station as a graphic artist. It was a defining moment in my career, and this is how it happened: One summer I was watching Howard Duff on the *Mike Douglas Show*. He was an actor and part-time caricaturist. I thought his caricatures of various celebrities were so cool that I started doing them myself. At our local TV station, there were two well-known personalities, Charles Harness, the newsman, and Gene Sherman, the sportscaster. I drew a caricature of each and sent them to the station, which turned out to be a very smart thing to do. That night they showed my drawings on TV! People I knew actually called me and praised my work. As they say, timing is everything. The station had recently lost their artist in the graphics department, so they called me in. Since I was only 15, there were legal issues concerning a work permit. But I got it worked out and I started there. I got to do all kinds of graphic art the station needed. And that job indirectly led to me working at Disney. So if I hadn't been watching the *Mike Douglas Show* that random summer, my life could have been very different.

Bill: Pastels, right? After all, no Photoshop back then!

Ron: Pastels, magic markers … and a hot press. I learned how to work a hot press. I shot a lot of slides. For every piece of artwork you did, you had to shoot a slide. And it would all end up on camera. I was still very interested in animation, though. I even brought in my Super 8 films and suggested we could do some commercials. In those days, everyone thought animation was a very expensive business, that without a bunch of fantastic equipment you couldn't do it. My little Super 8 films proved otherwise, so I convinced them. Soon I was making little animated commercials. They even built an animation stand for me, which they let me use on my own after hours. When I was 18, I made a 15-minute animated short called *Shades of Sherlock Holmes*. It was in color. I did all the animation, cels, backgrounds, voices, and soundtrack.

Bill: Did you have pegs?

Ron: I had pegs … just two pegs. I did it with a two-peg system. They were just little wooden dowels. I punched the paper and cels with a regular paper puncher.

Bill: You made it yourself?

Ron: I made the cells. I painted them. I did everything.

Bill: When you color painted, did you order from Cartoon Colour?

Ron: I ordered a lot of stuff from Cartoon Colour. They sent the rolls of acetate I needed for my cells. I used much thinner acetate and cut it quite a bit smaller than normal, but it worked. I figured out how to make my own x-sheets and a sound track too. It was all pretty crude. It did get some local attention, though. I think my background is different from a lot of people in the industry. After I graduated high school, I knew I wanted to go into animation, but I didn't know how. For a time, I was considering school in New York, at the School of Visual Arts. I even went to New York all by myself, on my very first plane flight, to see the school. In the end, I backed out. I got scared. I grew up with my mother and we didn't have much money. So I continued to work at the TV station until this news guy from the San Fernando Valley visited the station and saw my short. He knew some people at Hanna-Barbera. Based on that simple connection, the TV station flew me out to California. Iwao Takamoto and Bob Singer at Hanna-Barbera looked at my portfolio and my film. Much to my surprise, they hired me as an in-betweener. I packed up my stuff and moved to California.

Shades of Sherlock Holmes, Ron Clements, 1971. Courtesy of ACME.

Bill: You were 18?

Ron: Nineteen, at this point. I took an evening life drawing classes at Art Center while I was working at Hanna-Barbera. Unfortunately, the work was seasonal. I got laid off after about three months.

Bill: What show did you do?

Ron: All classic, very famous Saturday morning TV shows: *Inch High, Private Eye, Speed Buggy, Butch Cassidy and the Sundance Kids.* I also worked on *Yogi's Arc*, which had some of the classic Hanna-Barbera characters in it.

Bill: Was that before off-shore?

Ron: It was. It was probably the lowest point animation ever reached. Hanna-Barbera had a limited way of doing animation. It had started out really good too: *The Flintstones*, *The Jetsons*, *Top Cat*. But by '73, they figured out that they could get away with less and less. It was so limited, it stopped moving altogether. Even while I was working there, I really wanted to work at Disney. I called the personnel department, but they told me they weren't hiring anybody. They had just finished *Robin Hood* and laid off a group of people. But then I found this film magazine at a newsstand on Hollywood Boulevard with John Canemaker's article about Disney's talent development program. Disney was actually looking for young people around my age. It was almost an advantage not to have much experience in the industry. After Walt died, animation production almost got phased out. But *Jungle Book* was such a success that they decided to keep it going. A lot of the artists were getting pretty old, however. So they were pretty much forced to open their doors. Those interested were instructed to contact Don Duckwall, the executive in charge of the program. So I did. He told me to come in and bring my portfolio. My portfolio and film passed their initial test. But I then had to go before a review board of veteran animators. It was made up of Frank Thomas, Ollie Johnston, Milt Kahl, Woolie Reitherman, Eric Larson, and a few other key people. Fortunately, I made it past the review board and was accepted into the program. But there were still a couple four-week trials I had to endure. That's just the way the program worked. Every four weeks, for eight weeks, you had to do a personal test to stay in the program. It was very intimidating. The first four weeks was hell. I went from sheer excitement to pure panic as I suddenly found myself surrounded by really talented people. They knew how to draw. They knew the environment. I was from Iowa!

Bill: Do you remember your first tests?

Ron: My first test did not go that well. Eric Larson suggested that I do something with Sherlock Holmes, since my film featured that character. But my design was not at all a Disney-type design. I was frozen for three weeks. I was actually working on a walk cycle for three weeks. In the fourth week, I added a Watson character, who was a little King Hubbert–ish. I had more fun with him. But it was close.

Frank Thomas and Ron Clements, 1976 © Disney.

They saw a little spark with what I did in that last week, so I got to stay. That was enough for me to relax and start to feel more comfortable. Then I did much better on my second test, a test with the rabbit character from *Winnie the Pooh*. They liked that test. Before I knew it, eight weeks had passed. If you could make it through that, they hired you. That was the official start of my Disney career. I was an in-betweener at Disney working on *Winnie the Pooh and Tigger Too*, a featurette at that time. And even though I was officially employed at Disney, I still did personal tests in my spare time. I had a fairly ambitious idea to do one with Cruella De Vil. It went over really well. Frank Thomas and Ollie Johnston came into my room after they saw it and sort of bowed to me. That was probably the biggest thrill of my entire career. Suddenly, everyone at the studio knew who I was. It was definitely a transformative moment. At the same time, I was still scared. That test went over so well. But honestly, I still didn't really know what I was doing. Frank asked me to work with him. He wanted to be my mentor. I had originally thought about working under Milt Kahl. But I soon learned that Milt didn't really mentor anybody. You dealt only with his assistant, Stan Green. Working with Frank was a fantastic opportunity. He was a brilliant animator, actor, entertainer … just an incredibly smart, talented guy. I learned a lot from Frank as I became an animator on the *Rescuers*. Back then, there were only a few books on the animation process, such as the Preston Blair book, and Frank and Ollie wrote an amazing book after they retired. But animation is something you learn best from working with someone. You can get the ideas and concepts from a book. But in the end, you need a mentor, someone who can teach you how to do it, how to become an actor with a pencil. For me, that was Frank.

Bill: **How did your work evolve under Frank?**

Ron: We talked about basic concepts, things that inform the world and characters you create. Frank was very interested in getting into a character's head. In order for a character to be alive, you need to know what he's thinking all the time. What a character says can be completely tangential to his thoughts and intentions. The physical movement is an expression of those thought processes and personality. And, of course, we talked about drawing. I worked and worked at drawing, because it was never my big strength. Drawing was my frustration. Oddly enough, it was the same for Frank. He was almost masochistic, in that animation always seemed such hard work for him. Ollie, on the other hand, made animation look easy. Frank was a perfectionist. And it was a struggle to find that perfection. Even he said that in his entire career, he probably did only a few scenes he was really happy with. He was the right person for me to learn from. Like a lot of beginning animators, I wanted to do too much. I wanted to put too many ideas into a scene. You just can't communicate that way. And a film is essentially a process of communication between your characters and the audience. You're communicating your characters thought processes, and you're manipulating the thought processes of the audience at the same time.

Bill: That's a great way to put it.

Ron: I felt like I was struggling. Some scenes would be good, others not so good. I wasn't consistent. And I was slow. Then they gave me some multicharacter scenes involving the swamp volunteers. They were not major characters in *The Rescuers*. But I discovered that when you are dealing with that many characters, you have to simplify. And that helped my animation. Multicharacter scenes are supposed to take longer, but my footage suddenly went up when I was doing six-character scenes.

Bill: That's straight footage, not character footage, right?

Ron: Yes, straight footage. They didn't really count character footage then. They do now. Anyway, I had been doing two feet a week, or two and a half feet a week. With the multiple characters, I started doing four and five feet a week. Then I realized that some of the stuff I was doing in those multicharacter scenes would have worked fine in the one-character scenes. I was forced to simplify and focus on what was important. That helped me understand the process better. After the *Rescuers*, I moved on to *Pete's Dragon*. I may have hit my stride on that film. I felt more comfortable. The feeling of fear was gone. And I got fast. I was doing eight feet per week.

Bill: Was Don Bluth directing you?

Ron: Don Bluth was directing me. He gave me little sections of continuity to work on, and he would do a couple of drawings for each scene. That really helped, since drawing was still a challenge. If I had a few drawings to work with, I could work a lot faster. That was a good experience. And my footage had increased so much that I became a supervising animator on *Fox and the Hound*.

Bill: Did you skip *Small One*?

Ron: I skipped *Small One*. I went straight to *Fox and the Hound*. I was assigned the character of Big Mama, the owl, voiced by Pearl Bailey. But unlike my experience on *Pete's Dragon*, *Fox and the Hound* wasn't so easy for me. I was changing. I was starting to become more interested in story development. Even on the *Rescuers* I wrote story notes and sent them to Frank or Wooly. Basically, I was getting frustrated with working on little pieces. You had no control over the entire movie. I found myself more interested in the big story, the big picture. At this point, as an animator, I sort of fell into a slump. I was an intuitive animator. When it felt right, it was right. But if I wasn't feeling it, it just wasn't there. I sort of plowed through *Fox and the Hound*.

Bill: Did you continue to work on Big Mama?

Ron: No, I didn't. Big Mama was part of my frustration. She was a fun character, and Pearl Bailey was a great voice, but she was outside the movie. There was nothing really happening to her. She wasn't experiencing the story firsthand. So after a while, I asked to be taken off Big Mama. I wanted to work on the fox. In the end, I worked on some key scenes with the older Copper and Todd. I also did some stuff with the widow, where she takes the fox out and leaves him in the game preserve. Nobody wanted those scenes. But I found the traumatic nature of that scene interesting. I had a similar experience as a child. I talked my mom into getting a dog, even though the apartment we lived in didn't allow them. We had to sneak the puppy in. When the landlady found out, I had to take the dog back to the animal shelter and felt miserable. So, I had a connection to that scene and wanted to do it. But even then, I started feeling that the position of animator was not my calling. I wanted to get into story. It was a hard period for me. I felt so frustrated.

Bill: How did Disney feel about that?

Ron: They didn't want me to stop working as an animator. I had to push hard. I did finish *Fox and the Hound*. Then I went into story on *The Black Cauldron*.

Bill: What year was that?

Ron: I guess around '80 or '81.

Bill: Did you work with John Musker on *Fox and the Hound*?

Ron: No. I knew John. But we didn't work together. He animated on different parts of the film than I did.

Bill: When John came into the training program, you were already an animator, right?

Ron: Yeah, I was already an animator. John came in with the CalArts guys, all of whom contributed to the film in some fashion. In fact, *Fox and the Hound* was kind of a historic movie, since so many people touched that film. Frank and Ollie actually started it. They did preliminary animation. Then Don Bluth and his team worked on the animation before they left Disney. Henry Selick worked on it. You worked on it. And *Fox and the Hound* was the first movie that involved the CalArts generation: John Musker, John Lasseter, Brad Bird, Tim Burton, and many others.

Bill: As you became more interested in story, did you have any previous writing experience?

Ron: As a kid, I liked to write. I wrote short stories, scripts, and my comic books. I even wrote a novel when I was 11 and sent it to publishers. At Disney, the first script I wrote was for a project called *Hero from Otherwhere*, which was a combination of animation and live action. They had a script, but I thought it wasn't very strong. During a short break, I read the book and, on my own, wrote my version. And I did this very fast, in just a week. I then submitted it without any editing whatsoever. That was a stupid thing to do. I don't think I did myself any favors, and they rejected the script. But I had gotten the bug and wanted to write scripts, even though I didn't know how to professionally do that. A couple years later, the Disney Channel had just started up. They had this *Twilight Zone* type of show called *Future Tense*, and I had an idea for a story that I pitched. They liked it, and I turned it into a script. When it came time to shoot the pilot, they selected two scripts, one of which was mine. It was a science fiction story about a guy stranded alone on a planet who ends up developing a relation-

ship with a shape-changing alien that has been there for thousands of years. It was a fun experience. I spent time on the set and watched the production as it developed. This was also the moment when I began to consciously think about directing. When you're concerned with the big picture, the full trajectory of a film's narrative, directing is the only way to maintain control over your vision.

Bill: **When did you begin to work with John Musker?**

Ron: Despite being one of the young rebellious CalArts guys, the studio made John a director on *Black Cauldron*. It was the idea of Tom Wilhite, a young executive who was open to new ideas. The older directors didn't like that at all. After Frank and Ollie left, Don Bluth was running the show. But he clashed with the CalArts guys. They had different ideas and were not afraid to express them. Brad Bird was particularly outspoken. A schism developed quickly. Finally, Don Bluth and his people quit. The studio was then left with a bunch of talented, but unruly young talent, which could be quite scary for a fairly conservative company. Ron Miller, Walt's son-in-law, who was now running things, thought the answer was to bring us all together on *Black Cauldron* under a group of older guys just promoted to director. But I don't think that was a great experience for many of us. There was now a new schism between the younger and older guys. So John was

John Musker and Ron Clements, 1989 Ursula © Disney.

pushed into the role of director and was also working on the story. That's when we started to work together. I was also assigned to work on the story. That was my first time working with storyboards, and John and I had very strong ideas about the overall momentum of the narrative. But I think the older directors just wanted us to board the sequences and let them worry about the overall story.

Bill: **Is this when you and John bonded?**

Ron: Pretty much. We had similar ideas. Unfortunately, most of those ideas were not shared by the other directors. Eventually they put us in a room to work on stuff that was never going to be used in the movie. It was "additional story," that is, story never intended to be used. That was a bad experience for both of us, but we discovered we did have a lot in common. We were almost the same age. We were both raised Catholic, and we were both from the Midwest. We both were even cartoonists for our school papers. John was also an incredible caricaturist. And caricature was what helped to eventually land me at Hanna-Barbera and then Disney. It was easy to be friends. Anyway, we were both put on probation on *Black Cauldron*.

Bill: **They took you off the picture?**

Ron: No, we were on the picture. But we wouldn't be for long, if we didn't change our attitude. It was that kind of probation. But it didn't matter in the end. Joe Hale was the producer on *Black Cauldron*. He was very sympathetic to our group, but ultimately he had to choose between us and them. He chose the older guys. I guess it was a good thing, because there was no project slated for development after *Black Cauldron*. Since I've always been a big Sherlock Holmes fan, I had come across this book called *Basil of Baker Street*, which was about a mouse Sherlock Holmes. I thought it was perfect for a movie adaptation. But I was working on the *Rescuers* at the time and didn't pursue it. Well, now seemed like the perfect time to pitch the idea. I brought it to Joe first, and he brought it to Ron Miller. Ron not only wanted to make the movie, but he also saw an opportunity to put all these young disgruntled people to work on an alternative project to *Cauldron*. So John became the director and I worked on the story. Later, Burny Mattinson was brought on to keep us from going too radical. *Basil* developed slowly over the next year and a half. Then everything changed overnight. Saul Steinberg, who was a corporate raider, was trying to take over Disney. Evidently, if he succeeded, he was going to dismantle the company and make a huge profit. All of us working on *Basil* had no idea what was going to happen. It was a precarious time. Finally, Roy Disney and the Brass brothers came in and saved the company at the last minute. And Ron Miller left.

Bill: So, Eisner and Katzenberg came in.

Ron: Sweeping changes. For a time, they didn't even know we existed. We were such a small group, and Ron Miller had been our producer. We used to joke about whether we should tell anybody we existed. A lot of stuff happened at this time. There are a lot of stories.

Bill: We should stay focused on your personal experiences.

Ron: We had to pitch *Basil* all over again to Michael Eisner and Jeffrey Katzenberg. It was weird. We had worked on this film for a long time. Suddenly, we had to pitch it as if it were a new idea. Well, they liked it. It was greenlit. But Michael reduced the budget and gave us a strict time frame. We had ten million to spend, and we had to finish in about a year. So, we did.

Bill: You did *Basil* in a year?

Ron: We did. But we had previously worked on the film for over two years, so we had lots of boards, reels, and the cast. We jumped straight into production.

Bill: Basil himself is a manic-depressive. How different was he on the screen from what you guys originally envisioned? Didn't they ask you to tone it down a little?

Ron: We had to tone it down. That's why Burny Mattinson was put on the picture. *Basil* was indeed manic and eccentric. And we pushed that even more early on. Burny carefully pulled us back, allowing for some eccentricity and quirkiness, but nothing too extreme. The film was done

Andy Gaskill, Ron Clements, and Randy Cartwright. Disney characters © Disney.

very fast. Fortunately, it was animals wearing clothes, which is probably the easiest kind of animation to do. Everything turned out for the best, I think. *Black Cauldron* was costly and took four years to make. We finished *Basil* in a year, it was cheap, and it did better at the box office.

Bill: **Don't forget to mention the name.**

Ron: Well, we did hate the title change. To us, it was always *Basil of Baker Street*. But there was a marketing issue. Eisner and Katzenberg had come to Disney from Paramount, which soon released *Young Sherlock Holmes*. Big names were associated with that film: Steven Spielberg, Chris Columbus, Barry Levinson. I think *Basil* was green-lit because they were still riding high on that movie. When it finally came out and didn't do that well, Eisner and Katzenberg were worried about any association with *Sherlock Holmes*. So the title was changed to *The Great Mouse Detective*. We hated that name.

The Great Mouse Detective, 1986. © 1986 Disney.

Bill: **What about the secret memo?**

Ron: I don't think it's a secret now that Ed Gombert wrote that memo. He was a very talented story guy at the time. Peter Schneider was newly installed as the head of production, and the fake memo was attributed to him. It basically said, "Not only are we going to change the title of *Basil of Baker Street* to *The Great Mouse Detective*, but we have also decided to go back and change the titles of all previous Disney films. From this point on, *Snow White and the Seven Dwarfs* will be *Seven Little Men Help a Girl*; *Pinocchio* will be *The Little Wooden Boy Who Became Real*; *Cinderella* will be *The Girl with the See-Through Shoes*." I think he changed all the titles except the *Aristocats*. Peter was incensed! They wanted to fire whoever wrote that memo. Eventually, it died down and nobody got fired. But that memo has a life of its own. It was eventually the basis for a *Jeopardy!* question, and the *LA Times* wrote an article about it.

Bill: **Were you and John the sole codirectors of *Great Mouse*?**

Ron: No. Burny and Dave Michener were also directors. John and I were sequence directors. And as for me becoming a director, I should backtrack and say that it was due to Ron Miller leaving. He was the original producer. When he left, Burny became the producer. But he didn't feel he had time to both produce and direct, so they were looking for another director. I asked Burny to consider me, and he went with that. I guess that was my big break.

Bill: Did you and John do sequences together?

Ron: No, and we still work that way. We split a movie into sequences and then divide them up. We don't actually work on the same sequences. That's always been part of our process. There was also no screenplay on that movie. Most of the Disney movies didn't have one at that time. We did our own writing for the sequences that we boarded. Somehow, we were able to maintain consistency. We both did a lot of

Vincent Price, Burny Mattinson, Dave Michener, Tim O'Donnel, Ron Clements, and Matt O'Callaghan—Recording session for *The Great Mouse Detective*, 1986 © Disney.

The Little Mermaid, 1989. © 1989 Disney.

writing on *Basil*. And that reminds me of the "Gong Show," which was something Eisner brought with him from Paramount. Occasionally, they would gather a lot of the creative people at Paramount to generate new material by simply pitching ideas freely. This was called the Gong Show because the response required a simple gut reaction, yes or no. So we had to do this too. A bunch of us had two weeks to each come up with five ideas to pitch. As I was looking around for ideas, I found this book of fairy tales that included *The Little Mermaid*. I'd heard of it, but never read it. It didn't take long to discover that Hans Christian Anderson's writing was very visual, almost cinematic. It leapt off the page. There was so much potential,

I was curious why it hadn't been made into a movie yet. But as I read further, I could see why. It's a story that starts out sad, and then it gets sadder and sadder. Then she dies in the end. Depressing, but it intrigued me. A few days later, I had an idea. I thought of making the witch a villain and putting this sort of ticking clock in the story. I wanted this ironic twist where the prince falls in love with her voice, but she gives up the voice. And I had a way to give it a happy ending. I got so excited that I couldn't sleep. I wrote up two page treatments on five different ideas, but I thought *Mermaid* was the best. Two weeks later, when we gathered, Michael asked us to pitch our best idea, not all five. When I said *The Little Mermaid*, they immediately said, "No. That's too close to *Splash*." Nevertheless, they said they would read all the two page treatments. I was very disappointed. Then, two days later, Jeffrey Katzenberg said that he and Michael saw potential in *The Little Mermaid*. They wanted to put it into development. And for a while I was sort of in charge of that.

Bill: **Was John involved with it?**

Ron: John was not involved at this point. They were focused on finding a writer. Initially, they wanted Michael Christopher, the Pulitzer Prize–winning writer on the *Witches of Eastwick*. He was interested, but then backed off because he felt his take would be too dark. That's when I went to John and suggested that we collaborate on the screenplay. We pitched the idea to Peter Schneider and he agreed. *The Great Mouse Detective* was also coming to an end, so both of us were looking for a new project. At the same time Jeffrey Katzenberg, prompted by David Geffen, was trying to lure Howard Ashman to Disney. They showed Howard a number of things in development, both live action and animation, and he was most interested in writing the songs for *Mermaid*. We met him in New York with a 12-page treatment and, for two days, we went over it, figuring out how and what songs could be worked into the story. And Howard a great idea. Howard went on to direct the musical "Smile" in New York while John and I returned to California and wrote the script.

Bill: **How did it turn out?**

Ron: Jeffrey loved the script! He was ecstatic about it. Now, if you know Jeffrey, he tends to run either hot or cold. He's either going to hate it or think it's the best thing in the world! Fortunately, he didn't hate it. We had to do some rewrites, of course. But the script held its own. And when Howard finally finished the musical *Smile* and came out from New York, he started working on the songs with Alan Menken. But before he even got on the plane, he and Alan had written *Part of Your World*. Things moved very quickly from that point.

Bill: So this long running collaboration between you and John began with *The Little Mermaid*?

Ron: Right. That defined the entire way we work on a film and a script. And we've always written the first drafts of our movies. In many cases, we've brought in writers after that. But on *Little Mermaid*, it was just John and me for most of the movie. Howard Ashman did some key writing toward the end, though. For a long time, he declined writing, which surprised us. He's a great writer.

Bill: How do you two share the writing process?

Ron: We work out the story together, though I'm more structure oriented and John's more into dialogue and business. John always starts the script. He improvises quickly on paper. And he doesn't write complete scenes, just ideas or segments of scenes with bits of dialogue. He generates page after page of material like that. He gives all this to me, and I flesh it out, edit, add my own stuff, and turn it into a linear narrative with a logical structure.

Bill: Does he literally write it or …?

Ron: He doesn't type. He uses note paper.

Bill: Longhand!

Ron: Longhand. And he just fills these binders up.

Bill: That's what you get?

Ron: That's what I get. I read every word, make notes, and then turn it into a script. And I never show him anything until I finish. Only then does he find out what I used and what I tossed out.

Bill: Whole script?

Ron: The whole script.

Bill: So he does a pass and then …

Ron: Yes. He does a whole pass. Then I do a whole pass. But his pass is very fast. He writes so quickly. I'm slow. I do a lot of methodical rewriting and editing. The funny thing is, by the time I give him the script, it's like something he's never seen before. He writes in such a stream of consciousness fashion that he doesn't remember what he initially wrote. Sometimes he can't even distinguish between what he wrote and what I wrote. Consequently, his reaction and critique is much better. He's not attached to anything. It's like reading someone else's work. So he makes his notes, and then we go back and forth till we're both happy.

Bill: **While you're writing, is there anything else going on?**

Ron: Sometimes visual development is going on at the same time. We like visual development to begin as early as possible, because we want it to influence the script. We like to be as flexible as possible. Even regarding our script—we always think of it as a first pass. We don't think of it as the finished movie. It shows the potential of the movie. Again, there will always be rewriting.

Bill: **How are you and John guiding visual development at the very beginning? Are you side by side in everything?**

Ron: We are side by side. Our basic approach to visual development is not to inhibit it. We want to be as open as possible. And if we see something we think is really good, we'll work it into the script.

Bill: **So you meet with the visual development artists and brief them on the general tone?**

Ron: Exactly. We have a definite sense of the story and the visual concept from the beginning. On *Princess and the Frog*, we pitched that to John Lasseter with just a visual outline of the story. We hadn't written anything. We just had pictures that roughly told the story in three acts. We pitch the story to the people we bring on to do visual development as well. We talk about what we're going for and then let them do what they do. We don't want to constrain or limit our team. They need to have a good deal of creative freedom. When they come back with stuff for us to look at, then we start to steer them in more specific directions. A good example is the Shadow Man, the villain in *Princess and the Frog*. Sue Nichols did some drawings in which the shadows surrounding Dr. Facilier weren't mimicking his movements. They were doing other things. They had a life of their own. Better yet, they could reveal his intentions. We thought that was just a cool idea. You have to be flexible and you have to foster a creative environment. Great ideas can come from anywhere.

Bill: **But when do you hand your script over to the story team to start boarding? At that point, you can't be so flexible, right?**

Ron: We were brought up in the old Disney system. There were no scripts. You didn't start with continuity. You started with exploring all kinds of possibilities. Most people want to go right to continuity. But you need to explore before you do that. You need to explore a lot. That was Frank's basic philosophy: "Explore, explore, explore!" He would say, "You're given a scene. Before you do anything on that scene, come up with five different ways to do it. Don't just go with your first idea.

Force yourself to think of five different ways in which you might do the scene. Then pick the one that you think is best. Then you've explored a little bit, and then maybe you have a little something extra." That's essentially the Disney approach. Even though we have a script, we still want them to explore before they think about continuity. And for the board artists, we just want them to focus on the pictures, no dialogue. It's how we were trained. Get the visuals and the tone first. Dialogue is the last thing you worry about. Good boards should be able to pitch themselves. The pictures themselves should be able to tell the story. Dialogue can clarify and amplify, but we never want to rely on it to communicate the story.

Bill: Do you and John split up everything?

Ron: No, not everything. Casting, for example, we do together. We'll both sit through every part of the audition process. Layout, color, postproduction we do together. It's only in animation production that we split the film up. And even then, we don't divide it up until we pretty much have 25–30 sequences, which is roughly an entire movie.

Bill: Do you guys ever argue over how the sequences are divided?

Ron: Well, we quibble over the songs, because they are the most fun to do. If it's a musical, of course. Oddly enough, we don't have a huge problem with dividing a film up.

Bill: Do you generally take a certain type of sequence?

Ron: Yes. John tends to do the action or comedic sequences. I tend to do the quieter, more emotional parts. But that is not the case all the time. Sometimes we'll do the opposite. I've done some action sequences, and he's done some very emotional ones. The good thing about dividing it up is that we have a sense of ownership of our sequences. It also gives us a sense of objectivity concerning the stuff we're not working with every day.

Bill: How do you guys handle voice casting?

Ron: It's a big process. It takes months, usually. Once we have a script, we'll start auditioning actors. Even if the dialogue may change, it doesn't matter, as long as we have a sense of who a character is.

Bill: You use a casting director, right?

Ron: We use a casting director. We provide notes, suggestions, even the names of certain actors. It's important that a casting director knows what we're thinking. But even then, we're still rather flexible. Even if we have some very specific ideas, we're not afraid to make adjustments every now and then and go against type. And we prefer that actors audition, especially for musicals.

We'll go to New York. We'll go to London. It doesn't matter. We just want to see and hear them. We rarely use an actor that won't audition. Of course, we've done that with big name actors. It's pretty much impossible to get them to audition!

Bill: **Have you ever written a character with an actor in mind?**

Ron: The Genie in *Aladdin* was written for Robin Williams. We definitely were thinking of him right from the start. But that can be dangerous. We invested ourselves in writing this role for Robin, and for a time we nearly couldn't get him! We had brought him in and showed him the boards. Eric Goldberg had even done a little animation test to show the concept. He used a track from one of Robin's comedy albums. Robin liked it, but there was a problem during negotiations. We thought we might be forced to come up with an alternate. And that was just impossible. The Genie wasn't a role. It was Robin Williams! That's how we wrote it. Fortunately, we got him. And there was a similar case on *Little Mermaid*. We wrote the character of Ursula with Beatrice Arthur in mind. But we couldn't get past her agent or manager. I think they were somehow insulted because we wanted her to play a witch. It was frustrating. But Pat Carrol stepped into the role and did a fantastic job. In the end, we try not to write for a particular actor. That can cause you a lot of problems.

Bill: **The voice is the most important thing, isn't it?**

Ron: Now that's the truth. Any animator can tell you how important it is to have a good voice to work with. A good voice inspires the performance. So much can come out of that. If you saddle the animator with a voice that doesn't really come to life, that doesn't generate pictures in his head, it makes his job a lot harder. There are so many actors that have a lot of charisma on-screen. But when you reduce them to just a voice, the charisma is gone. Sometimes, to make sure a voice works, we'll do drawings that specifically sell that voice, that bring it out even more. Sometimes, we'll even do test animation.

Bill: **Does it get hard sometimes, finding the right voice?**

Ron: Certainly. On *The Princess and the Frog*, the hardest voice to cast was Prince Naveen. We had a few possibilities, but nothing felt exactly right. Finally, we took what we had to John Lasseter to get his opinion. But in this case, even he wasn't sure. He suggested that we play our options to a group of women and see what they responded to. And that was a smart idea, because we wanted the prince to have a romantic appeal. He needed to have a romantic voice. Bruno Campos blew away the competition. That voice of his was extremely popular with the ladies!

Bill: **A novel idea. A preaudience test.**

Ron: Yeah, that's how he got that part. Even though he's a totally handsome guy.

Bill: When you record your actors, what kind of direction do you provide?

Ron: We obviously talk about the character and what they're thinking. But we don't overdirect. Most of the time, you tend to overdirect when you first start out. You want to give people more direction than they really need. As John and I gained more experience as directors, we tended to believe that you should direct only when needed. Generally, we'll let the actor first play the role the way he feels most comfortable. If we feel like there's something that's not working, or there's something we're not getting, then we'll direct them. Most of the time, you're just telling them to do it faster, slower, or maybe with a laugh or a whisper. But you also need to remember to listen carefully. Once you've written a script, you often have a predetermined reading in your head. You want certain lines to be read in a very specific way. But that doesn't necessarily mean that it's absolutely the best way. The good thing about animation is that tape is very cheap. Let the actor try things. This is where animation gets to play with spontaneity. You want to capture that line as it has never been said before. And, most likely, if you asked the actor to do it again, he or she just can't repeat that exact performance. But you got it.

Bill: What about rehearsals?

Ron: We don't really rehearse. If we do rehearse, we record that rehearsal because something great might happen. But our process is all about takes. We do a lot of takes. And we tend to play a lot. We'll have an actor read an entire scene two or three times. Then we'll start focusing on individual lines.

Bill: Do you record actors together?

Ron: Not usually. Occasionally, if actors are really playing off one another in a scene, we try to do it. But it's tricky. Normally we just record actors individually.

Bill: When you're doing your reels, you're doing the scratch track, right?

Ron: We do scratch tracks. We didn't use to. In fact, we were reluctantly dragged into that. But we do it now, and it sort of works.

Bill: You didn't do that on *Mermaid*?

Ron: We didn't do it on *Mermaid*. Well, we didn't do it exactly. We had a script reading of *Mermaid* with random actors, because we wanted to get a feel for the script. But when it came time to actually record the songs, we did a reading of the whole script with the real actors. This was at a recording studio in Hollywood called The Record Plant. It's kind of a historic thing. The funny story about that recording is that someone forgot to push the record button! Seriously, Howard and

Alan were playing the music, and the actors went through the entire script doing the dialogue and singing the songs. But nobody pushed the record button. We had to do it a second time! After that, we recorded everybody individually. Then we put everything together on story reels.

Bill: That was it? The movie was done?

Ron: No. Very little of that recording was used in the final version of *The Little Mermaid*. The actors were too rehearsed. It just didn't have that natural feeling. So we went back and did rewrites. We even added new scenes that brought the film to life. We got that spontaneity back. After all, you only have to get it right once. But if you have an actor say the same line over and over again, they'll start giving you the exact same reading over and over. Now we do the story reel scratch. We do everything scratch.

Ron Clements, Jodi Benson, and John Musker—Recording session for *The Little Mermaid*, 1989 © Disney.

On *Princess and the Frog*, John was Prince Naveen. Rob Edwards, our cowriter, was Dr. Facilier, I was Ray, and just people in the staff helped out. That's why more and more animation people are becoming voice talent. Darnell, the big frog hunter, was Don Hall, our head of story. And Two-Fingers, who just mumbles Cajun, is Paul Briggs, another one of our story guys. Scratches are done very often with just people that work around the studio. And when something works, you just don't want to give it up.

Bill: How much did you revise your story reels?

Ron: If I could show you the story reels of *Little Mermaid*, they would look so crude compared with the story reels that are done nowadays. Story reels are getting more and more hyped up. They have aftereffects, full sound effects, and music.

Bill: The *Mermaid* reels looked like the old-fashioned story reels.

Ron: Yeah, they looked like the old-fashioned story reels. There was minimal source music that Alan played on the piano, and a few sound effects. Jeffrey's reaction was, "I love the script! I love the songs! I don't love this. Uh … Why don't I love this?"

A lot of it had to do with the fact he wasn't used to watching story reels. He wasn't used to seeing an entire movie from beginning to end with just still drawings.

Bill: What about Michael Eisner?

Ron: For people who aren't used to seeing story reels, it can be very difficult to judge if something is working or not. Michael Eisner really had a tough time. Jeffrey got better. Eventually, he could read story reels. The story reels today are so polished that they feel like a real movie. With all the bells and whistles, it's easier to see what's working and what isn't. It's also important for selling a movie now. You have to have all those bells and whistles.

Bill: Plus, it does help communicate the vision …

Ron: Right.

Bill: … and take your vision further.

Ron: I would say so. On *Princess and the Frog*, we did something we had never done before. It's something John Lasseter brought from his experience with digital animation at Pixar. In digital animation, before any animation is done, the scenes will be blocked out. The camera moves are all there and the basic idea for the lighting and the blocking are there. The characters wouldn't be animated, but they would be going through their motions and hitting their marks. John Lasseter suggested we do that as well, because in the past the emphasis in storyboarding was not on cinematics. It was about character and the clarity of storytelling. If it's approved for production, then we go through the workbook pass, where we break it down and define each scene. We define how long it's going to be and how the camera will move. That's when we give the scenes numbers. But …

Bill: That would be when the cinematographer basically comes in, right?

Ron: Right. We have the layout in our head.

Bill: He is kind of like your cinematographer, isn't he?

Ron: Very much so. So then we would have a workbook, which would be the guide for layout. That's what the animators would work from. But we never filmed the workbooks! On *Princess and the Frog*, we actually did that. We filmed with the staging, the preliminary lighting, and the basic blocking. Most of the time, we used the character drawings from the storyboards. If we couldn't, we would have the layout guys add their own drawings. Basically, it allowed you to watch something that felt like a finished movie, before the animation was done. And the animators could see clearly how their scenes connected with the ones around them. Better still, after the scenes were animated, that just made the cutting process much easier. We also noticed that we did less reanimation after the fact, with things like hookups or anything that didn't work with the layout. In the end, it strengthened the movie. I'm not sure why we didn't do that before. But this was something John brought to the team.

Bill: **What about your crew? How involved are you in selecting your story crew, lead animators, and other artists?**

Ron: Like the actors, casting your crew is critical to the success of any project. Experience is your best teacher here. There are people you just click with, who speak the same language. We've used Rasoul Azadani as our head of layout on every film since *Aladdin*. On *Princess and the Frog*, he wasn't with the studio anymore, but we managed to bring him back. Ian Gooding

The Princess and the Frog, 2009. © 2009 Disney.

also goes back to *Aladdin*. Recently, he's been our art director, and his sense of color and design is incredible. On the other hand, our head of story, Don Hall, we had never worked with before. But when we saw his work, we just knew we wanted him. Casting a crew is just critical, especially when it comes to animators. They can do anything. They can assume the role of any character in your film. And they like to work on different stuff. But animators often get typecasted just like actors. There are certain guys you think of for certain kinds of scenes. Andreas Deja, for example, has mostly worked on villains in the past. He's done the most famous: Scar, Gaston, Jafar. Then he asked if he could work on Mama Odie in *Princess and the Frog*. He felt a connection to the character and wanted to do it. So we let him. Andreas is someone we know. We know his work. We trust him. We can let him step outside of his normal role because history suggests that he'll do something good.

Bill: How do you organize your lead characters and your animators?

Ron: We always have a supervising animator for all the lead characters. When we cast that animator, that person is in charge of that character. And we want that animator to own that character. They need to take possession of it. If the character is being pulled in the wrong direction, doing something that's out of character, we want to know! John and I don't want to dictate or micromanage, but we want consistency in the overall product. In any studio, you want a core group of talented people that not only understand the process, but also thrive in it. We want our supervising animators to be happy with their assigned crews. That isn't always the case, however. If things aren't working out, if changes need to be made, you do it. But having that core group that always comes back for more is essential. That's your crew. You will rely on them.

Bill: As directors, do you generally work through the supervising animators?

Ron: Yes, we do. We certainly try to look at all the scenes with each animator, but that's not always possible. But before any scene is shot, we like to see them early, and we need the supervising animator there. We want to make sure that everyone is on the same page. If you don't, someone will make a beautifully animated scene that simply doesn't work. It has to go, and that's a painful experience. It happens. But you want to do everything you can to prevent that from happening. John Lasseter helped by introducing the concept of animator dailies. It was something he picked up at ILM (Industrial Light & Magic). It's a good way to maintain a consistent dialogue with your supervising animators and their teams.

Bill: What did the animators think about dailies?

Ron: Some liked it, others didn't. Regardless, we wanted to encourage the animators to show their work at the earliest stage possible. Some artists simply have a hard time showing and talking about their work when it's so rough. But they get used to it. They quickly see how much their work can benefit from the process.

Bill: So it's just you and John together?

Ron: Yeah, John and I are there, the supervising animators are there, and all the other animators are there too.

Bill: Looking at it by sequence?

Ron: If we can go in order, we do. But sometimes you have to skip around. Then we talk about them. Obviously, it can be a challenging experience. Bad ideas are just that—bad. They get torn down quickly. But when there's potential there, everyone recognizes it, no matter how much work it may need. And sometimes you have that "wow" moment. You watch a scene that just blows everyone away. The clapping and hollering follows quickly. You can also salvage scenes that appear to be lost. If an animator gets stuck, the collective brainpower of all the teams put together can often reveal a way out. At the end of the meeting, we have pages of notes and ideas to help move the project forward. And it makes everyone feel like they're a part of one big team.

Bill: But at the end of it all, you and John have the final word, right?

Ron: Right. I think John and I work well together because we have similar sensibilities. Sure, we argue over some things. But even our arguments are part of the process. You want the best idea, so we have to defend our positions. It's the only way to find out whose idea is better for the project at hand. And yes, you need more objectivity than emotion. It's not easy all the time. But if you have a strong relationship, it works. I can also firmly say that not all directors work this way. Brad Bird is a very talented director who works differently. He thinks very cinematically. He visualizes a movie entirely in his head in a very specific way. Then he communicates that vision to his team. If you compared that with us, Brad is probably not as collaborative as John and me. His process is just different. When we have a movie concept, we don't start from as specific a place. We like to let in as many ideas as possible. They can come from anywhere. John and I want to foster the most creative environment possible for our people. Our process then acts as a filter to find and isolate the best ideas. It's everyone's job to participate, not just perform one task and go home. The problem is, you'll get so many good ideas but a lot of them won't work. The trick, in my opinion, is to say yes to the right things and no to the wrong things. If you can master that, you'll be just fine!

Bill: How do you keep a unified vision? There's so much art to look at when you're making a feature-length movie.

Ron: It gets easier over time. The hours you're working may get worse, but the process gets easier. The most critical phase is the beginning. This is the time when everyone has a different movie in their head, even if you've already made the pitch and have a rough script. The movie doesn't exist yet. As a director, you need to direct. You need to communicate with everyone working under you, so that you keep them focused on making the same movie, telling the same story, the same characters with the same tone and overall style. Once you've established that, then a more natural evolution can take over. Everyone has a sense of the narrative. They know who the characters are. They know what the movie is supposed to look like. Then you're guiding more than directing. You can let your team do what they do best. The movie now exists and everyone can see it. It's just a matter of finishing it.

Bill: OK, I think Ron wants to ask you more about your influences.

Ron Diamond: Yes, I do. Are there any artists, films, or directors that have influenced your own development as a director?

Ron: Well, we already talked about the early stuff and Walt Disney. I think the *Wizard of Oz* had a big effect on everyone of my generation. It was such a big, wondrous annual event to watch on television. I'm also a big fan of Frank Capra and Billy Wilder. They're very different directors, but their movies just get me. *It's a Wonderful Life* is probably my favorite movie. *Mr. Smith Goes to Washington* and *It Happened One Night* are also great Capra flicks. In fact, *It Happened One Night* definitely influenced *The Princess and the Frog*. I can't tell you how many times I've read the script for Billy Wilder's *The Apartment*. I love that script, and *Some Like It Hot*. I should also mention that I'm a big science fiction fan. Stanley Kubrick's *2001* was a mind-blowing experience. And, of course, I don't think anyone of my generation can forget *Dr. Strangelove*. But I'm also a big fan of James Cameron, George Lucas, and Steven Spielberg. They make these blockbuster popcorn movies, which could be boringly repetitive. Yet every time, they don't hold back. They're always trying to take us in another direction. They want to give the audience an experience they've never had before. That's what I want to do. That's what John wants to do. We don't really think of our films as kids' films. We think of them as films for everybody. They're not art films.

The Princess and the Frog, 2009. © 2009 Disney.

We're just not those guys. We want to please and entertain a general audience. That's always been the Disney philosophy. I still believe in that. I always think of the person in the audience who's had a really bad day and isn't in the mood for a movie. If you can get that person to forget about their day or their problems, if you can get them emotionally involved in a story and characters, then you've truly achieved something.

Bill: **Of all this stuff that you've done, is there a scene or a sequence that's your favorite or most successful?**

Ron: You mean sequences I've directed?

Bill: **Any moment from any of your films.**

Ron: I don't know if this is the right answer, but there's a moment in the making of a lot of these movies where something changes for you, and the movie becomes real in a way it hadn't before. I remember on *Little Mermaid* this sequence John directed and a scene Ruben Aquino animated. It was Ursula undulating with her tentacles and dancing during the witch's song. Seeing Ursula come to life with such fluidity got me. It was so cool. It made me think, "This movie could really work!" And on *Aladdin* there was a scene, also John's sequence, that Eric Goldberg did in which the Genie was singing and dancing to this Cab Calloway bit. He had these huge hands in the background, and he was strutting in a spotlight. It was great to see that come to life. I love musicals. I love the way you can use songs to tell a story. When I was a kid, I enjoyed *Singing in the Rain*, *The Music Man*, and *Mary Poppins*. The King Louie sequence from the *Jungle Book* is also one of my favorites. Just being part of the "Under the Sea" sequence on *Little Mermaid* was a fulfilling experience.

Bill: **Well, you are responsible for bringing the musical to animation.** *The Little Mermaid* **basically reintroduced that genre.**

Ron: Thanks to Howard Ashman and Alan Menken. We learned a lot about musicals from them. After all, there are good musicals and bad musicals. The definition of a bad musical is when a movie suddenly stops and everybody sings a song. Then the movie starts again. A song should be integral to the story. A narrative shouldn't be able to move without it. It conveys something essential about the story. There was actually pressure to cut "Under the Sea" from *Little Mermaid* early on. Like most of the movies John and I make, it was always too long. But fortunately, the song was too great to lose. There was also pressure to cut "Part of Your World" before it was all in color. That song tells the audience about Ariel's dream. You can't leave that out. My one regret in terms of length pertains to *Hercules*. I love that movie. But if we could have had a couple minutes more screen time, that movie would have been better.

Hercules, 1997. © 1997 Disney.

Bill: Do you think there's anything about growing up in Iowa that still resonates in your work?

Ron: Absolutely! I don't think it's a coincidence that John and I are both from the Midwest. It's a different attitude. We have always been fascinated by Hollywood, but simultaneously a little repelled. Basically, the Midwest has a more down-to-earth attitude. I think you tend to identify more with regular people. The snob or elitist approach just doesn't interest me. I want our movies to reach everybody. I think movies can be funny and smart and popular and crowd pleasing and really good at the same time. Some people may disagree. But I would say that we tend to make movies for a midwestern audience more than the "Hollywood audience." Basic values are also a constant theme. *The Princess and the Frog* addresses what's really important in life, as opposed to shallow things that can often take precedence. In *Aladdin* and *Hercules*, we were definitely poking fun at superficial values, even Hollywood values. I especially love the way *Hercules* mocks the merchandising and corporate aspect of Disney. I hate the fact that people think our movies are corporate and merchandise driven. For better or worse, we've always made the movie that we wanted to make and never worried about anything outside that. We've told the story that we wanted to tell. We've never really aimed at an audience other than ourselves. And we're always hoping people will like the same stuff we do.

John Musker and Ron Clements, 2002 © Disney.

3
John Lasseter Interview

John Lasseter © Pixar.
Photo: Deborah Coleman.

I knew John Lasseter when he was a regular guy, a guy you could just have a cup of coffee with and shoot the breeze without ever suspecting he was the most powerful figure in animation. I'm talking about last week.

That's right. I consider this perhaps one of the most remarkable qualities of this most remarkable man: that in the 30-plus years I have known him, he has remained unbelievably real in the face of fame and fortune. Of course, he has made some of the greatest animated films of all time, built the world's most successful film company, and now heads one of Hollywood's major studios. But on a personal level, he is just such a good guy.

The coolness that is John is not as well known as his industry accomplishments, but in some ways, I think it reveals a different greatness.

decorations, his nutty costume, and his boys having a wild time, you'd know his head was in the right place. He approaches everything in his life with an astounding amount of energy, imagination, and care. No one benefited more from this than the artists he worked with, and for, at Pixar.

John collects trains, and a few years ago purchased the full-size steam train owned by Disney legend Ollie Johnston. Ollie was very old and infirm and had not even seen his train in years. John had the rusty engine and cars restored to perfection, trucked to Disneyland, and loaded onto the tracks that ring the park. On a ruse, he brought Ollie to Disneyland "to sign autographs." As Ollie sat in his wheelchair at the New Orleans Square Station, his train came puffing around the corner, whistle blowing, John Lasseter at the helm. John put Ollie at the controls. There wasn't a dry eye in the park.

Other people have made hit films, run studios, won Oscars. It's his genius in life that makes John Lasseter very special. We interviewed John at Pixar.

Bill Kroyer

Bill: When did you first discover animation, and at what point did you think you'd get involved in it?

John: My mother was an art teacher, so I was always surrounded by the arts. I drew all the time. But cartoons were my favorite thing. It was primarily the Walt Disney films that I saw at the theater. Sometimes you would find cartoons on the *Wonderful World of Color*, and I liked them too. But the cartoons that were most readily available were the Warner Brothers' cartoons, especially Chuck Jones and his Road Runner and Bugs Bunny stuff. Even in high school, when it was not cool to like cartoons, I'd still hurry home to watch. And I was always drawing. I took every art class that I could.

Even on Sundays, when my mom took me to church, she would hand me a pad of paper and a pen or pencil. I would sit still and draw.

Bill: **What did you draw? Flipbooks?**

John: Yeah, I did flipbooks. I used to love making flipbooks on the edges of songbooks. There was a nice wide margin, and it was so easy to flip. Pads of paper could be difficult, if your drawings weren't real precise. Songbooks also made that great noise as you flipped. I would make quick sketches, lots of moving stick figures.

Bill: **In high school, did you already know that you wanted to go into animation as a career?**

John: When I was a freshman in high school, I found the *Art of Animation* by Bob Thomas in the library. I think I read it from cover to cover about five times. It was such a great book, and I kept checking it out all through high school. It had never dawned on me before that people actually made cartoons for a living. People actually got paid to make cartoons! Now, this is going to make me feel old, because this was long before videocassettes, but the Wardman Theater in uptown Whittier, which only charged 49 cents a ticket, was showing the *Sword in the Stone* around the time I found that book. I was so excited. I had my mom drop me off at the theatre because I couldn't drive yet. And it was such a fantastic experience, watching Milt Kahl's animation. Of course I didn't know at the time it was his, but it was so impressive. When my mom picked me up, I remember telling her in the car, "I want to work for Walt Disney. I want to be an animator." She turned to me and said, "I think that's a great goal to have." Later, when I was at CalArts, I realized that it was very rare to have that kind of support at an early stage. I was fortunate. My mother was an artist and an art teacher. She always thought that the arts was a noble profession.

Bill: **How old were you?**

John: I was around 14 years old. Then I got the Preston Blair book, copied those walk cycles, and made more flipbooks. One of my friends even had a Super 8 camera that shot single frame. So we shot a lot of material. In fact, I just recently found the reels and gave them to the archives here at Pixar. And my dad also found an old notebook containing all of my Preston Blair walk cycles. Anyway, I had a great art teacher in high school, Mr. Bermudez, and he encouraged me to start writing to Disney Studios. Then one day, I received a letter from Ed Hanson, the manager of the animation department, inviting me to the studio. They were really supportive of young talent at the time, so I went over and showed them my high school artwork. They said, "For college, you should get a basic art education. We'll teach you animation. We have a training program here now." This was right at the beginning of my senior year of high school, but I was already accepted to Pepperdine University. Everybody in my family went there: my mom, my brother, my sister. It was affiliated with our church, the Church of Christ. Then I got another letter from Disney Studios. It was Jack Hannah telling me about the new character animation program at CalArts, which was starting in the fall right after my graduation. I begged and begged my mom and dad to let me go. They were always so supportive that they finally gave in. My mom wanted me to go Pepperdine, but she saw what a great opportunity this would be for me. I was the second person accepted to the program. Jerry Rees was the first.

Bill: So, after about 60 years, Disney suddenly starts a unique animation program just in time for your high school graduation. That's good timing.

John: I know. It was staggering. And it wasn't just me. Brad Bird was coming out of high school too. Besides us, the first class included John Musker, Darryl Van Citters, Harry Sabin, Doug Lefler, Jerry Rees, Nancy Beiman, Bruce Morris, Mike Cedeno, Joe Lanzisero, and Brett Thompson. Tim Burton, Mike Giaimo, and Chris Buck were in the second class. But both were so small that they combined the two classes right away. We were essentially one group.

Bill: I've heard that the instruction wasn't too great at the time, that all of you were pretty much self-taught.

John: Well, a few teachers at CalArts were great. Bill Moore, the design teacher originally from Chouinard, was phenomenal! He changed the way I saw everything. Ken O'Connor, the legendary Disney layout artist, was amazing—he would bring amazing original art from the studio to teach us layout. T. Hee taught caricature. We really had some fantastic teachers. It was an amazing place in time. They brought out of retirement a lot of former Disney artists and animators. Jack Hannah, who had directed most of the Donald Duck shorts, was head of the program. He was an also an ex-boxer, a real fighter, and that helped when it came to developing the program. He asked me to be his student assistant in the summer of 1975, so I actually got to work at Disney Studios right after graduating high school. Jerry Rees and I spent the summer going down to the Morgue to pick out scenes and Xerox them. We had complete access. Back then, the artwork wasn't considered that valuable. We were collecting a ton of material for the program. That summer, I also got to pal around with the guys currently in the training program: Glen Keane, Ron Clements, Andy Gaskill, Ron Husband, Randy Cook, Randy Cartwright, Ed Gombert. Eric Larson was there, of course. Just talking to these guys made it a great summer.

Bill: Did you stay at CalArts for the full four years?

John: I went all four years and got a BFA in film.

Bill: During those four years, did you ever contemplate directing?

John: Due to the structure of the program, you had to play with the basic concepts of directing. The first two years gave you a foundation. The last two years were about taking those skills and making a movie. You just did the storyboarding and some basic animation. They didn't want you to put in any color. I made this film about a lamp that's alive. It was called *Lady and the Lamp*. T. Hee was a governor at the Academy at the time and suggested that I enter it in the Student Academy Awards. I actually had to wait till the following year, but it won. After that, I entered my senior year film, *Nitemare*, and it won too. I'm the only two-time winner of the Student Academy Awards. And one thing that really got to me was seeing people watch the movie, seeing how it entertained them.

Bill: That was a different time. Those films were simply made to demonstrate animation.

John: Just animation.

Bill: And yet you obviously demonstrated the story. You went beyond thinking in terms of just animation.

John: These were originally called "tests." I don't know what really happened. I was ambitious, and I simply wanted a well-defined beginning, middle, and end. From the very first test, that's what I was into. I wanted to tell a story through my animation.

Still from *The Lady and The Lamp*, 1978. (Courtesy of John Lasseter.)

Bill: Disney just couldn't overlook a two-time award winner, right?

John: They actually offered me a job after my junior year, after I finished *Lady and the Lamp* and before it won the Student Academy Award. But I turned them down in order to finish my degree. This was a noteworthy achievement in my family. My mom finished college. Even Jack Hannah had a degree. I wanted that too. Of course, Disney made it clear that I wasn't guaranteed another job offer if I said no. But I did get a second offer after *Nitemare*. I didn't start right away, though. My brother had studied abroad while at Pepperdine. He spent a year in Europe, mostly in Heidelberg, Germany. He came home such a different person that I knew I wanted that experience too. As a family, we only traveled to Yosemite and Tahoe, stuff like that. So I told Ed Hanson that I would start at the beginning of September, and I spent my summer traveling around Europe by myself. When I returned, it just so happened that I started the Monday after Don Bluth and his animators left the studio.

Bill: What was that day like?

John: They left that Friday, and I walked in with nothing but enthusiasm and sheer excitement on Monday. I made it to Disney! Unfortunately, everyone was walking around with this, "What are we supposed to do now?" look on their faces.

Bill: You missed out on the Don Bluth era.

John: Yeah, I missed out. But from my perspective, it wasn't really a big deal. The answer was simple. Let's move forward and make movies! I have to say, and I tell this to a lot of young people, that time at Disney Studios was a dream killer. I experienced the absolute obliteration of my dream. There was a lot of fear, I think, over all this young talent coming in from CalArts. There were guys on top that had paid their dues and were now in charge. But they were in charge through attrition, not talent. It didn't make a difference how good we were. They didn't want to hear it or see it. Fortunately, we had unbelievable support from Frank Thomas and Ollie Johnston, Woolie Reitherman, and Eric Larson, the last of the great Nine Old Men. They were excited to teach us. They wanted to pass the torch off to us. In hindsight, we're truly fortunate that Frank and Ollie published *Disney Animation: The Illusion of Life*, so that everything was written down. But I remember clearly being told by the management, "We don't want to hear your ideas. We just want you to do what you're told. If you don't want to do that, there's a line of people outside that would love to come in and do that." As soon as I heard those words, I knew if I were ever creatively in charge of anything, I would never say anything like that to anyone. Because with three sentences they made any interest I had in the project disappear. I didn't care about the studio any more. There was far more creative energy put into the *Eddie* shows* than anything we were actually working on.

Bill: Did you learn anything about directing during your Disney period?

John: I learned what not to do.

Bill: Is that because you didn't get a chance to direct?

John: I never took no for an answer. That's why I got in trouble with Ed Hanson. I was so excited about the inception of computer animation. I started collecting these tapes that SIGGRAPH was putting out, which were bits of computer animation. This was before you and Jerry Rees came back with *Tron*, and I'd love to hear your take on that moment in time. It was life changing for me. In fact, I can pinpoint three life-changing moments. The first was simply reading the *Art of Animation* by Bob Thomas as a freshman in high school. Then I saw *Star Wars* on opening weekend at the Chinese theater. The way that film entertained me and everybody around me was amazing. I immediately said, "That's what I want to do with animation." So many people were excited about special effects, but to me it was about animation. Lastly, I remember clearly the day that you and Jerry showed me your very first *Tron* dailies, after coming back from Magi. It was the light cycle sequence that you guys storyboarded and choreographed with Chris Wedge. It was amazing.

Bill: Did we take you to a sound stage and show you that? At the time, we could only film it out on 70mm.

John: No, it was a test. But it just blew me away. And I remember talking with you and Jerry about using this for backgrounds and putting animated characters to it. I even started talking to Glen Keane about it. Of course, I mentioned this to Ed Hanson and received the expected no. But Tom Wilhite, who was head of production for live action at the time, had a great eye for recognizing young talent. He sort of plucked Tim Burton and me out of the group. They were developing *Where the Wild Things Are* with Maurice Sendak, and he took some development money and let me work with Glen Keane. I storyboarded a little *Wild Things* test. Then, after *Tron*, we worked with Magi on a 30-second test that incorporated Chris Wedge's computer graphics. That's when Chris and I became best friends. Together, we mapped out the process of moving the camera and inputting simple shapes that represented the characters. Then we did photo stats, just like when we animated with live action. Glen did the animation while I took on more of a director's role. I was working with

* The *Eddie* shows were a series of irreverent live puppet shows hosted by animators Darryl Van Citters and Mike Giaimo. The Disney staff would stand outside and watch the show through Van Citters's ground floor office window. The name comes from the life-sized cardboard cutouts of Eddie Fisher and Doris Day.

and overseeing the computer-generated side of the project. We literally had to invent digital ink and a paint system that had tone mattes. This was 1981. Years later, when ILM (Industrial Light & Magic) did *Roger Rabbit* with tone mattes and a traditional optical printer, I showed the test to them. They were blown away by what we did back in '81, on a computer! Anyway, we were completely caught up in pioneering never before seen techniques in computer animation. We knew what we wanted to do, and we had no choice but to figure out how to do it. We had to open up a new path, with brute force if necessary. It was so much fun. Needless to say, I wanted a project that we could apply this to. At that time, John Debney, who was my good friend and a young staff composer at Disney, read *The Brave Little Toaster* by Thomas Disch. John knew my *Lady and the Lamp* from CalArts and thought the story and I might be a good fit. I read it and loved it. After Wilhite got an option on it, Joe Ranft, Brian McEntee, and I started developing it as a feature. At the same time, I was finishing the *Wild Things* test. My plan was to show the test and then pitch the feature. And I wanted to direct it. Of course, Ed Hanson wouldn't have anything to do with this. In fact, he made sure it got sabotaged. He came in one day with Ron Miller and said I had to pitch my idea. We weren't even finished working on it yet. Clearly, Ed had worked Ron over beforehand. Ron saw it and asked, "What's this going to cost?" "It'll cost the same as a regular animation feature," I replied. It was hard to swallow what he said next. The whole thing is kind of funny in retrospect, because I've become real good friends with him and Diane. Now he says, "Did I really say that?"

Bill: What did he say?

John: He said, "The only reason to do computer animation is if it makes it cheaper or faster." He then got up and walked out. About five minutes later, I get a phone call instructing me to see Ed in his office. Ed only had one thing to say, "John, your project is complete, and your employment with Walt Disney Company is now terminated." That was it.

Bill: That literally happened after Ron Miller left?

John: Yeah, that was it. I immediately went to Tom Wilhite. He stepped in and managed to keep me on at Disney for a while. And I did finish the *Wild Things* test. But when Tom was replaced by Richard Berger as head of live action, I was laid off. Now, due to the computer research we were involved in, I was rather familiar with companies involved in computer animation. Tom and I had paid a visit to the Lucasfilm Computer Division. Unfortunately, they were still in the research phase. They didn't have anything in production. But they were excited to talk with me. The simple fact that someone from within Disney was interested in computer animation made them smile. They had been to Disney many times in the past. They thought it would be a natural place to develop computer animation. But, like me, no luck there.

Bill: How did you make the move up north?

John: It was the end of 1983, and I was kind of in limbo. I went to this computer animation conference on the *Queen Mary*, where Ed Catmull was scheduled to talk. I had no idea what I was supposed to do. *The Brave Little Toaster* was shelved, so any prospect of future work at Disney seemed dismal. Fortunately, after the lecture, Ed asked if I was interested in working with him and Alvy Ray Smith up at Lucasfilm as a freelancer on some tests. My previous work had focused on using computer animation for backgrounds. The characters were all done by hand. Ed wanted to challenge this. They wanted to do research in character animation using the computer. I immediately accepted and made frequent trips to the Bay Area at the end of '83 and the beginning of '84. It was supposed to be a one-month freelance job, but I never really left. We did *The Adventures of André & Wally B.* Once again, it was so much fun pioneering this new method of animation.

Bill: You started your career with an amazing string of short films. How did you come up with a new idea? And once you had one, did you develop them independently or did you have help?

John: Each one was slightly different. *André & Wally B.* was something Alvy sketched out originally. He wanted to develop an android, something like a *Star Wars* robot. But I was inspired by Ub Iwerks's animation in *Steamboat Willie* and *Gallopin' Gaucho*. We had to use geometric shapes, so I proposed something very cartoony. That's how *André and Wally B.* came to be. I did all the art direction, layout, and animation. Ed was overjoyed by how different it was. He wasn't expecting something so cartoony and fun. When it began to look like the Lucasfilm Computer Division would become its own separate company—it became Pixar in 1986—Ed mentioned that he wanted to make a new short film for SIGGRAPH, to make a name for ourselves. At the time, I had been experimenting with computer modeling by building a model of my desk lamp, and I thought maybe I could do something with that, but I didn't have any definite ideas yet. It was around then that I went to an animation festival in Brussels, Belgium. I had *André & Wally B.* and the *Wild Things* test. Everyone was blown away by what I had done with computer animation. The Belgian animator Raoul Servais was also there. I had always been amazed by his film *Harpya*. He said something really important to me, "No matter how short a film is, it should have a story. It should have a beginning, a middle, and an end." I came back from the festival thinking about the new film Ed had suggested. I knew I had to find a story for my lamp. At the time, Tom Porter was working with me and he had just had a baby. One Saturday, as I was sitting with this little baby, I noticed how the scale of a little toddler is what makes them so cute, the big head and the little arms. I looked at the lamp and started to think about what a baby lamp might look like. So I started playing with the scale of the original computer model of the lamp to create both a baby lamp and a parent lamp. Then I storyboarded an idea for a story using the two of them and started animating. The final film was only about a minute and a half long, but *Luxo Jr.* was born. It was accepted into SIGGRAPH and made the final selection in Dallas in 1986. People loved it. They were cheering even before it was over.

Bill: **This was all new.**

John: Yeah, computer animation was kind of a novelty to people outside the industry. When they saw it for the first time, the response was always, "Oh! This was made with a computer." With *Luxo Jr.*, I had just focused on the character and story. I remember at one SIGGRAPH screening Jim Blinn came over and said, "John, I've got a question for you." I thought it was going to be about Bill Reeves's innovative shadowing algorithm, which we had used for the lamps in the film. Instead, Jim said, "Was the parent lamp a mother or a father?" I knew at that moment we had succeeded. For the first time, a computer-animated film was entertaining the audience because of the characters and the story, not just because it was made by a computer.

Sketch, John Lasseter, *Luxo Jr*, 1986 © Pixar.

Bill: **That's a classic example of making people believe that animated characters have emotions. And that's so great about it, because they have no faces, they have no eyes, no arms or legs …**

John: It was a challenge for me. I always like to challenge myself. The lamps in the film are almost exactly the same as a real lamp—they only have a couple of degrees of rotation that a real lamp doesn't have.

Bill: **That accurate motion conveys to an audience familiarity, familiar gestures, things that make people believe that they can relate to a character. You got it right. It felt real. I'm sure that inspired you to move forward and take it to the next level.**

John: Absolutely. The next year I did *Red's Dream*, with a clown and a unicycle that was alive. After that was *Tin Toy*, which won an Academy Award. *Luxo Jr.* was actually the first 3D computer animation that was nominated for an Oscar. It didn't win. But in '88, *Tin Toy* was the first computer animation short to receive an Oscar. And then I did *Knick Knack*. In each case, I was both animating and directing. Ed Catmull's dream had always been to do a feature film. But that required money.

So we decided to do some television commercials, because that was the only way we could expand and hire more people. We started working with Colossal Pictures in San Francisco, who basically became our representatives for all the advertising agencies around. It was a great relationship. I loved making commercials; it was a fantastic learning experience for me as a director. There was a discipline that commercials had that short films didn't. In my short films, as the story grew, you were free to add a few frames here and there. Television commercials only allow 30 seconds to the frame. It was a challenge because the idea itself was usually a min-

Ed Catmull and John Lasseter © Lucasfilm/Pixar.

ute or 45 seconds long. But I actually enjoyed the challenge. The agencies came with an idea, a basic concept of an idea, and I would listen to them and the client. Every time I would take it and restoryboard it, thinking about the fun we could have with the product. I wanted to bring the product to life. I always had the confidence that I could bring any inanimate object to life. But in the end, you had to edit the idea down to 30 seconds. That required a kind of discipline I hadn't had beforehand.

Bill: Did these commercials provide the income you needed?

John: We were finally able to start hiring more people. The second animator we hired at Pixar was Andrew Stanton. The third was Pete Docter. Pete came straight out of CalArts and had been strongly recommended by Joe Ranft. This was the first time I had directed other animators. I was overseeing them, but I wanted them to feel like they had some creative ownership over the work they were doing. So I gave them commercials to create on their own, because I wanted them to come up with their own ideas and even share in the directing of them. My whole approach to directing was really inspired by the experience I had had with Dennis Muren working on *Young Sherlock Holmes*, back when Pixar was still

Pete Docter, Andrew Stanton, John Lasseter, and Joe Ranft, © Disney.

the Lucasfilm Computer Division. *Young Sherlock Holmes* was a project overseen by Steven Spielberg and directed by Barry Levinson. Dennis Muren, who was the director of special effects on the film, thought that maybe computer animation would work well for a scene in which a stained glass knight pops out of a window and comes to life. That really showed vision on his part because at that time, not a lot of people could see the potential computer animation had for this sort of thing. So we came in to work with ILM on the project. The whole thing was the complete opposite of my experience at Disney. There, when you turned in a scene, it went through layers of people to get to the director, and then the director's comments were relayed back to you. You never got to talk with the director personally, which made it hard to be sure exactly what needed to be changed and why. In contrast, every single morning Dennis had dailies, which was a screening of all the work done the day before. Everybody that was working on *Young Sherlock Holmes* would meet in the ILM screening room and share their ideas and give feedback on the work that was being shown. Dennis let everybody in the room have a voice. Of course, he had final say. But he listened. You felt like you were part of a team, and that made the work exciting. Later, when we got the deal with Disney to develop a computer-animated feature film, which turned out to be *Toy Story*, I looked back on my experience making commercials and especially working with Dennis and his morning dailies. We built a screening room at Pixar with this in mind, one big enough for all the animators working on Toy Story to come together and share ideas, with a screen big enough to let the animators see how computer animation would play on a full-size movie screen. It was definitely an adjustment for the animators, however.

Bill: One's art can be a very private matter. It's not easy to put it on the big screen for criticism.

John: Exactly. Years later, Andrew Stanton coined this fantastic phrase, and it's really one of our mantras. He said, "Be wrong as fast as you can." That's often a painful truth to accept initially. But the first draft of a script is usually bad. Revision is an integral part of the process. The first time you take the script and go to storyboards and reels, it isn't going to be right. In that first attempt at layout, aspects of your animation are going to be wrong. Very rarely does someone nail it the first time. Yes, you want it to be perfect. That's a natural feeling. But if you just hang on to it, if you don't let it go, you're just preventing it from becoming better, because you're postponing the feedback and improvement process. That's the irony. It needs to be wrong at first in order to ultimately be perfect. The longer you wait to share it, the harder it is to hear that necessary bit of constructive criticism.

Visual development, John Lasseter, *Toy Story*, 1995 © Disney/Pixar.

Bill: How did you ease them into that?

John: Well, it was mandatory. Everybody had to show their stuff. The initial stage was something we called "first blocking." It was something I had developed back on *Luxo Jr.* This stage is all about establishing the basic movements and timing. The last thing in the world we worried about at that point was facial animation and lip synch. This was about pantomime for all the characters. The difficult part for the animators was showing rough, unfinished work. I wasn't giving them time or instructions to complete or perfect anything. But they came around quickly. I explained that everyone would have a voice in the screening room, that it was about ideas. Obviously, some were more outspoken than others at first, and that caused a little confusion, but I told them to be open and inspired, and if they were confused, I would give the final direction. But the magic happened quickly. They became a close-knit team, closer than anything I experienced at Disney. This was a team working on a film together. They were inspiring each other. If one animator did a scene that took it to the next level, then that was a challenge for the entire team. "How do we improve on that?" became the question, and the animation got better as a result. There was one scene in particular on *Toy Story* that was animated by Mark Oftedal that perfectly exemplified this. Buzz and Woody are hiding underneath a tanker truck and arguing about what to do next. Woody finds the Pizza Planet truck and gets excited because he's found a way to get to Andy. But then he realizes that he can't go without Buzz. So he starts thinking and becomes really emotional. Now, when people get lost in deep thought, their eyes tend to lock onto some-thing instead of drift. The eyes immediately lock onto something and then dart back and forth. That's hard to do with hand-drawn animation. Using the computer, Mark made that moment happen. You felt like Woody was alive and really thinking. You could see this transition. I'll never forget that dailies. When Mark showed that scene, everyone could see what he had done. It reminded me of a time while I was at Disney when I went to Frank and Ollie for help on a scene. After they flipped my drawings, they quickly asked, "What's the character thinking?" They had immediately put their finger on the problem—I was just drawing animation, not showing what was going on in the character's head. Around the time we were animat-ing *Toy Story*, Disney was making *Pocahontas*, and we had to fly to New York for a press conference on this private jet. I happened to have an unfinished copy of *Toy Story*, so we all watched. Glen Keane was on the plane, and he, along with everyone else, was really struck by that scene of Mark's—by Woody's eyes and his emotion. *Pocahontas* was one of the most realistic bits of animation that Glen and John Pomeroy were working on, and they were having a difficult time with the subtle movements. But in the subtle movement of Woody's eyes, they could see that he was alive.

Character design, Buzz Lightyear, John Lasseter, *Toy Story*, 1995 © Disney/Pixar.

Bill: **In my opinion, that's the artistry of animation. You captured something so small, yet so important and relevant to the scene. You gave life to a completely inanimate thing. Glen was reacting to the magical artistry of animation.**

John: Right. Frank and Ollie always used to say that great character animation contains movement that is generated by the character's thought process. It can't be plain movement. When I was creating *Luxo Jr.*, I may not have included any eyes, but I clearly defined what part of this inanimate object was going to be the face. There needed to be a head, something facing forward. This was going to be the focal point of the character animation. You lead with the eyes first. Then comes the face and the body. If you don't have eyes, then you lead with the face. It always conveys that the character is thinking.

Bill: As a director, when did you learn the importance of delegating?

John: Delegation came a little bit later. There was such a tiny crew working on *Toy Story*. We were just making it up as we went along. Everybody had their job and I was directing. Consequently, I was intimately involved in every little aspect. Even on *A Bug's Life*, with the challenge of working with wide screen, I was still intimately involved in everything. When Pixar went public and *Toy Story* was a huge success, though, things changed. The pressure increased. It's hard enough just to make a good movie, but now you have stockholders to answer to. Steve Jobs, who was in charge at the time, decided to follow the business model Disney had used

Character design, Woody, John Lasseter, *Toy Story*, 1995 © Disney/Pixar.

with *Aladdin*. Basically, after a hit film you produce direct-to-video sequels. We asked a couple of our young animators to act as directors for these sequels, but we soon realized that this business model wasn't good for Pixar. We didn't want to differentiate between our projects and do some that would be second rate. Since we felt like the story we had come up with for a *Toy Story 2* had potential, we decided to put it on track for an actual theatrical release. This was the first time I was overseeing a feature project that I wasn't directing, and the pressure to put stuff into production was intense. My gut was telling me that it wasn't ready, but we had to "feed the beast." As *Bug's Life* was winding down, we started looking more closely at *Toy Story 2*, and it just wasn't coming together. I remember coming back from the publicity trip to Asia for *A Bug's Life*, completely jet lagged. I was supposed to go in and look at *Toy Story 2* the next day, but my family couldn't sleep, so we put on a laser disc of *Toy Story*. I hadn't seen it in a long time. I'll never forget watching it at that moment with my boys and my wife, Nancy. I said, "Man, that's a good movie!" I kept thinking to myself, "How did we do that?"

Bill: Did that give you any inspiration?

John: Nancy simply pointed out that I loved these characters. I loved Buzz and Woody. So when I went in the following day and saw how mediocre *Toy Story 2* was, I knew what had to be done. We couldn't let Buzz and Woody be in a movie that was anything less than the best we could make it. I stepped in as director and I brought back the original team: Andrew, Pete, and Joe, and Lee Unkrich, who was the editor on *Toy Story*, became the codirector. We had to do this right. Now, typically it takes four years to make a movie like *Toy Story* or *A Bug's Life*. But we had just nine months to make this movie and keep our release date. To make matters worse, we completely restarted the movie. This was around Christmastime, so I gave everybody the last remaining days of the year off. Meanwhile, Andrew, Joe, Pete, and I were still working. After the new year, we went up to Sonoma and completely reworked the story in two days. Then we returned to Pixar and I pitched the story to the entire crew. It was really good, and Andrew immediately started typing the script. But this is also the time when I hit a personal wall. I was tired. It was 1998, and I had been working nonstop since 1991. Not to mention, I had five boys at home. Nancy made something very clear to me. She knew this project was going to kill me. So, she wasn't going to support me on this unless I left for home every day at six o'clock and never worked a single weekend. That was the deal she put on the table. She laid down the law! I had nine months to make a movie. I said, "How am I supposed to do this?" "Delegate, John. You've got brilliant people that helped you make two movies. Just delegate," she said. Since I couldn't do it without her, I delegated.

Character sketch, Flik, John Lasseter, *A Bug's Life*, 1998 © Disney/Pixar.

Bill: Was that tough?

John: I just started assigning people various duties, and it was difficult. I could only check in on them as best I could. For better or worse, we just started making this movie. It was as close to improvisation as animation can get. Andrew would write something on Monday. Joe would storyboard it on Tuesday. Lee would videotape it and cut it by Friday. Layout was at the beginning of the following week, and animation was at the end of the week. Two weeks! It honestly was going that fast. Now Disney usually had to approve things for production. But Tom Schumacher said, "Don't let us get in your way. I'll try as best I can to help you, but just go go go." I'm not sure anybody believed we could do it. But we were having a blast. We just did it. And I did work some late nights and a few weekends. But, overall, I was out of the office by 6:30 every day. It was amazing. Everybody rose to the occasion. I delegated and they did it. It not only changed the studio, but I also started to recognize how I can direct people. If I give them more creative control, if I challenge them just enough, then they can achieve great creative satisfaction in rising to the occasion. And the project benefits from that success. The only problem we encountered was that we were working too hard. We pushed ourselves physically to the limit, and about a third of our people came down with repetitive stress injuries. That changed the way we worked at the studio, because we never wanted that to ever happen again. We adjusted in a good way, made sure everyone had ergonomically correct chairs, keyboards, etc. We even had massage therapists come in. So we were able to learn from that. The best lesson we learned, however, was to trust our instincts as artists. Working at that level, at that pace, we had to give our creativity free rein. There was no time to test anything. There was no time to second-guess our abilities.

Bill: Based on that experience, what advice do you find yourself giving young animators and directors?

John: One thing I always say to people in animation is, "Never forget the first time you hear something that makes you laugh or see something that moves you." Even though you'll see it a thousand times over before it's finished and it'll no longer make you laugh by then, never forget the first time. Because that's how the audience will see and feel it. It's hard, but I constantly remind people of that. Every day I try to put myself in the audience's shoes. Is it appealing, funny, and moving for them? Where do we want the audience to be? We have to take them on this wonderful journey. It's very easy in animation to get caught up in the details and lose sight of the bigger picture. I remember the Disney executives used to say, "I'm going for popcorn. You're boring me. Cut it. Make it faster." When you're directing, delegating, and keeping a larger vision in mind, one that includes the audience, you need to both trust your creative instincts and remember what it's like to be coming to the story brand new. *Toy Story 2* definitely changed Pixar. There was more delegation, and we started letting the leads have a little more creative control over their departments.

Bill: Talk a little bit more about how you direct your team.

John: As I mentioned before, I always looked back to my Disney days to find examples of what not to do. Managing creative people is arguably one of the most challenging tasks around. But I never had a problem with it because I always think about what inspires me, what plagues me, and what drives me as an artist. Looking back on those days, the motivation of my managers had very little to do with the movie, or even trying to make the movie better. It was politics. It was power. "Do what you are told to do," is what I heard. I just wanted to make the movie better. At Pixar, that sentiment was inherent in our approach to animation. I also think being up in the Bay Area, 400 miles away from Disney, was a blessing. Pixar may have been working with them a lot, but they couldn't micromanage us. They only occasionally checked in. Not to mention, we were a separate company. We were collaborators, not their employees. They had to diplomatically negotiate with us. They didn't control us. Technically, there were two producers, one from Disney and one from Pixar. We just worked off our instincts. And I started recognizing the simple truth that creative people want to be creatively satisfied. That's what drives them. That'll make them happy at the end of the day. Thus, in terms of managing them, you have to give them some creative ownership over what they're doing, no matter how small the task. Again, as a young animator at Disney, I remember being shut down every time I creatively suggested anything. I just felt like a warm body that was supposed to shut up and draw. And that made you soon not care about what you were doing. Consequently, as a director, I try to set my crew up for success. When I give them an assignment, I tell them everything they need to know to do the job right, but I don't tell them how to do it. I want to see what they'll come up with; I want them to have creative control over the task. What I do as a director, I try to figure out what information they need so they can be successful the first time. Oftentimes, you'll come in and someone has worked a week on something, you look at it and it's completely wrong—but I never blame them, I blame myself because I didn't set them up for success, and give them the right piece of information. I love, actually love, coming in and seeing something new and being blown away by someone's work. You're asking, "How did you do that?" and getting so inspired. Like Mark Oftedal's scene with the eyes darting, or the amazing Doug Sweetland—on any shot he animated I was always like, "Ahh, how'd you do that? That's amazing! How'd you think of that?" I'd often look at something, and it would give me ideas I would never have thought of otherwise—which is what collaboration is all about. That's what is so important about giving people a little creative ownership. Not only is it much more satisfying for them, they can make the whole project better in ways you can't even imagine.

Bill: **In your opinion, what constitutes a great animated film?**

John: You want to make movies that stand the test of time. In spite of everything I learned on *Young Sherlock Holmes*, it's nowhere to be found today. It's not on people's lips, not like *Bambi*, *Dumbo*, or *Pinocchio*. The great Disney animated films will never go away. New generations will always discover them and fall in love with them. That's what great animation is all about. It's what you strive to achieve. Because when you work really hard on something, you want it to be for something that lasts. For instance, I met this family up in Sonoma that was so excited to tell me that their grandmother was a cel painter on *Snow White*. The pride with which this family spoke of her really touched me. A cel painter, after all, wasn't the loftiest job back then. But generations of that family will always be connected to *Snow White*. I want the families of everybody at Pixar to be able to feel that kind of pride. I want them to say, "My daddy worked on *Toy Story*," or "My wife worked on *Finding Nemo*."

Bill: **What's the most unique aspect of Pixar's methodology? What makes you truly different?**

John: I think it's about sharing ideas. This goes back to the idea of creative leadership and the importance of dailies. The entire studio was designed with the way we run dailies in mind. We have two screening rooms and a theatre, and everything is set up so people can come together as a group and creatively share ideas. That mentality is the foundation of how we work, and it pervades everything that we do: animation, modeling, lighting, layout. Again, I thank Dennis Muren for teaching me that important lesson. We are also a filmmaker-led studio, which is in contrast to most other studios. Most other studios are executive led. Now that doesn't mean that a director can do whatever they want. But they're able to focus on the creative vision. Because a movie has to be something you believe in. It's like your baby—you're going to live with this movie for years, help it grow, and then send it out into the world. It ends up being like a product of your DNA. And when you watch any Pixar movie, you can see this. You see Andrew Stanton in *Finding Nemo* and *WALL-E*. You see Pete Docter in *Monsters, Inc.*, and especially in *Up*. You see Brad Bird in *The Incredibles* and *Ratatouille*. You see me in *Cars*, *Toy Story*, *A Bug's Life*, and *Toy Story 2*. That, I think, is what differentiates us from an executive-led studio. When we have a project that we feel compelled to develop, it's not going to be subject to the producer, the development executive, the head of development, the head of the studio, and then finally, the chairman. Yes, everybody wants to make a good movie. But under those conditions, it's too easy for the project to transform into a negotiation of mandatory notes from too many people. It's especially bad when you're dealing with contradictory notes and comments—the amount of energy that gets wasted is unforgivable, and the likelihood that you'll insert a bad idea, just to appease someone, increases. At Pixar, we bet on people, not ideas. It's the ideas of those creative individuals, that talented group, that are going to make a great movie. When Ed Catmull gives a talk, he always asks, "How many people believe that the most important thing in a movie is a good idea?" Half the people raise their hands. Then he says, "How many people think it's a good group of people?" Half the people raise their hands. What Ed then points out is that you can have the best idea in the world, but if you give it to mediocre people, it will become mediocre at best. On the other hand, a mediocre idea given to great people will become great, because if they know the idea's not working, they'll throw it out and come up with something better. That's how it is at Pixar. People really put themselves into their projects. I never feel like I'm just assigning something to them. And speaking

Concept Art by Armand Baltazar for *Cars 2*, digital, 2010. © Disney/Pixar.

of ideas, Ed also came up with a great strategy for people pitching new projects. It's mandatory that every director come up with three good ideas, not just one. All three have to be something you'd put your heart and soul into. This prevents anyone from becoming emotionally invested in just one idea. If that idea doesn't pan out, I want them to be able to keep moving forward. I don't want them to come to a creative standstill because they're stuck on that one concept. Coming up with three ideas is not always easy. Sometimes we say, "Nope, not good enough. Come back with three more ideas." But in the end, they love the freedom. They recognize that they're not only free to create here, but they're part of a talented group of filmmakers—and that's going to help them develop individually over the long run.

Bill: **That indeed sounds like a unique environment.**

John: We call that core group of directors the "creative brain trust" at Pixar. The brain trust was something that happened organically at Pixar. It was not thought out or planned. We weren't applying a business model that someone learned in grad school—even the name *brain trust* was a term someone else used for it that just ended up sticking. It started on *Toy Story*, with that core group of Joe Ranft, Andrew Stanton, Pete Docter, and myself. Over time, that group grew to include other artists that wanted to make great movies, like our editor, Lee Unkrich. We developed this really strong bond, and even when we all started directing our individual films, we were never far from each other. And, as I said before, showing your reels to other filmmakers is mandatory, just like showing your work at dailies. This was something we took from our early days. Everybody wants to delay, keep it close to their chest until they get it perfect. That's when Andrew would say, "No. The goal is to be wrong as fast as you can. Just keep showing it. Always show it." You're going to be wrong! It's fine. We'll all collectively work and help make it great. That's what we do here. We help each other. And in this scenario, there are two important rules. First, there's no hierarchy of ideas. It doesn't matter where or from whom the idea comes. If it's going to make the movie better, use that idea. That's really important. Second, there are no mandatory notes at the studio. In the early days on *Toy Story*, there were notes from executives that we had to account for. But many times, Andrew and I would read notes that simply missed the actual problems in the film. They'd be poking at one thing, but the problem was actually way over here, much earlier in the film. So sometimes taking a note literally isn't the right thing to do. I also learned that when you say that notes aren't mandatory, suddenly everyone listens. They want feedback, after all. They want the film to be better. So the process becomes more engaging. And everyone has to take responsibility for contributing to this exchange of ideas. They have to take ownership of the process. It's not about power. It's not about position. It's about making the movie the best it can be, so honesty is essential. When I was working on *Toy Story*, Steve Jobs said to me, "John, the computers I make at Apple, no matter how successful, will have a life span of about three to five years. Then they're so obsolete that they become basically a doorstop, or a boat anchor. If you do your job right, these films can live forever." In all of our films at Pixar, and everything I've ever done, even the short films, you can see what Frank Thomas and Ollie Johnston taught us—that there has to be emotion, feeling. Your audience has to be emotionally invested in the characters and the story. For instance, in *Up*, the first ten minutes is such a tour de force that you nearly feel like crying.

Bill: **Greatest ten minutes of the movie.**

John: It's mind blowing. In fact, Pete visualized those ten minutes without dialogue from the very beginning. It immediately reminded me of what Chuck Jones once said, "With great animation, you should be able to turn the sound off and still know what's going on." How can we tell this story point visually? That's a question I constantly ask at the studio. The dialogue is going to go in one ear and out the other. Moreover, it's going to be dubbed in over 40 languages. You've got to get it right visually. In every Pixar film, there's a lot of visual storytelling, and it's very sophisticated. We use everything to tell the story: lighting, music, etc. In Hollywood, I often get asked, "How have you made ten successful pictures back to back?" That's not an easy feat to achieve for a live-action studio. I think a big part of it is that everything we do here is about telling a great story. We don't put something into production because we simply need something in production.

Bill: The director is indeed on the top of the pyramid, and very few people get to experience what it's like to make those kinds of decisions. But you and Pixar are different in that the movie, the story, doesn't necessarily come from the top.

John: I always listen to ideas, either when I'm pitched three ideas or when I'm just talking to people. And when I think about an idea, two questions come to mind. First, where is the emotion in this movie going to come from? It's not like a joke that you can insert later. Emotion is the foundation of this building you're about to construct. Second, is this a place I want to visit and become a part of? Is this a place I've never seen before? This is also part of the foundation. You can't go back and change it once you've begun construction. Plot and characters can change over and over. But this world and its source of emotion are constant. When Andrew pitched *Finding Nemo*, it took an entire hour, because he had it all worked out in detail. At the end he said, "What do you think?" "You had me at the word *fish*," I said.

Bill: Is it always that easy?

John: No, sometimes it takes longer. Sometimes you have to go back to the drawing board. But it was like that with Andrew on *Nemo*, Pete on *Up*, and Brad Bird on *Incredibles*. In animation, especially computer animation, where it's such a monumental task to make a film, it's easy to get lost in the details. But you can never lose sight of why you are making this film. You have to remember what made you want to do it in the first place. That's why the foundation, the emotion and the vision of this world, is so important to get right. Once you've got that, it's OK to be wrong on the other stuff at first. We'll make it better. Pixar is a place where it's safe to be wrong. Ed Catmull created that environment, because we're always trying to create something that no one has ever seen before, and if it's not safe to be wrong, it's almost impossible to get something new. I often say Hollywood is like trying to be a trapeze artist in a deadly circus. You train hard to come up with a spectacular new move that will amaze the audience. But as you're up there, pondering whether or not to try it, you notice that not only is the net missing, but there are also poisoned spikes down there. At Pixar, not only is there a net, but it's full of fluffy pillows. You feel safe trying that new move.

Bill: And a crane to pull you back up.

John: Exactly! We want you to get back up and try again. And people do! It's quite intoxicating, working at a studio of pioneers. We're creatively driven, and we *want* to be inspired and motivated by others, both inside and outside the studio. We were filmgoers before we were filmmakers, and we want to make movies we want to see—entertaining films that engage all age groups. Everyone in the audience should have fun, not just the kids. I've heard executives in Hollywood paraphrase P. T. Barnum, saying, "You'll never lose money by underestimating your audience." Well, we want to overestimate our audience. We assume they're smart, especially the kids. Hollywood usually aims for the lowest common denominator. We aim high.

Bill: That's quite an impressive example to set for the industry.

John: When I was working for Disney and visited the Lucasfilm Computer Division in November 1983, I was amazed by the talent there: Loren Carpenter, Rob Cook, Bill Reeves, Eben Ostby, Alvy Ray Smith, and Ed Catmull. I asked Ed how he managed to hire such great people. He said, "It's easy. I just try to hire people who are smarter than me." He was utterly secure and comfortable with letting someone else's talent shine. It made me laugh because that wasn't at all the case at Disney at the time. All of us were being creatively squashed: Tim Burton, Brad Bird, John Musker, Jerry Rees, Henry Selick. That's not how we want it to be at Pixar. We want people to have a chance of a career at Pixar, a chance to shine. That's why we believe in mentoring. We want to bring in up-and-coming talent and help them grow. We don't want to recreate Disney in the fifties and sixties, where they didn't hire anybody, just relying on the Nine Old Men for years and years until suddenly it was the early seventies and they realized the studio was nearly empty!

Bill: As a studio, how would you briefly describe Pixar?

John: Steve Jobs once said about Pixar, "We're in a golden age." But I always disliked that because "golden age" usually means there's an end to it. And when I recently described Pixar as a family to Ed, he said, "When you think about family, there really is no such thing as a golden age. You meet someone, you fall in love, you have your first baby, and then your family grows and grows. The kids grow up and go to college. Then they get married and you end up with grandkids. It never stops. There's never one single 'golden age.'" Each person, each family unit, is special because a family evolves over time. And Pixar continues to evolve, just like a family. We look for new talent. We have an internship program for college students, where they get work experience, and we get the opportunity to work with young artists who are eager to create. These are the young artists and animators that are going to help our studio and the industry evolve. When Brad Bird first came to Pixar, Ed and I told him that the thing we worry about the most is Pixar becoming complacent, thinking that we know what we're doing or stopping innovating. We didn't want Pixar to become a place that stifles creativity. We'll never allow that.

Bill: This has been absolutely great. Thanks, John.

4
Andrew Stanton Interview

Andrew Stanton © Disney.

Like so many of the directors in this book, Andrew Stanton dreamed of someday working for Disney. Unlike the others, Disney never hired him.

Instead, he had to be one of the founding creative members of Pixar to make it to Disney. He was a writer attending a pitch meeting on the first *Toy Story* when he first set foot on the studio lot. That unconventional path reflects an unconventional career, taking a story artist with little computer experience to the director's chair on two of this biggest Oscar-winning computer-generated (CG) films of all time, *Finding Nemo* and *WALL-E*.

Andrew loved telling stories, and it was his great good luck to land at Pixar, where story is valued above all else. Perhaps more than any other Pixar director, he has an additional visibility telling stories about telling stories. As an educator, I have found his quotes, articles, and interviews about story to be particularly cogent, precise, and valuable. Check out his TED talk online!

Andrew once said that when he started his career, he was surrounded by artists whom he knew had more talent as writers, animators, painters, designers, and storyboarders. The one thing he knew he could do was outwork them. What can never be achieved by mere effort is his profound gift for recognizing the core emotional heart of a story.

Unlike most directors in animation, it was the written word, not the sketch or drawing, that defined his creative process. Andrew can draw—well–but his way of visualizing an animated film through writing is a method young animators should study.

We interviewed Andrew at Pixar Animation Studios.

Bill Kroyer

Bill: When did you first become interested in animation? How did you start your path toward this career?

Andrew: I think I'm pretty cliché for a lot of people of my generation. It was before DVD and VHS. I saw the few Disney releases that would come to the theater. I watched the *Bugs Bunny* reruns on TV. Animation was just barely in my life. Whenever I could find it, I would watch it. I would even endure the last ten minutes of Lawrence Welk on Sunday nights just to make sure I didn't miss any of the first frames of the *Wonderful World of Disney*! I never thought of animation as a career option. It was just something I loved. But I liked theater, film, and music … things that I thought I might follow. I bet a lot of people have similar stories. Then I discovered CalArts through a handbook in my guidance counselor's office and its animation program by Disney. Once I knew that existed, it was like Devils Tower in *Close Encounters*. I had to go. Come hell or high water, I had to go! And when I finally made it in, after my second year of college, it was like finding my own species. Before, there was no one else like me around. Suddenly, there were a hundred people like me! That's when I just knew down to my very core that this is what I wanted to do.

My path was rather normal for the mid to late eighties. Unless you were working for Disney, there was no such thing as full-time employment. You worked for a couple of weeks, a couple of months, project to project, show to show, commercial to commercial; I was all over the place for two or three years. I worked for Ralph Bakshi, for Bill Kroyer and Kroyer Studios, and I worked on a lot of freelance projects. But it was only because I had made some student films that I was picked up by the *Spike and Mike's Festival of Animation*. It was then that I bumped into John Lasseter, who was representing Pixar, and over many years we built up a friendship that ultimately turned into employment and what got me here.

Bill: Why didn't Disney hire you?

Andrew: I applied to Disney three times and was turned down each time. In fact, I remember finally admitting that to Tom Schumacher when we were working on *A Bug's Life*. I had already proven myself and he just kind of went pale and said, "You're not going to hold that against us are you?" I said, "No, I'm not." But the first time I ever entered that lot professionally was to pitch *Toy Story* to Katzenberg.

Bill: Wow, that's amazing! Your first pitch was *Toy Story*?

Andrew: Yep.

Somewhere in the Artic, Andrew Stanton, 1988. (Courtesy of ACME.)

A Story, Andrew Stanton, 1987. (Courtesy of ACME.)

Bill: After John hired you at Pixar, what was your first role at the studio?

Andrew: Again, I lucked out. I had no interest in computer graphics at all. I had never even touched a computer. John, was a maverick.... All of the guys were sort of mavericks at the time. It wasn't about people understanding the tools; it was about the tools servicing the talent. And he was one of the few guys that was able to employ people with that philosophy. All I wanted was a job! But he was the first to hire me for what I could contribute as an individual; I wasn't just a pair of hands. Pete Docter then came about six months later, and it was just the three of us for the longest time. We did commercials for about two and a half years.

And we got to do it all. Even when one person was directing, another was boarding, and another animating. We shared everything. We were this little trio, a think tank. This is when my real film education began. My time at CalArts was about learning what I didn't know. Then my first five or six years at Pixar was about actually learning it and being able to iterate quickly. Working on a commercial every 12 weeks really allowed you to get better and better. It was a great practice run for suddenly having to leap into a feature three years later.

Bill: Did you learn the whole pipeline, where you're modeling and rigging?

Andrew: Yes. I can't say I was good at it, but I learned enough to know what the hell I was talking about and sound like I was good at it! Later, someone else was hired for that job and I never had to do it again. But yeah, I learned the whole thing. It's funny, it seemed to me we were standing on firm ground. Now when you look back, it seems that this was a pioneering moment in the creation of feature CG movies. I just didn't recognize it at the time. I didn't realize that I was learning a skill that would become incredibly useful and allow me to be somewhat of a professional simply because I was there first. At the time, I just thought I was learning something that I couldn't use anywhere else.

Bill: What was your role in getting the first *Toy Story* feature in production?

Andrew: I wanted it so badly! *Toy Story* was always the thing, the project I wanted to get off the ground. So the minute we got the OK to make the movie, it honestly felt like we were kids playing house. "What do you want to do?" John says, "I'll be the director." Then Pete says, "I want to do the animation." And I said, "I want to work on the story." Joe Ranft was actually in charge of the story, but I wanted to be involved. Because I animated for so many years, I think everybody assumed, including me for a while, that I would be an animator once we got into production. But it just didn't stick. Once I got my hands dirty in writing, I really had no other interests. And I really lucked out. For the next five years, I observed how movies are written, and I was very fortunate to work with both bad and good screenwriting, to see what the difference was. The person I learned a lot from was Joss Whedon, who worked with us for about a year. It was from those writing sessions, even sometimes just gag sessions, that I started to appreciate the craft of screenwriting. Again, it was like a think tank. We would talk, he'd go away and write, and then come back and we'd refine our choice of words. But eventually Joss had to leave. Almost a year is a long time for a screenwriter to stay out of Hollywood, and his career was definitely going. So I remember thinking, "Well, I think I can do this. I can take a crack at this. After all, they can't fire me. This is not what they are actually paying me to do. I'll just keep doing this until someone tells me to stop." Two years later, the movie was like gangbusters. That I would be a screenwriter, that I would enjoy writing, it was something I was intimidated by or not appreciative of beforehand.

Bill: **You started with the Disney style, which of course is storyboarding, visual storytelling, right?**

Andrew: I somehow separated that from writing, though. In my limited mind, I thought, "No, I draw pictures and I think of funny stuff." I never thought about writing for adults and for smart people. Once I finally realized that screenwriting is cinematic dictation, that it's putting in words what you picture in your head, I said to myself, "I can do that!" I never had a problem picturing what I think should happen on-screen. The whole process was then demystified.

Bill: **Do you still see any difference between storyboarding or brainstorming visually and just sitting, imagining, and writing it out?**

Andrew: I don't think it's an either/or situation. I think they're both needed. It's certainly been proven that you can make a movie without one of them. But having lived with both and trying to be an expert in both, I can't imagine not having both tools. You know, the biggest advantage for storyboarding is that it's closer to what will finally happen on the screen. It's the image. It's the final translation of what will be up there. It also makes your brain think about how to translate emotions, intentions, dramatic shifts, everything through movement, through visual terms and not being dependent on exposition and on words. But the written word forces you to think about the bones, to think about what you're doing and how it all connects. You can hide behind funny drawings. Pretty pictures can trick you into standing on broken bones and not know it. I think it's really a combination of the two. If you can be strong in both, then you're only going to be that much stronger and closer to getting the better product at the end. Even if I were only making the movie for myself, which is the mind-set I always have, I would use both techniques every time.

Bill: How did writing lead to your first directing opportunity?

Andrew: By the time we finished *Toy Story*, I had been involved in every step of the production. That wasn't my intention; it just happened. Since John and I had spent so much time together making commercials, whenever we hit a difficult spot or needed a second opinion, he would call me in. And I know there were a lot of people on the back end that were thinking, "Who is this asshole that is coming in suddenly and making changes? Why does his opinion matter?" Well, John, Pete, Joe, and I were this little band that was just smarter together than apart. And we would find any excuse to rely on each other to strengthen or fix something. When that was all over, John and I wanted to make this process official and give it a name. So we called it "codirector." But we also recognized that this notion of codirector was different from the usual suspect … the shared directing. For us, it was more a Batman and Robin relationship. I was Robin. I was just there to be a counterpoint to the larger vision at hand, to help modify it. But after I finished working on *A Bug's Life*, I was just too greedy. I realized that I didn't like just one part of the process. I loved the whole thing. And in a way, I think I've always loved the whole thing. I have brothers that are five years younger and twins, so my home came with a built-in audience. I was always putting on a show, always finding some way to entertain them. Honestly, I never consciously desired or was attracted to the role and title of director. Since I just wanted to put on that big show, I found myself accidently falling into that role. And John and I were so in sync…. It was almost psychic. But little things began to frustrate me. "It's not going to kill it, one way or another, if it goes green or red," I would tell myself. "But I like green, he likes red, and it's his picture. It goes red." And so I saw the writing on the wall. That maybe another film or two down the road the resentment may start to rise. And at no point ever did I want to feel resentment. I was so grateful and I really enjoyed what I was doing; I always wanted to have a healthy relationship with Pixar and John. When the time came, I thought, and the idea presented itself, then maybe I would take the wheel and see where I could take all those little differences and points of decision making and …

Bill: It's pretty clear that you needed to be a director.

Andrew: Yeah, but I didn't think too hard about it. We had such a healthy atmosphere that I knew something would have to change, if any kind of resentment appeared. And things were moving in that direction. It just wasn't there yet. But things worked out for the best, because we had to evolve and grow anyway. I still feel so lucky. We were isolated up in Northern California, cut off from the way the rest of the world made movies and the typical politics that ensue. We just did what made sense, which is a radical idea, apparently, in the world of moviemaking. And regardless of where we were in the process, we were just honest with each other. That's what holds us together, and I think it has shown for the entire 20-year run, so far.

Bill: *Finding Nemo* was your first solo project, as director?

Andrew: Yeah.

Bill: How did that come about? Did you simply stand up and say you had a great idea for a movie, or did they tell you to come up with something?

Andrew: Actually, I don't think they would have been too surprised if I had asked to be a director on *A Bug's Life*. But at that point, I knew the difference between creating your own story and just working on an idea. *Toy Story* came from this honest love of being in the world of your toys, and what it's like to have a new toy. It sprung from that childish imagination and curiosity about whether a toy wants to find us, if it's lost, or if it has a life of its own behind that closed door. *A Bug's Life*

A Bug's Life, 1998. © 1998 Disney/Pixar.

was more like an assignment. We said, "What if the grasshopper and the ant fable was turned on its head?" It didn't come from this place of inner love or childhood fantasy. It was much more of a chore to get right. I remember saying at the time to my wife, "I only want to work on ideas from now on that are so compelling that I can't stop myself from getting out of bed to work on them." So I waited until I had something that just needed to be on-screen. I mean, I was certainly developing it over time, but I was waiting for that right moment. Basically, I would always fantasize about living in the underwater world and growing up on the ocean. When I was a kid, my dentist had a fish tank in his lobby. I even used to think how weird it probably was for the fish to watch humans have their teeth worked on. But I knew those two notions weren't enough to tell a story. That was just a scenario and a setting. I needed more. Then one day I was out with my son, who was four or five years old at the time, and I was feeling that pressure to have real daddy–son time, since I had been working too much. As I started saying, "Don't touch that, you're going to poke your eye out," or "Don't run into the street," I realized I was pissing away the entire point of the afternoon, the reason I was with my son. I was the good father with the best of intentions, and I couldn't get out of my own way. Then it hit me. That was the missing link. That's a real and interesting issue for parents. So, just shortly after *A Bug's Life*, these three ideas came together and I had it. You can tell I'm always thinking about another film while I'm working on one. Actually, knowing that I have the right ingredients was really the catalyst that made me want to direct. It wasn't ever the desire to direct. I guess that's a long way of saying it was the idea that drove that decision and nothing else.

Bill: **One of the landmarks of that film is the incredible cast of characters. And there are a lot of them! I always use that movie as an example of characters that are genuine, not only the nature of their role in the ocean, but their personalities and stories. Did you set out to have such a gigantic cast of characters?**

Andrew: No, and this is starting to become all too familiar. I have this little idea for a little film. Then it ends up being the whole ocean or the whole universe. My intentions are small, but my executions are big. I don't know how else to put it. I know it sounds cliché, but you know your story once you know your premise. The premise on *Nemo* was "fear denies a good father from being one." Once you have that, everything else will fall into place. Everything will have to service that premise. For example, even if the most remote character is interesting to you, you'll now have the discipline to keep them to only three shots with their three lines because you now know the premise. No matter how much a character and sequence inspires you to stop and explore, you have to keep the big picture, that premise, in mind. Otherwise, you're basically saying, "We've got somebody really good looking in this film, let's just keep shooting him or her and screw the narrative." It's a very sexy trap that you shouldn't fall into.

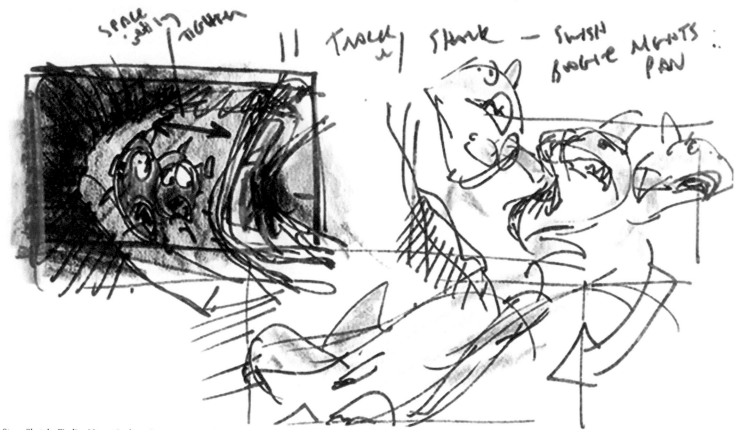

Story Sketch, *Finding Nemo*, Andrew Stanton, 2003 © Disney/Pixar.

Bill: How did you come up with the character Dory?

Andrew: Dory was interesting. I knew I was going to separate a father and son, and I knew I needed a guide to take the father on this journey to find his kid. But I immediately fell into the cliché of just making him male. And it was actually the character Gill (that Willem Dafoe plays) that I had in mind during my early drafts. Then I read about how goldfish have a memory of three seconds. I thought that was a hysterical problem. It was too good not to give to a major character. Wouldn't that be a great problem, if your guide keeps forgetting everything? But I couldn't find a funny way to do it, without it getting old really quick.

Tom Hanks had just been on *Saturday Night Live* and did the short-term memory skit, so I'd seen some examples. But ultimately I felt stuck. Then my wife had the *Ellen DeGeneres Show* on in the background one day, and I heard her change the subject five times in one sentence. It just clicked. Honestly, it was one of those lightning bolt moments. I asked myself, "What if it was a girl? What if it was platonic? I've never seen that." It's the "Why not?" and the "Why can't it be like this?" that drives me. Even on *Toy Story*, we wanted to get rid of all of those weird myths that limit animation, not only outside the industry, but also inside the industry itself. It had to be a musical. It had to be a fairy tale, things like that. But there is so much more that you can do. And that's how Dory came to be. And even more so, I realized that she was a surrogate for the child, that she was playing the role of Nemo for the dad. That way, I could have Marlin grow and change on this journey, even though his son technically wasn't with him. And that gave a distinct strength to the film, which is something I'm always looking for.

Bill: **Ellen DeGeneres, a bigger part? She wasn't just cast that way?**

Andrew: I've made a rule never to write for a character, never to write for an actor. That can easily screw you up, if they don't say yes. But I had writer's block if I didn't think of her as Dory. So, this was my pitch. I sent her the script. She read it, and when she called I said, "Hi, Ellen. I'm Andrew Stanton. I wrote this part for you, and if you don't take it I'm fucked." That was it. She said, "Well, I better take it."

Bill: **And then you made a bold move of not casting Brad Pitt.**

Andrew: And there was so much pressure!

Bill: **Albert Brooks was an unusual choice. Most people would have never thought of him. How many people did you go through until that idea hit you?**

Andrew: He was actually my first choice. But then I got talked out of it. Some people thought he might be too old. So I went with another actor for a while. And he was incredibly professional. He didn't do anything wrong. But ultimately, the casting wasn't right. I was treating the father, Marlin, too much like a straight man. We needed to be entertained by his uptightness, and it's a short list of people that can be anxious and worry that aren't off-putting. So I went back to my first instinct, which was Albert.

Bill: **In a movie that big, there is so much work to do. Your team is essential. Where do you start? How do you put a team together?**

Andrew: Well, when you don't know them, you have to go off their résumé, what they've done before. You even have to talk with their former employers and associates. But I'm a real believer in plain chemistry; I've witnessed the benefits over and over again. It's like putting a garage band together. You're looking for a bass player, so you get a couple of guys together that seem to like you and go from there. You just know when they fit. And you can't necessarily know ahead of time or even explain that moment of realization. Once it works, you're just suddenly able to understand why you're choosing them. I truly rely on my discernment skills, sometimes to a fault.

Bill: **Do you have any thoughts about what the greatest qualities or attributes of an animation director might be? And do you feel that your skills fit that description?**

Andrew: You mean director of an animated film or an animation director?

Bill: **A director of an animated film.**

Andrew: It's funny. I prided myself on believing you shouldn't have to think differently from any other director. But, if I'm really breaking it down, there are differences that you need to be aware of. At the end of the day, there shouldn't be any difference concerning the fundamentals. I mean, you should have a great sense of story. You should have a great sense of momentum, timing, and drama, so that you can not only come up with great ideas, but also, more importantly, recognize when you're not getting it. You have to recognize when it's not happening. Otherwise, you're going to spend most of your time diagnosing and fixing problems that should have been avoided. One of the big traps I see directors fall into, at least at a place like Pixar, is that when they first start, they're already at the top of the pyramid. If they succeed and survive the whole drama, they think they were the sole reason for how it all came together on-screen. The truth is, if they did their job right, they were the facilitator of all those great ideas. But they didn't come up with all those ideas. And they shouldn't think they have to. But a lot of new guys think they have to. That's the trap. I've always said, "Your job is not to be the one with the answers. You should be the one that *gets* the answers. That's your job." You need to make friends and get to know your crew. These folks are your talent, your bag of tricks. And that's where you're going to find answers to the big problems. And it's going to be different on every movie, unless you're trying to make the same movie twice. That's the job. It's pretty universal too. I would not say it's unique to animation. The only thing maybe unique to animation is that you don't get anything for free. There's no pretty sunset that you suddenly get to shoot. There's no little five-and-dime store where you stumble upon a cool prop. There's no wonderful improv. No, you have to decide every pixel. It's incredibly daunting. Seriously. When I made the transition to a live-action set, everybody assumed that I would be overwhelmed. But, no matter how many questions I received that day, no matter how crazy it got, it was never more than 50 percent of what I'm used to on a day here. Here you have to juggle so many different moving parts, parts that will never be seen in the same room together for months. There is just no such thing as spontaneity in animation, other than recording sessions with the actors. So, you have to have the skill of coming up with an exciting idea. Then be able to deconstruct it into the 50 parts that will ultimately produce that exciting idea. And then, not only assign each part to your crew, but also keep that idea alive in your head for months until you see the pieces come together. Hopefully, you're right. Hopefully, it works. But you never are. Then you figure out why it's wrong and do something about it. I once had a cameraman on a live-action set say, "I don't know how you do it. You see the picture, the scene, before we've even rehearsed it or put people on the set." I wanted to say, "Buddy, you haven't met anybody in animation!" I mean, that's what you have to do. In the world of storyboarding you have to picture it ahead of time, and then it becomes a quest to find that image as you embark upon this great construction project for the next year and a half. As a director of animated film, you truly are the vision keeper. The movie will not move forward without that. For better or worse, other mediums can progress even if the director doesn't quite know what he or she is doing. It just doesn't work that way in animation.

Bill: What's the ratio of visualizing the sequence as opposed to visualizing something somewhere along the way? You have probably experienced both.

Andrew: Well, I'd say it's three to one, three not working and one working.

Bill: Really?

Andrew: Yeah, I'd say that's the average. It may be well known in animation, or maybe it's unique to my experience at Pixar, but making movies is messy. And there's an organized way to do it, where you're not spending a lot of people's money. And there's the chaotic way to do it, where you're spending irresponsibly. Either way, you have to accept that it will be messy and there will be issues. Outside the arena of filmmaking, the world often seems structured on the notion of "cross your fingers and hope for the best." But I think that's a flaw. You see, Pixar is really good at fixing problems. We're organized around the expectation that things will go wrong, things will suck. Consequently, there is this constructive mentality waiting to kick in, waiting to creatively address and fix this issue. We don't cross our fingers here.

Bill: So that's another way of expressing that crash and burn phenomenon, right, where every picture seems to go at one point?

Andrew: Yeah. And there are many degrees of that. On *Toy Story 2*, we encountered a huge mistake in the middle of production. On *Toy Story 3*, just a tiny speed bump. All movies reveal an ugly face to some greater or lesser degree.

Bill: What about music, effects, atmosphere? Do you see and hear this stuff as you're creating the story?

Andrew: Hmm, atmosphere. For me, I would say tone, and this is speaking as a writer-director. I can't write unless I've decided on what the tone is going to be. Or I write until I see a tone develop, then I rethink it again. As for music, I pretty much create the soundtrack to my films while writing, even for those films I'm just attached to as a writer. All these things help me develop the story and put me in a creative mood. Whatever black magic tricks conjure up your boyhood imagination skills, you need them.

Bill: What were the toughest issues you encountered while making your first big film?

Andrew: Well, it's a lot easier being number two than number one. I know that! But when you're next to the president and go to every cabinet meeting, you find yourself thinking, "I can do this." Then suddenly you're the person in charge, and you're immediately sobered to the fact that nothing moves forward without you. Every problem is your problem, and every answer has to be facilitated through you. Even though I had been close to it on two films, I truly had no idea what that level of pressure was like. And a lot of things went wrong on *Nemo*. There were casting problems. I hit a big impasse with the narrative. I had some morale problems with some of the leads. And, of course, they all seemed to come to a head simultaneously. Then I had my *Jerry Maguire* moment when I was on vacation, at least that's what I would call it. I woke up sweating in bed, having a panic attack, and questioning my ability to do any of this. I literally typed out a mission statement, sort of, just to get it off my chest. And I woke up the next morning with some clarity. By the time I got back from vacation, I was thinking, "That's your job Andrew. That's what you need to do. That is what a director does. Even if you made the decisions that created the problem, you're also the person that needs to make the necessary decisions to get out of it." That was the big turning point for me. That's when the film went from bad to good.

Bill: What's the toughest thing about being the director?

Andrew: It's the loneliest job. You may have all these people around you, but nobody knows what it's like to be in your shoes. I mean, they see you, they're aware of your job, but at the end of the day they're not privy to the unique variables of that production. And it's rare that directors talk to one another. If they do, it's between projects. You see each other at either the awards ceremonies or some other kind of function. And veterans in the business have definitely felt your pain. But, man, what you really want is a suicide hot line to somebody else who understands your job. Someone you can talk to when you're in the middle of it! But when you're in it, it's just you. And that's a lonely place to be.

Bill: How did you feel about *Nemo* when it was finished? Was it a good buzz? Did you feel confident?

Andrew: No. I mean, I knew it worked. I remember feeling that this is the movie I wanted to make. But was this what the rest of the world wanted to see? I was in no way confident that I had done that. I'm way too much of a Protestant, I guess. Well, someone once told me this joke. "What did the Protestant say after he fell down the stairs?" He says, "I'm glad that's over with." And that's just it. My mind immediately goes to the deepest, darkest possibility. "It's all going to suck!" "It's all going to fall apart!" I feel superstitious about allowing myself any sort of optimism in advance. So, I try not to let that pessimism influence my decisions during the making of a movie. But it can be hard to control. As for positivity and optimism, I have to earn it along the way, somehow. I'm chasing that pure, sincere adulation and praise. Growing up, I had to work hard for that sign of affirmation, so maybe that's where it comes from. Anyway, for *Nemo* it took two weekends at the box office and a lot of reviews for me to admit, "OK, OK, they like it!" That was really bad. I'm not proud of it. I'm not proud of that at all.

Bill: How did you go from *Nemo* to your next picture, *WALL-E*?

Andrew: After *Nemo* and *The Incredibles*, Pixar's name and reputation were gaining a tremendous amount of momentum. I remember thinking, "Wow, we're in a place where people may actually come to theaters just because it says Pixar, regardless of what the movie is." I told myself, "If that's true, aren't we artistically responsible to put something out there that nobody else can, as opposed to something that's safe. We need an idea that would never have had a snowball's chance in hell of coming out otherwise." I already had the *WALL-E* idea. In fact, I started writing *WALL-E* while I was still working on *Nemo*. But it wasn't ready, and I didn't have the guts to settle on that as my next project. Only after the massive success of *Nemo* did I finally decide that this should be the next movie. And it still amuses me that I never had to sell *WALL-E*. Seriously, a silent robot, a dystopian world, and the near absence of human beings: who would let you make this movie? But whenever I would pitch it to anybody that I respected, any of my animation or film peers, it was easy. They saw it. I quickly realized that the only thing I was fighting was the preconceived notions of what an animated movie should be, or even what a movie should be. So I thought, "Well, if I have the protection of the Pixar brand, then we should just go for it. Let's go there!" After all, there really is no "there" to be scared of. And that was the challenge that I loved, in the same way I felt challenged on *Toy Story*. This doesn't have to be a musical fairy tale. It doesn't have to be this expected formula. We don't have to create that situation where people say, "I know what a Pixar film is. It has this, this, this, and this." Listen, if the idea is good, that's the only formula you need. And if you do it right, that will always be the only formula. Any other comparisons or similarities are just coincidence. Or maybe it's a director's taste. But there is no rulebook, and there never will be one. I just really, really love challenging and breaking the mold. I loved that *Up*, *Ratatouille*, and *WALL-E* all came out in a row. I just hate limited thinking!

Wall-E, 2008. © 2008 Disney/Pixar.

It drives me nuts. And, sadly, I saw the collective masses at the time starting to do this. Maybe I'm just getting tired, old, and a little jaded. But, for me, it was such a conscious effort to prove that animation, starting with *Toy Story*, is a medium that's not just for kids. It's for all ages, and it can be whatever it wants to be. It's just like Brad Bird had said. My utopian view was to elevate animation to the level you find in France or in Japan, where, just because it's animated, doesn't mean that it's simply kids' stuff. But in this country, no matter how many films we make, that stereotype is hard to escape. You feel like Sisyphus, just perpetually rolling that boulder up the hill.

Bill: **Are you conscious of being influenced by the other directors?**

Andrew: Yeah, it's far too much of a film geek world here. We all speak in movie talk. People that aren't as film centric feel that they have a lot of learning to do when they come to Pixar. They have a lot of movies to watch, just to even understand what the hell we're talking about when we're in meetings. We don't ever set out to literally mimic something, because there is no interest in that. But we also don't want to fight the fact that we're all influenced greatly by others. The more you learn about your favorite artist, and the more you learn about the world that they grew up in, you start to see their timeline. Then, for instance, you recognize the Jimi Hendrix in Prince. It's a natural part of evolution that you're infected, in the most positive sense of the word, by those filmmakers that you connect to, those speaking a language that you just get. It speaks to something deep down inside you, and it compels you to talk back, loudly. You can't really think about creating something from scratch. All you can do is take this language you've been taught and express yourself as best you can. That's when it becomes original.

Bill: **Do you feel that you've changed as a director from picture to picture? Can you see a change from how you worked on Nemo to how you worked on WALL-E?**

Andrew: Definitely. Of course, you get more comfortable with yourself. You learn to listen to your voice. With each film, you learn how you tick, when you're productive versus unproductive, and how you work and interact with those around you. You become more aware of yourself as a director and take ownership of that. I get why Spielberg, Eastwood, and Scorsese put people on retainer. You form a family that really brings the best out of you. These people know you. They know that you like to work at this hour of the day instead of that hour. After I paid my dues to get to that point, I didn't want to have to teach somebody all over again. I've always felt that there's a finite amount of time to make a movie, and you can either be spending dollars fixing problems or making it great. You can't do both at the same time. My motto is, "Be wrong as fast as you can, because you need to be smart about how you use your time." I'd rather be spending my Monopoly dollars on making a movie better instead of trying to fix a film. Knowing yourself as a director and surrounding yourself with the right people is key. And there's a learning curve there. It's a process.

Andrew Stanton, Conducting Research for *Wall-E* © Pixar. Photo: Deborah Coleman

Bill: How would you say your process is different from that of other Pixar directors?

Andrew: Hmm, I know there's a ton of differences between myself and the other directors at Pixar. But … I'm blanking here! Maybe it's because we were just talking about this the other day. Anyway, it's a small one, but maybe it'll make me think of some bigger ones. Some people are more specific and plan out their shots in story, and they board it. They put it on reels and then they make those shots in layout. As I discovered on *WALL-E*, I like to let my characters play and experiment, even if that meant more work for everyone. So I'd tell my animator, "You're not wasting your time creating animation that I'm going to throw away, you're helping layout." Then I'd explain, "I want you to take these characters and do this little scenario." Basically, it's like bringing the actors onto a set and letting them rehearse in front of you. Then I would send my digital cameraman in and I would find interesting ways to shoot it. I find that animators are often unconsciously animating to the camera, as if the camera has a fixed position. You establish a pretty picture, and then you put the actors in and they will

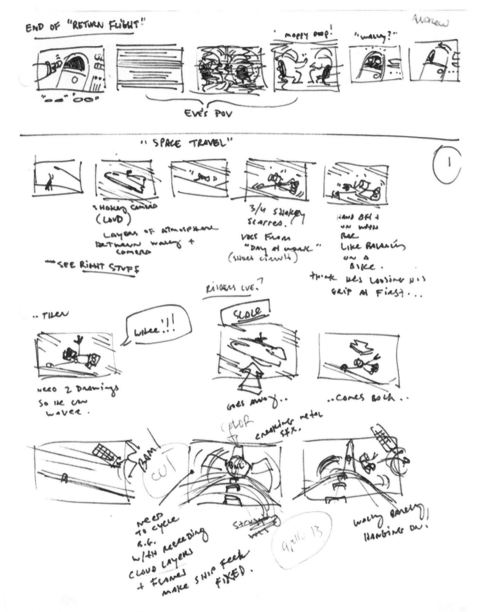

Story Sketch, Andrew Stanton, *Wall-E*, 2008 © Disney/Pixar.

stage themselves in a specific way. I can't help but think we're robbing ourselves a little bit, at least in our medium of three-dimensionality, from some added realism. Let the animator work in this 3D space! Of course, some stuff won't hold up, but you can actually add a little spontaneity to this preplanned world. You can *find* shots instead of simply playing shots from the board. And you can even have a happy accident that works in your favor. Obviously, there is a danger of creating too much extra work. But I found a way that works. Other than that, my writing process comes to mind. On *Nemo*, I learned how to write surrounded by a gang of people. Consequently, I can only do so much in isolation. I actually need to be in the writer's room, in the pit, pitching it as I go. I like to have a partner or, better yet, partners to bounce ideas off.

Bill: **What do you think an "Andrew Stanton movie" has that makes it uniquely yours?**

Andrew: I don't know. If I'm lucky enough to get the chance to make more films, I'll probably discover that along with everybody else. I remember John Lennon saying once that someday people were going to figure out that every song he'd ever written was about his mother. It's like that. I'm sure there's something like that in all of us. There's an itch you just can't scratch. But you're going to keep trying. It forces us to do what we do. I know I have certain tastes, and I know there's a reason for that. I was in a small town, a little seaport town that had a Swedish dance hall that during the summer would turn into a movie theater. A retired B movie producer that still had connections with foreign distributers ran the place. So every summer, he would play hit films from foreign countries, along with local films from the previous year. For a kid in the seventies and eighties, the exposure was unique, and you lined up to work there. It was your own little *Cinema Paradiso*. On weekends, I would be watching *Star Wars*, and on the weekdays, *My Brilliant Career*, both three times in a row. I've realized that my attempts so far with *Nemo* and *WALL-E* had been to create a sort of art house–blockbuster hybrid film. There's a feeling when done right, that only a foreign art house can produce, and I'm addicted to it. Likewise, there's a spectacle and near-childish wonder that only a blockbuster can conjure up. And I think I've never wanted to give up on either in making a film.

Bill: **Was there a moment that you wanted to achieve on *Nemo* or *WALL-E* that you just couldn't pull off?**

Andrew: You're going hate me. No.

Bill: **Wow!**

Andrew: Well, we're lucky. This medium of animation, especially computer graphics, allows you to do things again and again. You sort of have infinite reshoots until the calendar runs out. It's a wonderful luxury. In fact, you have no excuse not to make a great film. It makes me very unforgiving when selecting the next project. Again, that takes me back to my experience in live action. Everybody was shocked that I was so comfortable, as if I had always been doing it, working and talking with everyone.

I found myself constantly explaining that I hadn't worked with 200 computers for the last 20 years. I worked with 200 human beings! I'd spent all day talking to people that do a job. Whether they're using a computer or raw materials to make a costume, their mind essentially works the same. Of course, I had to learn some new terminology and methods, but the goals and intentions are fundamentally the same. It's amazing how drilled into people's unconscious it is, that because there's no face, because there's no living human being on the screen, that animation is some distant and inanimate petrified process. I was just talking about this with my editor. Warner's had announced, "We're making the *Bugs Bunny* short." And my thought was, "You know, if you could resurrect Chuck Jones and Michael Maltese, then maybe I'll get excited and believe you'll make a great *Bugs Bunny* short." Seriously, the Beatles are no longer a band, so would anyone say, "They're making another Beatles album now." It's this weird disconnect.

Bill: **In animation we don't have the possessive credit in the title. Animators stay behind the scenes in an animated film.**

Andrew: Yeah, I feel lucky that we're in a building where there's a commune of moviemaking minds. At least, in your day-to-day life, you get the respect of a Lee Unkrich film, of a Pete Docter film, a John film, and an Andrew film. It's talked about like that. So you're deluded into thinking that's how the world sees it. But I know, in the end, that to everyone else it's just a big cartoon that a bunch of geeks made somewhere.

Finding Nemo, 2003. © 2003 Disney/Pixar.

Bill: So why leave the paradise of CG to go off and shoot a live-action movie?

Andrew: It was not about leaving animation. I've just always been idea driven. Like I said, I'm only going to immerse myself in a project that I badly want to see on-screen, so badly that I'll get up even when everything's going wrong. That's always been the requirement. That's how it worked on *Nemo* and on *WALL-E*. And after those films, I didn't have another animated idea that felt right. But I had this hybrid idea, something I'd always wanted to see since I was 12. I started out as a John Carter fan. So I just wanted to see somebody finally put something on the screen. It was never my intention to do it. I just wanted to be alive when it happened! In the end, it was just the circumstances of having the great idea

Production meeting, *John Carter*, 2012 © Disney.

at the moment the property was available again, and I was simply more excited about it that than anything else. It's just about the ideas. That's very consistent with me.

Bill: What's the toughest part of your job now?

Andrew: All the compromise involved. In animation, you write it on a piece of paper like a script, and then you translate that to boards. You write it out like a comic book. Then you edit that together on video, or digitally, and put music and your own voice to it. You can edit like that forever. But you get to a point where you can watch this chicken scratch drawing, with your bad voice and some music from a CD, and just tell that it works. Somebody may actually pay money to watch this! That's when you know it's good enough to go into production. It's ready for the very expensive shots that you're not going to leave on the cutting room floor. Basically, if you count all the drawings, you've made about five movies. Think about that. You've got five movies worth of material, but you can only choose one.

Bill: Do you have a favorite scene or moment from one of your films?

Andrew: Yeah, I do. It was one of those moments when I felt like I was still learning, getting smarter, and finally understanding how I could tell a story. I understood the camera better. I understood the lenses better. I understood lighting better. It's the scene where WALL-E is next to EVE and she discovers that the lighter creates a flame. They stare at it while *Hello Dolly* is playing and WALL-E suddenly wants to hold her hand. So much work went into making that scene, planning every detail so that the moment would be perfect. I had a clear image in my mind of how I wanted this world to look through the lenses. And at that moment I was aware that my education made my vision possible. I mean, sometimes you feel it's beyond you, like they're going to find out that you're no good and just fire you. But that was just one of those perfect concert-esque moments when I felt like I had the entire orchestra behind me, and I knew exactly how to use every player in it.

Ron Diamond: Well, can you tell us about a specific time that you were unclear or stuck? How did you use your resources to work through it?

Andrew: It's usually story problems that force you to seek the help and advice of others. As a director, the one thing you lose fast is objectivity. You're basically asked to stare at yourself in the mirror for three or four years straight. After a while, all you see is every little imperfection, every hair on your head, every bump that's wrong. Objectivity becomes this valuable commodity that you don't have access to. And it always tends to be the major, if not the main, ingredient to getting out of a story problem. So you have to seek help from somebody else. Then it just becomes the art of knowing the right people to talk to. For a long time, we had this huge hiccup on *WALL-E*. The minute *WALL-E* arrived on the *Axiom* in space, about 30 minutes into the picture, we suddenly went to a bay window to find this sleeping captain as the ship was docking. We wanted to show the captain waking up in order to convey the automated process of this new world. It seemed logical. Let's use this automated process to wake up the captain and introduce a new character. But as we went along and made the rest of the film, there was a growing disconnect. The investment in this character, this captain, wasn't paying off. This problem was identified at a brain trust meeting. That's what we call it, anyway. It's an environment that makes you smarter. We just work better together as a group. As we learned on *Toy Story*, we jammed better this way. And when the critical minds get together, you have no problem getting rid of something you spent four months working on. You just see it clearly. And that's what happened. I could see clearly this scene and character didn't work in the bigger picture. It's all about being around the right people, the right method of criticism, and the excitement of finding something better and cooler as a result. It started out with just John, Joe, and me, and then Pete Docter and Lee Unkrich. Now it's evolved to include a couple of other names, and over time it does change. But the method remains the same. You show them your film, and they tell you what they think. These guys are your peers, not voices from above demanding changes. You listen, you swallow a pill or two, and you get better. And so we realized that we had to stay with WALL-E at that point. We had been telling the story through his eyes, and we couldn't just suddenly change that. It didn't work. And trust me, no matter how hard those corrections are, you can't impose any limitations on your story and try to work around them. You have to open your mind and find a way. In this case, I had to do a little pruning so that I could truly see the beauty of this garden. Yet again, so much of this process involves problem solving. You really need to create an environment that is supportive and conducive to tackling tough issues, because they will happen.

Bill: **One more question. If you were to look back to your time in college, and say you knew you were going to take this path, what would be the most important thing for a young filmmaker to learn about being in animation and ultimately becoming an animation director?**

Andrew: You get this question countless times over your professional career. There's two ways to look at it. First, you have the question of what you should learn in college. The answer: Drawing! And don't ever give it up! This is a visual medium. At the end of the day, you're visually putting something on the screen, or you're even visually mapping out how to attack a live-action shoot. You have to be able to draw it out. It cuts through so much bullshit. A picture really does speak a thousand words, and in our profession it can save a thousand bucks. I bet it even could save a thousand lives! Even if you never have to use it directly, it's just a great skill to have. Second, you should be making movies every chance you get. College assignment or no college assignment, it's just one practice run after another. And it's not just about the chance to learn a trade skill or two, but this is how you build up your filmmaking muscles—your instinct! When I finally got to sit in the driver seat and got stuck in a real bad place, I didn't go to what I had been taught in class, what some lecturer told me. No, my mind raced back to when I was making home movies as a kid. I noticed the sun was setting, that I'm making a goofy video with my brothers in the backyard, we've borrowed my dad's suit, and he's coming home soon. I have to get it back in the closet or we're screwed! How do I still get the shot? How do I pull through? It's a muscle memory that you're going to rely on. It's just like parenting, when you realize you're repeating what your parents did, even though you firmly pledged not to do so. When you're in a visceral mode, you're instinctively going to go with what you remember, not necessarily with what you want to do. I think it's like that, anyway. So whatever means you have, whether that's YouTube or something else, make movies. Do it again, and again, and again, and again! And now that I think about it, there's something else. I would have told myself to trust my instincts and stick with the philosophy that you have no control over what opportunities will arise.

But always be ready to have your stuff out there for people to see. And always be available and give 200 percent to anybody you're working for. You have no control over when that opportunity is going to come. When it does, you want to be ready. I don't care if that's ten years later than you wanted or ten minutes after getting your bachelor's. That's what I would say.

Interviewer's note: After this interview, Andrew completed *John Carter* and returned to Pixar to direct the sequel to *Finding Nemo*, *Finding Dory*.

Bill: **When we last talked, you were in the middle of making your first live-action movie. Did you learn anything on that movie that you're now going to take with you as you move forward?**

Andrew: Yeah, I learned a ton. I definitely would stick with what I had said before about the building of the muscle memory. You're never going to regret that. With live action, it was invigorating. I remember going around and trying to get advice from people with live-action experience, and I got some pretty heavy hitters giving me their fortune cookie quick synopsis and advice. It may be a bit cliché, but it's so true. I was talking to the director, George Miller, who did *Road Warrior* and *Mad Max* and stuff, and he said, "Plan everything, but then be completely prepared to throw it out on the day that you're shooting. But if you don't plan, you're going to be screwed."

It's basically, in a more practical way, what you were just reminding me of, what I said about getting that experience that will … or as we put it, muscle memory. Because that's exactly what you need to do. You may riff off of all your planning because the weather may change or somebody comes up with a better idea. With live action, you just don't have time on your side. Whether it's the time that you've rented the space or the time when the sun is in the right place in the sky, time is something you don't have. No matter what's changed, you have to work within the time you've got. So you have to think so fast on your feet, and if you already rehearsed it a million times, even if it's a different way in what you're going to do, it pays off tremendously. That just was a truism every day.

On the (live-action) set I was working with a very experienced crew. Most of them were people who worked with J. J. Abrams all the time. Everybody kept saying the same thing. They asked, "What's it like to work with (animation) people?" I said, "It's not like I sit and work and talk to computers all day." I have 20 years of experience with talking to artists and individuals, and I just happen to be indoors all the time. But they do your job.

I know you know this, but it was fascinating to see that everybody gets dumb for a moment when they think about the world of computer animation or digital filmmaking versus live-action filmmaking. What people don't realize is that they're very similar. It's just the tools are different. You're still asked to be a ringleader and corral all these people into doing one idea, and when you look at it from that point of view, there's really no difference.

So in a weird way, other than the physical endurance test of being outside and moving very fast and doing all this work in six months that normally I had the luxury of maybe a year and a half to do, it was exactly the same. It was just, "How do I coordinate all these people under one vision?" I didn't feel like I was out of my depth or out of my league when it came to coordinating and planning it.

I remember the camera operator was incredibly shocked that I always knew exactly what I wanted something to look like or what I wanted a shot to be before we had even walked the set or had looked through an eyepiece. I realized that's from the muscle memory of just being a storyboard artist for so many years, where you just have to see the movie before there was anything to help you with it. That's a luxury that most people don't have to think about. They like to actually just be surprised and wait until they see what's in front of them, and I can see both sides of the coin.

Bill: You had mentioned that live-action people have an abstract approach to what a movie is. It's the event that somehow gets captured, whereas an animation person looks at a movie as the thing that's actually on the page, on the picture plane. You're instinct was natural. You said they were amazed at that.

Andrew: You're so right about the fact that live-action people always think it's a completely different animal. They have some strange ideas, especially in CG now, where we deal with dimensionality and lighting issues and literally cinematography that's using the same conventions. It's really come together.

John Carter, 2012. © 2011 Disney. John Carter™, ERB, Inc.

Bill: I'm curious. Now that you're working in animation again, did your experience in making a live-action movie have any impact on how you're now working? Are you changing anything at all?

Andrew: Well, I can't say it has come in to changing methodology of how we make it because Pixar certainly has perfected its style of making movies as far as the production flow. In a weird way, I felt like when it came to production flow and management of staff and planning out how the production is going to work, Pixar is an incredibly highly evolved being. It has a benefit that very few studios do, where it's like this summer stock crew of people who have been putting on a play again and again for two decades. You have all this time to, almost to a fault, refine the process of how to put on a show.

So there was a level of organization and having your shit together for how to put it through the machinery. It just made us very impatient. When you're watching a live-action movie, it's so by the seat of your pants. It's almost a fairground carnie level of just chaos, which was shocking because we have such high respect for movies.

I'm sure there are some people that might say it was not a good thing that I came back to animation because I have no patience. Now that I've been out there and I've seen what you can do in a day and what you can do in an hour, I've seen people literally fight sandstorms to get the shot for half, if not a quarter, of the pay of some of the people that work here with no cereal bar and no scooters—none of this.

My respect just only went to a higher degree for what people will do to get the movie right. I was already sort of a hard, fast worker *relatively on the scale* working at Pixar, but when I came back, I thought, "Why can't we get it now? What can we get now? What can we do?" I was really pushing. I still do, though I've slowed down a little bit.

I don't know if I feel bad about it so much because I feel like there's a subtle sense of complacency that can happen when the deadline is farther out than a week. It's good to have deadlines that are built in within a couple days. It just keeps you at a certain kind of pace.

Bill: When you do live-action movie, as you said, you always assemble this brand new community that stays very tight for a short time, and then they dissipate and they're gone again; whereas at Pixar, as you were just mentioning, you have this group of day players who have been on this job for 20 years. So in one respect, you get that comfort level of falling back into this down comforter of people who know what they're doing, but would you say each project has to bring its own special kind of excitement and uniqueness to get those people jazzed together again as a family?

Andrew: Yeah, but it's not that black and white because we're always trying to do slightly more projects than we have the manpower for at Pixar, so the exact casting of who's on a crew isn't always the same people, so you don't really put your foot in the same river twice. But all these people who you're working with have had the same university training from the same college in a way, so there's definitely a commonality of lexicon, and there's always some core group of people who you've worked with before.

But there's an overall sense that this is just the speed and the pace and how a movie is made here. I can't say what's worse or what's better. They're just very different animals when you look at it with that lens.

The only thing I have a hard time embracing coming back to animation is the lack of spontaneity. You have to plan the spontaneity. You have to do extra work to make it possible to have things be spontaneous. It just is not inherent in the process. Maybe you get it sometimes in gag sessions for a brief time, maybe you get it from a couple recording sessions depending on the actor you're working with, whereas live action is nothing but spontaneity.

It's not for everybody. It's just one of those things where it literally feels like one is an indoor game and one is an outdoor game, regardless of whether you're literally indoors or outdoors. There really is that kind of difference.

Bill: **I know what you mean. Do you seek that a little bit more in your recording sessions now?**

Andrew: Yeah. It's funny. I found that what I assumed was going to happen and what I heard happens and what typically does happen with people who come from a technical background in the moviemaking process, particularly if they come from a computer or a digital background, is that they're going to be scared of the actors if they work in live action.

I found it the opposite. I couldn't get enough of working with the actors. I loved it. I think that that was more a personal thing because I had come from doing a ton of theater and had almost become an actor myself until my last year in high school. I pretty much hung out with all the theater guys equally as, if not more than, the animation guys at CalArts.

So I think that was more a dormant love that I just didn't think I was ever going to go back to again, but I did when I suddenly found myself literally getting to rehearse scenes and adjust performances on the fly and see an immediate result. You never shoot anything that's longer than a couple of minutes, as opposed to animation, where you record the line, select the take a week later, then you cut it in, and maybe three weeks later you get to finally see what you thought your choices were. To be able to just keep adjusting within minutes and hours on the same day, I just felt like somebody who had not been let outdoors for 20 years and could suddenly just run at the pace my brain went. That is the hardest thing to adjust back to.

Bill: **Do you see, for that reason, some merit in the mocap blocking that some studios do, where they actually let the animator put on a suit and the director sits there and fools around developing the scene with him?**

Andrew: I actually totally get it. I had to do a ton of mocap (motion capture) on *John Carter*, and I remember I was very surprised that I was so pro. Mark Andrews and I worked really hard in advance trying to figure out the technique that we were going to want to use that seemed smartest. We had a lot of knowledge about all the options that we had, and there was no reason to be afraid of it. If you really know your history, all that stuff that we had admired in animation in *Snow White* and *Cinderella* and *Sleeping Beauty* or even *One Hundred And One Dalmatians,* there was all this live-action actor reference that was not rotoscoped, but it was definitely referenced as a starting point for an animator to add their touch to it, their specific stamp to it. To me, it was just following with the latest technology doing the same thing. Why not lay down digital foundations and tracks based on actor choices?

This is way too wordy, but I know with your background, you'd get this. By having references of what the live-action actors did on set, it gave me ammunition, and hopefully the animators courage, to do *nothing*—because an animator tends to want to think, "This might work. I want to show off what I can do. I want to make all these great choices for the scene," and they end up making their characters move all over the place, even when they think they're being minimalistic.

I would sometimes show what the actor was doing in the scene that somebody was animating. I remember showing them this one scene and I asked, "What's the actor doing in this scene?" They looked and looked and looked and said, "Nothing." I said, "Exactly. That's why it works so well in this scene. He's just being." It's the last choice animators make. It takes a lot of discipline and courage to just consider that one of the options when you're animating is doing nothing.

Bill: **That's really a perceptive observation. When your stock and trade is making things move, you feel that if they don't make a move, you're not doing your thing.**

Andrew: Right. I wasn't thinking about this so much in advance, but it certainly became a great tool and by-product of it. I just thought, "Geez, we're paying for these great actors, and I know we're trying to do a level of realism that hopefully you'll buy that they're literally in the real world, breathing the same air and talking to these live-action actors." So I need all the help I can get to start off in the strongest place. Had we been going for a more extreme exaggerated hybrid look, I might have done it differently and not done mocap at all or done a very different limited use of it.

I get that it's just a tool to help you and you should use it however you need to use it, so I don't have some hard, fast rule about it.

Bill: **I guess you can't really use it in *Finding Dory* because it's hard to block fish, right?**

Andrew: Yes, but we do have humans. We have a *Lady and the Tramp* kind of universe. I'm not against it all, if it helps. They may not want to admit it to themselves, but they find, at least here at Pixar, that "it's a nice deviation from the norm, and suddenly makes this job a little more interesting, as opposed to how I did the last job." Sometimes that's still OK as an excuse to try it, but the minute it becomes an extra step that we don't need in the process, then I question it.

Bill: It's funny. We always accuse screenwriters of saying dialogue is the most interesting tool you've got, so they want to use lots of dialogue, whereas animators seek to do the scenes almost wordlessly. We often put down screenwriters for not being able to write visual scenes and instead resorting to dialogue. It's interesting that you're saying the same analogy with animators. Because their favorite tool is motion, they have to suppress their ego a bit and look at a performance by an actor who may have an internal motor that's generating the scene without much motion. That's a revelation in a way.

Andrew: Yeah. You can look at any movie that you pick as a favorite—let's say live action—and every actor is different about how physical they are. It's kind of endless with choices. It's almost like choices with playing an instrument. I feel like, why is it that I watch these animated movies and I'm starting to see the same kind of shrug and the same kind of gestures all the time?

Finding Dory, 2016. © 2016 Disney/Pixar.

All that really tells me is that they're clichés simply because they're the first things a lot of animators think of, and it shouldn't be their final choice for the scene. They should be thinking a little bit harder about the context of the character they have, the world they're in, and the other characters they're doing the scene with. It's a lot more thinking, and a lot of people either sometimes get a choice or maybe they're limited by the direction they're being allowed and given. The grammar of motion choices for animated characters is much smaller than it should be.

Bill: **It sounds like you're feeling really positive that all these career experiences have continued to add arrows to your quiver.**

Andrew: Yeah. You try really hard not to think of it like a career because I think that sends you down the wrong path. I just try really hard to be appreciative that I get to make another movie and make sure that it's good enough that people want to watch it. It's pretty much the same thing, but now I just feel like the new place I'm at is a little older and I get tired quicker.

Bill: **Pace yourself.**

Andrew: Yeah. I always do, but the further you go, the more you really appreciate the people you work with, and you appreciate every little good moment that you find in a movie because you start to realize how hard it is to achieve that, and how rare it is to get those.

Bill: **Did directing John Carter change/influence the way you direct an animated feature?**

Andrew: Well, it at least confirmed one thing: that I naturally work at a much faster pace than animation will allow. In animation, you make hundreds of micro-decisions on a scene over its existence (which can be 3–6 months, depending.) In live action, you make maybe a few dozen decisions on a scene—but within an hour. I like to make a decision and move on. Lingering is the Devil. If you stare at yourself long enough in the mirror, you will keep finding things wrong with yourself. So, when I returned to animation, whenever I could, I moved it along.

Bill: **Where there any challenges revisiting characters from one of Pixar's most loved films?**

Andrew: Not really. Yes, there's a luxury to already knowing some of your characters, but that advantage lasts for maybe 6 months, and then your dealing with (hopefully) new problems in new situations. If you're doing it correctly, *all* stories are "original films" even if they are sequels.

Bill: Having now directed five feature films, what advice you would pass on to budding film directors?

Andrew: The "auteur theory" is bullshit. Yes, you need to have a vision and a passion to tell something, but once you've infected everybody with that, your job becomes how to help your crew make that vision. Movie making is a team sport.

Andrew Stanton, Angus MacLane, and Steve Pilcher, *Finding Dory,* 2016 © Pixar. Photo by Deborah Coleman.

5
Brenda Chapman Interview

Brenda Chapman © Disney.

Brenda Chapman kept making history when all she really wanted to do was tell stories.

From her first work at CalArts, everyone knew that Brenda had a special talent as a story artist. She ended up in a profession that was overwhelmingly male and, as a result, would find herself standing out—for a variety of reasons.

By her own admission, Brenda bristles a bit at the idea of being the one brought in to provide "the woman's point of view," but that intrinsic contribution to the projects she worked on proved consistently, uniquely valuable.

It's tough enough to be outnumbered by your male counterparts, but when you have a naturally quiet, shy demeanor, it is even tougher to rise to the head of a boisterous story department. Brenda managed to do that through the strength of her talent and the genuine camaraderie she established with her fellow artists.

She was the first woman to be head of story on a Disney feature, and what a result: *The Lion King* remains the biggest 2D hit of all time. She became the first woman to codirect a major Hollywood animated feature, *The Prince of Egypt*. She was the first woman selected to direct a feature at Pixar, her own original story called *Brave*.

Brenda did not have the opportunity to finish **Brave**, but there was no mistaking that the originality of the lead character, Merida, her struggles, and her relationship with her mother, was pure Brenda. There has never been an animated female heroine quite like Merida, because there has never been a story artist, or director, quite like Brenda Chapman.

We interviewed Brenda at Pixar with a follow-up by phone.

Bill Kroyer

Bill: Where did you grow up?

Brenda: A little town called Beason, Illinois. It's outside of Lincoln, which is outside of Springfield. That's right. If you stuck your finger right in the middle of Illinois, that's where I'm from. Corn and beans [*laughs*].

Bill: Tiny little town … went to a little, tiny high school?

Brenda: I would have gone to a very tiny high school, but Beason High School closed down my eighth-grade year. So we had to be bussed into Lincoln, Illinois, which had 250 in the class. I went from a class of 15 kids to 250, which was huge culture shock.

Bill: Did they have art classes at that school?

Brenda: Yes. It was the art class where they sent all the troublemakers.

Bill: When did you first start drawing or being interested in art?

Brenda: Oh, I drew since I was little. My mom was very artistic, but she only had an eighth-grade education. My mom's story was that her favorite teacher saw her talent and wanted to talk to her grandparents about it. Mom was raised by her grandparents. The next year that teacher wasn't there. Her grandfather was on the school board, and he didn't feel education was worth it for women, nor should they be encouraged by silly teachers. So when my mother was in eighth grade, he pulled her out of school.

I was the youngest of five, and she saw that I was really interested in art. So she really encouraged me. We used to play a game at home called the scribble game. I'm sure a lot of people play it, where you make a scribble and then you hand it to another person to make something out of it. We would do that back and forth. It was the most amazing thing. I do that with my daughter now. She loves it. It really stretches what you see.

Bill: When did your interest in drawing start morphing into an interest in animation?

Brenda: I think the first animated film that I saw in a theater was *Cinderella*, and I'd watch *Wonderful World of Disney* every Sunday, and *Bugs Bunny* every day after school. But I didn't seriously start thinking about it until the end of high school, early junior college. I just knew I wanted to do something where I could draw. Of course. I don't draw anymore, but … [*laughs*] actually, that makes me very sad.

One day, when I was watching a film on-screen and the credits started to roll, it just hit me, "Oh my God, people do that for a living. That's what I want to do!" It was just sort of this … revelation.

Bill: So how did you find out where to go after high school? How did you decide?

Brenda: Well, I, as everyone who initially wants to get into animation, wanted to work for Disney. My sister had a friend who had a cousin who worked for Disney in the live-action division. I got his number and he agreed to talk to me, so I called him. He was very nice and got the number of Disney Features for me. I called and talked to Ed Hanson's assistant. She sent me brochures on CalArts. That's how I figured that one out.

Bill: **You were one of those people who had the fortuitous coincidence of CalArts being there when you came of age. It had never been there before.**

Brenda: Yes.

Bill: So she said CalArts, and you applied?

Brenda: Yes, but I was rejected the first time. So I worked really hard with a new art teacher at the local community college in Lincoln. He was not remotely interested in animation, but was very interested in helping me meet my goal. So he sent me off to life drawing classes, and to dance class to draw the dancers. He really worked hard with me, and I was accepted the next year. I was and still am very grateful.

Bill: You went to CalArts in the character animation program.

Brenda: Yes.

Bill: Not a lot of women in that program.

Brenda: No. There were … I want to say five. Four or five of us out of a class of 28, I think.

Bill: That must have been overwhelming at first, going from Illinois to California.

Brenda: Yes [*laughs*].

Bill: You'd never been around anyone in animation, suddenly being around all these fanatics.

Brenda: It was great, actually. It felt like "Oh my God, I fit in here!" We were all just people who never fit in at home or our schools that much, and suddenly we were all in a place we wanted to be. And it felt right. So, that actually was great. The rest of CalArts, on the other hand, was a bit of a culture shock for a girl from a small town in the Midwest, with the nude pool and all that stuff.

Bill: All of a sudden you're getting taught all these things you've never been taught, right? You probably had never heard of color theory, you've never heard of character design. That must have been pretty stimulating.

Brenda: Yes.

Bill: Was it difficult? Was it exciting? Did you take to it like a duck to water or did you struggle?

Brenda: It was difficult and exciting, but it was a struggle. I'd never been given any of those classes before. I still remember a design project I did during the first week or two, where Bob Winquist, our design teacher, had us depict movement with a rectangle, a triangle, and a circle. You know, it was very simple. So I just slapped them on there at tilted angles—you know, to show movement! Bob looked at it and just said, "Oh no, no, no." He kept coming back to it as a bad example. I can remember just being mortified. It was just a mess up there.

Bill: The Bill Moore thing, right?

Brenda: Yes, but it was Bob Winquist who had taken over the class. It was the same assignment, basically. He gave me another chance to do it, and he liked it! I'd definitely learned something in his class.

Bill: **What was your goal when you entered CalArts? Did it change as you stayed there?**

Brenda: [*Laughs*] Yes. Well, I think everyone goes in wanting to be an animator. You know, because that's the one part of the industry that's always in the limelight, at least it was when I was growing up. But, as I spent three years there, by my last year what I was really enjoying was cre-

A Birthday, Brenda Chapman, 1987. (Courtesy of ACME.)

ating the story: the puzzle of putting together a story, the structure, the characters, and all of that.

I was working on my final film my last year there. Joe Ranft had come in and started teaching story to the freshmen. He just came by to say hello, and he saw my boards up on the wall. I did this little pencil test film called *A Birthday*, about a little old lady who is alone on her birthday. He looked at my boards, and he asked me, "Ever think of going into story?" I hadn't, you know? [*laughs*].

From that point on, I started thinking about it. When I was putting my portfolio together for a job at Disney, my teachers were saying, "Oh, you'll have to apply as a cleanup artist, just to get in." So I dutifully put in a portfolio for a cleanup position, but wrote a note on my cover letter that I'd eventually like a story-related position. I had included my storyboards and a video of my film just in case. And then, much to my surprise, I got hired as a story trainee at Disney!

I was put in a training program with Rob Minkoff as my mentor. He gave me story tests to do initially. After my first review, I was excited because I got to work on *The Little Mermaid*. I worked on a few of the sequences with Roger Allers, who was my main mentor there.

They hadn't really assigned a head of story yet. It was just a bunch of guys working together. They were very inclusive, very supportive, and very helpful. I didn't feel like I was, "Ooh, there's a girl in the room." They just welcomed me in. I was just one of the guys, which was really nice.

Bill: **Were you learning things beyond what you learned at CalArts?**

Brenda: Yes! Pitching! No one warned me about having to pitch a storyboard, because I was the little quiet one sitting in the corner. Put me in a party, and I'm over in the corner, you know, watching everybody. I'm not good at it, but I've learned I have to get up and talk. That was the hard part.

Bill: **But, like you say, it's not only essential to the story, it's pretty essential to the directing, isn't it?**

Brenda: Yes, it is. Big time. Joe took me under his wing and taught me a lot, but I think the ones who really influenced me were Roger Allers and Ed Gombert. Roger really can pitch a story.

Bill: **What makes a good pitch?**

Brenda: Well, for each person it's different. I mean, if you watched Vance Gerry pitch, he didn't put on the character voices or anything, but he just kept you focused on that board. He kept you really riveted into what he was talking about. But Joe, on the other hand, would get into the characters, and he'd goof off, and you'd still get it. It's an individual approach.

I think what helped for me is that I loved how Roger could just be a chameleon and become the characters in a not overt way, where you're not trying to look at him and see the faces he's making, but you really could feel it. It always cracked me up because I remember him pitching in his flip-flops and his leopard-print Bermudas, and an ugly green Frankenstein T-shirt with his red hair and his beard. It took me a long time, but that's what got me going. I'd pretend to be Roger in that outfit when I got up and pitched. That got me over my own nervousness, and now I just do it—instead of pretending I'm a bearded redheaded guy [*laughs*] with a Frankenstein T-shirt and flip-flops.

Bill: **Did you stay in story?**

Brenda: They did ship me off to cleanup to improve my drawing skills for a few months. I worked on *Roger Rabbit*, which was also a lot of fun. That was quite an experience and probably the hardest cleanup job I could ever have been given. I had to match weasels to oil spots on the live-action stats.

Bill: Tough doing cleanup on *Roger Rabbit*—though you're happy you have a check.

Brenda: Yes, I was very happy to stay employed. It was pretty demoralizing, but I saw it as an opportunity. They gave me another chance, basically. So I worked hard. Charlie Fink was head of development at that time and what they said to me was "When something comes up, a small project we could use you on, we'll give you a call." So I kept calling him up, at least once a week.

"Have anything yet?" [*laughs*]. I think just to stop me bugging him, he got me onto some shorts. And that's when I started working with Joe, on the Public Service Announcements with Mickey, Donald, and Goofy. Joe used to tease me about one of them because it was driving me crazy.

It was the "Buckle Up" song. "Buckle up, Uncle Donald, buckle up! Quack, quack" [*laughs*]. Joe would just start singing that to me. And I'd say, "Ugh … [*laughs*] stop!"

Bill: You were doing story on all these?

Brenda: Yes, I was doing story.

Bill: How would that work? They would come to you with a concept or a script?

Brenda: Tim Hauser would write out script pages and treatments, but it wasn't like a full-on script, no.

Bill: He'd get a sequence and say, "Explore this?"

Brenda: Yes.

Bill: Would you be working alone on your own sequence?

Brenda: Yes, but what I will forever find amazing is that when I'd hit a block, I could have someone come in. We were all constantly going around the corner to the other story artists, kicking things around, and showing our work. So I never really felt alone that much.

I'd board something up, and then they'd come in and have ideas, and I'd think, "Whoa! Great idea!" So I'd go back and work their ideas in. It was great, collaborative, and a whole lot of fun.

Then *Rescuers Down Under* came up, and Mike Gabriel and Hendel Butoy were looking for artists to work on that story. They liked what I was doing so I was transferred over to feature, which was great.

Bill: How was it different on a feature? Were you given more responsibility?

Brenda: Yes, I wasn't a trainee anymore. I'd become a full-fledged story artist, which was awesome. That was a lot of fun, working with Mike and Hendel and Joe as the head of story. It was a really fun experience.

Bill: This is your first kind of important experience because eventually someday you're going to be the director working with the story crew. So talk about exactly how they worked with you, and what you thought worked well in that situation, and what you learned from it.

Brenda: Well, we would get an outline for a sequence or script pages, but I always felt we were free to vary—that the pages were just sort of a jumping-off place. We were allowed to explore. We were all aware of what the other story artists were doing. We were in a big bull pen basically, with just cubicle walls dividing us off.

We would get the pages, and Mike and Hendel would give us feedback on what they were really looking for. So I would do what they asked for, but Joe encouraged me to offer up any other ideas I might have by boarding them on the side if I had time.

It became a joke, in a sense, with Mike and Hendel, and me too. I'd pitch the sequence that I thought they were looking for. They'd say, "Well it'd be great if you'd …" And I'd hold up a drawing and say, "You mean like *this*?" [*laughs*]. So I always seemed to have in my back pocket the notes that they were talking about, which was kind of fun. Occasionally, they'd catch me when I didn't have them, but … [*chuckle*].

The big thing for me on that one, I think, the big success that people noticed, that moved me on to be a more senior artist on *Beauty and the Beast*, was the scene of the boy and the eagle at the nest. Joe had tried it, Ed had tried it, Roger had tried it. They were trying to get a scene between the boy and the eagle without the eagle talking, and get across all the information that they needed.

It always came off really stiff. The eagle talked, and it just never felt right. I was sort of the low man on the totem pole so I said, "Can I give it a try?" I was remembering this Roy Disney film, *The Legend of the Boy and the Eagle*.

I remembered how expressive that bird was. So I went to Glen Keane, and I was talking to him about it, because he was going to animate the eagle. We talked about it and I boarded it out, and they really liked it, and that's what's in the film now.

Bill: Do you remember how you analyzed that and came up with the solution?

Brenda: Well, mainly I had the boy ask the questions that would lead to the information that we were trying to get across, but in a childlike way. I was approaching it from the little boy trying to communicate with this eagle, and the eagle understanding what he's saying, but not able to vocalize it. So, the response of the eagle was in how it turned its head, and the boy understood what the eagle meant.

And so, the boy could vocally respond in the way we needed that gave the information that the father eagle was dead. It was just little bits of information that they tried to get across but could never figure out how to without dialogue. You know, I learn by my own mistakes, as well as from other people's. I'm the youngest of five, so [*laughs*] I'm well trained in watching, "OK, don't do that, don't do that." But that scene got me noticed to move on to other projects.

Bill: *Beauty and the Beast?*

Brenda: Yes.

Bill: And how long were you on that?

Brenda: A year and a half, I'd say almost two years.

Bill: And what sequences did you do?

Brenda: I worked on the opening scene with Belle going through the village. Roger Allers and I partnered up a lot on bigger musical sequences. I worked with him on "Kiss the Girl" on *The Little Mermaid*. We also partnered on the ballroom sequence to the title song of *Beauty and the Beast*. A lot of people touched all the scenes, but the one that I am most proud of is where Belle and the Beast argue, where she bandages his wounds after he saves her from the wolves. She tries to bathe his wounds, and he yells at her, then she yells back at him. It's just this back and forth, but he's cowed by her scolding him.

Storyboards, *Beauty and the Beast*, Brenda Chapman, 1991 © Disney.

BE GOOD NOW. I
WON'T HURT YOU...

IF YOU'LL JUST HOLD
STILL...

ROAR!!

Storyboards, *Beauty and the Beast*, Brenda Chapman, 1991 © Disney.

Bill: Did you pretty much come up with the dialogue and everything in that scene as well?

Brenda: Yes.

Bill: What could be a better directing school than story, right?

Brenda: Right! You are given the opportunity to be mini-directors. You have someone that you still have to answer to—the director, and you're given your limits as to where to go—but you are in control of that sequence.

Bill: You're staging, you're writing, you develop character performance, you're often thinking how to compose the shots.

Brenda: Yes.

Bill: At this point, are you thinking about being a director?

Brenda: Nope, nope. [*Laughs*] No.

Bill: So, what's next after *Beauty*?

Brenda: After *Beauty*, I went into development again, and I worked closely with Chris Sanders and Kelly Asbury. We were having a good old time over in this newly acquired building, and I was working with Mike and Hendel. We were dabbling in *Fantasia/2000* (it was *Fantasia Continued* at the time). I'd developed the whale piece. It didn't turn out quite as I conceived it, but its still the flying whale thing.

    Then Mike sort of broke off and started working on a version of *Swan Lake*, which I was very interested in because I love magic and fairy tales and that kind of stuff. I'm always looking for a new take on one. So Chris and I started really working hard on that. That's where I met Joe Grant. Mike brought him in, and what a wonderful guy! Very inspiring. But then *Swan Lake* got canned because of Rick Rich's *The Swan Princess*.

Bill: What did you learn from Joe Grant that you hadn't learned from anyone else?

Brenda: Just his very simple way of executing an idea. He didn't put anything in environments, he just had little character sketches and ideas, and just really simple, little gags. At face value, it looks like, "Eh, it's just a throwaway gag," but then you look at it closer and you realize, "No, that could be a character trait, that's a little deeper than just a little throwaway gag."

    But also, just his whole attitude, his whole outlook on life, was very reassuring. Here's this guy with this incredible history and this incredible talent, and he was sitting here listening to your ideas like you were an equal as opposed to looking down at you. He was just a great guy. You could ask him anything and he'd be there to help you.

Bill: So when *Swan Princess* killed the project …

Brenda: I had gone in to Tom Schumacher and said, "You know, I'm really interested in being a head of story. If you think I'm ready for it, I think I'm ready for it."

I was aiming for *Swan Lake*, thinking this was the project for me. The project that I so wanted to avoid was *King of the Jungle*, as it was called at the time. Then *Swan Lake* tanked, and guess what they offered me? [*Laughs*] I thought, "Aw," but then, I thought, to work with Roger again would be great. He was one of the directors, and George Scribner was the other director at the time.

Bill: So did they make you head of story?

Brenda: Yes, I was head of story! We were the B project, you know. Everybody was going for *Pocahontas*, because Mike had left *Swan Lake* too and started up that movie. Tom told me they were going to send us to Africa, and I said, "Ah, I don't want to go to Africa. I like Europe, I want to go to Europe." But they made me go to Africa.

How stupid was I! I have never had a trip like that, ever! There is this weird thing, now, when I talk to people who have been there. It's as if we're this weird little society, "Oh, you were abducted, too?" You go there, and it feels like you've come home, it's the weirdest thing. I don't know if it's just the knowledge of this origin thing, or what.

Bill: You went to Kenya right?

Brenda: We went to Kenya, and it was just amazing. It was life changing.

Bill: You came back inspired? That's how the project really got kick-started?

Brenda: Yes.

Bill: You guys, the story crew, were all carrying the water on this, right?

Brenda: Yes, Linda Woolverton had done some treatments, but one of the first things I did was to kill off a couple of characters that I thought were taking

Roger Allers, Brenda Chapman and Chris Sanders, Research trip for *The Lion King*, © Disney.

away from the main characters. When George left the project and Rob Minkoff came on, Linda left the project as well. And then we started working with Irene Mecchi and Jonathan Roberts, the two writers that were brought on. They were great because they were very collaborative, so we could go back and forth. I could hand out the pages to the story crew, and they had freedom to go beyond them. Then Irene and Jonathan would come in and polish up, plus what the story artists did. It was a really lovely back-and-forth relationship. Because sometimes writing versus story can be a little contentious.

Bill: **As the head of story, were you spending more of your time managing than drawing?**

Brenda: That was the first inkling of how hard it was to do both. I eventually had to say, "Look, you have to ask one or the other of me, I can't do both." So they opted that I be in the meetings and be able to be a liaison between story and the rest of the film. I boarded and wrote the Mufasa ghost scene before anything else. That was one of the scenes they wanted to look at early on. I do not take credit for that scene visually—that was Chris Sanders—but I wrote the "remember who you are" aspect of the scene.

It was just sort of a placeholder until we knew what was said between Mufasa and Simba in the first act, "Remember (what I said to you back in Act I, Simba)," and then it just stuck and it fleshed out into the scene that is in the final film.

I've never been a great draftsman, but I was always clear in getting ideas across.

When you want to really "wow" an audience with visuals, I was not the person you'd give that scene to. So I asked Chris Sanders to come in and do a couple of those things to help me sell the idea. He did these amazing, beautiful pastels of Mufasa coming through the clouds. I'd done these chicken scratches and told him this was the idea [*laughs*]. And then he really made it sing, so that was a fun thing to do.

Bill: **How long were you working on that picture?**

Brenda: I was on it a little over two years.

Bill: **Did you stay until the story was finished?**

Brenda: No, I jumped ship just before story was finished because I was going a little crazy. Things were changing all the time in layout just because things were seeming old, and I was becoming the veto person. I had to go to layout sessions and have to say, "No you can't change this. No you can't change that," and it was just a joyless part of it.

So by the end I said, "You know, it's in good shape, I don't think it's going to fall apart if I'm not there to say no." So, Don Hahn let me move on. I was kind of getting burned out by some of the politics in the studio, so I just needed to take some time off.

Bill: What did you do then?

Brenda: That was when Kevin Lima was doing *A Goofy Movie*.

Bill: You guys had already married …

Brenda: We got married while we were on *Rescuers Down Under* in 1988.

Bill: So he's working, he's making enough money.

Brenda: Yeah [*laughs*], well I didn't quit. I just took some time off. He was doing *Goofy Movie* in Paris, so I'd take little breaks, going to see him, different lengths of time. And then, I started working on *The Hunchback of Notre Dame* with Kirk Wise and Gary Trousdale because I had such a great time with them on *Beauty and the Beast*. They were a wonderful pair to work with on that movie. And then *Hunchback* started.

Bill: Were you head of story on this one?

Brenda: No, no, I just wanted to be a story artist. And that's when the whole Jeffrey Katzenberg thing started happening. I had sort of gone to battle for my story crew for bonuses, because they were giving bonuses out and the story crew always seemed to get, you know, meager pickings after the animators. I thought, "Well, wait a minute," [*laughs*] "you know we put a lot into these things." So I went to bat there, and I guess I caught Jeffrey's eye by doing that, along with the success of *The Lion King*. So when he left, he called me and wanted me to go help set up the story department over at DreamWorks.

I was ready for a change [*laughs*]. Joe Ranft was supposed to go over there too. I think Jeffrey had in mind that Joe would direct and I would be his head of story, but then John Lasseter talked Joe out of going and Joe ended up at Pixar. I thought, "Oh no! Wait!" [*laughs*]. So Joe, when he brought me up here, said, "I hope that makes up for me abandoning you," and I said, "Yes, Joe." But when Joe went to Pixar, that's when the directing thing came up with Jeffrey. I had never really thought of it for myself; I really loved story. I still love story.

Bill: So it was Jeffrey's idea?

Brenda: It was Jeffrey's idea. Joe was gone. They'd tried other people. He just didn't trust anyone, and he knew me. So he asked me if I would direct *The Prince of Egypt*. At first I said, "No. I really think I'll best serve you if I can just set up your story department." They kept looking, but he wasn't satisfied with anyone, so he just said one day, "Brenda, you're directing until we find someone better." I think he expected me to just stick to it, cause once I got into it, and started going on my path, I didn't want to give it up to anyone else anymore.

Bill: **Were you the sole director to start?**

Brenda: To start, but there was always the knowledge that there would be these other two, somebody else coming on from Amblimation, because they were going to fold them into DreamWorks. So, I was waiting to meet them for a while. It was interesting, because it was hard just waiting for someone I'd never met. I'd met Steve Hickner before. He was a sweetheart to me when I first started working at Disney.

But I'd never met Simon Wells, so I was kind of nervous. Jeffrey, who—I have to give the man his due—is very loyal to people. When he was in that mode [*laughs*], he gave Simon a really hard time at first, protecting me, because Simon's a talker, and I'm not.

That was hard, but I just made it clear to Simon that it wasn't coming from me. So we stuck together, and we became a really close-knit team. I think initially they wanted me to just take over the story and have Steve and Simon do the animation, layout, etc. I said, "No, story is going to permeate the whole movie." So, I fought for them and they fought for me. We actually were a really good team.

The Prince of Egypt ©1998 DreamWorks Animation LLC.

Bill: What were your feelings then, and what were your first decisions on what you felt needed to be done? Were they waiting for you to lead everything; were you supposed to just have these big meetings and start saying, "Set it up this way, set it up that way"?

Brenda: Yes. I mean, we were standing there, six of us in a room, and we didn't even have pencil and paper yet. But having been at the early stages of *Lion King* and *Beauty*, and even *Rescuers*, I knew how to get something going. It was what was coming down the road that made me a little nervous.

I knew how to get people started on visual development. I knew how to get people started on story. I've observed it for so many years at Disney. I thought, "OK, I can do that." The terrifying part for me was going into actual production, because I hadn't been involved in animation since cleanup on *Roger Rabbit*. You do your own film at CalArts—that's the closest I had come to production!

Bill: Plus it was a brand new studio. They didn't have established departments.

Brenda: Exactly. But the nice thing was, there were some really experienced people who came over. And they were willing, even though I was inexperienced, to work with me, and teach me, and guide me along through their departments. I had Don Paul in effects. That was the scariest department for me. "I'm looking at all these squiggly lines, what does it mean?"

For backgrounds and the design style, I had Kathy Altieri and Richie Chavez—both were my art directors—and I had Lorenzo Martinez as head of layout. So I had all these people who'd done it for many years. Simon had done it before, so I was happy to leave layout to him because he has such a great cinematographer's eye. It was a great collaborative process. You just have to trust the people that you work with.

Bill: When you came on the project, what state was the story in?

Brenda: You had that chapter Exodus, in the Bible [*laughs*], that's it, that's where we were.

Bill: That was it?

Brenda: Yes. Susannah Grant had done a treatment with another writer, but it turned out not to be the direction that Jeffrey wanted to go with.

Bill: So even though you were the director, you were actually head of the story.

Brenda: Yes, at first.

Bill: And you're pretty much starting to say, "Here's how we have to pull this into shape."

Brenda: Yes.

Bill: Did you break it down and basically start assigning problems to a group?

Brenda: Yes, and then as time progressed, you know, pretty quickly I'd asked Lorna Cook and Kelly Asbury to be coheads of story. That was how we got Kelly to come to the project. He wanted to head up a department, and Lorna was willing to partner with him, so then I could hand that off to them as I started getting into production more.

Bill: So what did you end up doing as the project grew? Because you're basically blazing a new trail, right? You got a brand new studio and you end up with a three-director system.

Brenda: Yes.

Bill: Which doesn't often happen.

Brenda: No.

Bill: Which I would imagine makes it exponentially more difficult to coordinate.

Brenda: It could have been. I think that's where Simon, having done it by himself, and me, having watched how two directors can clash or work well together, and Steve, having been in the trenches too, decided to make it work. It's like again watching examples and saying, "OK, I won't do it that way, and maybe I'll try that way."

Also, being a person who doesn't like to work in conflict, I always try to make sure people are getting along. I'm always aware of the vibe in the room and how things are going. I'd heard Simon could be a tough nut to work with, but he's a great guy. He can use that British accent and make it sound like he knows exactly what's going on. I can remember in one of the story meetings, I looked at him, he said something, and I threw a story pad at him. And he looked at me and he just started laughing, and from then on we were really connected as partners. And Steve was always a good guy. He would just stick with you, no matter what.

Bill: Did you guys end up supervising the departments together?

Brenda: We divvied up. We worked very closely together in story and animation because we felt like those two you cannot break apart.

Bill: Did you do all the pitches together, and look at the reels together, and take notes together?

Brenda: Yes. We insisted on that, and then Simon took layout, I took backgrounds and effects, and Steve took cleanup. We would all meet together in sweatbox and give our final notes together. It was a good system. We worked really well together, because we all (agreed that) story is king.

It's the glue that holds everything together. The layer on top of that is the characters, and how they act, which has to be cohesive (with story). I felt like we were successful in doing that.

Storyboards, Brenda Chapman, *The Prince of Egypt* ©1998 DreamWorks Animation LLC.

Storyboards, Brenda Chapman, *The Prince of Egypt* ©1998 DreamWorks Animation LLC.

Storyboard, Brenda Chapman, *The Prince of Egypt* ©1998 DreamWorks Animation LLC.

Bill: **You had never supervised backgrounds before that?**

Brenda: Nope, I hadn't.

Bill: **How did that work?**

Brenda: Well, I got very lucky. Like I said, I had Kathy Altieri as an art director, and we had two heads of backgrounds, Paul Lassaine and Ron Lukas. Kathy and I had been really good friends at Disney, we're still really good friends, so we had a language where during the first few sessions Kathy would do the talking for me. If I knew there was something I wanted to change, she could figure out what it was by my "stutterings." And then, by a few weeks into the movie, I was able to give those critiques myself … without stuttering.

Bill: Who was the production designer?

Brenda: Derek Gogol. Kathy and Richie were there prior to Derek, and actually Richie did a lot of production design as well. We had basically two different worlds, the Egyptian world and the Hebrew world. Richie took the organic aspect of the Hebrew world, and Derek really led the Egyptian world, and then they blended it all together.

I'd met Derek on *Lion King*. He'd done some early work on that and I was really impressed, so I asked Jeffrey to take a look at his work. Then when he came in, he did these giant things and Jeffrey said, "Wow!" [*laughs*]. So Derek knows how to wow an executive. Draw big [*laughs*]. But he's an incredible designer, and he works in live action a lot as well.

Bill: So you guys had a good thing to key off of when you were directing?

Brenda: Yes.

Bill: So you were art directing with a story sense, right?

Brenda: Yes, I come from story and so everything has to support that.

Bill: Jeffrey, in later years, became famous for swapping directors and story people. Did you have a lot of swapping on that film?

Brenda: No.

Bill: You stayed pretty consistent all the way through?

Brenda: Yes, we did. It was a very different time at DreamWorks. I think we had a very humble Jeffrey for that time. I think he was very bruised from his experience at Disney, and I think he was very grateful to those of us who jumped ship and followed him to come and help him create this other studio. I was there because I really wanted people in the industry to have options. If there's a guy who knows the business Disney knows, it'll thrive. What if we had another studio that could thrive?

Bill: How did you feel when the movie was finished?

Brenda: [*Exhales deeply*] Tired [*laughs*].

Bill: Did you feel like you had made the movie that you had set out to make with the story?

Brenda: Yes, Simon and Steve and I were pretty happy. None of us are particularly religious people, so it was an odd choice of directors, or so I thought. But in the end, I thought that we made it more palatable to people of all kinds.

Bill: Were there any big surprises or disappointments as the picture went on?

Brenda: I found sometimes it was hard to maintain a consistency of the flow. The Egyptian priests were supposed to be these wacky, really funny characters, and then the subject matter just didn't sort of allow that. To me, they felt a little out of place. I was a little torn about some of the tonality that went on and the inconsistencies in the film. I think the most frustrating part is being told, "Don't worry about budget, just be creative, do your thing," and then, at the end, it's, "Sorry, you can't spend that." It's like, "Well, if I'd known, I could have planned better." That was really frustrating. I feel like the crowds in the Exodus look a little, um, funky.

Bill: That's a pretty big lesson.

Brenda: Yes [*laughs*]. Well, it was a huge lesson, but it wasn't like I had a choice in the matter.

Bill: Was he aware of these changes? Did you tell him?

Brenda: Um ... I tried [*laughs*]. But I didn't get very far. He was great with me, I have to say. I don't want to belittle him too much, but I also felt that he was sort of losing sight of the bigger picture for animation. At Disney, he had many other things to keep him occupied, and then when he got into DreamWorks, animation was it. I think he really believed that live-action writers could solve all the problems.

Bill: Why did they have such a hard time working with animation writers?

Brenda: Because I think they were not used to the process, the preediting process. A writer in live action will write their script, and they'll do the changes back and forth with the director. Then, they'll go shoot that script, and then they edit the movie. Whereas, in animation, you're testing the script constantly, you're testing the story and you're totally ripping it apart and putting it back together. You're totally ripping it and they can't deal with it. They feel like they've already gone through that process in their own writing of it. The mistake is letting them get so deep into it and feel like they've given you gold. It's just a whole different animal.

Storyboards, Brenda Chapman, *Spirit: Stallion of the Cimarron* © 2002 DreamWorks Animation LLC.

Storyboards, Brenda Chapman, *Spirit: Stallion of the Cimarron* © 2002 DreamWorks Animation LLC.

Storyboards, Brenda Chapman, *Spirit: Stallion of the Cimarron* © 2002 DreamWorks Animation LLC.

Bill: So, you were frustrated on *Sinbad*, you pulled out of that. What happened next?

Brenda: I stayed for a little while, trying to develop a couple of other projects. I felt like I'd been on that movie twice already. It was like *Lion King*, which to me, was the story of Moses, and then I did the story of Moses on *Prince of Egypt*, and then *The White Seal* was the story of Moses, so I tried to develop a fairy tale of my own, an Irish-based fairy tale about selkies. And that didn't fly. I was really tired, so I just said, "You know, I'm moving on." I left and touched down a few places. I worked as a story artist, very briefly, on *Where the Wild Things Are* at Universal with Eric Goldberg. Very briefly. That project went under pretty quickly. Then I went over to Sony because Sandy Rabins and Penney Finkleman Cox were my producers on *Prince of Egypt*. That felt a lot like DreamWorks to me, where the producers were really basically the directors.

Bill: And you didn't like that.

Brenda: I didn't, no. Then Joe called me and I ended up at Pixar, working on *Cars* as a story artist, thinking that's all I wanted to do ever again [*laughs*]. I just felt so beat up by the end of it.

Bill: Did you go on the *Cars* road trip?

Brenda: No, I didn't. I missed that.

Bill: They did it before you got there?

Brenda: Yes.

Bill: *Cars* was a tough story!

Brenda: Yes, but by the time I got here, they'd gone through most of it. I got on right as they were really trying to nail it down for production. The story of my life is always being hired because I'm a female [*laughs*], except for at DreamWorks.

Bill: Was your story work gender specific, or just story stuff?

Brenda: I got gender stuff. He wanted me on because he felt they needed a female perspective. So [*laughs*] I was trying to do that. But it was well on its way. I think it was more of a "Will I fit in at Pixar and does Pixar fit in for me?" I think it was a test run.

Bill: What did you do when *Cars* was over?

Brenda: Well, before *Cars* was over, I started thinking about a couple of ideas which included the one that I'm working on now. I got the idea, so I went to Mary Coleman and Sarah McArthur. I don't know if they want me to direct or not, I just have an idea.

I wondered, "Should I pitch it?" How do I go about that? Next thing I know, I'm having lunch with John, thinking that I'm just talking about the possibility of me directing. And he's like [*claps her hand*], "Hear you have an idea! What is it?" So I have this impromptu, over-the-lunch-table pitch, which I was not prepared to do, but he liked it. And I've been working on it ever since.

Bill: **And suddenly you're a Pixar director.**

Brenda: I still pinch myself [*laughs*]. "How did I manage that?" And I know how I managed that—Joe. You know, Joe was the one who really believed in me and got me in here and had them thinking about that already, before I even knew that I was thinking about it.

Bill: **Well that's the Pixar power. They recognize talent. So now you're the director. Now you're going to take this project all the way through.**

Brenda: Yes, and let me tell you I had no idea what directing meant until I got to Pixar, because at Disney and at DreamWorks it was, "OK, here is your composer, here is your editor, here is your writer." You're just told these are the people you're using. And here, it's like, "Well who do you want to edit the film? We've got all these people you can meet. Who do you want to be a composer?" And I'm like, "How do I choose a composer other than I just like their music?" I was having to go through and figure out, "How do I make the right decision for the film, and not just taste-wise, you know?"

Bill: **So how do you? What's your method?**

Brenda: [*Laughs*] Well, I met with a lot of people. The hard part was I tried to get a lot of people I worked with in the past to come up. And out of fear of losing their jobs, moving, and all this … none of them would come. So I had to listen to my newfound work friends up here as to who they would recommend. I found Steve Pilcher, my production designer, through Ralph Eggleston. I saw his work and was sort of wowed by the variety. He's just so prolific. He was the best interview I ever had, trying to get someone to work on the project. We're sitting out in the atrium, and I decided I wanted to ask him to be my production designer. But I knew I was going to have to sell him, because he'd had some tough times at DreamWorks as well. So (we) sit down, and I say, "Here's what the story's about. It's a fairy tale. And, um, you know, it's a princess." [*Laughs*] And, you know, I start just the general thing of telling him about it and seeing him sink in his chair.

But then I start telling him about the character, and the story, and the location, and pretty soon he's like this [*leans forward in the chair, wide eyed*]. And then he had all these ideas. It was the best going from, "Oh God …" to [*gasp*] "Great!" You know, being really into it.

Bill: And with Steve, that gets you a lot of energy.

Brenda: He's the best PR I've ever had! I mean, just in the building, he'd put his stuff on the walls and I'd meet people at the coffee station who'd say, "Oh my God! Your film looks so great!" [*laughs*]. And it was all Pilcher's work. I mean, he's amazing.

Bill: I heard a story about John Lasseter walking into one of your early meetings and looking at Steve's stuff on the wall.

Brenda: Yeah. He's amazing. He just asks me what I'm looking for, and he does what Steve does. There's no executive telling him he can't do something or telling him to do it a different way. We finish each other's sentences. We're really on the same page, and it's a real pleasure to see him shine. I know he had a blast working with you.

Bill: Did the art direction end up changing or affecting the way you approached the story at all?

Brenda: It was complementing. The thing about Steve Pilcher is that he's always questioning what I'm looking for. He'd question me about the story, or question me about a feeling, and so we influenced each other along the way. I really love how it's turning out. The big question mark for me was, what is the film going to look like? I'm used to 2D; I'd never worked in CG (computer generation) before. So I see all these beautiful paintings he did, and beautiful drawings. But what is it going to look like when it is actually rendered? The first couple of shots that I finally saw, with finished lighting and everything, I was like, konk [*motions to jaw dropping*].

Bill: Was story an easy thing for you on this project? Did it seem to flow pretty well?

Brenda: Well, yes and no. Initially, I didn't know how they worked up here, really. I just knew they always did brilliant stuff. I was a little surprised when they were surprised that I worked in a room by myself for a year and a half with, occasionally, Kiel Murray or Mary Coleman coming in and kicking (around) ideas. But I was pretty much cards and writing on my own. I would have a structure, you know? And then I would show it to someone. But they were always surprised that I would have a beginning, middle, and end. Because what I did notice was that they would have brain trust sessions here where they would just show the first two acts, or just the first act. And I was always like, "How do you critique something if you don't know where it's going?"

But they always managed to do it! And do it brilliantly! So who am I to say that's not the way to do it? But I can't do it that way. I'd always have to start here and end there.

That was sort of a surprise to them. But I also told my movie idea to the story crew on *Cars* early on, when I was just beginning to develop it. They saw me working in my office, which was still over there in the *Cars* area. And Steve Purcell really liked the story; he liked the heart of it. So he was always shoving drawings under my door. And Joe was saying, "Oh you should get him as your head of story. You should talk to him." I was thinking I had someone outside that I wanted, but

I told myself, "Just look at the stuff he's giving me already. He's so into it." So he's my head of story.

Bill: **How has the CG production experience been going for you? Did they teach you? Do you just fumble along yourself?**

Brenda: A little of both [laugh]. Brad Bird had said, "It just seems like you're never going to get there, and then suddenly you start seeing stuff. You just have to take it on faith for the longest time." Which is, you know, absolutely against his grain and a bit against mine, too. But, I was at their mercy in that sense. And they were at the mercy of getting it all build and going through all the stages of it. I can still remember my first sets review.

Bill: **Looking at the 3D?**

Brenda: Yes, but it was like, "OK, we've got some hills here and rocks and da da da … does that look like about the right amount?" I was stumped. What

Sketch, Brenda Chapman, *Brave*, 2012 © Disney/Pixar.

is the context of this? It was just stuff up there and I had no idea what I was looking at. And you know, it turned out we

Sketch, Brenda Chapman, *Brave*, 2012 © Disney/Pixar.

hadn't gone through a few steps. I asked, "Is there anything equivalent to workbook in this place?" And that was a whole big debate and issue. We've got a workbook session now, but it's not quite the same as what we had in 2D. But it informs all the departments what we're all doing and can put everything in context for me, so I know what I'm looking at when I see it on-screen.

Bill: As a director, do you worry about appearing to not know what's going on? Do you ever have a mask? Have you ever tried to just fake it and walk through it?

Brenda: I think at first I was terrified because here I am at this place and there is a general disdain for my past work. I mean, for the old Disney films. The purpose of Pixar was to not do fairy tales, and not do musicals and simpering princesses and all of that. And here I am bringing a fairy tale in, but wanting to do something really different. So on that level, I was really worried that people wouldn't want to work on the project, or (that they'd) look a little askance at me. But, I'm a horrible faker, so I just have to be honest. (I'd say,) "Sorry, I need people to guide me here a little bit." And they were great. Again, the people that I met with and hired in the lead positions were very willing to teach me what I need to know to make the right decisions. Now I feel like I have knowledge and I'm moving forward pretty well. But, I was met with enthusiasm rather than disdain, which was what I was really afraid of.

Bill: What's your toughest task as a director now?

Brenda: You know, I think it's the challenge of the brain trust.

Bill: By the "brain trust," you mean the Pixar group that comes in and critiques your film?

Brenda: Yes.

Bill: Having just to listen and face up to those guys?

Brenda: It can be difficult.

Bill: Do you absorb? Do you argue back? Do you discuss?

Brenda: I usually can't get a word in edgewise to argue back between Brad and Andrew Stanton and John. Pete Docter and I are usually just sitting there going, "Hmmm …" [*laughs*]. I have to absorb because I don't really have an alternative to go to. But sometimes it's hard because I feel like either they've missed what I'm trying to say or they all have their own opinions of how they want to do it. I have to try to decipher that. And they're all very strong, they have very strong ideas and strong opinions. I'm not saying that is a bad thing, I'm saying it's great. But when they are coming from different places, it's really hard to try to take the essence of the note and go forward with it, when there are like three different essences, so to speak.

Bill: But you're not required to agree with their notes?

Brenda: No, but it's a fine line you walk, I think. Because they want to feel like you heard them. You don't have to go to the letter of their note, but you have to try to figure out what it is that's behind the note, the reason for the note. And sometimes those notes change. That's been the problem for me. I have been pushed back twice for sequels since Disney bought Pixar. So I've had this extra-long time for people to keep messing with the story, and I feel like it's sort of made it a little harder. But at the same time, I do feel, looking at this last screening, it's gotten a lot better. So, it's hard, and it can be confusing at times, but it's not like having to go in and Jeffrey giving you a mandate saying, "This is what you have to do! And so you're going to do it!"

Bill: It's an unusual directorial challenge to have such a long period to keep the crew motivated, to keep things on track.

Brenda: Well, for me, it's easy because it's my story. It comes from my heart. It's inspired by things that are personal to me. So I find ways to keep it going, and my challenge has been to try to keep the crew motivated. I'm constantly amazed at how they find that thing to keep moving forward. My story crew and my editorial crew have just been fantastic.

They just keep plugging along, and I don't hear or feel a lot of grumblings about, "Ugh, I'm ready to get off this thing." I know they try to hide that from the director, but I also can usually pick up on that.

Bill: You said your inspiration came from personal things?

Brenda: It comes from my daily life with my daughter—because she's a real daddy's girl. And she and I are like this [*fists bumping each other*] all the time. She's been like that since she was four years old. She just kicked in somewhere, right after being a toddler, and we've been butting heads ever since. So it's sort of taking that idea and putting it in another fantasy world, so to speak, and letting it have the emotion that builds up in action and adventure. It's not a girly movie, yet it's fueled by a mother and daughter story.

Bill: How do you think you're different as a director today than you were six years ago when you started this?

Brenda: I think coming out of false assumptions that I'd always had about Pixar. About what it was to have that creative freedom. I thought it would just be Valhalla, you know?

But it's hard. Yet the pain you kind of go through to get what you need for your film enriches you, and it enriches the film. It's just having to dig a lot deeper story-wise. That's the thing: they put you through the paces here. I understand where they get sort of disdainful of that other age of animation in the late 1980s and 1990s. Because in comparison, those are more surface than what they do at Pixar. They really dig deep here, and I really appreciate it now. I mean in *Up*, there are so many levels emotionally and filmic to that movie. I just love it.

Bill: **So you're not required to be a technologist to be a director here.**

Brenda: No. Thank God. I do feel like I know a lot more than I did when I started, but I still can't touch the brainiacs that work here.

Bill: **Have you thought about what's next?**

Brenda: I am only beginning to dip my toe in those waters, because I've been so all-consumed with this one that it's been hard to think about the future. But I'm getting there, and I haven't found it yet. I know I need to do something different. My gut was to just do another fairy tale and make up something else. But, I feel like maybe I need to broaden that a bit and look elsewhere.

 Interviewer's note: Between these interviews, Brenda was removed from *Brave* for "creative differences." However, she won the Academy Award with codirector Mark Andrews when Brave was named Best Animated Feature Film by the Academy.

Bill: **Although you left the project, what's your final appraisal of how the whole thing came out? You had to feel good that your original conception of the mother–daughter relationship was intact. And, of course, you must have been happy to win an Oscar.**

Brenda: I was really happy with how it turned out. Of course, there were things I would have done differently in some of it, but for the most part, it was the story I was trying to tell. It felt really good. There were parts that I had been asked to take out while I was still at Pixar, but they had somehow worked their way back into the movie, which was really good to see because I thought they were integral to the story. The award was a really good ending to a really difficult time, so that was great.

Bill: **Didn't you take your daughter to the ceremony?**

Brenda: Yes, I did. We only got one ticket. They only allow you one guest, so I was really torn. I wanted to take her, but I felt like I should take Kevin too. But he was very adamant that I take Emma because it was our story. She had such a great time.

Bill: **That was a poignant ending, I think.**

Brenda: I think so, too.

Bill: Weren't you the first female director of an animated film to get an Oscar?

Brenda: I think so, actually.

Bill: You had a situation where you were kind of in limbo. You were off of the movie, but you couldn't work on anything until the picture was over. What was happening then?

Brenda: I was working on my own stuff. We had agreed that anything I worked on, on my own time, when I was at home, they would not take. I was working on three different books. None of them are finished, of course, but they were ideas that started coming forward. It was a lot of fun. It really helped me get through that really hard time.

Bill: You were approached to do some consulting on another project, right?

Brenda: After *Brave* was released, I was free of Pixar, so I was free to take other jobs. I had been offered different things, but the first one that I really took was a consulting job with Kathleen Kennedy at Lucasfilm on an animated project that George Lucas had started, but it was having trouble.

Bill: She's obviously one of the most powerful women in the industry. Meeting her, she still has a really wonderful blend of grace and elegance and niceness, along with the fact that she really gets things done. Did you learn anything from her in your time working with her?

Brenda: I really admired just what you said: her grace and her dignity, but yet her humanity. It just made things clearer that you can be kind and be in this business. You can be tough and get things done. I've never seen her belittle anyone in the room. I've only seen her be straight. She tells the truth. She tells it as she sees it, but she never needs to take anyone down to do it. She just does a really great job. Watching her, no matter what level of person she's talking to—the hierarchy in the company—she's the same. I really admired that.

Bill: It's a good thing to imprint that.

Brenda: Yeah.

Bill: How did you end up back at DreamWorks?

Brenda: Jeffrey has this sense of loyalty, which I really appreciate. The day after I was taken off of *Brave*, he called me and said, "Come home." He literally said those words. I couldn't and I wouldn't even remotely be ready to do anything like that emotionally, but it was just so great to know that he still felt strongly about my abilities. I helped him start DreamWorks, and he remembered that, but I think he also feels that I can do a good job. That was just really validating and helpful at the moment.

Bill: That was a great thing for him to do. When you were able to then finally go over there, how did that discussion go? How did you fold back into the work there?

Brenda: Initially, I think they were hoping I would bring an idea and develop it. But because I didn't want what had happened to me on *Brave* to happen again, I wanted to put some things in place to protect me and whatever idea I brought in. We couldn't quite reach an agreement that they were comfortable with, or that I was comfortable with, so I just said, "Show me what you have in your stockpile of project ideas." They had five or six things they showed to me that they thought I might be interested in, and there was one that I really was. I've been writing, and I just turned in a first draft with my writing partner, Irene Mecchi. It's been a blast.

Bill: Did you work with Irene on *Lion King*?

Brenda: Yeah. That's where I met Irene.

Bill: But she's a writer. She didn't come from a storyboarding background like you did.

Brenda: No. It's what I really like about Irene. She was the first writer I had worked with that seemed to really enjoy the process of animation and understand that it's a collaboration and it's not about being an author of a movie or a story. It's about working with other people. She loves working with story artists. She really enjoys that process. It's great because animation is such a collaborative process that to work with someone like that as a writer was great and very rare at the time.

Bill: All of your formative years in story were done, really, doing storyboards—telling stories through pictures. Do you draw much, or are you doing it completely through words?

Brenda: I don't draw very much anymore, and I am mostly writing. I'll do a scribble here and there for my story artists or whatever to get across ideas. I'm so rusty, and there are so many people who can do it so much better. I sort of get lost in the storytelling. I've been enjoying writing because I think I have a slightly different approach, a different perspective, because I write in a visual way. I understand the boarding process, so that's sort of in my head as I'm writing. I don't overdescribe, but I try to give enough so that the artist can run with it.

Bill: Do you find that you're able to visualize the movie equally well without drawing by just writing?

Brenda: Yeah. It's in my head as I write. I'm visualizing it as I write. Of course, when you get the artists on it, things change and it comes into its own thing, as all of these movies do. But yeah, I do. After *Brave* I thought, "Maybe I should just get out of animation and just write." And while I was writing my stories while I was still tied to Pixar, I just found myself visualizing and visualizing and visualizing. I thought, "This is what I love. I can't just leave it on a page. I need to see it." I realize that I do still love the community and the filmmaking of animation.

Bill: Do you see any scenario where you would be able to start pursuing your own original ideas again in animation, or would you be looking for some other way to do that?

Brenda: I think I've decided that I will still write my stories, but I want to put them in a book form that clearly states that it's my story, "That's what I did." Then if a studio wants to option it, that's great. I think I need to create the story on my own without the committee and put out what I feel is the pure vision of a story that someone creates. To be able to say, "This is a story I created. If you want to make a film out of it, great." There will be no question about paying for it, credit, and all of that stuff—or going through the hell of being taken off of it and having to struggle to stay connected to it.

Bill: It sounds like you're still dealing with that conundrum where, as you said before and you know so well, animation, by its nature, is a collaborative medium. You have so many people involved. But as the creator, you still have the sensitivity about putting your own idea, which you know well, through that process.

Brenda: I guess I just contradicted myself. I think the difference is that for *Brave*, they asked for my idea. They asked me to write it and create it. I collaborated with my story artists, and Irene was working on it for a while. I do like that. And everything I've ever worked on before has been either an adaptation or purely collaborate. *Lion King* had been around for so many years in development that God knows where that story originated.

Bill: So was *Hamlet*!

Brenda: *Hamlet* and *The Ten Commandments*. They always said *Hamlet*, but I always felt like it was *The Ten Commandments*. Then I ended up doing *Prince of Egypt*, and I thought, "Oh, God. I'm doing this story again." I guess because *Brave* was so close to my heart and I realize that any story I come up with on my own is going to feel that close to me—I think what I was trying to do was just get a guarantee that they wouldn't take me off of it. It wasn't about claiming absolute authorship, but it's like letting me nurture it to the end with the crew, with my team. But if they weren't comfortable doing that, if I was going to be connected to a story, I felt that I would rather write a book and then hand it over and let them do what they want to do with it, if they want to buy the story. But if not, that's OK. I didn't make *Brave* by myself. I created the concept by myself and I did create that story. I had it planned out before many people were on it, but to create it visually as a film takes so many people.

Bill: You had a very emblematic experience of anybody who brings a story into the animation business. Like you said—especially with these big features now in big companies—there's so much going on and there are so many things pulling it each and every way. I really, seriously doubt if anybody ever had a story come in one way and come out exactly the way they thought.

Brenda: I think that's why I would like to write stories as books. Then I can see something all of the way through. The book I'm working on now does morph and change when you make it into a film. That's where the collaboration really kicks in.

Bill: I guess I should wrap up with this one question. Admittedly, you're one of the few women in this book. Looking back on all of this and your perspective on what you've done so far, do you feel it was a different experience for you? Had you been a man, do you think you would have done what you've done? Do you feel, going forward, that you bring something different or your experience is distinctly different because you're a woman and not a man?

Brenda: I think, definitely, my career has been affected by being a woman. It bothers me because I often wonder if I would have been as successful if I had been a guy because so often I get hired because I'm a woman.

When I started at Disney, Ed Hansen sat across the desk and said, "The review board liked your stuff, but we really need to get a woman. We're getting a lot of flack for not having a woman in stories. You're the right price, fresh out of school. And if you don't work out, we can let you go and try someone else." It was that blatant.

I know I got hired because I am a woman, but I felt like I also had to work harder to prove that I should stay. But then once I got in, the artists were great. I was mentored by a bunch of guys that really didn't seem to care one way or the other whether I was a woman or not. I think Joe Ranft called me to help out on *Cars* because he felt like it needed a woman's perspective. I think I've gotten a lot of opportunities because I'm a woman, and I hope that I can live up to the trust I was given to do those things. But, honestly, I feel like if I had been a guy, I would have probably gotten lost in the shuffle coming out of CalArts.

Bill: I don't know. I have to say that my personal experience in animation is that it really is kind of a true meritocracy because there's such a weird collection of human beings that get into it. But at the end of the day, people do recognize real talent, and they don't care where it's coming from. That's been my experience. It crosses genders and races—and personal hygiene.

Brenda: [*Laughs*]

Bill: I don't think you would have been lost in the shuffle. I think that was a revealing comment that when you got with the artists, if you didn't have it, they wouldn't have reacted to you the way they did.

Brenda: I don't know. But thank you for that!

6
Nick Park Interview

Nick Park © Aardman.

Animators like Ollie Johnston taught us, "There is more humor to be heard on the street than you could ever hope to invent yourself. You merely have to listen for it." Since he first broke out onto the world stage with his 1989 award-winning stop-motion short *Creature Comforts*, Nick Park has shown himself to be an astute observer of average people. When you come to know him and enjoy his company, you can see where the personalities of Wallace and Gromit originate. As Gilbert and Sullivan sang, "But in spite of all temptations, to belong to other nations, he remains an Englishman." The way Hayao Miyazaki's films are unapologetically Japanese, and Tomm Moore's films are Irish, Nick delights in the unique characteristics of his working-class neighbors. Aardman is not in London, an international center of animation production, but in the smaller city of Bristol, where they can be closer to average people.

Ron Diamond: At what age did you realize that animation existed? And when did you think about it as a possible career?

Nick: I grew up with all the Disney films and the cartoons on Saturday morning TV. I was probably six or seven years old when my brother told me that animation was actually created from drawings. I had never thought about it like that before. And I was definitely a fan. I watched whatever I could find on British TV. *The Wombles and the Clangers*, which were these little mousey creatures that lived on a strange planet. They didn't speak. They just kind of whistled to each other. There's a whole range of stuff that Oliver Postgate and Peter Firmin did throughout the sixties and seventies that really influenced me and got me more into the process of animation.

Ron: But when did you think that you'd actually like to do that?

Nick: That was some time later. Art was always my thing. I was never really good at anything else. And everyone knew this, so they supported me and pushed me in that direction. It gave me a buzz, really. When I was ten, I loved doodling and inventing my own cartoon characters. I even remember drawing my characters on badges that I could put on my blazer. I used to dream of how great it would be to have my own characters one day.

Ron: What were those characters like?

Nick: My first character was this rat called Walter, and that had nothing to do with Disney. I saw this documentary on mice and rats that inspired me. Anyway, I made flipbooks until I discovered that my parents had a movie camera. It was an 8mm Bell and

Howell that could take single frames for animation. What are the chances, right? I had been practicing by making flipbooks, and suddenly a camera falls into my lap, one that takes single frames! What would have happened if I didn't find that camera?

Ron: How old were you?

Nick: I was 13.

Ron: How did you figure out how to go from flipbook to camera?

Nick: My dad was a photographer, so he introduced me to lighting and angle points. It was really my dad who showed me how animation works. He'd once had a go at it. He made a promotional video for a company. He gave me all kinds of ideas. It wasn't just going from flipbook to camera. He said I could use paper cutouts, move cups around the table, and bring clay sculptures to life. I'd seen the work of Peter Lord and David Sproxton, who were doing this Gumby style of animation for kids TV. That was a big influence. I started animating everything I could find. I was also heavily influenced by Ray Harryhausen, who made dinosaurs out of coat hangers and foam rubber. My dream of making movies started very early. I even looked at books on Alfred Hitchcock and how he storyboarded. I spent all my time doing that from age 12 upwards.

Ron: Did you take classes at school?

Nick: No. I came from a small town in the north of England called Preston. It was a million miles away from anything to do with film. Never mind Hollywood, it was a three-hour train ride to London! Even Liverpool was 30 miles away. All I could do was go to the library and read books about a world that seemed so far away.

Ron: Do you remember any of those books?

Nick: There was an amateur movie magazine called *Moviemaker*, and it had its own version of the Oscar awards. Anyone could submit a film. I used to be in awe of those awards. I wanted to win one!

Ron: Did you?

Nick: No. I did submit films, but all I received were a few kind notes from the judges.

Ron: What kind of stop-motion films did you make?

Nick: When I was 15, I was actually making live-action stuff. I was really into horror films. There was this salt marsh near my house, and I made a bunch of tentacles from some hoses and filmed my friend being dragged away by them. It was supposed to be this unseen monster bubbling in the water. After it gets my friend, I envisioned the bubbles turning red with blood.

Ron: Were you ever the subject of any of your films?

Nick: No. It was mostly a small group of my friends. I was on the camera.

Ron: Did you use the drawings from Hitchcock to help you understand cinematography?

Nick: Yeah, that really interested me, because an early influence was always comic strips. For a time, I wanted to be a comic strip artist. There's a famous comic in the UK called *Beano*, and I dreamt of being a Beano artist. Comic strips are frames, after all. It's like a storyboard. When I saw Hitchcock's storyboards for *Psycho*, the combination of writing and boarding became clearer. I was never confident with writing in the beginning. So that helped me with the process of bringing a character to life. Honestly, my first film wasn't exactly a film. I didn't know anything about peg bars and registration. I had notepaper, and I drew Walter the rat walking. I didn't even plan the cycle of walking! I just started with the first drawing and worked through.

Ron: How did he walk?

Nick: Very badly [*laughs*].

Ron: Did you study the motion of walking? Did you look at Eadweard Muybridge or anything like that?

Nick: No. I think I may have seen stuff in passing, but I just picked things up wherever I could find them, whether that was watching film competitions on TV or reading books in the library. My first film was Walter walking for a couple of seconds. Then he comes across a bottle of cider, drinks it, and falls over. That was it. I sent it off to Kodak, but it never came back. I never got it back. The funny thing is, I should've given up at that moment. But I didn't. My mother was a dressmaker and she always had bags of material. So I took some colored felts and made my own Walter the Rat felt toy. And I made a film that took me one day. I didn't even have any lights. I set up an easel in front of the living room window with a camera. You could see the sun going behind the clouds and exposure changing. It's called *Rat and the Beanstalk*. You see these human legs walking through the frame while dropping some beans. The beans grow into a giant beanstalk. Then Walter comes along, climbs the beanstalk, reaches the clouds, and finds a bottle of cider. After he drinks it, he hears the giant coming. As Walter runs away, the giant trips over the bottle of cider and dies. The end. That was my first story.

Ron: A lot of animators are interested in either the process, in story, or a blend of the two. Were you more interested in story?

Nick: Yeah, I was very attracted to story. I think very early on. Obviously at that age you're not intellectualizing it or thinking about structure. But I really liked telling stories, and this was a natural outlet for me. I was better at using a combination of images and language to tell a story than simply writing something down for English class. However, if I had to write a sci-fi story or a comedy for class, I rose to that challenge. I loved to make people laugh, and my stories were always ridiculous!

Ron: **When did you become aware of David Sproxton and Peter Lord as filmmakers?**

Nick: Around 1975, I became aware of them through this character called Morph. He was on a children's TV show on BBC, a bit like *Sesame Street*. Animators were employed to do these sketches and skits. Morph appeared in these little vignettes that Pete and Dave made. At first I didn't know who made them, but I found them inspiring. Then later, when Morph appeared again, there was a segment about the artist. He was sitting at his desk, and there was this plastic Morph sitting next to him. Next thing you know, I'm in my attic doing clay animation.

Ron: **And so you instantly became the director of *Wallace and Gromit*?**

Nick: No! It was a slow and long road, really. I tried all kinds of stuff along the way. Influences were to be found everywhere. There was Terry Gilliam, and Monty Python was big in the mid-seventies.

Ron: **What did you experiment with?**

Nick: I emulated Terry Gilliam a lot. I played with more dinosaurs in the vein of Ray Harryhausen. The Disney style attracted me too, but I could never afford the necessary materials. I tried using tracing paper, but it just wasn't good enough. Eventually, I was rather torn between meticulously drawn animation and more spontaneous techniques, where you can work in front of the camera with less planning. A good example was the show *Roobarb and Custard*. The drawing was very spontaneous; the lines didn't have to be precise. There was this green dog called Roobarb. Bob Godfrey was the animator. I've always been a big fan of Bob Godfrey. Everything was intentionally wobbly, and there was a distinct humor that came with that. And that's when I started to like working with Plasticine. You can act in front of the camera without too much planning. I planned in storyboard, but a lot of my best ideas came as I was doing the animation. I like that. I liked the freedom of improvisation. And I created even more characters. There was a dinosaur and a caveman character in *Murphy and Bongo*. But the whole thing was out of focus. I wonder if I could go back and fix that digitally …

Ron: **After you graduated from high school did you know what you wanted to do?**

Nick: At the time I didn't. I always thought this would be a hobby, nothing more. I did a two-year program at a foundation art school in Preston. There was painting, sculpting, printmaking, everything. But I had this bias toward filmmaking, and I continued making films at home. My tutors were actually amazed when they found out that I did animation. I didn't mention it because I didn't think it was serious art. I thought serious art was painting and still-life drawing. I was trying to be a real artist in that program. As it turns out, everyone loved the animation I had been making at home.

Finally my dad said, "Why don't you apply to film school or art school? Go to a school where you can study filmmaking." It was strange. I had never thought about that before. I didn't think someone from Preston would be able to do that. I applied to Sheffield Art School and the Royal College of Art in London. But I couldn't afford the train fare to London for the interview, so I went to Sheffield.

Ron: **You only applied to two places?**

Nick: Yeah, it was a good thing I got accepted. I spent three years at Sheffield studying video photography. They knew I loved animation, but there was no program devoted to it. Still, they liked my stuff and let me specialize in animation. That's all I did. I made a couple of puppet animation films, and one using chalk on a blackboard.

Ron: **What happened after Sheffield?**

Nick: I applied to the National Film and TV School near London. I thought that was the place to go, since it's a postgrad school, and there was an animation course. I learned a lot about the basics of filmmaking and editing at Sheffield, but it was more of a crash course in cinema. I really enjoyed the history of film and studying directors like Orson Welles and Hitchcock.

Ron: **Did you study lighting and write essays?**

Nick: Absolutely. One of my essays was about German film of the 1920s: *The Cabinet of Dr. Caligari*, *The Last Laugh*, Pabst, and all these other filmmakers, many of which moved to Hollywood. I really enjoyed that cinematic look back then. In fact, that forest atmosphere Fritz Lang created in *Die Nibelungen* (1924), the way he used the atmosphere in the trees, that's what I was thinking of when I made *Curse of the Were-Rabbit*.

Ron: **What about other filmmakers? Who else from the world of cinema influenced you?**

Nick: I kind of pick up everything and anything along the way. Hitchcock is definitely one of my favorites. The way he filmed; there are loads of his films that I haven't seen. But *Rear Window* and *Psycho* just spoke to me. But I tend not to refer to specific scenes. It's the movement of the film as a whole. That's what grabs me.

Ron: **And the National Film and TV School?**

Nick: That was another crash course in film studies. The school was founded in 1972, so it was a relatively new institution. It was fantastic. I loved it. And I was not the first animator to go there, but definitely part of a stream of animators that started coming out of that school.

Ron: Had they been teaching animation since the beginning?

Nick: Not specifically. There were animators like Phil Austin and Derek Hayes, who were a few years before me. They also went to Sheffield. I was following in their footsteps, and I looked up to them.

Ron: Who else was there with you?

Nick: Joan Ashworth, who's now professor and head of the animation department at the Royal College of Art. She was the only other (stop-motion) model animator there that I can recall. Mark Baker, Tony Collingwood, and Ken Lidtser were there. Mark Herman, the live-action director of *Brassed Off* and *The Boy in the Striped Pajamas*, he was there too. There were so many talented people there. Mark Baker's *The Hill Farm* is one of the best animated films ever made. He's an animator's animator.

Ron: Was there any competition? Did you collaborate and share notes? Or did everyone just want to make great films?

Nick: There was never any sense of competition. We were all quite different filmmakers, which made it easy to support one another. On top of that, the animation department was young, and there was always that feeling that you weren't being taken seriously. That made us pull together. We were a close group.

Ron: What kind of lectures and teachers did you have? Do any stand out in your memory?

Nick: It was predominantly live action orientated. Even though I was learning great skills, nothing was focused on what I wanted to do. Nothing stands out in my mind. The whole school was that way. It was a lot of old fifties' film studios with video and editing rooms back then. Video was just coming in. It's different now. But I was there when we got the first stop-frame animation camera in 35mm!

Ron: How long were you there?

Nick: Over three years.

Ron: And you did two films?

Nick: I did bits and pieces of things, both for other people and school exercises. By the second year, I had to start thinking about my graduation piece. That was when David Fine came to the school with some clay animation. It was really good. It made me think of my early experiments with *Walter the Rat*. But it was these characters that I'd been doodling since art school that got me. I went back to my old sketches and found this one particular character, whose name I then changed to Wallace. He's an inventor. He's building a rocket in the basement of his house; that was going to be the joke. At the time, I was in this student work program at Elstree Studios with Jim Henson's outfit. They were making *The Dark Crystal*, and I was just hanging around making tea for the special effects people. That's when I came up with the idea. I was thinking of the rocket blasting off through the house and how I'd do the effects. I dropped that idea in the end, but that's what got me going. I immediately started animating. Originally I had a cat character, but I just found it easier to make a dog out of clay, with the big paws and the big ears. I did some testing, and I was amazed by what you could do with clay.

Ron: Can you talk a little bit about creating your characters, going from lump of clay to a well-defined identity?

Nick: The beauty of clay is that it doesn't have to be too polished, or too smooth and sophisticated. You don't want it to be mechanical and lifeless. I really admire what certain people are doing with computer animation. Still, only in very recent films have I seen a human-

Nick Park's doodles of characters.

ity come through. The beauty of clay animation is that the animator is actually in touch, physically, with the character on every frame. You're imbuing life into that character. You are the actor. And I'm quite sure if you animated a Disney princess in Plasticine, it might be impressive. But that's not what I'm after. That's why my stuff is blobby, thick, and handmade. There's a natural humor that comes with that. And that's important to me. On the other hand, there is a much needed balance. If you're not careful, it can look too simple, or just plain bad. I have to reach this point where the figure is comically and deceptively simple. Wallace's hands, for example, are thick and like bunches of bananas, which is something you find in eastern European animation. I like to emulate that, I think, more than Disney. It's more Simpson's than Disney. Everything moves in a basic way, and there's a softness that emerges. That's the key for me. I want you to see the story through this medium that exists in a self-contained and believable world.

I loved the process of drawing and designing a character, modeling him in clay, and then animating him on film. You get all the cartooniness you can create with clay, with the elasticity of their limbs and facial expressions. You also get a 3D film-making quality. You can light the set and the camera angles. For me, it was this perfect blend of animation and live-action filmmaking. It appealed to that side of me that loved that history of filmmaking and my favorite filmmakers. I could use the cameras the same way Hitchcock did, or Orson Welles. I was making a live-action film, but on a small scale.

Ron: Your actors never talk back.

Nick: And your actors never talk back [*laughs*].

Ron: When you were making *A Grand Day Out*, is that when you discovered this very personal artistic approach?

Nick: To a certain extent, yes. The characters of Wallace and Gromit were actually developed in one day. And Gromit, at the time, had a mouth. I had even done some recordings for his voice. But as we were filming a scene, I couldn't reach his face

EXT. BANANA LANDSCAPE. 'A GRAND DAY OUT'.

Early Wallace and Gromit on the Moon, Nick Park, *A Grand Day Out*, 1989.

to put the mouth on. So I just moved the eyes. That's when I realized I could do everything with the eyes. Gromit was suddenly born. He didn't need a mouth. He became a very introvert and very intelligent dog. Gromit is the opposite of Wallace. As two characters with two distinct personalities, the dynamic between the two of them was born.

Ron: **So that was the beginning of *Wallace and Gromit*. Did you make the whole film at the National Film and TV School?**

Nick: It took some time. It wasn't easy doing everything by myself. It is a mini-live-action movie, after all. I wrote the script with a friend in a London pub. I was never confident when it came to writing, so he helped out a lot, especially the jokes. David Fine and Alison Snowden also pitched in. They helped make props sometimes. At one point, I even had a guy come in and do the lighting and camera. He couldn't stick around for too long, so I learned everything I could from him. In the end, it was pretty much a one-man show. A year and a half later, I realized I'd shot only five minutes of the film! To make matters worse, no one could really explain what I was getting into or what I needed. It was all trial and error. After a year and a half, all I had done was one page of the script, a five-minute scene of Wallace and Gromit building the rocket in the basement. I had 19 pages left to go!

Ron: **What did you do?**

Nick: I was running out of time and money. The film school gave me an extension, but I soon realized that it was going to take forever to finish. I went to see David and Alison in Canada at the National Film Board, and I remember someone saying, "Can anyone think of how to cut this down, just find an ending with what he has?" I'd also met Peter Lord and David Sproxton and invited them to the school as lecturers. They were the only people I knew who did this kind of animation. When they saw what I was working on, they asked me to come work with them for the summer. It was a great opportunity. I could be an assistant animator. But I felt

Nick Park and Peter Lord © Aardman.

like a director with a vision, and I didn't want to neglect my film. Pete and Dave understood. They offered me a part-time job instead, so I could have the necessary time to continue. It was a way of earning money and making my own film.

Ron: **You made the whole thing yourself?**

Nick: Yeah, I did. It took about seven years altogether.

Ron: **Did Pete and Dave give you any help or advice?**

Nick: They did. And I learned a lot from making commercials for them. It was the right place for me to be. I could grab someone and ask them to light a scene or make some models. Joan Ashworth did one scene, in fact, where the robot on the moon dreams of skiing the Alps. It's a great black and white scene. Joan was setting up a studio in London at the time, and she just offered to do a scene for me.

Ron: *Creature Comforts* **also was a school project, right?**

Nick: No, it wasn't. The concept was developed as I was finishing *A Grand Day Out* at Aardman. A group of us got together with the idea of making collaborative film. Besides me, it was Barry Purves, Richard Goleszowski, Pete Lord, and … I might be leaving someone out. We decided to take these animated conversational pieces and do something a little different. We used real-life recorded conversations and then animated characters around their voices. In this case, we made all the characters animals at a zoo. We even took the idea to Channel 4, and they liked it. The project got going very quickly. It took me three months to make that film, but it was finished at the same time as *A Grand Day Out* because I had a proper crew. I had model makers and people to handle lighting … all money from Channel 4. It was fantastic. It came together quickly. Suddenly, I went from unknown student to a director with two films.

Ron: **And two Oscar nominations within the same year.**

Nick: Yeah. That's right. I didn't even realize you could be nominated for an Oscar for short animated films. It was an amazing time. On the other hand, I always dreamed of this moment when *Wallace and Gromit* would come into the world. Suddenly, I had a film that stole the limelight.

Ron: **Did you get any attention for** *Wallace and Gromit*, **or was everybody focused on** *Creature Comforts*?

Nick: It was all about *Creature Comforts*. Even before the Oscar, it was getting all the attention at festivals. It was a funny, clever idea, something that hadn't been done before. People loved it.

Nick Park animating dancing chickens on "Sledgehammer", 1986 © Aardman Animations 1986.

Ron: An Oscar is a nice graduation present. You must have had a lot of people trying to fund your future projects and steal you away from Aardman.

Nick: Yes. But everyone knew I was part of Aardman. Pete and Dave made me a legitimate director in the company. And everybody seemed to want *Creature Comforts* commercials. But it wasn't just the Oscar. We had a lot of success with Peter Gabriel's "Sledgehammer" video. But I do remember the change. I went from an unknown animator to a director whose hand everyone wanted to shake. It was both funny and strange.

Ron: Did you feel different?

Nick: It gives you a lot of confidence. And it's suddenly easy to raise money for projects. It was also good for *Wallace and Gromit*. The BBC wanted more.

Ron: Were you also doing the Heat Electric campaign at that time?

Nick: Yes, we did. *Creature Comforts* spawned a whole series of commercials. But it was a different process, so we were picky. The original wasn't scripted. But commercials are always scripted and feel contrived. You never believe that they're real people. So, we got real people, and they became more popular than the original film!

Ron: Talk about recording and animating those voices. It wasn't scripted, so how did this work?

Nick: Well, it (*Creature Comforts*) was an experiment. At first, I took a documentary filmmaking approach. I decided to go to the zoo and record what people were saying about the animals. Then I would go back and reverse it; it would be the animals talking about the people. But it was too hard to record properly. It didn't work. Then I tried interviewing people directly. But they always said the same thing about the animals. Finally, we made the interview as much about them as the zoo. Suddenly, they started talking about themselves and the animals. We also just went out into the street and interviewed people at random. It was great material to blend and edit together. I remember this Brazilian guy. He was perfect. I just

Creature Comforts, 1989 © Aardman.

went to this flat in London and asked him about his life in England. I think this was the first time he had a chance to vent. He went on and on about the cold weather, his tiny flat, and how he hated the food. It was perfect material to work with.

Ron: Isn't he a celebrity?

Nick: He later became one in Brazil. I lost contact with him after making the film, but then later connected with a friend of his.

Ron: **These tracks were all recorded on tape, right?**

Nick: Yeah, it was all on tapes. I then put everything on a two-disc cassette and did the rough edit myself. In fact, I recorded a lot of it on a Sony Walkman. That's why some of it sounds fuzzy.

Ron: How many commercials did you direct for the Heat Electric campaign?

Nick: I did the first five. I can remember the tortoise, the cat, the penguins, and the parrots.

Ron: They were very popular?

Nick: They went ballistic in the UK. I think they're still in the top ten of the 100 best commercials in the UK.

Ron: I assume that totally changed Aardman.

Nick Park © Aardman.

Nick: It took us in a new direction.

Ron: Is this around the time you met Colin Rose?

Nick: Yeah. Colin Rose was based in Bristol at the BBC. He wanted to set up a center for animation in Bristol. In fact, he put me in touch with Bob Baker, who was a writer and script editor for *Dr. Who* in the seventies.

Ron: Was this the first time you worked with a proper writer?

Nick: It was indeed the first time I worked with a proper writer. We hit it off quickly. And this was good for me, because my ability to write scripts wasn't very strong. You know, with *Grand Day Out* and *Creature Comforts* we didn't really have a structured story, in any traditional sense. I had a script, but it was all over the place. I needed something that was more presentable, and Bob really helped. In the beginning, I thought he would throw out most of my scenes. I had penguins, various gags, and a chase scene with a train. But he didn't. Instead, he gave me structure. He said, "You need to put that there, this here, and move that to the end. That way you can find the story." Everything just came together nicely. I always enjoyed storyboarding, but moving from script to the storyboard is a big leap. The storyboard has to bring to life what the script intends. But it's not words. It's the film. You have to execute it visually.

Ron: It's very cinematic. Did you reference anything on the storyboard?

Nick: It was more in the back of my head. I'm never thinking about anything too specific. But I think I had Hitchcock in mind, and Ealing too. After all, it was all about that quiet lodger, and those discomforting hallways and stairways.

Ron: The Heist (1989)?

Nick: Yes, *The Heist*. Again, I didn't refer to anything specific, I just had certain movies in my head. Of course, don't forget that I had Tom and Jerry in mind when I wrote the chase sequence.

Ron: Did you ever publish that storyboard?

Nick: We did. We published a storyboard book for the film. We also did one for *Close Shave*, which compares the actual storyboard to the finished film.

Ron: And then you won another Academy Award in 1993.

Nick: Yeah, for *Wrong Trousers*. I think Julian Nott had a lot to do with that. He doesn't write any music until it's all locked in. And he obviously understood what I was trying to do, because he just brought so much to it.

He was also a student at the National Film and TV School. Even though I had been at Aardman for four years, I still visited, and

The Wrong Trousers, 1993 © Aardman.

that's where we met. He wrote lovely music for *A Grand Day Out*. He's brilliant. I learned a lot about music from him. We've had a great relationship since then. He's worked on everything I've done except *Chicken Run*.

Ron: **OK, let's go back to the BBC.**

After the Oscar, were they just giving you a blank check?

Nick: After *A Grand Day Out*, pretty much, and even more so after *Wrong Trousers*. Then we started talking to studios in LA about doing feature films.

Ron: **What came of that?**

Nick: We were hesitant. It was such a big step from making shorts. I always felt that both *Wallace and Gromit* and *Wrong Trousers* were the frustrated beginnings of feature films. They could be bigger. But it was a slow and challenging process to learn how to bring in more characters. I didn't know anything about character arcs.

Sc. 65. Shot 7. INT. DINING ROOM. NIGHT.

PANICKED PENGUIN TRIES TO BRAKE AND WALLACE AND GROMIT OVERTAKE.

TRACKING SHOT.

Sc 65. Shot 7. CONTINUED.

TROUSER FOOT COMES DOWN ON THE TRACK. PENGUIN GOES FLYING.

Sc.66. Shot 1. INT. KITCHEN. NIGHT.

WALLACE REACHES UP TO GRAB PENGUIN.

TRACKING SHOT

Sc. 66. Shot 2. INT. KITCHEN. NIGHT.

GROMIT ANTICIPATES A CATCH.

TRACKING SHOT.

Sc.66. Shot 3. INT. KITCHEN. NIGHT.

PENGUIN SALES THROUGH THE AIR.

TRACKING SHOT.

Sc.66. Shot 4. INT. KITCHEN. NIGHT.

GROMIT SMASHES INTO KITCHEN UNIT CUPBOARD

TRACK THEN STOP.

Storyboards, Nick Park, *The Wrong Trousers*, 1993 © Aardman.

Ron: How'd that go? That had to have been a lot more responsibility. You're in charge. You have to delegate.

Nick: Definitely. I had great animators, guys like Steve Box and Peter Peake. But I suddenly had to coach all these animators. I had to tell them when their work was a little wooden. I had to push them in the direction I wanted to go. That type of responsibility was new to me. This was our first foray into a more industrialized approach. It was a learning process, but we made it work. I think *A Close Shave* has some funny moments, especially that sheep.

A Close Shave, 1995 © Aardman.

Ron: Did you initiate the character development?

Nick: Yes, I assigned characters to specific animators: Steve Box took on Wendolene, Peter Peake had Shaun the Sheep, and Preston was Loyd Price. But there was always a collaborative atmosphere at play, as we created scenes in which these characters interacted. And I continued to play on a few of my favorite films from the past. David Lean's *Brief Encounter* was definitely in the background of our romantic scene in the wool shop. And when Preston became a cyber-dog, there was a *Terminator* reference in there.

Ron: It seems natural that you would next make a *Wallace and Gromit* feature. But instead, you decided to make *Chicken Run*.

Nick: By this point, we were serious about making a feature. Pete and I wanted to direct something together, and we thought it might be best to start with something fresh, not *Wallace and Gromit*. We had originally met Jeffrey Katzenberg at Disney, but now his

Chicken Run, TM @ © 2000 DreamWorks Animation LLC, Aardman Chicken Run Limited and Pathé Image. All Rights Reserved.

company DreamWorks was in operation. I was at Sundance with *A Close Shave.* After he watched it, he flew us to LA on his private jet to meet with Steven Spielberg.

Ron: What did you do?

Nick: I had this idea, which was just a couple of lines, and I pitched it to Steven and Jeffrey. It was a short version of *The Great Escape* with chickens. I had even done a sketch of a chicken digging its way out of a chicken coop. Steven said, "*The Great Escape* is one of my favorite films of all time, and I have 300 chickens on my farm. I love chickens." Needless to say, it went really well. I don't remember if it was three or five films over a ten-year period, but we signed a deal right there. That's how *Chicken Run* came to be.

Ron: But what about Aardman Animation (Studios)? You can't take ten years off, right?

Nick: That's right. We didn't want to stop Aardman from earning its bread and butter with commercials and short films. But it was a big change for the studio. We took on a crew of at least 150 people.

Ron: How'd that feel for you, as a director?

Nick: This was a whole new scale for us. *Chicken Run* had so many characters. We needed a lot of animators and a lot of backup for the molding process. As I said before, the challenge was keeping that same look. All these new animators had to reproduce our look. And with so many people working in front of the camera, things can change. One thing we did on *Close Shave* to combat this was to make replacement mouths for Wallace. We noticed that if we weren't careful, that would change quickly. We made them with different shapes and different syllables. There was a set of about 12 mouths.

Ron: **Was it for reference? Or were you actually replacing them?**

Nick: We were replacing them. For example, if Wallace were saying, "window," we'd have press molds to take his mouth through the syllables. Without those, it was a dirty process of molding and remolding. Sometimes we could ruin an entire mold and have to start from scratch. It could take forever.

Ron: **Were these made out of clay?**

Nick: Made out of clay. They're still malleable.

Ron: **The figures are about a foot tall, right?**

Nick: Yeah, Wallace is about that big. But I always had his sweater made of something more solid, so I could hold him without ruining the mold. And it also gives you something to plant the wire into for his legs. Armatures inside, but still with clay. Or sometimes we used latex rubber on the legs, because it just makes animating quicker.

Ron: **What kind of tools do you use to sculpt on the set?**

Nick: I tend to use wooden tools. Metal tends to nick too much.

Ron: **Do you use video reference when you animate?**

Nick: I used a lot on *Chicken Run* and *Were-Rabbit*. But on my latest *Wallace and Gromit* venture, *A Matter of Loaf and Death*, I probably acted every single shot, except those that were too difficult. It was a good way of telling the

Nick Park Animating Gromit © Aardman.

A Matter of Loaf & Death, 2008 © Aardman.

animator what I was looking for. They wouldn't follow it frame by frame, because that would be too realistic. I like things that are traditionally cartoony. But this was a good way to communicate with the animators.

Ron: **Essentially, it sounds like everything was a new experience for you.**

Nick: I knew my characters and sense of humor very well, but the studio process was entirely new. I couldn't write the story myself, or do the storyboard all by myself. Other people were involved now. And there were so many scenes. Pete and I sat down for about six months just to discuss them. Sometimes we'd rent a cottage in the Cotswolds, in the English country-side. We'd walk around and look at chicken farms. After that, we probably had about four hours' worth of stuff.

Ron: Did you get a chicken to help inspire you?

Nick: Well, actually, I had pet chickens. A lot of my films reference things I know well. For example, the furniture in *Wallace and Gromit* is a reference to stuff I had when I was a kid. But, and I'm not joking, my family had chickens as pets. They were like our dogs. My sister's chicken was a Rhode Island Red and called Penny. We used to make up this story that she eloped with her lover, the lone free ranger. That memory made its way into *Chicken Run*.

Ron: Did you bring anyone in to help with writing?

Nick: Peter and I decided we needed a writer, someone who knew about feature film structure. But we also wanted to maintain that quirky British humor. Once again, it was important to us to keep that Aardman style. Oddly, we couldn't find a lot of British writers who knew about feature film structure. Eventually, Karey Kirkpatrick was recommended, since he'd worked on *James and the Giant Peach*. He came in and loved our ideas. He loved British humor and Monty Python. Better still, he understood the simplicity of our shorts and wanted to develop that style into a feature. This big-picture vision was exactly what we needed. Pete and I tend to get bogged down in subplots. That's just the way I work, and I sometimes need a writer to come in and help. The three of us went off to develop this story with DreamWorks. And, of course, DreamWorks threw all these great storyboard artists into our lap. I had never worked like that before. It was very exciting.

Ron: But how did that feel, handing over your baby to someone you didn't really know?

Nick: It was difficult. You want to come up with all the ideas yourself. And we did a lot. But it was great to have that help. Looking back, every movie was a training ground. With *Close Shave*, we had to learn how to make a short with more people. Now, we had to learn how to animate chickens and keep an entire crew on the same page. The story was crucial. Basically, we did what we had always done. We learned and adapted.

Ron: Obviously DreamWorks could pull in good animators, but what about your style of clay animation?

Nick: They came from all over and worked closely with Pete and me. We worked the basic models ourselves and then let them elaborate on those figures. Then it went into molds, and they could make multiples of those characters. You're shooting the same character in numerous scenes at the same time. You need multiple characters. That's essential to the big studio process.

Ron: You described earlier your own personal way of working out the character's personality in clay. Could you apply those same principles in this big a project?

Nick: We wanted to apply those lessons to *Chicken Run*. But we were working with a different scale. We were dealing with a lot of chickens, and I couldn't create and give that distinct personality to all of them. *Chicken Run* wasn't exactly in the Aardman style.

Since childhood I've always wanted to put my own mark, my own style, on something. And I found it with Wallace and Gromit, with that extremely large mouth and his simple syllables. It reflected a northern English way of speaking. I think we got lost a little bit on *Chicken Run*. We had never made anything for the big screen before. There was confusion on our part. We used double frames. We tried mixture. We assumed we had to do everything more sophisticatedly, since it was for the big screen. But we soon learned that that just wasn't true. And making the chickens wasn't easy. You couldn't use feathers. They had to have that Plasticine clay look. But then we couldn't use that, or the figures would be too heavy. We ended up making them in molds. They were made of silicone and rubber. But the heads and hands were made of clay, the expressive parts.

Ron: **Did you enjoy the process? You had made four great films, three of which won Oscars. Now you're casting in the feature film world.**

Nick: It was an ambitious project. After three successful shorts, it seemed like the logical next step. And I liked the challenge it presented. Things might have been different if we didn't have a good idea. But we had a great idea. That was important. Looking back, I think I like it more now than I did then. The script was good. It was very funny. Although, people who loved Wallace and Gromit were a bit worried. They thought that a big studio might ruin or limit our quirky style. We tried very hard to retain our own voice. There were a lot of expectations involved, both from fans and the studio, who wanted to capitalize on that Oscar buzz.

Ron: **Did you insist on maintaining control and the freedom to carry your vision through?**

Nick: It was a good relationship from the start, but we definitely insisted. Don't misunderstand me. The studio also had their prerogatives, which they pushed. Music was a big one. DreamWorks was very excited about these two younger composers who had just worked on *Antz*, Harry Gregson and John Powell. They were great. I loved working with them.

Ron: **So, you finished the movie. And now you have more movies to make for DreamWorks. Did you immediately have an idea for a *Wallace and Gromit* movie?**

Nick: I had this idea of a vegetarian horror movie, in which a vegetable starts growing uncontrollably. It seemed perfect for Wallace and Gromit. It would be set in their small north England town, yet it would have all these references to Hollywood horror movies. It was a spoof of all these horror genres that I love.

Ron: **Did you learn anything on *Chicken Run* that helped you with *Curse of the Were-Rabbit*?**

Nick: Definitely. Learning how to get a movie off the ground in the Hollywood big studio environment was priceless. But now I had the chance to do something even better. I decided to codirect with Steve Box, and then we got Bob Baker back. The three of us together again was like going home. Actually, it was in the middle of *Chicken Run* that I started talking with Jeffrey Katzenberg about a *Wallace and Gromit* movie. When I first pitched the idea, he said, "Nick, I would love to do a *Wallace and Gromit* feature." And when we went into production, Jeffrey's comments and notes were helpful. It was amazing how we got this movie off the ground so easily. Steve and I also had full control over keeping that distinct *Wallace and Gromit* sense of humor and atmosphere. We went back to pure handmade animation, the clay. Even though the Were-Rabbit himself is made of fur, the style of the fur was a nod

Nick Park shooting *Chicken Run*, © Chicken Run TM @ © 2000 DreamWorks Animation LLC, Aardman Chicken Run Limited and Pathé Image. All Rights Reserved.

CR/SJ/2/0

to old movies, like *King Kong*. We were aiming for a certain vintage quality, and I think we nailed it. Being able to make *Were-Rabbit* with such ease and simplicity, I think, was the result of having to go through the *Chicken Run* process.

Ron: **What about the crew? Did you bring anyone in from the original shorts?**

Nick: Yeah, a lot of them came from the shorts, you know. We also had this huge team from *Chicken Run*, and they were involved as well.

Ron: **Were you able to make any changes or try anything new with the characters? Animation often has a very distinct pipeline, and studios don't want you veering too far off the path.**

Nick: I used the opportunity to rewrite and redefine Wallace and Gromit, because they had evolved as characters over the years. Even though I knew what they looked like, I decided to play with the way I molded them. And then there were all these background characters, the villagers. I wanted the quintessential townspeople from a classic horror film. Everything about the movie was an opportunity for me to create and invent.

Ron: **The character of Wallace takes a bit of a hiatus during part of the story, more so than in your previous films. How did that come about?**

Nick: Well, Wallace is the Were-Rabbit. He takes a back seat when the Were-Rabbit is present. In each film, I've tried to stretch their characters and their relationship. How much can Gromit put up with? How heroic can he be? They're like an elderly married couple. They know each other so well that they have that love–hate dynamic. It's great to play with that. What could be worse than your partner turning into a Were-Rabbit … and eating all your vegetables when your garden is your pride and joy?

Ron: **Are Wallace and Gromit based on real people?**

Nick: I have often thought that Wallace is just like my father; he reminds me of him. Sometimes I see him in Wallace's eyes. Well, my father didn't have eyes that close together! But my dad used to spend his time in the garden shed building things. He wasn't an inventor. He just loved to make things. He once built a caravan, a trailer that we used to go camping in Wales. After making *A Grand Day Out*, that's when I realized the similarity. Wallace is just like my dad, out in the shed building a trailer.

Ron: **Looking to the future, are you ready to make another movie? Are you going to develop new characters?**

Nick: Having made another short, *A Matter of Loaf and Death*, it was nice to make two feature films and then get back to shorts. After working in that big studio, it was great to do one for the BBC again. I think I got one note during the whole time I made that film. And that was in the storyboard, when they saw Gromit wearing a muzzle. They thought it might look too much like Hannibal Lecter. Of course, it wasn't meant to be a reference to that at all. It was just a dog wearing a muzzle. It was nice to make a film for myself again, because that's what I was allowed to do. I didn't have to worry about audience testing, or whether kids in the suburbs of Middle America could understand the accent.

Ron: **Did you animate on it?**

Nick: I didn't do any animation. It needed to be finished for the Christmas holiday. We only had eight months to make the entire half hour. I had about 20 animators working simultaneously.

Ron: **How many sets did you have going on at the same time?**

Nick: About 20–25. Every day. We were shooting the whole movie at the same time.

Ron: Had you prepared to guide your crew under those constraints?

Nick: Yeah, but they were well honed. They'd already worked on *Curse of the Were-Rabbit*. They were a good team. We also shot digitally for the first time as well.

Ron: How many cameras did you shoot with on each set?

Nick: One camera on each set, so no fewer than 20.

Ron: Did you ever shoot with multiple cameras before this?

Nick: No. A lot of the sets are built for a certain camera angle. And with model animation, you're filming on a tabletop set. There's lighting, rigs, and bounce boards crowding the scene. The animator can barely get in to cover two angles.

Ron: Did you ever have a situation where one of your animators has a different take on a scene and wants to animate something that you don't want?

Nick: No, I wouldn't allow them to do anything that I didn't want. Usually, it's so specific there just isn't room for anything like that. It's all there in the storyboard and story reel. I find people respond best to very specific directions. Things do change, of course. If I wanted something in one shot, but something goes wrong halfway through, I'll maybe cover it from another angle instead of reshooting. Reshooting gets very expensive. Normally you can't afford to do it. That's why the boards need to be well planned and your instructions clear and specific. I'm not someone who can easily farm it out to people. It's in my head. I know I'm surrounded by great artists. They have good ideas to contribute, and I let them do that all the time. But this is my vision. That's what we're bringing to completion here. I'm a bit of a megalomaniac, I guess. I like working with specific animators, model makers, and even set builders. After working together for so long, I don't have to say that much. They've all done it before. They're good at it. They know how much chunkiness or how much softness to give things. As a team, we also know where the problems are most likely going to arise.

Ron: You know the world.

Nick: Yeah, I know the world of Wallace and Gromit. But you wanted to know about future ideas, right?

Ron: Yeah.

Nick: I've got lots of *Wallace and Gromit* ideas. I could keep making shorts. I love making shorts. You don't have to wait four years to see your joke on the screen. And in that four years, you have too many chances to screw up a great idea. I like the freshness of short films. There's a great satisfaction about doing feature films as well. And I still have ambition for another *Wallace and Gromit* feature. Currently we're doing an episode where Wallace and Gromit present a show about eccentric inventors and the history of inventing.

My colleague and chief animator on the last few movies, Merlin Crossingham, is going to direct. I'm involved with some of the writing, but hopefully I'll be settling down soon to write my next feature. It's something I've had in mind for quite a while. It's all clay animation. I just want to take my time writing it. It's not Wallace and Gromit, I'm afraid.

Ron: **Do you sit down at a computer and type it up yourself?**

Nick: I like story. I've learned to love writing over the last few years. I want to go as far as I can, just get it all out of my head. Then I'll seek the help of other writers. I want to make sure I have my own ideas down first, before people come in and

pull it in different directions. In the beginning, I never exposed my ideas and my approach to story too much. I was very self-conscious. Even now, for example, I am afraid of just referring to other movies. Even though my films are known for that, it's not really what I do. I like the idea to have its own sense of itself. A lot of movies are just spoofs. That's the basis of their idea. But I think an idea should fly on its own wings, so to speak, and have some originality. *Were-Rabbit* and *Chicken Run* were in a sense both spoofs. At the same time, they were more than just that. I watch a lot of movies. I love movies. But I don't want to analytically go back and plot out how references get into my movies. During writing and development, that needs to happen organically. If there was too much planning in that respect, I don't think it would turn out very good.

Wallace & Gromit: The Curse of the Were-Rabbit TM & © Aardman Animations Ltd. 2005 © DreamWorks Animation LLC.

Ron: When you're talking about point of view, are you talking about directorial point of view or the character's point of view?

Nick: There are many choices as to where to put the camera and how to tell the story. I guess a key question for me is whose point of view is it. Obviously, in *Wallace and Gromit* the main protagonist is Gromit, and you tend to have his reaction to everything that happens, especially his now famous reaction to Wallace's jokes. Everything revolves around Gromit. He's the lynchpin. Whether I'm writing or filming a scene, I always ask one question. Who is it about? You need to know whose point of view you are following. I think that's a key part of storytelling.

Ron: Is that something that you learned on *Chicken Run*?

Nick: Yeah. But it happened instinctively. I didn't analyze it after the fact. And I suppose now I've learned a bit more about it. But sometimes you do need to stop and think. You need to realize when a scene is getting out of control. It's discipline, really. On the other hand, there does need to be freedom and spontaneity. The beauty of shooting in model animation is that it's not very strict. And I like a lot of freedom in the editing room. I truly believe that a film is made in the editing process. I don't want to take anything away from all

Story Sketches, Nick Park, *A Close Shave*, 1995 © Aardman.

the other aspects of filmmaking. But we edit the story reel thoroughly. We chop and change constantly as we're making the film. No matter what you write or conceptualize, it may not work during that actual shooting of a scene. You have to go back and figure out why it's not working and make changes. You can have a lot of great scenes, but you can't make a great movie out of all of them.

Ron: Do you do a lot of retakes?

Nick: Sure, that happens. Sometimes the scene just doesn't work. If it's essential to the movie, it needs to be fixed.

Ron: Is it about character performance, or is it just angle?

Nick: It's often about the idea. It's too complicated. It's not clear to the audience. In *Loaf and Death*, there were two silent characters, the love interests of Wallace and Gromit. Fluffles, the poodle, has a slight character arc, but it's also a very important one. Basically, I was trying to do things that were too complex for a silent character. She was going to be an accomplice of Piella, the villain, and then have this turnaround. But it was too much for a silent character to carry. She couldn't retain any innocence, since she's involved with a murderer. So we made her more of an unwilling accomplice. She was used by the murderer.

Ron: Did you try shooting her as an accomplice first, or just conceptually realize that in developing the story?

Nick: It was in the original storyboard and script. But to get her to that point of crisis and turn on the villain, there just wasn't time for that arc. So we decided to start later in her story, where she's already tired of doing this. She's already been pushed too far against her will. It's really Gromit that sets her free. And in the end, when she witnesses the demise of her mistress, Wallace says, "Fancy a cup of tea after all that?" Gromit then does this gesture, essentially inviting her to stay. We wanted to give her some dialogue, but it was too much acting. This is more akin to live action, where a small look will say everything. Her not reacting said everything. Sometimes less is more. Nearly always less is more, actually.

Ron: It's a good rule of thumb.

Nick: And it's great with animation.

Ron: Your characters are so far removed from reality, but their expressions and simplicity are far more valuable than trying to get something that is so heavily articulated to look human. That's what I love about your work.

Nick: I think that's why I take a page from the playbook of many live-action filmmakers. When you're filming and then editing conversational scenes, there's a reason why you cut to someone at a certain point in the sentence, especially when the other person isn't talking. You capture something in their face as they're absorbing the other person's words. And capturing that essential moment, I think, happens in the edit. That's where you learn about the process of refining it down and focusing on only what you need.

Ron: How often do you review your cuts?

Nick: Every day, all day. As the animation drops in, that informs the other shot, and that can sometimes surprise you. A scene just works wonderfully or is utterly overacted. You might realize that you went overboard when you acted out a scene for the animator. I think that's where I first learned how little I actually need to do, how less is more. At the beginning of *A Grand Day Out*, when Wallace decides to go to the moon, he says to Gromit, "I know we'll go somewhere where there's cheese!" Rather than have Gromit do some hilarious reaction, he just doesn't react and looks at the camera. That says it all, because he connects with us, the audience. I actually stole that from *Trading Places*.

Ron: **Before we end, I'd like you to take a moment and think about a short film. It could be something you saw either a long time ago or recently, but it's a great short film. If you could make the whole world watch one short, this would be it.**

Nick: Well, I already have a dilemma. I have two favorite shorts. One is funny. The other is beautiful. Can I talk about two?

Ron: **OK.**

Nick: It's just difficult. Um, well my, probably my top film of all time is *Tale of Tales* (1979) by Yuri Norstein. It's hard to explain, though. It's just a beautiful film. But that's what art really is. It's hard to put into words, because it's not words. In this case, it's a film. It's a provocative story about this little creature, and … Honestly, I'm not sure what it's about. For me, it's like a song that you love, but you have no idea what it means. You don't know why you like it, and that's part of the mystery and the beauty of it. A lot of explanations have focused on Yuri Norstein's history and his experience during the Second World War. There's a lot of talk about childhood, innocence, and dreams. I wouldn't get too specific. It's just the artistry, the different layers, and the humor and warmth surrounding this boy and this little creature. You can't help but feel and see the very notion of childhood. It's magical.

Ron: **And there's another one?**

Nick: Well, for pure comedy I would say *The Big Snit* (1985) by Richard Condie. Pure comedy. This film made me laugh so much that I wanted to be an animator and to do comedy. It's this very offbeat kind of humor, and his style gives his characters this goofy, yet cool, look. I still feel influenced by it to a degree.

Ron: **Thanks for talking with us, Nick.**

Nick: My pleasure.

7

Tomm Moore Interview

Tomm Moore. Photo: Dylan Vaughan.

It takes a certain kind of personality to navigate and thrive in (or should I say survive in?) the big studio environment, where multimillion dollar budgets create a bureaucratic quagmire. Tomm Moore is not that personality – thank God.

It wasn't purely by choice that Tomm's path to animation director pointed away from a big studio career.In his native country of Ireland, that opportunity didn't exist. And unlike some of his classmates who chose to seek their fortunes in Hollywood, Tomm believed there were stories to tell close to home.

As cofounder of Cartoon Saloon, the animation company in Kilkenny, Ireland, his two animated features, *The Secret of Kells* and *Song of the Sea*, have a magical, unique connection to Eire in style and content.In a country where myths and legends might be whispered from behind every stone, his films seem to have listened to those voices.

Tomm is an incredible draftsman and designer. Working in a smaller production setting allowed him to have much more of a hands-on involvement with the films, resulting in a personal touch that is not easily achieved in studio productions.

Making animated feature films outside the structure of big studios is a rare achievement, and it wasn't accomplished easily. Tomm describes the lean years as "living on tea and toast." This is not a metaphor.

But "staying local" had a huge upside. You don't mistake a Tomm Moore film for any other film.With a beautifully distinctive art direction style and authentically Irish stories, they are literally a world apart from a formulaic studio project.They remind us that animation is a global art form.

Bill Kroyer

Bill: Talk a bit about where you grew up and when you first started enjoying art … when you first started realizing you had some artistic inclination.

Tomm: I moved from Northern Ireland to Kilkenny just before I started primary school. In my family, early on I was being praised for drawing and my sister was being praised for singing. That was her "thing," and drawing was mine. There are photos of me when I was three years old beside a drawing of a cartoon dog that I had decided was Popeye's dog. So it was kind of early on that I started designing characters and so on. I was encouraged from the start by my parents. When I was around 11 or 12, my cousin came over from Canada with American comic books, and I really loved those. Up until then I'd, only seen comics like *Asterix* and *Tintin*: French and English and Belgian comics. By comparison, the American comic books seemed like they were really well drawn—anatomically at least.

And like most teenagers, for a while I wanted to be a superhero artist, and I spent a lot of time trying to draw Batman and stuff. I guess the next big step for me was joining Young Irish Film Makers in Kilkenny, which was kind of a mix of a youth group and a filmmaking group. That's actually where I met Ross Stewart. He was the art director on *Secret of Kells*;

he's working here in the studio with me on the next film too. A lot of people who really shaped my point of view I met in Young Irish Film Makers, as a teenager.

Bill: **You were just a teenager?**

Tomm: I was about 14, yeah. We had an opportunity there. It was already a special place. Mike Kelly, who was the artistic director, was from Kilkenny originally, and he set up Young Irish Film Makers in Kilkenny. We didn't know how lucky we were because that was such an unusual thing for a small town in Ireland to have. I mean, now every kid can make a movie on their phone, but in the 1990s it was still exciting just to have access to filmmaking equipment—which I suppose I mistakenly thought was the real value in the place. But Young Irish Film Makers is still very relevant because that teamwork was what was really important. It wasn't the fact that we could use the equipment. It was the fact that we were learning how to work together as a team. Because I was crazy into comics and animation, I convinced Mike to let us set up a little animation and comics department. I'd wanted to try and make cartoons because of seeing news footage on TV of Don Bluth. There was a TV show here in Ireland called *The Late Late Show*, and I remember my parents getting me out of bed and letting me stay up and watch Don Bluth on *The Late Late Show*, way past my bedtime. I remember trying to get cels to make my own animation. My dad is an engineer, and he had some overhead projection acetate. I remember trying to make cel animation with those, but I had no camera to shoot them on. So I made these animation cels with no way to shoot them! That was part of why I went to Young Irish Film Makers—just to get the stuff they had there to start playing around with animation.

Bill: **It sounds like you're saying you were the first one to bring animation to the Young Irish Film Makers. They were primarily a live-action filmmaking support group?**

Tomm: Yeah, me and Ross Stewart. That was pretty much it. And it wasn't really on Mike's radar cause he came from a kind of theatrical background. And because of that, he focused on the drama and he allowed us a kind of free reign on the art side of things. That was the real beginning of Cartoon Saloon, I suppose. We made our first comic there and got it printed, and made our first experiments in animation.

Bill: **Did you have any art in school? Did you have any formal training at all?**

Tomm: We had an art teacher in secondary school. He was very encouraging too. Because the Don Bluth studio was in Dublin, it had always been in my mind that I might like to go and be an animator there. That seemed like kind of a dream job. Just a generation before, I don't think growing up in Ireland you would have ever imagined that was a possible career. It just sort of turned out that by the time I'd finished college, they (Bluth Studios) were gone [*laughs*].

Bill: Did you ever visit the Bluth studio?

Tomm: Yeah, Ross and I visited. We were about 14, just after we joined Young Irish Film Makers. A friend had an aunt—nearly everybody in Ireland seemed to know somebody who worked in the Don Bluth studio! They were working on something—I think it was *Troll in Central Park*—and they were really unhappy and everybody said, "Don't do it, it's awful." They were saying it's just mundane work. I remember telling my mom when I went home that I didn't want to be an animator anymore because Don Bluth had the only good job and everyone else was miserable [*laughs*]. There was one guy who was into making little short films out of Legos. He was using the line tester to make his own short film out of Legos. He seemed kind of an independent, so I don't know what became of him. But everyone else we met in studio … they weren't in a happy place. And Ross and I kind of left going, "Let's make comics." That way we can just tell our own stories and do all the drawings ourselves. It just seemed like such a big machine. It really put us off.

Bill: Wow, anti-inspirational.

Tomm: It was the opposite, yeah. It was such a pity. I get the feeling we got an unfairly negative impression of the Bluth studio that day, just from the people we met and the time in the studio's history when we visited—I have since met many artists who worked there who thought it was a highlight of their career back when the studio began and the atmosphere was great and exciting.

But after we visited, I remember telling my mom, "It feels like somebody draws the back legs of the dinosaur and someone else draws the front legs. And it just felt so much like a production line." Whereas in Young Irish Film Makers, we just did everything ourselves, from soup to nuts. It was a funny thing because I still loved animation, and bit by bit I kind of got the bug again. I remember going to Ballyfermot College in Dublin—which had been set up by the Don Bluth studio—and for both myself and Ross our stated objective was to get strong enough drawing skills to be comic book artists. But I really got the animation bug again because I loved it and I was surrounded by other people who loved animation. I felt that I'd misunderstood the whole process until I got there and I realized that it was an art form. I got really really excited about it again. I remember seeing a poster for *The Lion King*—just a regal lion's silhouette and a sunset on a bus in Dublin—and really getting a strong feeling that I wanted to be part of the animation world after all.

Bill: Who was running the program at Ballyfermot? Was it a professional filmmaker?

Tomm: Larry Lauria had been there, but he had left the year I started. Again, we were in this kind of weird in-between place like while I was in Ballyfermot. The Don Bluth studio was packing up and going to Arizona, but the Disney studio in Paris kind of took over as the kind of uh … what's the word?

Bill: European destination.

Tomm: Yeah, as a sort of local sponsor. Glen Keane came and gave a talk a couple of times—that was really inspirational. A lot of the past pupils from Ballyfermot had gone out to LA and had work, like Richie Baneham and Colbert Fennelly. That was kind of the dream that everyone had … that they could make that leap into the 2D renaissance that was soon to be happening in the nineties in the states. I remember Glen Keane, when he was working on Tarzan, came and gave a big lecture, and his son Max was attending Ballyfermot College when I was in my final year. Max was in his first year, I think, so there was that kind of connection. I know Nora Twomey, who I met in Ballyfermot and who set up the Cartoon Saloon with us, did an internship during Tarzan with Disney Paris. So that was the kind of oversight that I felt we had. But otherwise, all the teachers were mostly Don Bluth artists who hadn't gone to Arizona. We also had great life drawing teachers and a visual language course by a teacher who was a fine art painter. Those were very valuable parts of the course, I feel, looking back on it all.

Bill: So you were studying animation at Ballyfermot? Did they give you a degree in animation?

Tomm: No, we got a diploma. Ballyfermot was the only option rather than going abroad at the time. And it was free education and actually attracted a lot of people from around Europe because it was a pretty good course. It was based on the Sheridan College course. And because people had been hired for Don Bluth and then for Disney Paris and even to LA, it attracted a lot of people. You know, it was a pretty cheap option. I mean, it's in a pretty grungy part of Dublin, pretty working class. You know, back then you'd go to college every day, and on the way you'd maybe see cars on fire and kids riding around on horses and stuff. But that kind of toughens you up as well, I suppose. I think it's much nicer now, though.

Bill: What kind of films were you making when you were a student? Were they individual hand-drawn films? Were you doing team projects? Or were you just doing exercises?

Tomm: Mainly experiments. Mostly experiments. Once I got to Ballyfermot, it was very much just the exercises in the curriculum. But, I mean, I met my wife in Young Irish Film Makers, and we were very young, having our first—our only—son, Ben. He was born in my first year in Ballyfermot, so I immediately had to work, to make some extra money. So right from the start I was doing work after hours. I was working on CD-ROMs and doing educational jobs. Paul and I started collaborating and that's how we set up the company. So maybe the more creative stuff I did at the time was some of that work I did for hire, until I got into my final year and I was able to make my own final-year film.

Bill: And what was that film?

Tomm: Well, for my final-year film I had originally developed what was going to end up being the *The Secret of Kells* with Aidan Harte and some of the other artists in my class. Aidan had been in Young Irish Film Makers with me and had also gone to Ballyfermot a few years after me. We'd done a lot of artwork and begun writing it and realized it was bigger and more epic than I was going to be able to do as my final-year film—even as a group project—so I decided just to do an exercise for my final-year film, kind of an elaborate show reel piece. It's called Bimble Bamble. It really just ended up as an elaborate line test of a witch preparing for Halloween night—based on illustrations for a poem that Nora and I had worked on in second year. It was a rostrum camera exercise first … just making illustrations and moving the camera over them. I developed it a bit further in third year but never really finished it. It only exists in boxes in my attic now, thankfully!

In the meantime, I was developing and working on the pitch material for *Rebel*, which is the original title we had on *Kells* to show to Channel 4. We had a connection there through Young Irish Film Makers to Channel 4 schools who had produced a film with YIFM the year before.

So a lot of my third year was kind of dividing my time between work for hire, for the Cartoon Saloon, which was me and Paul and the others working in our bedrooms, doing development work for what was going to become *Secret of Kells* to pitch to Channel 4, and trying to do my final-year film. It was a busy year.

Bill: You were already formulating your plan for that first movie. Was that the very first thing that Cartoon Saloon did? You went right to Channel 4 and pitched the idea?

Tomm: Yes. And they made an offer that we—thankfully Mike Kelly in Young Irish Film Makers kind of advised us—decided not to take because that could have been the end of the project. You know, they could have just bought the materials that we presented and chosen to do nothing more with it. What we decided to do instead was apply for a grant thru YIFM to continue developing it with the group we had assembled in Ballyfermot. It was the year 2000, so there was a Millennium Arts and Culture scheme, kind of a bridge between leaving college and work. We applied for some money and got it—a really tiny amount of money to live on—roughly the same as unemployment benefit. But it was also about the same amount of money we'd been used to living on in college, so it didn't seem that hard for us really. It was a way to kind of keep going as a group, and Mike Kelly gave us space in Young Irish Film Makers. So I kind of dragged everyone I met up in Ballyfermot back down to Kilkenny with me. We set up Cartoon Saloon that way and tried to get *Secret of Kells* off the ground, you know, very naively.

Bill: So you had some state funding to get started, and you all moved into the offices at Young Irish Film Makers. How did you move forward? Were you doing other freelance or were you completely focused on doing *Secret of Kells* at that time?

Tomm: Well, the thing is, when I was in college I discovered *The Thief and the Cobbler* by Richard Williams, and I was mad about that. I'd gotten the animation bug so bad that I thought this was the ultimate art form. Maybe even more than the film itself … the documentary that I had on a VHS tape where he was really passionately speaking about making *The Thief* and was so inspiring about the potential of animation as an art form—even though I was discovering this long after he lost the project and everything had gone bad for him—I was just stuck on this documentary that showed a moment in time where he was talking about doing commercials in order to make his own film and about how animation could match Rembrandt one day, all that inspirational stuff. And I really sort of spiritually signed up to do something like that. It felt like a great way to balance making your own art and making a living. I remember telling Alex Williams, his son, about this years later and he nearly fell under the table laughing. He said, "You got your business plan from my dad?" [*laughs*]. He thought that was ridiculous. But that was our business plan. We would do commercials, or whatever paid the bills, in order to be able to make our own feature. And that was the dream that everyone signed up for when we first came down to Kilkenny.

Bill: That's what you did? You started doing commercials? How did you get work?

Tomm: We were lucky because it was the year 2000, and it was just the start of that whole Internet dot-com bubble. Paul and I, while we were in college, had been doing work for CD-ROM companies and early Internet companies. We were doing website content work and e-cards. But it was a meager living. You know, we lived on beans and toast mostly.

Bill: That's how you were keeping the flame burning? So you literally had no competition in Ireland right?

Tomm: Except for Brown Bag Films. They're a massive company now, but they were only a couple of years ahead of us at Ballyfermot. They were really just getting started then too. They were more focused at that time on shorts and other types of projects, not features. And of course Gerry Shirren, who's now our managing director, had set up a company called Terraglyph Productions in Dublin out of the ashes of the Don Bluth studio. He gave us bits and pieces of a feature that they were doing. He gave us trailers to animate for them, and if they didn't have time to animate their next pitch, we would animate that too. So we made a little allegiance there with Gerry, and he gave us a lot of advice as we were starting off. It's kind of ironic that 15 years later we hired him as our managing director. He is one of the only people in Ireland who'd been part of the business side of animation since the early days. He had been a production manager and then managing director of Don Bluth's studio and then his own place. So he's one of the only people who knew the business inside out.

There were one or two other small companies, like Monster Animation, but it was pretty much a wasteland compared to these days.

Bill: **You had no rep, nothing like what we would call an agent or anything here in the United States? Nobody out there beating the bushes for work for you, right? It was all kind of word of mouth?**

Tomm: Yeah. I remember Paul and I went to Gerry's office and he showed us his calendar for the year. Prior to this, the only experience we really had was the work for hire that we had done in college, and suddenly Gerry was showing us all the industry events. He said, "You're going to have to show up at all of those and meet people if you're serious about getting your feature produced." And we just took it that that's what we would do. So, even if we were going over on a wing and a prayer with very little money—you know, sharing hotel rooms, flying Ryanair, and having to drive long distance to get to the conventions because we didn't have the money to fly a normal airline—we kept showing up. And Paul very quickly became the producer. We started calling him Paul Hollywood Young cause he was the one who was willing to go out and be the kind of baby kisser and hand shaker and meet people.

Bill: **You're trying to raise a kid. You're trying to support a family. It's pretty hard to make a living. Was there ever a point you thought, "Maybe I should think of something else?"**

Tomm: Yeah, very often over the first ten years. My wife was in art school but ended up retraining as a teacher. She became the breadwinner, the sustainable income for the family. And I was really lucky that she was willing to do that … sort of lucky that there was a certain stability that allowed me to take the risks. There were plenty of times where we had to lay people off and it looked really bleak. We didn't know if we would be able to keep the lights on. We made this big announcement that we were going to make this feature film, and then it just felt like it would be too humiliating not to do that. I always think about this guy that I knew that gave up cigarettes. He had told everyone that he had given up cigarettes because he knew that then he'd be embarrassed if he started smoking again. So, much like that, we told everyone we were going to make this feature film. I remember at one point kind of worrying that I had wasted my twenties. I was around 27, the studio was about six years old, and the project still wasn't in production. It was scary. I felt that if I'd given up then, I'd lost the jump on all of my friends who'd gone to work in studios right after college.

Bill: There's that saying, "Jump off the cliff and build your wings on the way down."

Tomm: Yeah!

Bill: You were six years in and doing development work, and you actually nailed a story reel. How did you approach making *Kells* into a real project?

Tomm: We were learning everything: how to run a company, how to run a studio, how to work with other artists. We were all a group of peers at the beginning, and we had to learn about the hierarchy that was necessary and the sacrifices that were going to be necessary. It had ups and downs, of course. It was about 2001 that we'd done enough footage that we thought was going to be actual production footage when we realized we were just going to have to recut into a promotional trailer. We brought that to

Color Storyboards, Tod Polson based on rough storyboards by Nora Twomey *Secret of Kells,* 2009. (Courtesy of Cartoon Saloon.)

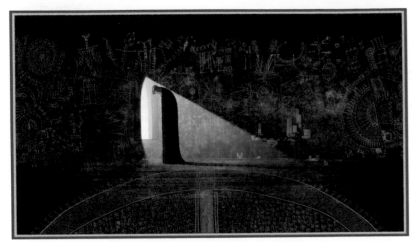

Scene Illustration, Ross Stewart, 2006, *The Secret of Kells*.

Scene Illustration, Lily Bernard and Adrien Merigeau / characters Barry Reynolds, 2005, *The Secret of Kells*.

Cartoon Movie, which is an event very much geared toward allowing different-sized companies and different coproducers to meet each other. We made our own trailer for what was to become *Secret of Kells*. It was originally called *Rebel*, and it was quite a different story. But it was always based on the *Book of Kells* and that period in Irish history and the mythology surrounding it. We presented that at Cartoon Movie, and Paul had met Didier Brunner on the bus going in. Didier was talking to someone beside him, about how he needed extra animators on the *Triplets of Belleville*. Paul, being cheeky, would never miss an opportunity. He overheard this conversation and butted in and went, "Oh we've got a studio!" He invited Didier to come to our pitch just to see what our studio was like, because he was looking for someone to do ten minutes of *Triplets of Belleville*, which he didn't know how he was going to get finished in time. That's how we met Didier and Vivian Vanfleteren, the Belgian and French coproducers of *Triplets*. As it happened, it was perfect timing. Didier was looking for the follow-up project to the *Triplets*, and so he kind of came on board then and he started to really show us the ropes of how European coproductions worked. He became the lead producer at that point, and because he believed in us and took us seriously, the Irish Film Board and Irish broadcasters took us more seriously then too. Prior to that, we seemed to be just a little outgrowth of Irish Film Makers, which was seen as kind of a kid's organization or whatever. The fact that we were coproducing with an established producer like Didier (meant) we got taken much more seriously. He really showed us the ropes and helped sculpt the film artistically as well. He brought on Fabrice Ziolkowski, as a screenwriter, to work with us on the script and to help rework the story. We were very much animators trying to come up with stuff we wanted to animate.

Fabrice really taught us about sculpting it into a proper script. I remember painful meetings with Didier and the head of the Irish Film Board where they were just chucking away concept artworks—we had all this artwork but too many ideas really for one film. They said, "There's no place for this." But we were like, "Ahh, but we want to do that part." I really learned the wrong way, the hard way. You know at Pixar, they talk about story, story, story. We were really about art direction, animation, art direction, animation. And I had to learn that story was most important the hard way.

Bill: **It's always fascinating, isn't it? How hard work and determination add something, but so many people have a moment of luck, just a moment of chance that causes a great thing to happen. It seems that happened there, the fact that Paul interrupted Didier. A very lucky bus ride.**

Tomm: Well, he's such a show bizzy person! I don't think I would have had the guts. So I was lucky that Paul was that way. You know what they say with luck, "You make your own luck." The fact that Paul was willing to show up and be kind of cheeky like that is what made it happen. I guess just the "showing up thing" is the thing I always tell young people … that if you stay in your room drawing, nobody will ever know what you're doing. But if you can be cheeky enough to show it to people, you might have a chance.

Bill: **It got you going.**

Tomm: And then suddenly it was a totally different problem. Too much work! At the same time that *Kells* was getting started, a show Aidan Harte had created and developed, *Skunk Fu!*, was gearing up as a Flash production, with a totally different talent pool coming in. It was really exciting, kind of an amazing time around 2005. We were suddenly responsible for two projects that together were worth around ten million euros, which was a big change from sort of living on beans on toast. So, it was a big change. We had to move out of Young Irish Film Makers. They're based in an old orphanage. They're still there now. But we quickly outgrew that space. It was a real emotional thing for me. It was almost like leaving home. We had to rent the premises that we're in now and expand into this space.

Bill: **So you've really just had those two homes right?**

Tomm: Yeah. They're kind of the places I grew up in.

Bill: **You guys are not traveling gypsies at all. You're homebodies.**

Tomm: Yeah, that's how it turns out. We have to travel around the world to promote our stuff. But other than that, yeah.

Bill: It must have been tough to staff up. Other than Brown Bag, you're the only thing going in Ireland. Did you seek international filmmakers? How did that work?

Tomm: Well, due to the nature of the coproduction we knew that some of the work would have to be done in France and in Belgium. The budget was pretty low for the ambition of the project. Our first estimate was about eight million, and we knew we couldn't raise that. So Didier and the line producers said that the maximum was going to be 5.5 million. And we had to figure out a way to make it for that. That was a learning curve too. Because of that, we decided to focus on preproduction here. I fought pretty hard to do about 20 minutes of animation here too. We did all the preproduction. So the team here was about 40 people that we hired from around Europe—a mix of some old hands and plenty of new recruits from the colleges around Europe.

Bill: You were making the transition from operating as an independent animator to a director of a big project. Were you and Nora splitting the roles on that project?

Tomm: That's when Nora Twomey came on as codirector. Nora had done two narrative short films already while I was developing the feature. The most I had directed at that point was a commercial and some little experiments. I hadn't really ever directed anything of any scale, and suddenly I was faced with a feature. That's why I asked Nora to come on as codirector and we started working on the storyboards together after she finished her second short film. Ross Stewart was starting work on the final designs with me, and the team started to grow out from there. We put out an APB, "Okay we've finally got the money and we're going to make this." So some people that had originally been part of the team came back. Our cleanup supervisor, Martin Fagan, had been a cleanup supervisor for Don Bluth, for example, but had gone into illustration after that. Some artists who had been with us at the beginning, like Fabian Erlinghauser, Barry Reynolds, and Tom Caulfield, came back to work on the film now that it was finally in production—in the meantime they had been in other studios around the world.

Bill: Did you have a conversation with Nora about how you might codirect? Did you ever sit down with her and say, "You handle this. I'll handle that"? Or did you just kind of get started and work side by side most of the time?

Tomm: We both knew our strengths. And I knew I really wanted Nora to help, especially on the story side of things and on the voice recording. As it happened, that was the main area that she influenced on the movie. But she was also deeply involved in all the aspects of the film. She had a point of view on everything and was head of animation. But because I'd been carrying the movie for so long and was seen as captain of the ship, we decided on that slightly unusual Pixar thing of director and codirector. It was clear I would have final say, but we didn't have to debate about things too often, thankfully. Nora was generous enough to be OK with that. I was only 28 at the time and felt a bit insecure and overwhelmed. I was very lucky to have had her support and talent and experience.

Bill: What was it like starting to direct a big group of people? You're well known now for being very hands on your films. You do a lot of the drawing, a lot of the layout yourself. Were you able to do that on the first film? Or did you find yourself having to suddenly become more of a director of others as opposed to an artist making the actual art?

Tomm: I think that might have been one of the most challenging things for me at first, that I had to let go and delegate. But I felt that it wasn't so bad in the end, because most of the people that were working with me were improving whatever ideas I might have had. I learned pretty quickly that I was better off directing good artists than trying to shackle them. I think that was one of the first lessons I really learned as a director, that giving the crew some kind of space to have ownership generated better results. But in the beginning, I think I was a little insecure—for example, I grew a beard to try and look older—and maybe a bit too controlling on *Kells*. We had a very small team that controlled the look of the film, and I had Barry Reynolds and Fabian Erlinghauser, who did most of the posing for the whole film. I did some sequences, but they did the lion's share of it. That was basically the solution that Nora and I came up with, because of the nature of the coproduction, that we would try and control things with a very small team of people that we trusted here in Kilkenny. Preproduction would basically encompass all our direction. It was our chance to direct all the design, the key backgrounds, the animation, and then we would following that by going to the other studios during production.

I'd had dinner with Michel Ocelot, who had done *Kirikou* with Didier prior to that, and he gave me a lot of good advice. He likes to draw and design a lot himself, but he gave me a lot of advice about how to work with a bigger team and deal with the compromises of a coproduction. Paul Bolger, who is an animation director here in Ireland, also advised me about how to control the whole production through preproduction. So that was what we tried to do. One thing that we did that was a bit controversial, but it worked out really well, was where we'd make a scene illustration which was basically a final style frame. It wasn't just a concept, it wasn't like, "Ah it's going to look something like this." It was *exactly* what we wanted the final film to look like. And very often we'd use the background as a production background. You know, we put the characters on and treated them in Photoshop as if they'd been composited and added effects—exactly how we wanted the final film to look. Ross Stewart and the background supervisors, Adrien Merigeau and Lily Bernard, did about 200 of those in collaboration with the character artists. We had a blueprint of the whole film even before production left Kilkenny. We did a lot of notes and a lot of model sheets and a stupid amount in preparation. We were paranoid about that side of things.

Bill: In 2D you have the ability to work that way because the image is what it is. You don't have to make the subsequent transition into 3D with all the problems of lighting, texturing, etc.

Tomm: We did have a problem with this style in that a lot of traditional animators immediately reacted to it as being wrong. You know, they went, "Uh, it's full of tangents. We'll fix it." We're like, "No, no. We want it to look like medieval art." We had to do a lot of explaining to animators and background artists that that was a look we really wanted. So that took a lot of preparation. That was something we kept a close eye on, all through it. The whole production was very design focused.

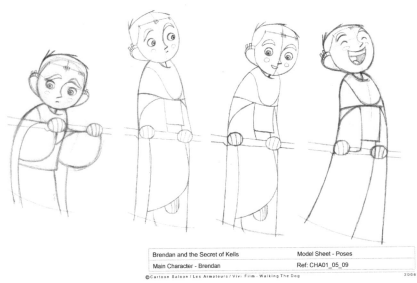

Brendan Model Sheets and final designs, Barry Reynolds, 2005-2007 - *The Secret of Kells*.

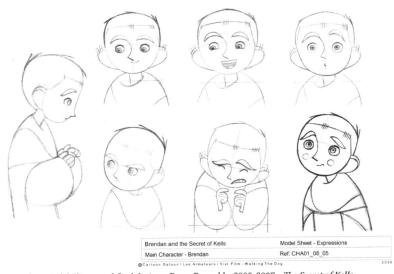

Brendan Model Sheets and final designs, Barry Reynolds, 2005-2007 - *The Secret of Kells*.

Brother Aidan Character poses, Barry Reynolds - *The Secret of Kells*.

Bill: Do you remember what was the most meaningful advice that made you modify or change what you had previously been doing as an individual director? What was the advice that was most helpful to you?

Tomm: I'd say it's from Didier and Michel Ocelot. It was funny when I told Michel Ocelot that he was telling me the same thing Didier had said. He said, "That's amazing. We never agree on anything" [*laughs*]. But the one thing that they both said was to keep pushing away from any kind of copycat stuff, where they could see that some of the work was really inspired but some of it looked overinfluenced by Bluth or Disney or whatever. They said that the only way your work is going to stand out is if you very much try and get your own look, you know, your own style. And that was confusing for me because I had all these influences impacting my work and was very reverent toward them. For me, back then, it would have been a compliment to be compared to those artists. But I kind of understood fairly quickly that they meant that, "You're only going to look like a cheap copy of those bigger productions, if you look too much like them. So, finding your own look and your own style and your own voice was going to allow you to stand out from those other productions—as much as you might admire them."

That was an interesting thing for me. I think it's something that comes much more naturally to animators and artists on the mainland of Europe. But I think that because Ireland is Anglophone, and we're so influenced by the U.S., we have a tendency to think that if it looks a bit like an American production, then its good. You know what I mean? It's bad if it looks too weird or unusual. So even though I've been a major fan of all that Hungarian and eastern European stuff and Richard Williams and all that, I think I felt that Didier really gave us a mandate to push it further, to go more in a different direction and have our own voice, and not to try to copy anyone else.

Bill: I think that was one of the most distinctive things about the *Secret of Kells*, the fact that it did have that distinctive look. It felt different. You could look at one frame and say, "This is not another production from anywhere else. This is something from Ireland." Almost all directors identify themselves as primarily storytellers, but you've been saying that story was really your biggest challenge. How did you find yourself growing as a storyteller?

Tomm: I never imagined myself as a director when I was younger. I never separated the idea of being an artist, an animator, a designer, and a director. I never thought of them as different things. And it was only through making *Secret of Kells* that I really learned that you could even have somebody that can't draw be a great animation director. I started to really value that when I started working with Fabrice on the script and working with Nora, understanding that Nora's skill set was much more rounded than mine. Whereas I was superfocused on the art, she had more of a sensibility about filmmaking in general. Of course, my background in Young Irish Film Makers came into play then, because I learned a lot there about film appreciation. All that started to come into focus and I started to understand the difference between being a director and being an artist. They don't necessarily have to be the same thing.

Bill: And what is the difference? What would you say are the qualities a director must have?

Tomm: I think the challenge is for a director to have an overview, to put the project first all the time, and not to fall in love with the details, especially in animation. I learned about editing by editing *Secret of Kells* with Fabiene Giro. I remember wanting to keep scenes in just because I liked them and to cut scenes because I felt they were "off model." And the editor was like, "No, it won't work if you take it out." And I was like, "Aw damn" [*laughs*]. I was really learning the hard way. And I still feel like I really am learning a lot. I am just lucky to be surrounded by people much more talented than me, so I can work on having more of an overview.

I remember … I think it was some Chuck Jones's quote that really resonated with me, that there's two kinds of talent. There's the little scrabbly insecure talent you might have about your own work. Then there's another talent that you need as a director, which is being able to identify other people who are more talented than you and have them work in the direction of your vision. That's actually much more important than the first talent. And I think I had that, because I managed to get a lot of very talented people working with me [*laughs*].

Bill: So as you were approaching the completion of your first film, *Secret of Kells*, how did you feel about it? Did you feel like you were successfully achieving what you wanted to achieve? Did you have any crisis moments, either like artistically or production-wise, that you thought jeopardized what you were trying to do?

Tomm: Well, it was such a difficult production and such a challenge for the studio that there were a number of moments where we were afraid that the film wouldn't get finished. In the end, we even went over budget and had to borrow from friends and family just to get it done. So, there was an enormous sense of completion that I hadn't wasted my twenties. I was turning 30. I had finished this huge project. But on the other hand, I'd learned so much at every stage that it was quite painful. Particularly in story, you know. Fabrice had delivered a very classically structured script, which was a great foundation. But I still learned a lot thru the storyboarding process with Nora and Remi Chayé. I feel like the third act was possibly compromised by decisions I had made to cut scenes at board stage. Even though I'm still proud of the film, I think I learned a lot, and all the good things about it are mostly because of a talented and dedicated crew. Any failings are my fault. I just felt that I'd learned so much about tone and every aspect of actually directing and making a film that I immediately wanted another bite of the apple because I felt I could do better. I was very proud of what we'd done. I felt particularly happy that those visuals that we'd done in 2005 were exactly on-screen in 2009. The visuals in 2005 were like a distillation of all our ideas since we were in college in '99. So I was proud of the fact that that had carried all the way through. But I learned so much as a filmmaker and could see where I could improve in the other areas that I couldn't take too much pride in.

Bill: How did you feel about the reception of the film?

Tomm: First, I was really depressed, because we put so much work in and it kind of disappeared. It was a really amazing story. I'd won the Director Finder Series Award with the DGA (Directors Guild of America). They bring a European upcoming director, live action or animation, to the U.S. and introduce them to agents and stuff. I remember I was there the week that Lehman Brothers was collapsing. I had this really strange week of planned meetings where agents were like, "Yeah, yeah, sure kid whatever." And they were packing up their offices! Tom Sito came to a screening, which was nice of him. But it wasn't a great week to present the film in LA because of the economic turmoil. But I did get to visit all the studios and made great contacts and started to sow some seeds out there. I'd come home and I sort of felt, "Wow those studios over there, like Pixar and Disney, are amazing playgrounds. Maybe I actually really want to go and work there after all and get a real job." *Secret of Kells* was released and didn't make much of a dent in the box office at all. It was well reviewed, which was a saving grace, because that gave us a bit of hope. But the Irish public just kind of ignored us. It was kind of depressing, you know. I think we had the classic struggle with the Irish audience—we were coming too much out of nowhere for them. They had never heard of us and maybe didn't trust that the film was worth a gamble compared to a better known brand. So I was a little depressed about that. We did a little bit better in France, and we won an award in Annecy, which was a really massive moment for me because Annecy had been such an amazing part of the journey. Going to Annecy was something that we'd done every year as part of our schedule.

And then slowly but surely it started winning awards. And all through 2009, just as I thought the journey was over, we kept on winning awards, kept on getting noticed. The sales agent kept on making more sales. It ended up being shown all around the world. And then in the end of 2009, we were nominated for the Annies, which we were like, "Ah this is amazing. We've been kind of noticed by the big boys or whatever." I remember booking the tickets for the Annies and we really felt that the Annies was the end of the journey. So, when we got nominated for the Oscar, it really came out of the blue. It was such an amazing feeling because we'd gone on this trajectory of being really high when we finished the movie, really depressed because it kind of disappeared, and then it slowly built up to something beyond belief ... that we were going to the Oscars! It was like we were rabbits in the headlights at the time. We just couldn't believe that it had gone that far. The goodwill of the animation community in the U.S. had really reassured me. So many of the people I met over there were saying, "You're crazy, don't come out here looking for a job. Keep going, make your own movies. This is amazing what you're doing." They would always say, "You're living the dream." And I was always going, "No, *you're* living the dream. *You're* working in a dream studio where you get served free pizza in the swimming pool and all that kind of stuff." But a lot of people really helped, and that was the major boost to me as a filmmaker and a very uplifting for us as a company. It really put us on the stage worldwide. The Academy taking us seriously that way really helped a huge amount. I always say there's three stories when you make a movie. There's the story of trying to get it made, of how you got it made—the story of making it, like how you spent your day for three or four years—and then there's the story of what happens afterwards. And they're all different stories with their own arcs and structure.

Bill: Would you say that Oscar nomination was a huge boost to the next movie? As far as getting financing and getting support ...

Tomm: There was a little part of me that was kind of thinking, you know, maybe it's time now to cash in my chips while I was ahead. And that really made me fully commit to making the next movie. I think after the Oscar nomination we got a little bit of tinsel in our eyes and we thought, "Maybe we could, you know, go big." We wasted a year because we got the notion that maybe the next one could be a bigger movie and we could get financing in the States. We took a lot of meetings with big studios. I feel like we wasted a lot of time because ultimately I think we knew in our hearts that the independent route was going to be better. We went back to plan A. Plan A was the European coproduction model that we learned on the *Secret of Kells*. One thing I learned was that there are movies that you can develop that you're willing to work on with a big studio and plan for it to be a commercial enterprise, and there's movies that are too personal and have to be made independently. There's no point trying to make a personal independent project into a big studio project, because you'll only have your heart broken. I remember talking to Brenda Chapman around that time, and she encouraged me to keep going with my own independent way of making the movie.

Bill: In a small studio like yours, I assume you were so immersed in finishing *Kells* that you really didn't get started on *Song of the Sea* until it was pretty much wrapped, right?

Tomm: As soon as it was wrapped, we made a trailer, a little conceptual trailer, with some of the crew that were still around. And then it had to go on the shelf.

Bill: Tell me again that story of where you got the idea for *Song of the Sea*. You were at a holiday with your family and …

Tomm: I was in the west coast of Ireland, and my son was only ten at the time, so it was a long time ago. We were in Kerry actually. We were sketching on the beach and there were seals that had been killed all along the shore. It was kind of gruesome, you know. It was kind of shocking. And it just tied into so many things I had been thinking about as we were developing *Secret of Kells*, about heritage and culture and those old stories and how they were being forgotten. It felt like there was a race to be as far from our heritage as possible and to kind of redefine ourselves as Europeans or whatever. It felt like that stuff was going to get forgotten. That was in my mind when I discovered those seals on the beach. I was talking to the woman that we rented the cottage from down in Dingle, and she was saying that it was a tragedy that the fisherman were frustrated with the fall in fish stocks and were taking out their frustration by killing the seals. I'm also interested in animal rights, and I found it disturbing. She said that this wouldn't have happened years ago, that there would have been a respect for the wildlife and a belief in things like selkies, that seals could be souls of the dead, people who could have been lost at sea. I thought about it from the point of view of my son's generation, that a lot of those beliefs and stories and that kind of way of interacting and seeing the environment in that kind of immersive way was being lost. Ross Stewart gave me a book called the *People of the Sea*, which was a collection of stories from the early part of the twentieth century about the beliefs of people all around the west coast of Ireland and Scotland, about selkies and those kind of stories. I read that, and so it was kind of ticking away in the back of my mind. While we were developing *Secret of Kells*, I wanted to do something that dealt with the loss of those stories, a way to try to reinvent them for another generation in a different way.

Bill: I think that's the most emotional genesis of an idea I've ever heard of for a feature film. You had this terrific idea for *Song of the Sea*. You wrap up. You get the Oscar nomination. Now you've got all this experience as a director on your first movie. How do you go about making the second movie? What's different? How do you begin?

Tomm: The first thing I did was I thought I could be Hayao Miyazaki and storyboard it instead of writing it. I crashed pretty quickly. I found myself with too many ideas. The Irish Film Board was funding the development. They were really happy with the Oscar nomination. It was a bit of good news that year and a pretty bleak year for the country, so they were really happy to fund and to

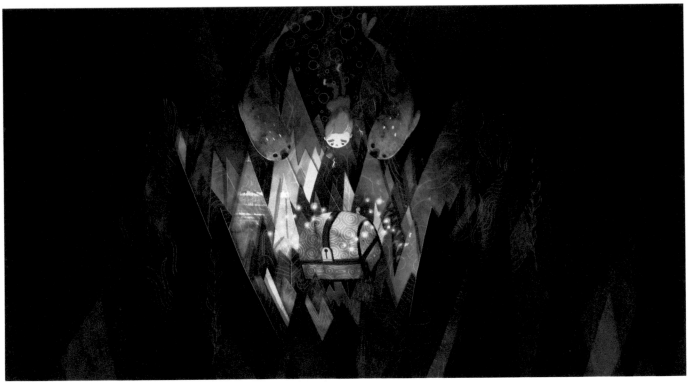

Concept art, Adrien Merigeau, *Song of the Sea*, 2014. (Courtesy of Cartoon Saloon.)

Concept art, Tomm Moore, *Song of the Sea*.

develop the idea for the next film. That was to keep us going, and they introduced me to lots of different writers. They felt that I should work with an Irish writer, and they would fund that. There were so many different writers that had a lot of experience. I felt pretty sheepish saying no to them because they were pretty established, especially the live-action writers. But one guy stood out, Will Collins. He was about my age and he had just gone back to college. His first live-action feature was in production, and he'd sent me an e-mail that made him seem uncannily perfect for the job. The joke I always make is that my wife thought he had been going through our trash or something because the e-mail was so on the ball for what I was looking for in a writing collaborator. He said his favorite movie was *My Neighbor Totoro* and that he had just finished his first feature, which was set in 1987 on Halloween night—which was when I wanted to set *Song of the Sea*. Even some of the sample scripts he sent—one was a short film based on a sleeping giant off the coast of Ireland! This was all a bit unbelievable to me. And so I called the film board and asked them about him. The creative director said, "Oh I was so glad you like his stuff. He's a really great new talent and I'm really happy that you'd work with him. We are always happy to work with him." So, it all was very positive and reassuring. We met

Illustration/background by Adrien Merigeau, Characters Tomm Moore, *Song of the Sea*, 2014. (Courtesy of Cartoon Saloon.)

up, and sure enough it worked out great. Ross had gone to work for Laika for a while, and so I had asked Adrian Merigeau, who had been one of the background supervisors on *Secret of Kells*, to be the art director. It was me and Adrian and Will for a long time, just developing and trying to get the story into shape.

Bill: You were talking earlier about becoming more of a director of other people, but this movie starts to be formed and you are doing foundational drawing, right? You started drawing a lot of designs, a lot of concepts for scenes, locations, everything.

Tomm: Yeah, maybe even more so than on *Secret of Kells*. Although I'd done a huge amount of drawing on *Secret of Kells* over the years before it went into production, when it was in the final stages of editing, music, and compositing I didn't have to draw as much for that project, so I could start putting my sketchbook energy into a new idea. So at that point, when it was in postproduction, I think I started putting a lot of my drawing energy into the new ideas for *Song of the Sea*. I think it was an outlet, you know? Sometimes I think focusing on the next one, when you're stressed on the one you're working on, can be easier. I think I heard Andrew Stanton talk about positive procrastination, where you allow yourself to doodle and daydream about the next project when you're stressed about the project you're working on. That certainly happened for me with *Song of the Sea*. I was already thinking about it and doing drawings while *Secret of Kells* was still in production. Adrian and I went on quite a lot of research trips to the west coast and did a lot of research drawings. We both agreed that we wanted this film to be more atmospheric, more based on watercolors, and to have that kind of dampness, natural, traditional media feeling all the way through. We wanted it to have a real sense of being hand-drawn, which was ironic because we actually moved from paper to TVPaint for the animation. But for the backgrounds and for the overall look, we wanted to keep a really, really hand-drawn kind of organic look to it.

Bill: **So you're wearing two hats now. You're a director, but you're also an owner of a studio. I assume you had to let most of your crew go from *Kells* and then bring them back when you started *Song of Sea*. That must have been a tough thing to do.**

Tomm: Yeah, it was a painful moment. We were about 80 people in the studio during production of *Secret of Kells* and *Skunk Fu!* Then we shrank back to about 15 people. It felt strange because we'd sort of grown up to this point, and then suddenly we hit this kind of rock and we had to shrink back down. I think we'd learned enough from the previous productions that we knew if we could get another bite of the apple, we could do it better. Thankfully, since we went into production on *Song of the Sea*, you know, we've maintained a crew of around that size and the studio has started to stabilize a bit. So we learned the hard way.

Bill: *Song of the Sea* **was a different production using digital production methods. Did it make you go faster?**

Tomm: It was about seven years from the rough idea to the time it was finished. But actual production was about 24 months from the time we had the finance locked in. It was a lower budget than *Secret of Kells*, and it was with more partners. We were working with five coproduction partners, but they were all people that we'd either worked with in the interim or I'd worked with on *Secret of Kells*, so they were all people that we fairly well trusted. The one thing I'd learned in the meantime from Adrian, seeing how he directed his short film *Old Fangs* and from working on *Secret of Kells*, is that I knew I'd enjoy it more if I loosened up a bit. Then I'd get to do more artwork myself. So I kind of came up with a way to have the supervisors from the other studios come to Kilkenny and work with us in the room while we were developing the final look.

Storyboards, Tomm Moore, Remi Chayé, Nora Twomey & Ross Stewart, *Secret Of Kells*, 2014. (Courtesy of Cartoon Saloon.)

Then they could take that torch, that flame, back to their studios and light the fire from there. By delegating that way, and by having Nora as head of story, with her and Darragh Byrne able to focus totally on the editing of the animatic, I got to do a lot more storyboarding and a lot more character design. I did a lot more of that stuff I had always wanted to, but still had that support structure around me. I kind of organized it in a slightly more, hopefully more, collaborative way than *Secret of Kells* on purpose.

Storyboards, Tomm Moore, Remi Chayé, Nora Twomey & Ross Stewart, *Secret Of Kells*, 2014. (Courtesy of Cartoon Saloon.)

Bill: So the other studios were like your sequence supervisors?

Tomm: Yeah. The supervisors from Denmark and Luxembourg came over and even contributed to the model sheets. They did animation tests with us and had ideas for how we might tweak the character designs. It felt the opposite to *Secret of Kells*, where we made these telephone book–sized documents of rules for the character and location designs and said,

"This is how it's done." We allowed them in a bit more, and even let them pose their own sequences. So they would pose a sequence here in Kilkenny, I'd approve the posing, and then they would go back and do the full animation with their team in Denmark or Luxembourg. That way they had ownership of those sequences and it felt like they gave it more because of that, rather than feeling like, "Oh we're just following orders."

Bill: But hadn't you done more foundational work so that it kept more unified? Both in story and design? It doesn't look like a production that was done all over the place. It looks like it was a unified film.

Tomm: I think that's because a lot of them had worked on *Secret of Kells* and were used to the style and the way we worked. TVPaint helped, because on *Secret of Kells* I felt the style kind of saved us. Even if people would draw off model, the style was so unusual that people couldn't tell. Stuff that was making me and Barry Reynolds, the character designer, really annoyed, audience members didn't notice. They just thought, "Oh it's meant to be like that." Whereas on *Song of the Sea*, we just had more communication. I felt that drawing over TVPaint was actually the biggest advantage over paper. On *Secret of Kells* I might draw over and e-mail the correction, but then it would be printed out and interpreted again by the animator. With TVPaint, I could draw directly on the file and give notes directly that way. So that helped to keep it consistent.

Bill: You did a lot of that personally on the film?

Tomm: Yeah, but after posing and storyboarding, a huge amount of it was trusting the crew. We had it well cast, you know, so I don't want to say that I controlled it that way. I touched the animation more than the backgrounds. Adrian touched nearly every background. But once the composition was locked and the character posing was signed off, I tried to let the animators have a free hand and to trust the supervisors too.

Bill: Did you feel you were happy with the final product on *Song of the Sea*? Did you get pretty much the vision you wanted?

Tomm: Yeah, much more so than *Secret of Kells*. *Secret of Kells* was a learning project, whereas on *Song of the Sea* I felt much more comfortable. There were hairy moments where I wasn't sure how it was all going to come off, and there's still story issues and stuff I'd like to improve on. But overall, I felt that the emotion and the tone was the one I had in mind. That kind of melancholy tone that I had in mind right from the start, and the look of it and everything. I was much happier, I think, overall with *Song of the Sea* when it was finished.

Concept art, Tomm Moore, *Song of The Sea*, 2014. (Courtesy of Cartoon Saloon.)

Concept art, Tomm Moore, *Song of The Sea*, 2014. (Courtesy of Cartoon Saloon.)

Bill: And that movie was not coming from someone unknown, but from an Academy Award nominee. How was that reception different? How was the release of *Song of the Sea* different?

Tomm: Oh, it was so different in so many ways because it was sort of that difficult second album. Jamie Bolio, who we had originally met during the whole adventure when *Kells* was nominated, was now working with us and GKIDS in a PR role. She was focused on introducing the film to all the studios she had contacts with. She set up a six-week tour. I think I met you during that time. We stayed in LA and we actively campaigned for a nomination. But I remember coming home and being conscious of all the great movies that were in competition that year, including the beautiful Ghibli movie *The Tale of Princess Kaguya* and the *Lego Movie*, so I just didn't feel there was enough room for us. I felt we'd sort of had our day and I was going to be able to tell the grandkids I'd been Oscar nominated once. I didn't really expect that we could do it a second time. So it was pretty amazing to get nominated again!

Bill: You did an unusual thing. Instead of going right into your next feature, you did the short sequence from *The Prophet*. How did that come about?

Tomm: That actually is an interesting story because that wasn't "after." We'd been approached after *Secret of Kells* to work on *The Prophet* really early on, even before Roger (Allers) was involved as the overall director. It seemed like it was going to be the perfect job to do between one feature and the next, but it ended up having to be produced at exactly the same time (as *Song of the Sea*). I came under a lot of pressure from the coproducers on *Song of the Sea* not to do that sequence of *The Prophet*, because they didn't want my time divided. I was lucky enough that by then Ross had come back from Laika and was willing to codirect it with me, that little chunk, and that was the only way I was really able to do it. We had to do it in parallel with *Song of the Sea*. There was a period of six to eight months where we were in intense production of both at the same time. And then in Toronto, at the film festival, we had the *Song of the Sea* premiere and I had to rush directly to *The Prophet* premiere right after it. They were both on the same day, one after the other. So that was another once-in-a-lifetime thing, to walk a red carpet and then walk the red carpet again right after.

Bill: **I didn't realize you were doing those simultaneously. How do you keep your head in both films like that? It must have been a challenge.**

Tomm: Again, I have to say it comes down to an amazing team. We were able to do all of *The Prophet* in the same room. I just had to come in early and work on the storyboards and stuff with Ross on weekends and after hours. Thankfully I'd started the boards of *The Prophet* after the animatic was locked for the *Song of the Sea*.

Concept art, Tomm Moore, *The Prophet*. © 2015 Gkids/Participant Media.

Bill: Where did the new feature idea come from?

Tomm: A few years back, Ross and I were attending a master class that Brenda Chapman was giving in Dublin. As we sat over lunch in our favorite vegetarian restaurant, we came up with the bare bones of what *Wolfwalkers* was going to be. It was just something that Brenda talked about, where you take a lot of things you love and a lot of things you hate and kind of join them up. At the time of the English Civil War, there had been this interesting belief in what they called the Man-Wolves of Ossory. They weren't quite werewolves. They were kind of like benign wolves that would lead lost people home through the woods. There were all these different legends about them, and they were supposed to be pagans who hadn't converted to Christianity for St. Patrick. They had been cursed by St. Patrick. When they fell asleep, a wolf would leave their body, almost like an avatar-type thing and kind of explored the world that way. Oliver Cromwell had tried to symbolically tame the country by killing all of the wolves. Ireland had actually been called Wolf Land around that time, because there were so many wolves. So, those are just two aspects that we felt could be knit together kind of interestingly into a story. So we came up with the idea of the wolf hunter coming from England, coming over trying to claim some land in Ireland and to have a better life for himself under Cromwell. But his child makes friends with one of these natives, who also happens to be a "wolf walker." The end of our pitch is that the daughter of a wolf hunter turns into a wolf and ends up being hunted by her father. He has to actually turn into a wolf to save her.

We are only getting started properly on it now because I had to take a year to travel after the craziness of the Oscar nomination for *Song of the Sea*. I learned after *Kells* that you can't really do anything else for a few months after the Oscars because there's other festivals around the world then that want to screen the movie. And usually the local distributor will tie the local release in their country to a big festival screening, so I have to show up and help promote the movie there. Most of last year was taken up with promoting *Song of the Sea*. In fact, next week I'm going to Japan for the Japanese release of *Song of the Sea*, so it's kind of a long process.

Bill: Still promoting!?

Tomm: Yeah, two years later. Because we're not with one big huge distributor like Disney that can just put it out everywhere at once. It gets released territory by territory, you know. And then each territory has their own plan. It's even opening in mainland China in August.

Bill: They're pretty stingy about those release spots in China. You're lucky. Is it being dubbed in Mandarin or subtitled?

Tomm: It's Huahua Media, and they had to go through the censor to get it approved. It's going to be like a G kids' type limited release in China, but they're going to release it dubbed. They've done a lot of work with the Chinese market to prepare it, so fingers crossed.

Bill: It will be interesting to see how it does there, how it might resonate with the Chinese audience. Because *Zootopia* was a story of a country girl coming to the city, that aspect of the movie felt personal with the Chinese and the audience connected with it.

Tomm: The distributor told us was that they were encouraged by the fact that there was a very high number of illegal downloads already in China. So I was like, "Wow, that's a good thing?" But actually, they see that as encouraging, that people were interested enough to find it online.

Bill: That's the good and bad. Now you are on your third movie as a director and a studio owner. What's different?

Tomm: The studio owning part has gotten easier. We've hired Gerry, and we have a room full of accountants. It's become much more organized. It's not the lunatics running the asylum like it used to be. There was a steadiness to the studio because a TV series called *Puffin Rock* was running all through *Song of the Sea*, so that meant we had a TV series department keeping the studio steady during that time. That led straight into Nora's film *The Breadwinner*, which is the first in-house feature the studio has produced that I haven't had a lead artistic position on. I did some very early storyboards, some character design, and some concept design for that. But I'm in that nice creative producer role where once or twice a week I see the latest work and go, "That looks brilliant" [*laughs*]. I'm pretty hands off there, so I'm in a much nicer position than I'd ever been before. I'm quite lucky that most of the days I'm in the studio I'm just focusing on *Wolfwalkers*.

Bill: The unique thing about an independent studio is you don't have a release date target. A complete production schedule is not set, right? You're proceeding in more of an independent way on this movie.

Tomm: Yes. We have a lot of partners that are already interested, but we've been keeping them at bay because we really want to develop it independently. It's the point of this type of movie. Nora's interested, and so am I, in developing projects that are more commercial and have a wider release and everything. But this one I feel is like the third and possibly the last of these kind of Celtic folklore–inspired films that we will do. I feel it goes in the box set with the other two. I don't want it to be too influenced by anybody outside. And I'm pretty determined and sure that I can make it for a reasonable budget, like the other two, and keep it pretty independent. The studio is busier than ever, and we have plans hopefully for the next few years to keep the crew busy. We have to fit the production in there. So there is a certain amount of pressure that *Wolkwalkers* has to slot in at a certain point after *The Breadwinner*. That way, we continue on with the same crew, hopefully. There is an internal pressure, just production-wise, that we have it financed and in production so that we don't lose crew again.

Bill: **You're a relatively young guy, but it has taken you a lot of years to get two credits under your belt. The third one will take a few more years. What do you have in mind for yourself as a director in the future?**

Tomm: I had a plan up to 30, where I just wanted to get *Secret of Kells* done, right? And here I see myself facing 40 next year. I feel like the last 10 years just flew. Like all my plans went out the window. And it's kind of scary. It feels like if each production is going to take ten years, I'm only going to be able to make one more feature film. It's kind of the price you pay for the freedom of being an independent producer. I'm still inspired by the Young Irish Film Makers. I still think that Mike created an environment where people could be creative and dream and come up with stuff. A lot of amazing stuff came out of it. Not just us but amazing drama groups, people who have amazing careers in live action. Even people who don't work in film feel like they got a lot out of it. So I ultimately hope that when I stop directing movies, I can focus on letting Cartoon Saloon be the right environment for younger directors to come in. I'd like to be something like … how Didier was for me to somebody maybe younger and more talented than me, and in that way help other directors make their own movies here in the Saloon.

Bill: **Knowing what you know now, if you could go back and change anything or do something different, is there anything that you'd do differently?**

Tomm: I think I'd be less tense and uptight and kind of trust the process and the flow a lot more. I found *Secret of Kells* an incredibly stressful production overall, mainly because I was so overwhelmed and uptight. I looked pretty skinny at the end of *Secret of Kells*. I was really stressed the whole time. The big thing I learned on *Secret of Kells* is that it's how you spend your day. It's such a big chunk of your life, so many years of your life, that if you're not spending your day in a way that is positive, in a way that you feel is worthwhile … even if the movie comes out and it's a total disaster, if you spent your day with people that you love and people that you respect and admire and have learned from, it isn't a waste of time. Whereas if you have a nightmare production where you're stressed all the time and the movie comes out crappy, well then it's just awful. So I'd much rather build an environment where I enjoy what I do every day so that at the very least, I've enjoyed the process. The final product is what it is.

Bill: I think when people look at your work, the thing that makes it so exceptional is the fact that you've maintained not only a personal kind of stamp on the films, but they also have a unique feeling in the world of commercial features. They really feel like they're from your land. It sounds like you paid the price to make it happen, but you are very satisfied that you've done it.

Tomm: Yeah, I feel really lucky in so many ways. I can't even count all the ways that I'm lucky and how many times it could have gone the other way. I could have been the guy at the bar saying, "I nearly made a feature film once." I feel lucky. Lucky to have met so many great people that ended up working with me too.

Bill: If you were giving advice to young artists, what do you tell them? How should they start to form their careers?

Tomm: I think the cheeky thing. Everyone says to draw or practice, and you're going to do that anyway. If you love animation, you're going to be doing that anyways, so the advice I usually give is be cheeky. Don't be too much of a, "Gee whiz I could never talk to that guy. He's too famous or whatever." Talk to everyone. Be cheeky. And usually people are nice. That worked for us anyway.

Bill: Yes, that cheeky moment on the bus talking to Didier was a very important moment for you.

Tomm: I really think that. Be cheeky and go up and talk to people and make contacts and ask for feedback and take feedback. If you get feedback, take it and don't be insulted because that's the most precious thing you could get from a more experienced artist.

Bill: You're really an inspiration to a lot of people, Tomm. It's a great story how you've made it all work.

Ron: You know the only aspect of your filmmaking that we really didn't cover was the soundtrack aspect of it. How did it go for you? I mean, how did that process evolve for you?

Tomm: For both features, it was definitely the area I had the least experience in. I'd been at the voice recording for Nora's second short, which was an Irish-language short. I purposely went to that to try and understand that side of things. Prior to that, my only experience was scratch and being delivered a track to animate to. When we were looking for actors, obviously we had a wish list and we were lucky enough on both productions to get the wish list we wanted. For the adult actors, it was just a pleasure to work with them because they were people that we were fans of first and they got the material. So, you know, generally it went really smoothly and they added a huge amount. It was one of the best parts of the production for me because it suddenly felt that much richer to have those experienced actors. For the kids, it was a bit harder. We had to audition a lot for both productions, and for *Secret of Kells* they were completely unknown kids. That's where Nora was a huge help. I guess I was a bit intimidating or scary or something to the kids, but Nora was able to be gentle and coax the performances out of them. Fabrice, the writer, came to the voice recordings too, so I had a lot of support during the voice recording for *Secret of Kells*. Similarly, Will was at the recordings for *Song* and Nora was voice director again, so it was a great experience too.

Bill: What about music?

Tomm: We asked Kila, who were an Irish band, kind of a modern folk and world music fusion. They were already on board for *Secret of Kells* when Didier said that we needed to work with a composer, somebody who had experience composing and writing a score, not just talented musicians. So he introduced us to Bruno Coulais, and I remember at the time I hadn't seen much of Bruno's stuff. I had only seen *Microcosmos*, which was a really interesting documentary about insects that he'd done the score to. But Didier made sure I saw some of his other features and I loved the music. Most importantly, Bruno was open to collaborating with Kila. He wrote demo tracks to the animatic that some of the animation was done to. For example, the sequence where the little forest spirit Aisling sang needed music first before being animated. The *Secret of Kells* was a situation where I'd been really nervous and really uptight through the whole production. Even with the music, I think I nearly lost Bruno because I was giving too many notes at the beginning! I learned so much working with him and Kila on *Kells* that I wanted to change how I worked on *Song of the Sea*. So, where the *Secret of Kells* had a lot of demo work and then the actual recording done in a short period of time at the end, for *Song of the Sea* I asked Bruno and Kila to work together again because they'd enjoyed the collaboration on *Kells*. But we realized it would be so much richer if they had started collaborating right from the start of production. So the guys from Kila and Bruno would come over during the storyboarding process and do spotting sessions with me and come up with ideas, very often even story ideas. They influenced the movie, and it was very much more collaborative than, "Here's the movie. Write music to it." One example on *Song of the Sea* was that I had a lot of flashbacks storyboarded where the main character, Ben, remembered his mom before she disappeared. They were visual flashbacks, and Bruno suggested that we use the singer Lisa Hannigan's voice as an aural reminder and that we didn't need to be so literal and see her at the same time. He recorded her singing and then threaded that all the way through the soundtrack. In that way, he was part of the filmmaking process where we were deciding what was going to be visual and what was going to be aural in the storytelling. And then at the very end, which was fantastic on *Song of the Sea* but which we didn't have on *Secret of Kells*, we had a live orchestra. It was an amazing experience for me! To have labored at this thing for years and then suddenly in a couple of days an orchestra plays the score to the picture and it's immediately a hundred times richer and feels like a new movie again. It's like you're rediscovering it again. That was the best part I think.

Bill: **Is this changing your approach to the new movie? Are you going to involve composers earlier? Songwriters earlier?**

Tomm: Yeah I hope so. *Wolfwalkers* is not as musical like *Song of the Sea*. What's interesting for *Wolfwalkers* is that we have another element in that there's an English element. Two of the main characters are English, so we want to bring a little of that English folk music in somehow. I've already started talking to Bruno and Kila about that, how we might do that. I hope that they'll be just as involved this time, even though it probably will be more limited than on *Song of the Sea*, given that there aren't actually songs being sung on-screen. I would still like them to be part of that. I feel very protected when I work with those trusted collaborators. I feel like I know I'm going to get a good result.

Bill: **It sounds like you put most of your voice directing into the casting. If you get the right person for the thing you're envisioning, it sounds like it goes pretty well for you, right?**

Tomm: Yeah, and I mean not to take from Nora's role because without Nora as voice director, especially with the kids, it wouldn't have worked. She work shopped with the kids a lot, and she'd even make little drawings beside the scripts to kind of remind them if it's a happy emotion or whatever. But I think with kids, a lot of the time, it's about picking the best take, the most natural take. Whereas with the adults, Brendan Gleeson changed his character from how we'd imagined it. When he came into the recording booth, he had ideas that we hadn't thought of. He even asked us to change things about the character in *Song of the Sea*, which required changing the storyboards. But we knew he was right. There was a certain amount of collaboration, but certainly with Fionnula Flanagan and Brendan and those type of people … they were such pros that we were just blessed and it made our jobs very easy.

Bill: **You have a very different story, because a lot of the other guys have that problem of bringing some kind of individuality into a massive studio system. To me, it's a very inspirational story, especially for animators, because I've always had this feeling about animation and that there's always the idea that one person with an animation desk could make a movie. You are one person in a country that really didn't have an infrastructure at all, didn't have much of a professional community, didn't have a studio history, didn't even have funding, but ended up being able to make two** famous and well-received movies and is on his way to making another one. That's a very inspirational story. We really appreciate you being part of this book.

Tomm: Thanks for asking me. I'm really looking forward to reading this!

Ron: One last thing. Is there a short film that you saw early in your career that inspired you, excited you, that kind of remains either a talisman or an inspiration?

Tomm: It's hard to put my finger on one. We were really lucky. There were a couple of opportunities to see short films when I was a kid. Channel 4 had a collection called the A to Z of animation, which we video recorded and kind of wore out the tape rewatching it, looking at different and amazing films. There was a *Masters of Animation* series …

Ron: John Halas.

Tomm: Yeah. And I think RTE, the Irish broadcaster, bought it as a filler, you know. But I loved it. I used to see amazing eastern European animation there, and it was a real eye-opener. But the one short film I loved is *Sisyphus* by Marcell Jankovics. I just think that's pure animation. Yeah, I talk about that one a lot. I'm still hoping to make something that has that level of expressiveness and draftsmanship.

Bill: Have you seen the CG (computer-generated) version?

Tomm: No. They did a CG version? Oh no.

Bill: It was pretty good, actually. But it's nothing like the 2D one. Because the 2D one … it's the irrational, illogical way he switches from the sort of anatomical to purely stylized that no computer could ever come up with.

Tomm: Years ago, I would have been more interested in diagrammatic stuff and UPA and really design-y stuff for design sake. But as digital 2D has moved more into that area, I'm more and more interested in things like *Sisyphus*, which uses literally the language of line to express what's going on for the character. Like *The Tale of Princess Kaguya* last year from Isao Takahata. I think that's interesting because, as CG advances, the argument for 2D has to continue to evolve, just like the argument for painting had to evolve after photography, I guess. You know, we had to find what was unique about that language and what made it different. I think *Sisyphus*, the 2D version at least—I haven't seen the CG version—really shows something about the language of drawn animation, something that drawn animation could do that I think would be pretty hard to replicate digitally.

Bill: I'd totally agree with you on that. I feel that when the right topic comes along for 2D, it will be a big hit. It will be a commercial hit, which is the thing that's keeping the studios from getting back into 2D. They just all think CG is what the audience wants.

Tomm: Yes, it's really interesting. We had a conference call yesterday on a big project that we're going to take on in the studio. I can't really talk about it too much, but I was really surprised and happy that both the producers and the director in Los Angeles really wanted 2D. He's talking about *One Hundred And One Dalmatians*, he's talking about *Robin Hood*, and I was like, "Wow, really? OK, great!" He wanted it to be scratchy and drawn, and I thought, "Ah, that's interesting."

Scene Illustration, Lily Bernard, 2007, *The Secret of Kells*.

8
Chris Wedge Interview

Chris Wedge.

I first met Chris Wedge at an animation festival in Majorca, Spain. We spent a lovely afternoon on a beach with Bill Plympton and Shelly Page of DreamWorks swimming and eating fresh grilled squid. For someone who has made such an impact on animation, I found him modest and soft spoken. By impact, I mean that Chris and his partners had done something no one has been able to do since the days of Max and Dave Fleischer. They built an animation studio on the East Coast that evolved to a large studio that produces feature-length films. Chris has spent his career in the small towns of upstate New York and Connecticut, fashioning films that compete with the best of Hollywood.

His work reintroduced to computer animation a cherished ingredient of traditional cartoons, the pantomime slapstick gag. What vaudevillians called "schtick" and what traditional animators called "business." Norm Ferguson's animation of Donald Duck with a comedy cannot be written; it is pure performance. Yet like Chaplin, its appeal is universal. While completing his graduate studies at Ohio State University (OSU), Wedge started experimenting in computer generation (CG) with getting the properties of squash and stretch necessary for such pantomime. Later, in the hit film *Ice Age* (2002) the character Scrat (which he supplies the voice for) led a return to this iconic style of animation comedy. At the same time, being a strong family man, he appreciates relationships being at the emotional center of a good narrative film.

I caught up with Chris Wedge via Skype at Blue Sky soon after his film *Epic* had been completed.

Tom Sito

Tom: So, you were born and raised in upstate New York, and went to State University at Purchase NY. Then on to Ohio State University, where you studied computer graphics under Charles Csuri?

Chris: Yep! For a little while.

Tom: That was one of the earliest programs in CGI (computer-generated imagery) in the U.S. Is that what first attracted you to Ohio State?

Chris: That's the only reason I was at Ohio State. When I was a kid, I got interested in animation before there was any such thing as computer graphics. I experimented with stop-motion animation because I didn't have to draw every frame. I could make one puppet and one set, then move it and make a movie. I went to film school and that's what I studied. With the help of Richard Rogers, a great independent filmmaker, I did my own course design in animation at Purchase College. Mostly stop-motion. Late in my stay there, I met the experimental film-maker Stan Vanderbeek through his son Max. Stan was crazy about computer technology. He'd been making avant-garde films at Bell Labs—I think by going in at night and having friends sneak him onto the computers. He'd shown me some stuff that I couldn't believe came from a computer, early 3D images from NYIT (New York Institute of Technology).

Tron, 1982. © 1982 Disney.

Ed Catmull and those guys were working on *The Works.* That stuff blew my mind. This was like 1977 or 1978.

When I'm finishing up at Purchase, I tripped over an opportunity to work at one of the first computer animation production companies ever: Magi Synthavision. It was in Elmsford, New York, which was, at the time, kind of a truck stop. There was a strip with a diner, a bar, and a bunch of tire stores and gas stations. Anyway, Magi was in a corporate office park behind it, and that's where we made a lot of animation for (Disney's) *Tron* (1982). That's where I did my first CG.

Tom: **You were right there when CG was just starting.**

Chris: I was in my early twenties and was suddenly right in the center of this brand new technology. I was one of the first animators, I believe, to even use 3D computer animation—which was done, by the way, through an arcane and tedious typewritten interface. There were no graphics cards in computers back then, or even color monitors. You could only type things in. There was no way to interact with the images at all. Everything was plotted and measured on graph paper and then typed into those green-type terminals you see in the movie *War Games* (1983).

Chris Wedge, Magi Synthavision, *Tron*, 1982 © Disney.

I was thinking at that time that if I were going to be an animator in the future, I'd have to know how to program computers. Some of the programmers and technical directors at Magi were able to make cool pictures with textures and lighting. But I didn't understand how they did it. It was around then that I met Chuck Csuri at SIGGRAPH, probably in 1984.

I was on a panel with him. I told him I was interested in the animation they were creating there. And he said, "Well come to OSU! I'll teach you how to program. I'll give you a TA (teaching assistant) stipend; you can do a degree in computer graphics and then teach here."

Tom: Such a deal!

Chris: So, I moved my wife and three-month-old daughter to Columbus, Ohio, and lived on a stipend of $500 a month [*laughs*].

Tom: I'm sure they appreciated it.

Chris: Yeah, they loved it … but it was, I have to say, that lab that fostered a seminal moment for me in computer animation. At that time, they called it the Computer Graphics Research Group (later ACCAD for Advanced Computing Center for the Arts and Design). It was a combination of master's degree students, both artists and computer scientists that were getting together to design computer animation software and use it to make short films. There was an incredible exchange of information. There was none of the competition, you know, the jealousies of proprietary technology that exist between production companies. There was just a free exchange of information. We could just develop ideas and techniques in a supportive artistic environment.

Ron Diamond: What was the driving force behind your making short films? Was it to make artistic films? Or was it to make scientific or medical films? There must have been a mandate of some sort.

Chris: It was an art program. There was a curriculum. The artists also learned how to program, including how to create 3D graphics. We also sat around and collaborated with the computer science students. Someone would say, "This would be a cool tool." And someone else would say, "Well, what if it did this?" And then you'd counter, "What if it did that?" Then you'd actually develop something and use it. Make a short film with it.

It's quite possibly the place where deforming geometry first started, as well as some of the first squash and stretch movies. I think I might have even made the first 3D CG animation that used squash and stretch, *Tuber's Two-Step*, by simply following Frank Thomas and Ollie Johnston's playbook. I just told myself, "Look! Here are the principles of animation! Let's just apply them to a computer, to computer graphics!" We were free to experiment like that.

We were also some of the first to experiment with physical models—assigning weight, gravity, and surface tensions to computer-generated objects. There was even that initial research into applying artificial intelligence to the way characters moved. Michael Girard developed a program called PODA. This was in the mid-eighties. You could have a multilegged character walking on its own over varied terrain. You could tell it to go faster or slower, and it would change its gait automatically. Tell it to turn this way and that way. These were tools that didn't exist yet in production, but have since evolved into crowd simulation and flocking techniques. That was the kind of research going on there. And it really opened my eyes. It opened my mind to what the potential for computer animation was going to be one day in the future.

You know, in a lot of ways we haven't even caught up to what was happening in that research environment. And most of the research at Ohio State was done for the sake of art. It wasn't necessarily research that formed the bedrock of what people consider CG technology now, but a lot of concepts were developed there. In those days, you couldn't do anything in CG without being the first person that had ever done it. A lot of the ideas that we have about textures, for example, and even the technology we use at Blue Sky, had a precedent in those early days at Magi. Most people don't even

Tuber's Two Step, Chris Wedge, 1985. (Courtesy of ACME.)

realize that many of our current tools can be traced back to those moments when everyone was first thinking about what you can do with computers.

Tom: Did you get a sense of what was happening when you began to work on *Tron*? And I heard you also did some stuff on Lasseter's *Where the Wild Things Are* test.

Chris: Right.

Tom: Before Disney pulled the cork on that, did you ever see yourself coming out to LA and working at Disney, or doing anything like that?

Chris: Oh, I had no idea what I was going to do. I honestly didn't have any idea. The animation industry was in the pits back then. (Hopefully I'm not offending anybody.)

Tom: No, you're right. It was pretty bleak there for a while. There were only one or two releases a year. The Disney feature, and maybe a Bakshi film. There wasn't that much exciting stuff going on. It was a hollow space between the exit of the "Nine Old Men" at Disney and a new generation of animators. And a lot of people were quitting Disney at the time … you know, Don Bluth, John Lasseter, and …

Chris: Tim Burton even went through there. A lot of the first-generation CalArts students worked at Disney for a while. Then they thought, "What am I doing here?" and took off. They went on to revolutionize the industry. It was a moment where no one was quite sure what was happening. I didn't know either. Magi (Synthavision) actually opened a studio in Santa Monica the very day *Tron* opened. We wanted to capitalize on all the business from the ad industry that would pour in after *Tron*. That was about the only look we could do back then.

Tom: But that all didn't happen when *Tron* underperformed.

Chris: That all went south about a year later. I have to say, I was, as I think a lot of people are at that age, more fascinated by the technology and the technique than anything else. And I was just trying to figure out how to make a living doing it. Our ambitions were well beyond anything that was realistic. Our ideas about what computer animation could eventually bring to filmmaking were beyond what we could do at the moment. At that point, it was 10 or 15 years beyond.

There was no such thing as software you could buy and put a studio together with. You had to write all the software yourself! You needed everybody! When we started Blue Sky we had a little bit of everything—a computer scientist, a mathematician, a producer, a businessman, and me. You needed all of those things to even … Now everybody knows what CG is. Everybody knows what Pixar is. There was no such thing back then [*laughs*].

Ron: Were you inspired at all by the people around you, in terms of what they were going on to do? Like Tim Burton? John Lasseter?

Chris: Yeah. I met John when I was at Magi. John was at Disney, and he was on the periphery of the *Tron* production when our rushes were coming in all the time. None of the animation on *Tron* was done at Disney, because they didn't believe in computer animation there. I guess they thought machines did all the work!

Tom: Lasseter said that's when the potential of CGI really started to intrigue him.

Chris: John was pretty fascinated by what he saw. So, he made a point of visiting us at Magi. And we became very fast friends. John had an office at Disney where he and Joe Ranft were cooking up ideas. I think *Brave Little Toaster* was something he was working on then.

Tom: Wasn't *Brave Little Toaster* supposed to be the next big CG project for Disney?

Chris: *Toaster* and *Where the Wild Things Are* were going to be hand-drawn and CG hybrid movies. John cooked up a test for *Wild Things*. A collaboration between Disney and Magi. John had Glen Keane did the (story) boards, and I modeled the backgrounds and animated the CG part. Glen then rotoscoped his animation on top of it. At Magi, we wrote a system that digitally composited it. Because until then nothing existed to do any digital compositing. You know, we scanned Glen's drawings, and then colored and shaded them digitally. Christine Chang wrote the program that did the digital compositing.

Tom: When *Tron* tanked, Disney pulled the plug. *Brave Little Toaster* was completed as a 2D film. And John went on to Lucasfilm.

Chris: Yeah, the project died.

Tom: Were you then burning to make your own films? Or were you just focused on a job?

Chris: I was always cooking up ideas. You know, at work, driving, or running, whenever you have idle moments. I was always piecing a movie idea together. Making a living just got in the way of that for a long time.

Tom: [*Laughs*] That happens …

Chris: It was just, "Well, I gotta do this first." And I always considered myself fortunate to even find a job making animation. I'll be honest, though, for all those years when computer animation was in its infancy, it was just as fascinating to use the technology as it was to think about what you were doing with it. "Look! Oh, holy shit! Look at this image. This works, you know? This works!" I spent a good part of my career just being fascinated by the technology. I just thought it was so cool. I think the breakout moment for Blue Sky was *Bunny*.

Tom: **Tell us about *Bunny*. That was something you did when you guys built Blue Sky after leaving Magi Synthavision.**

Bunny, 1998 © Twentieth Century Fox. All Rights Reserved.

Chris: That's a short film that I'd been working on behind the scenes from the time we started the company (Blue Sky). I waited for technology to "happen" as I modeled things in my spare time. In the process of creation, everyone uses a different formula. These days our development model for computer animation is a lot like that of a live-action movie.

Tom: **Since the company has grown so big, when directing, how do you supervise a large crew of artists, all with their differing tastes and opinions, and still make it feel like your own vision?**

Chris: You can't afford to make it on your own. You want to make sure that your colleagues are interested in doing the film that you want to do. So, it's a matter of corralling everybody and getting the collaboration on its feet. Of course, you make it yours as much as you possibly can, but at the same time, you want everybody on the crew—and our crew is like 500 people—to feel the same way.

You want everybody to own what they contribute. It's not just about me. There can't simply be a preoccupation with forcing my point of view on everybody. Along each project's four-year ride through development and production, everybody needs to be involved. Everybody should be having fun. If what ends up on the screen is a hit, we're lucky. We're lucky if it really resonates with audiences. And we've had that happen. But that isn't the only part of it.

Tom: **You started Blue Sky originally in Ossining, New York. The thing is you did something nobody had been able to do in a generation. You built a successful theatrical studio in the New York City area. Something that hasn't happened since the Fleischer Brothers left in 1938.**

Chris: We didn't start out with that plan in mind. We had a fortunate recipe. But it was never easy. It was *never* easy. It still isn't easy. We really struggled for years without any money. Six of us that started the company, we went through two divorces over it. People dropped off. People joined in.

Seriously, we didn't have any money for a long time. We had to scrape it all together. But we couldn't let go. We were developing very realistic-looking images with a process called "ray tracing," which simulates very intricate properties of light. We tried to prove to other people that it was viable. We'd go to ad agency art directors with a sheet of slides and say, "See all these realistic objects? We made them with a computer!" And they'd say "Yeah, well we can just shoot the real thing with cameras. What do we need you for?" It took a lot to get the buzz going.

As our business grew, we got some acclaim. People would hear of us. It was difficult staffing up because there weren't a lot of people in our area that had the experience we needed, but after a while we found some. Some people on the West Coast who would say, "Really? New York? Well, I'm not living in LA because I *want* to." So, we got some ex-pats back here, formed a relationship with (Twentieth Century) Fox, and then committed to making feature films. It was just the right time. But certainly I never started out in 1987 thinking, "You know what? I like those Fleischer movies. I'm gonna make a studio to beat the Fleischers!" It wasn't like that at all. I will say I always thought the Fleischer films had some grittiness that distinguished them from the California studios. I think some our stuff does too.

Ron: **So, back to *Bunny*. What was your creative vision for it? It was something a lot different than anything you'd done before.**

Chris: Oh yeah. A lot of the sensibilities that I was bringing to computer animation came from the 3D aspect of it, because I had made puppet films. And I used to love it! I'd spend three years making a seven-minute-long animated movie.

I'd make ridiculously detailed little sets and latex foam puppets with armatures. I'd spend all day just lighting a shot. Then I'd come back after dinner to shoot it, walking around the set turning the lights on with my eyes closed. I didn't want to see the set until I looked through the camera. I wanted to see a completely separate world. I just loved to live in there. I loved lighting. I loved the dimensionality of it. And so when we started Blue Sky, that's all I was thinking about. Nothing practical was going through my head at all. It was simply, "Oh, we could make things look like this! We could do this! We could do this! We could do this!" Nothing practical. I told you, I had been making $500 a month. I was beyond "Will this work as a business?"

So, *Bunny* came from all these ideas that I was bouncing off of my colleagues: Carl Ludwig, Eugene Troubetskoy, Mike Ferraro. We were getting the ray tracer up. First, it could make a shaded object, then a shadow. Then it could make a soft-looking shadow. And then it could make more articulate light effects. And then we could get the light to bounce between objects. We were just sitting there playing with it, modeling simple things, and putting them in front of the camera. And I just thought, "I want to make a scene, I want to make a CG movie that looks very natural. Let me make one with a furry animal, you know? Let me put it in an environment that looks natural and storybookish and dreamy, and then let me just insert my own strange ideas about what could happen there." I wanted to make images with this precise, cold technology that evoked dreams from my childhood—ideas from the time when I was confusing dreams with reality.

Ron: Could you have made it earlier?

Chris: We couldn't have made it earlier because the technology wasn't ready, and we just didn't have the time. We had to work. We had to make commercials and effects to keep the lights on.

Tom: **There's a thing about the fur in *Bunny*. That was some of the most successful fur done at the time. This was about six years or something before *Monsters, Inc.***

Chris: We developed some fur technology that we were using before *Bunny* came out, on effects work. Pixar's done this too. They'll do a short where to develop and showcase new technology. *Bunny* was that kind of the project.

Tom: **So, how did you come up with the idea for *Ice Age*? Was the pitch to Fox about that, the technology? I find it interesting that we live in an era in which a lot of animation is dominated by dialogue. You know, *The Simpsons* and all, and here you are making a movie that's heavily grounded in pantomime. It's a sight gag movie, you know? At Disney when we all saw it, we were thinking "Yay! Somebody is finally doing real sight gags again!"**

Chris: Well, you talk about this balance between what you want to do and what comes your way. *Ice Age* was a project that had been pitched at Fox by Lori Forte, who had a producing deal there. They said, "Sure, why don't you get a writer on it. You know, write this thing up." And so, she developed a screenplay for it. At the time, it was a typical "animals on a journey together adventure story." There was a lot of action in it. But it wasn't funny. It was actually pretty dramatic.

Chris: Chris Meledandri was president of Fox Family Films at the time and he knew I wanted to make features. He saw the potential at Blue Sky, and in the Ice Age script. He said, "Why don't we make this movie at Blue Sky?" I looked at the script and thought, "Yeah, it's OK. It's a pretty good story." Actually, it was one of the best scripts I had read that year, structure-wise. But then he said, "The only way Fox is going to do this movie is if you turn it into a comedy." If you'd read that first draft you would have laughed, because it had some dark moments. But those dark moments shaped the story, and with some adjustments in tone I knew we could do it. Besides, somebody was saying "greenlight." "OK. I'll give it a shot." And as we started thinking about it, it was a comedy of peril. Here's one thing that I believe very strongly about, the reason that so many animated films are so good. It's all about the process, no matter what anybody tells you.

Tom: **At Pixar, the late Joe Ranft used to say about story development, "Trust the process."**

Chris: You know, we're not all geniuses around here. We are simply fortunate enough to be engaged in a process where we can collaborate with people over time, where we can keep working the story over. So you start with a screenplay, but then you take a sequence and start to draw it and formulate new ideas. And you realize, "Wow, when I see that drawing, I realize that I don't need those two lines of dialogue." Or I show the drawing to a writer and say, "Look at this! Look at how the tone changes when you just see it happening this way." Let's try it this way!" You just keep working it. You get designs up, and they change the movie. You get into animation, and the animators discover things that inform the writing. You get voice actors that give the thing an attitude that surprises you. And then you bring that attitude back to the writing and the animation.

Tom: **And that's your way of working?**

Chris: It was not a typical live action studio development process at the time, where it was all script driven. Fortunately, the studio embraced it, though. They would let us take script pages, go work them in story (boards), and then come up with a different take or a different tone. And a lot of it was just happening naturally. We were searching for places to make the film more fun. And it wasn't in the plot [*laughs*]. It was in the business (pantomime). And all that business was visual.

Tom:　　In *Ice Age*, when Sid the sloth is trying to get comfortable on the rock … I remember seeing it and thinking, "Oh crap! Business!" Somebody is doing it, finally.

Chris:　　It was a lot of fun. I wanted to tell as much story with pantomime as I could. I can't tell you why it ended up that way. It was just, you know, the sensibility.

Tom:　　**But as the director, I know you made the decision to let that happen. You didn't say, "OK, we're wasting too much time here. Let's move on to the next plot point." You allowed that to stay there. You allowed the performance to play out.**

Chris:　　Look, every project is different. We were able to get those moments in *Ice Age* because the story was simple and strong. And here's a little design philosophy for animated film that I think works really well. You don't need too much plotting. You need just enough story to support the set pieces. Take an idea. And you see the characters run with it. At the end of the sequence, maybe they achieve a goal and you're onto the next thing. Then you run with that one. It's just set piece, after set piece, after set piece. The audience loves that. Another example of this was *Avatar*. You know, it's pretty simple structurally. You go for minutes at a time just riding a roller coaster! It's fun.

Ron: **So, what influenced you during the making of *Ice Age*?**

Chris: *Ice Age* happened when I was 40-something years old. I'd spent my life to that point thinking about animation. I'd spent a lot of time with the technology and a lot of time building a company. There were so many ideas in my head. There were influences coming from every corner. People looked at it and said, "Oh, you guys were looking at Chuck Jones!" And I was thinking, "No, not really. I was looking at squirrels out of my window, you know?" Honestly, the way they moved! They just move really quickly to a spot and stop, and then blink and turn their head. That's what we used as inspiration for Scrat.

You just work with it. Frank and Ollie said that animating a movie is like having a kid. That seemed true to me at the time. It seems even truer now. You pour everything you know into it, but you just have no idea how it's going to turn out. It just does. I think they were talking about being pregnant, and not

Sketch, Scrat, Peter De Seve, *Ice Age*, 2002 © Twentieth Century Fox. All Rights Reserved.

Sketch, Scrat, Peter De Seve, *Ice Age*, 2002 © Twentieth Century Fox. All Rights Reserved.

knowing exactly what was going to come out at the end. For me, it's more like raising a kid. After two or three years it starts to talk, and then after four, or five, or six, or seven years it talks exactly like you. And then you think "No, no, no, no, no … You need your own voice." So, you … encourage it to discover what it wants to be. You realize it's got to be its own thing.

And it really was that, I'd just go back to this process. That's what made *Ice Age* successful. We really respected the process, and we just let it become something. And the studio, which could have had issues with letting us experiment too much, embraced it too! Not that we didn't have tooth-and-nail arguments about how much of "this" or how much of "that" along the way. But, at the end of the day, I think they understood that that's what it takes.

These films get better as they age in production. You don't just start with a script and shoot it. You fiddle with it and it changes. It gets better as the characters come into focus, as more people understand them, and as more people contribute. There's an acceleration of ideas toward the end of the project.

Tom: I was also curious about the design. One of the things that you guys did on *Ice Age*, you went for more simply designed characters that were streamlined for action and pantomime. You made a conscious decision to step away from making a hyperrealistic National Geographic special on the Ice Age. Something with every eyelash and highlight rendered. What was the origin of that design decision?

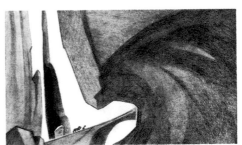

Chris: Well it's very simple, at the time we were possibly the one studio with technology that could pull off something photoreal. I mean, we had—and we still do have—fantastic rendering technology that can pull visual detail out of things, just by virtue of the fact that we simulate the physics of light.

We're still the only company that does it this way, with ray tracing. So, the capability wasn't an issue.

Environment design, Peter Clarke, *Ice Age*, 2002 © Twentieth Century Fox. All Rights Reserved.

What was an issue in my mind was, "Are we gonna be able to make a whole movie? It's gonna be our first feature film. Our technology. It's a little bit more expensive time-wise to use. How are we gonna ever get ninety, seventy-five, eighty minutes of movie on the screen?" Our longest project before that was eight minutes. There was a very practical conclusion. "Let's style this like crazy." And so, I started looking at illustrators and came up with the people that I thought could pull it off. And we stuck with that level of detail in everything. At the end of the day, we put more detail into the characters than we put into the environments.

Tom: **The environments looked very stark and stylized.**

Chris: I chose Peter Clarke to design those. He had a very cool geometric look. If we impose a style on the backgrounds, then people won't be looking for every vein, every leaf, and every snowflake. And then Peter De Séve's character design is organic and lifelike. They just kind of got it, you know? Your eye goes to the characters. And the background has its own … I don't know, simplicity.

Tom: **It's very successful. Now, one of the classic debates among people who do story work in animation, are the ones who say, "Character is derived from plot." And then other people say, "No, characters drive the plot." Where do you come down on that? I don't know if it's a chicken and egg thing.**

Chris: It is, completely! I mean, people say, "Oh yeah, the story is character." It's exactly the chicken and the egg thing. They've just completely come together. As you're developing the story, you'll say, "Well, here's my idea for it." And then you'll say, "OK, if that's the story, then who are the characters in the story?" You know, I'll back up even further, since most of my ideas start with an environment. It starts with a place. A lot of smart people will say, "Oh, I read a fantastic book. We should make a movie out of this!" [*laughs*]. I'm more likely to say, "I think it would be cool to go into a robot land! It would be fun to do a story in the Ice Age."

Tom: **So you start with an interesting setting.**

Chris: You first have to come up with a story that happens in that world, and then you start dressing it up with characters. Now, all these parts start to move. Then you start saying, "Well, I thought it was this character. If it's this character, then he's not going to do that in that situation, so that plot point doesn't work. Oh yeah … Well, maybe we should change the character. Nah, well maybe we should … Well, the character works so great in these other scenes! Maybe we have to change what happens here. Yeah, that's probably what we have to do." That's just the way it works.

What's the first thing the audience cares about? They don't give a crap about the story. They really don't care what the plot is. At the end of a movie, the first thing my 8-year-old son would say is, "Who's your favorite character, Dad?" He didn't say, "Wasn't it amazing that they thought to jump into the car at that moment before the house exploded?" It's never the plot points. What do you go to the movies for? You jump into somebody else's skin.

Tom: **When you start planning these films, how do you cast in terms of sound and music? Do you have actors in mind? When thinking of new characters, do you have certain sound in mind?**

Chris: Sometimes, yes. But you have to learn to be flexible.

Everybody has to be happy. But for me, I think about the character first. Honestly, I don't really care if it's a movie star providing the voice. It just has to work. And you know when it works, if you just look at images of your character and listen to voice tapes from actors. Casting is fascinating, because you'll think, "Oh, that guy would be perfect for our character. He's always like this in the movies. And he did this great role that nobody has seen. That would be perfect for our character." And then you look at the movie and think, "Oh yeah, he'd be perfect!" And then you listen to his voice alone and you realize that maybe a tenth of their effect comes from their vocal cords. Most of it comes from their face and their body. They don't work as a voice actor. You never know how they're going to sound until you play them disembodied.

Tom: **When you find an actor because you love his voice, you ask him to read. And they immediately think it's a cartoon, or some other silly voice.**

Chris: No, we get over that rather quickly, that process of casting a type. *Ice Age* is a great example. I was thinking, "OK, well we're going to have a funny guy do the sloth. We're going to have a serious actor do the tiger. And I'll get a big, deep-voiced guy to do the mammoth. And so, we'd put a drawing of the character up on the wall and play the tape. You'd hear a really deep voice and say, "OK, well I get that it's big, but what does it add?" Where is the irony?" I think the idea for Ray Romano came from Christian Kaplan, the casting director at Fox. Sometimes you are ready to let everything the studio says get under your skin" [*laughs*]. You want to just be, "*No way!* I'm not selling out just because that actor is famous!" But, then when I listened to Ray (who had a huge hit TV show at the time), the effect was pretty good. He doesn't necessarily have a deep voice. But when we played it—and I'm just saying we'd pin pictures of the characters to the wall and play the voice on a cassette tape—you thought, "Wow. I can see the drawing starting to move!" Attitudes, comedy, and timing come through the voice. And that's what Ray brought to it. His voice was deep enough to be plausibly coming from that character, but he had just the right attitude and delivery.

I guess what I'm saying is that it's all part of the process. You have to be open-minded. Go in with what you think it's going to be. But let it turn into what it wants to be.

Tom: **What about music? Obviously, you have a rough track when you're looking at reels. But does anybody ever come up to you and say, "We need Tibetan bells here, or zydeco, or something?"**

Chris: Those calls are usually coming from me. There's a reason why people try to work with the same crew over and over. I think it's because you come up with a shorthand, or your sensibilities align. You have magic formulas. I've been fortunate to have a little bit of that going on in the music. On *Ice Age*, we worked with David Newman, and he was open to a lot of suggestions. There was texture we couldn't get in the images that I thought we could get in the music. I had an overarching need to make this feel like it was part of a period. So we looked at ancient music. We looked at Inuit music. We looked at a lot of wooden instruments. The drums, flutes, and harmonies in the movie all come from Eskimo music. A lot of percussion textures. Then, just sweeping simple themes that I really liked. In *Robots*, because we were in a metal world, instead of using strings for all the big emotional moments, I wanted to use horns. So, John Powell put 11 French horns in a row [*laughs*]. Anytime you'd typically use strings for a romantic moment, or a sweeping emotional moment, we used horns. We even had the Blue Man Group banging on pots and pans for *Robots*.

Tom: **As you delegate responsibility, or as you cast people, do you feel that there are some decisions that you have to make personally?**

Chris: Oh for sure. If you're smart, you surround yourself with people that are either as good as you, or better. I hardly draw anything anymore because we've got an army of incredibly talented people that can draw better than I do. What's the point? I'll sketch things out on napkins and say, "Here's where I think the camera should be. And here's what I think, you know, maybe he's got his arm out this way!"

The worlds of animation and live action are really coming together now. I think it's even more apparent to the people in live action that are adopting animation techniques. They're using storyboards and previz and really working their stuff. And their previous techniques are coming in and influencing what we're doing in our action sequences. It is becoming more and more realistic looking. And you can just assume it's going to look a certain way. So, yes, you're delegating a lot to people. One of my favorite moments in the history of our company was when we were just getting *Robots* up on its feet. For me, most of the issues on *Robots* were visual, how the movie experience of being in that world with mechanical people was going to look and feel. We'd been working the story like crazy, and there was

Robots, 2005 © Twentieth Century Fox. All Rights Reserved.

plenty of frustration. So, we finally got some of our first characters and scenes up and running. The voice was recorded and we animated it. We rendered this beautiful thing, maybe just ten seconds of animation, and showed it to the crew at one of our general meetings. Everybody "oohed and aahed." One of our more cynical, "been-there-done-that" members of the story crew came up to me and said, "Well, here's where the movie gets bigger than the people that made it." So, it was that effect of everything coming together that makes it special. The process is the proof. It's bigger than any one person.

Tom: Yet, it's satisfying when as a director you can enable people to go further than even what they thought they were capable of.

Chris: Yeah, if you can get people to do that, you look like a genius. Honestly, you've got people that just love what they do. They don't need much encouragement to dig deep and produce the best work they've ever done … and it's in your movie!

Tom: So what do you think are your personal strengths as a director?

Chris: Oh, I don't know. [*Pause*] I'm a pretty good problem solver. I like to cast the most obvious solutions aside and keep digging for the better ones. I've got a lot of patience. I think that just comes from making animation for fun as you grow up. That's one thing a lot of animation directors probably bring to their work. If they've done animation on their own, they're fine with sitting there and figuring something out. However, I'm not the funniest person on the planet. I think I know what's funny [*laughs*]. And I know when it's not funny enough. You just have to keep pushing till you get it there.

Tom: How do you think your personal style as a director has changed over the years? If you could go back and redo *Bunny*, would you do anything differently?

Chris: There are always little things. I'm sure it's the same for anybody, you know? It's usually only done because you ran out of time. It's never finished. So, there are little things that bug me every time, but most people don't see that stuff.

Tom: The design styles of *Bunny* and *Ice Age* were in-house. But starting with *Robots*, and then with *Horton*, then *Epic*, you're working with a very strong illustration style of well-known artists like Dr. Seuss. How do you make that creative adjustment?

Chris: Well, *Robots* and *Epic* were collaborations with Bill Joyce. We had been trying to work together for a long time. For *Robots*, Bill would sketch his wild retro look and we would adapt it so that it could move expressively. I just love his style, so nostalgic and warm. I love the fantasy that he throws in. We embraced that and tried to organize and amplify it here at Blue Sky, to put it into a 3D world. We had to make it our own. At the end of the day, it's more evidence that it isn't

Character design, Rodney Copperbottom, Bill Joyce, *Robots*, 2005 © Twentieth Century Fox. All Rights Reserved.

just coming out of one person. Bill would come up with a concept, but we had to transform it, make it scale in our world. A lot of fine-tuning had to be done so that things could animate properly. So, all of Bill's drawings got filtered through a number of hands, but we tried to preserve the heart of it.

Tom: **And the same for *Epic*? Joyce was a producer on that film.**

Chris: The characters in *Epic* were inspired by the characters in Bill Joyce's book *The Leaf Men and the Brave Good Bugs*. It took us a few years to find the kind of support to get it green-lit (given the go-ahead for production). In that time, Bill Joyce had moved on to other projects, so he wasn't as involved as he wanted to be. Greg Couch (production design) and Mike Knapp (art director) really lived with that project for three years and made it work. Their stuff was beautiful.

Visual development, *Epic*, 2013 © Twentieth Century Fox. All Rights Reserved.

Tom: How about the Dr. Seuss stuff (Dr. Seuss's *Horton Hears a Who!*) His material was something that Chuck Jones had already done in the past, as well as Bob Clampett. You can't avoid comparison, the inevitable, "Is it truly Seuss?"

Chris: It's like anything you do. Once you're in the middle of it, you just embrace it. You make the best thing you can out of it. I didn't direct *Horton*; Jimmy Hayward and Steve Martino did. But Steve Martino was one of our art directors here, and he grew up with computer animation as well. He really went in and figured out how you make Seuss in CG. We knew we had a huge responsibility, because it was going to be the first Seuss feature. And it was going to be done in CG. We had to do it right. And Jimmy had a strong background in animation too! He was at Pixar for a long time, and he's a story guy. From Jimmy's perspective, we wanted to exaggerate the characters and the motion as much as we possibly could.

We did more extreme posing in *Horton* than we've ever done. That was just more of a technical challenge than anything. But in the end, you see the designs moving in an environment that looks fairly realistic, in a way that's impossible and hilarious. You see the whole thing coming together.

Tom: By contrast, *Epic* was your first foray into an action film.

Chris: I consciously wanted to make an action-adventure film that was not a pure comedy, though it would have comedy in it. I wanted to try in animation what I liked in live-action movies: live-action-type staging and more nuances. Make the environments more cinematic. It was a fun challenge. But animation has become what it is, for a good reason. It is a medium that is best used to exaggerate emotion and exaggerate character. In *Epic*, we kept to the action-adventure theme, but there was still that enhanced physics for action. We could have a

character jump 30 feet believably. In animation, we could do explosive, expressive action. It really was a great tool to get us into a story fantasy world in the most complete way possible. It can be used for more than just comedy.

Tom: **I'm curious about the use of a codirector. Most people want to direct alone. What prompted you to take on a codirector?**

Chris: The codirector title means different things on different movies. After a while on Ice Age I simply had too much to do. Carlos had really been stepping up so I elevated him from one of the animation supervisors to codirector. We were growing the studio too, so it gave him the opportunity to see every aspect of the production without all the weight on his shoulders. I'd say that decision paid off for everybody.

Otherwise each project works its own way. Sometimes two directors share all the responsibility equally, so they are codirectors. Other times it's more like one director has a lieutenant. In the end it's a way of acknowledging that the director didn't make the movie by him or herself. It's a massive creative collaboration, and the first collaborator is codirector.

Tom: **As they say, "A director is part artist, part commander, but also part salesman and diplomat." How did you deal with the political nature of the job? Dealing with the production executives at the studio?**

Chris: [*Laugh/sigh*] Diplomacy may not be my strongest suit. But you definitely have to do that. You have to be willing to put the time in to have these discussions. And the people on the other end of the phone are not always wrong. You have to listen and wonder if there's a better idea than yours. You have to be willing to do that. In every project, there's bitter debate at some point, but everybody's friends again at the end. It's just what happens. It's just very easy to get attached to your ideas to what you think is right. But, when the people who are paying for it don't agree with you, reality hits you straight in the face. That's when the salesmanship and diplomacy begins.

When we finished *Ice Age*, Chris Meledandri and I looked at it and thought, "You know, that bit's pretty funny. I can't even remember whose idea that was." "No, I can't remember either. I remember we were pretty mad about it." "Yup, yup. We probably shouldn't argue about this stuff anymore." "Yeah, you're probably right." And then we went right back at it on *Robots*.

Ron: **Sounds like Chris was a major influence as the head of Fox Animation at that time, in terms of helping you choose projects and supporting them.**

Chris: Yeah, Chris was a great collaborator. And it was his responsibility as studio head. Blue Sky is a big part of Fox Animation, but it's not the only part. The president of that division has a huge responsibility. These films cost a lot of money. The studio has a lot at stake. But don't let me characterize the whole relationship this way. We're talking about the diplomatic parts.

Often, they green-light a movie just because they love the idea. Arguments come over details. It's always in the scene, or a line, or something like that. "That joke isn't funny enough. We should write another one…."

Ron: **Do you ever find yourself taking notes from licensing and merchandising people?**

Chris: No, not so much. But there's definitely a marketing objective we have to consider. You want to make sure that this reaches an audience. This has to sell. So, there's a lot of attention paid to that. Little details come back from them. They give you perspective on who the audience is. I'll tell you another one of my favorite moments on *Ice Age*. I'd won an Oscar for making *Bunny*. I'd built a large animation company from scratch with a few of my friends. I had two (college) degrees [*laughs*]. I didn't need to be told how to make a movie. And I really didn't care about audience previews. I really didn't think it was necessary. The film was my vision. This is what it was going to be.

But the moment came when it was time to let an audience preview it. We had maybe 60 percent of the animation done; the rest was (story) boards. We took it to a mall theater on a Saturday, and there was a line of people going out the door and around the block. I walked down that line and thought, "Yikes, I have nothing in common with these people. Nothing. Nothing! That guy doesn't look like any of my friends. That one doesn't dress the way I do, and these people are going to decide the fate of my movie!" You know, guess what? They're the audience. The audience! So, I go in and sit down. Fortunately, there was a lot of goodwill already, because our Scrat trailer had been out for a while. Everyone knew that *Ice Age* was out there. When they saw that this was the movie, they erupted. I had this palpable sensation that the characters were reaching out of the screen and that the audience was reaching back—and I wasn't out of my mind! [*laughs*]! There was a distinct communication between the audience and the movie. And I thought, "I will do anything to make these people happy. I will do anything to make this work as well as it possibly can." And it was pretty obvious at that point what needed to be cut out of scenes, or if it was wise to kill off certain characters, or what needed to be made funnier. It was pretty obvious. So, I spent the next four months on *Ice Age* just fine-tuning it. It was like filing off all the rough edges on a roller coaster.

At the end of the day, it's about communicating with people. And it's about entertaining people.

Tom: **I want to ask you about "the one that got away." Was there ever something you wanted to get into a film, but had to let go? A time where you had to walk away thinking, "I had a much better idea here. Oh well."**

Chris: Oh sure. But it's not worth talking about. You really have to look at your ideas as just a fountain. You just have to let 'em come up and go away. If we don't use them, who cares? You throw your best stuff at it all the time. You just constantly throw your best stuff. You just don't hold back. "Well, I'll save that one for another huge, green-lit [*laughs*] animated feature film." There have always been a million tossed-off ideas. Who knows if they would have worked better?

Tom: Do you think you have a personal style? I mean, is there a style in your direction?

Chris: I'd like more opportunity to develop it and find it. But I also think that you work with your instincts in scenes. You get them where they want to go. I personally go for things that are a little quirky and odd. I go for the visually captivating, as captivating as I can get them. But I also like to monitor myself when I'm watching movies. I like to feel my heart. I like the emotional connection. If a film's working, you can feel it. Your heart's in it. And if it's not, if the story doesn't go the way you think is realistic, or there's something in there that doesn't go over, you drop out and you're not interested.

I think you're only interested if your heart feels like it's in touch with the characters.

Tom: What is the most bizarre, surreal, or the strangest moment that you've had as a director?

Chris: It'll be midnight, and you're in editorial. You're at your wit's end. You're having issues. This scene is never going to work, but we can't cut it out of the movie. Every once in a while you have to look at each other and say, "Relax. We're making cartoons, right?"

Ron: When you're coming up with a story, using things that are more over the top than normal, do you think, "You know what? This is right for that moment." Have you had experiences like that?

Chris: Oh, I don't know. Honestly, the sensation is more like, "What makes the most sense here? And what would be the most interesting and engaging?" There's never too much second-guessing. If it works for you, it should work for them. And if you can remove yourself for a moment and just listen … If people say, "I don't get that," you have to ask yourself, "Why aren't they getting this?" And then you realize, "Oh, that was just too oblique, you know? I have to set this up a little better." This is storytelling. You're telling a story, beat by beat, by beat, by beat, by beat. You're sitting around a campfire, and you're saying, "This is what happened. This is what happened next. And then this happened, and then *this* happened. And then he said this, and then he …," you know? That's what animation is about! You can't just depend on an actor to do something incredible and spontaneous … and you caught it (on film)! You're making the whole thing up, beat by beat. Meticulously, you know? I mean, that's the one thing unique about animation. The process isn't spontaneous. There may be moments of spontaneity within it, but the larger momentum just doesn't work that way.

Ron: Do you have a favorite director, or a favorite genre?

Chris: Oh, it's just what I'm in the mood for, you know? It's always just what I'm in the mood for. I'll tell you one thing, *Avatar* blew me away. I sat there watching it and I thought, "I'm an hour and a half into this, and I'm so glad I've got an hour and a half to go. I'm right in the middle of being transported to another place, with a story that's completely accessible." Another time I felt this way was in *Titanic*. Hey, it's not like I want to make out with Jim Cameron. But I just said to myself, "That is an incredible feat!" You know, to be able to transport you that far away.

Tom: He knows his genre, action pictures, and he tells them well.

Chris: One of my other favorites is Ridley Scott, obviously. I love his stuff. He's a stylist. And *Gladiator* is one of my favorites. You get to go back and dress in swords and sandals, and get to see what Rome looked like back then too. But it's a character story. It's a huge, powerful character story. And Terry Malick influences me simply because he can just sit and meditate on grass blowing in the middle of a compelling character story. One of my favorite films has always been Werner Herzog's *Aguirre: The Wrath of God*. It's a great movie for some of the same reasons. Here's a locked-off shot of a river roiling on its own for a full minute, to underscore the challenges lying ahead for these characters.

Ron: Do you have one short film that is important to you? Something from your past.

Chris: Well, I can think of quite a few. The first one that always springs to mind is *The Mascot* by Ladislaw Starewicz. He's a Russian stop-motion filmmaker from the 1920s and 1930s. He had a studio in Paris, I believe. Anyway, he made this short film about a sick child that wants an orange, but his mother can't afford it. As she's trying to figure out what to do, she's sewing together a little stuffed animal. A tear then falls into its stuffing, and it starts to beat like a little heart. It immediately comes to life and embarks upon an adventure. The story ends at the Devil's ball. Deep within the recesses of Parisian streets, where there is debauchery, fighting, goblins, and … Some of the most amazing, trippy stop-motion you'll ever see. Found objects and characters with onions for heads get torn apart. There are characters made out of balloons and broken wine bottles. It's very trippy, very cool. That's one I'd go to.

Tom: Getting back to the nuts and bolts of directing, what's your favorite part of the job?

Chris: I have two favorite parts. One is thinking up the story, before anyone's done anything. It's just the pure sitting around thinking about what it could be … "Wouldn't this be cool?" and then taking the accumulated effort of time and people and bringing that final product to the screen.

   My second favorite part is post (production). When we do the final mix. It's all done, and the things you do there actually have an impact in real time. That's when it's more spontaneous for me. I mean, everything else in the middle is fun, but those are the best parts.

Tom: OK, what's your least favorite part?

Chris: [*Pfff*] Well, I don't like getting excited about something and then have to watch it undergo intense scrutiny.

Tom: When it gets too crazy with approvals and stuff, and you have the little schedule of all the appointments you have to make, I know directors who would hide in the basement.

Chris: I haven't done that yet. I've pictured them carrying me out on a stretcher, but I haven't hidden … yet [*laughs*]. I'm the kind of person that, left on my own, would just go crazy. I like it when we're in production and they hand me a little schedule and every 15 minutes, or half an hour, is outlined. Then I run around like a doctor on rounds. I like that part of it, interacting with people and the excitement that follows.

Tom: Did you ever run into a creative gridlock? And how do you dig your way out of it?

Chris: All you can do is dig! All you can do is work on it. I mean, that's the only [*laughs*] solution I have. You just work on it. Sometimes, if I don't have the idea right off, or if I have a lot of ideas about something and when I have nothing left to say about it, that's when I think it's done. Maybe I'm more easily satisfied than other people. I don't know. But when I can't think of anything, usually I just say, "OK, well, that's the way that'll be."

Tom: From the time you first started directing up to the present, have you adjusted your personal time and personal style? There are some directors now who just make a point to say, "I don't care. At six o'clock, I go home. I'll go crazy!" And then other ones that say, "I don't mind staying all night if I have to."

Chris: Well, we work plenty of nights and weekends, but in animation we're fortunate, you know? We can go home at the end of the day. No matter how long you've been at work, you get to go back to your own bed. My family is very supportive. When we are getting into the grindy part of the schedule, I let everybody know, "It's going to be tough for like a year and a half. If I have to travel, or if I have to be at the studio, that's just what it's gotta to be." My wife has made huge concessions for the productions.

On *Ice Age*, we were stressed about whether or not we could actually make the movie. We were so stressed about the budget that most nights the lights were off at six o'clock. Most people took off at the end of the day, since we couldn't pay anybody overtime. But the lights in editorial would be on. That's where we would be. But it's not necessarily any easier now. The budgets have gone up, and the crews have gotten bigger. It just seems like there's more pressure.

Tom: When you are directing, did you ever have a moment where someone just goes off on a tangent, or reinterprets something? And you don't want to be the one to say, "Look. I got the stars on my shoulder, you don't. We're going this way." But, you know, you want to reason with them.

Chris: Years ago, a friend told me that probably the best political atmosphere in a studio is that of a benevolent dictatorship. You can be democratic, but to a degree. At the end of the day, people are looking for direction. That's your job. You're the director. You want to listen to people. You want to gather all the input you can, but you have to be able to tell people "That's not what we're looking for here, and this is why. This is the vision for this scene. I'm sorry, but that's not it. And by the way, this doesn't just happen to you, it happens to me every day." No one is given full creative freedom here. We're all working in service of the story. And when you take the whole crew together, you have the opportunity to multiply the power of your own vision exponentially. They add layers and layers of detail. And that's why it's so important to communicate the global vision of the movie as often as you can. You need to guide them. You're the director.

This is animation. You start with nothing. No actors. No sets. You start with nothing! You can talk about whatever you want at the beginning. There's a lot of talk. But until you start putting stakes in the ground, "Here's the story. This character is gonna be kind of like this. Oh, this is what he looks like, by the way. Oh, here are some lines for him. He could be like this! And here's a voice that could perform it." You know, the further you get into the movie, the more there is for people to react to.

For instance, in our voice recording sessions, in the first one, the actor is saying, "Well, I've never really done this before, and I don't quite understand what character I'm talking to here." We're in a recording booth with one person usually, because we couldn't get all the actors together—they're shooting movies in Australia, or Prague. You spend four hours recording and saying, "Yeah! I like that idea a lot!" And they're very self-conscious. So you say, "No, that was good! If you have anything else, try it!" And they try stuff. At that point, we've shown them artwork. But the next time we see them, months later, we will have cut the numerous voices into an animated scene.

When we show it to them, they say, "Oh my God! Oh, that's it! Oh that's what I'm ... Well, let me change this line! Let me read it this way! Now I get it. This is what I'm gonna do!" And that happens with everybody. They see how it all comes together and say, "Oh this how it should ... Oh, I get that guy now." There is an escalation of input, once people are focused on it. The more you share, the more people get it. And, the more focused the movie gets.

Tom: You're also directing your first live-action film (*Monster Trucks*) in Vancouver for Paramount.

Chris: Everyone who has ever directed told me if someone offers you a movie, take it! After *Epic*, I felt like doing live action was something I wanted to explore. What was similar and what was different. I'm having a lot of fun, and I intend to bring what I'm learning back to animation.

Ron: As far as becoming a director, how do you advise people just starting out? What should they study? What skills to hone? Do people ever ask you questions like that?

Chris: I don't know. I didn't go to school to be a director. I mean, I kind of have this thing. Chuck Jones said he didn't like people calling him an animator. He just didn't think that he deserved it. It sounded too high floutin'. He liked to be called an "animationist." So, a director? I don't know.

If you're going to be a director, you have to be able to tell stories in an entertaining way. And you have to have enough self-confidence so that people can't talk you out of it.

You have to feel as though everything fits. Everything in animation has to come together: the concept, the design, the style of the animation, the music, the pacing of the beats. The audience wants to feel as though they're in capable hands. They want to relax and have a capable storyteller sweep them away. Everybody remembers those movies. Everybody knows who those filmmakers are.

Tom: OK Chris, on that note, I think we got what we need.

Chris: Boy, and just look at the time! [*Everyone laughs.*]

Ron: Thanks so much.

Chris Wedge, © Blue Sky/Fox.

9
Roger Allers Interview

Roger Allers, Disney artwork © Disney. Photograph courtesy of Jennifer Sari © 2002.

The idea that "you have to have a life to be an artist" is perfectly represented in Roger Allers. Other directors came through Hollywood, CalArts, or Disney, but Roger took a different journey, and that made all the difference in what he brought to his art.

Roger studied fine arts, not animation, and then traveled in Europe rather than immediately pursue a career. When he finally caught the animation bug, he started in a town (Boston) with no animation industry and no animation professionals for mentors. Roger was the classic self-taught animator.

I met Roger when he (finally) came to Hollywood to work on a movie called *Animalympics*. On that film, we did our own storyboards and layouts for the sequences we animated. Roger's sequences are funny, melodic, and carefree—like him! Unlike the rest of us, when the movie was over he didn't dive back into the biz. He headed for Europe again with his new family!

He followed opportunities in Japan and Canada before he returned to California and landed, inevitably, at Walt Disney Feature Animation. Once he started in story, his unique perspective was evident. Roger has the friendliest, most supportive, most open manner with his fellow artists, a style that makes everyone on the team feel relaxed, safe, and energized. He will often approach a story problem from a different perspective, what could be described as "aesthetic humanism," and those ideas have made profound contributions to the projects he has worked on.

Despite operating in the production bull's-eye, Roger seems genuinely unaffected, even surprised, by the notion that economic and personal forces should ever be allowed to dilute creative ideas. To Roger, animation is a joyful thing!

We interviewed Roger at his home in Santa Monica, California.

Bill Kroyer

Bill: Where did you grow up?

Roger: Mostly Scottsdale. I was born in New York, but then I ended up in Arizona when I was six years old.

Bill: How did you end up in animation?

Roger: I always thought I was going to be an animator, even when I was a little kid. I was crazy about animation. I was a huge geek. I could not get enough of it! It started with *Peter Pan*, which I saw when I was five years old. It just knocked me out. I had all the Disney books and records, and, being an only child, that was my world. That's where I lived. When I learned that there were actually animators who made this stuff, that's when I knew what I wanted to do. I always imagined myself walking in with my portfolio and meeting Walt. Of course, it was Walt who was going to interview me. I had this whole fantasy. When I was about eight, I sent away for an animation kit from Disneyland. There was a part of Disneyland back then called the art corner, and they sold animation kits. There were books on the principles of animation and on how to draw the characters. You could even put together your own light table. And they gave you exposure sheets.

Bill: Had you ever seen one of these at the time?

Roger: I still have it. I can drag it out of the closet.

Bill: I'd love to see that kit. But we should continue.

Roger: All right. So I put it together and started animating. There was a walk cycle of Donald Duck with step-by-step instructions. I worked on that for a while.

Bill: Did you just flip them, or did they tell you how to photograph them?

Roger: You could send your animation back to the art corner at Disneyland, and they would film it. But I never did that. I just kind of taught myself.

Bill: Did you ever try to make films?

Roger: Not really. In high school I took art classes, and my father gave me an 8mm camera. It was a really bad camera, but I made some special effects movies. I discovered the principle of double exposure, so my friends and I turned ourselves into ghosts. I also made some stop-motion. But it wasn't very fancy. I just had to hit the button to get a frame! Anyway, it was a lot of fun. But by the time I was ready to finish high school, Disney died! I remember riding home from school and hearing someone say, "Hey, did you hear? Disney died! Ha ha ha ha!" I was so shocked. That was my dream. That can't happen! And I remember a couple of films came out after that. When I saw *The Aristocats* in college, I thought it was terrible. So, I thought I missed it. I was too late. I gave up on the whole idea and became a fine arts major at Arizona State University. I actually had applied to Arts Center—this was before CalArts—but I didn't make it. I was kind of shocked. They said I should go to a liberal arts college for a year. At that point, I just moved on and went to ASU (Arizona State University).

Bill: Did you finish college?

Roger: Of course! I have a fine arts degree.

Bill: Were there any artists or specific schools of artists that influenced your creative development?

Roger: I can't say there's really anything specific. For me, just the opportunity to study art history was extremely valuable. I really loved studying art in terms of its diachronic development. I remember these intense three-hour-long slide shows. But seeing the flow and movement of art over time, and how different cultures expressed it, just fascinated me. I think that gave me a good foundation. I can't really point to one artist in particular. You just draw on other artists and art from the past. It's intrinsic to anyone's development as an artist.

Bill: But how did you end up in animation?

Roger: Well, after college I was avoiding life. I lived in Europe for a year and a half. I met the girl who would later become my wife. There was a reason why *Peter Pan* was my favorite film! Honestly, I just didn't know what I was going to do. How was I going to exist as a painter? I had no clue. I was really running away. When I came back to the States, I worked in frame shops, framing pictures. Long story short, I wound up in Boston. And someone just happened to mention that Harvard has an animation department. I actually went over to Eric Martin, who was teaching animation at the time, and asked, "Do you ever let people, who aren't Harvard students, sit in on your classes?" He had me take a drawing test. Fortunately, I passed, and he invited me to come. By the time his course was over, I had a 15-second film. I combined that with my portfolio and got a job at Steve Lisberger's studio in Boston.

Bill: What were you doing?

Roger: Commercials, openings for TV shows, a children's show called *Make a Wish*, stuff like that. You would get about five or ten minutes of animation to storyboard. And you had to come up with the ideas and get them approved. Then you traced it on the cells, painted them, and shot your animation. That's how I learned to do it.

Bill: How long were you there?

Roger: I started there in '74, and then in '78 we were trying to get *Animalympics* together. But finding the right talent proved too difficult. We then moved the studio to Venice, California. So that was four years in Boston.

Bill: Were you doing your own layouts and in-betweens?

Roger: Yeah. I never had an assistant.

Roger Allers at Lisberger Studios. Photo: Darrell Rooney.

Bill: So is this where your skills developed?

Roger: Yes, and it was intense. Commercials and TV shows come with a lot of pressure. You have to animate fast!

Bill: Did you have any mentors or any animators accessible to you at that time?

Roger: Not really. I mean, we were all kind of on the same level. Most everybody in the studio was fresh out of college, mostly from the Boston area. A lot of people there had gone to school in Boston and there wasn't a great deal of animation support back then. We were all making our own way. We screened films in the studio and exchanged ideas. We didn't have any mentors. We just worked with each other. We'd all get together for movie nights and look at films and analyze them, teaching ourselves that way, but we didn't have any mentors. I would have loved to have a mentor. I'm so jealous of all the people who went to CalArts and then on to work at Disney. They got to work with the "Nine Old Guys"! Totally jealous of that. Actually, I loved working in that little studio and doing a lot of different stuff. And then we moved to Los Angeles to do *Animalympics*. And we had great camaraderie there, too. It was at that studio that I met guys like Bill Kroyer and Brad Bird.

Bill: We loved that studio because you could design your own sequences and board them and everything …

Roger: My ice skating flamingo … It was fun. And then we started on *Tron* and then I ran away, and went to travel …

Bill: Let's just stop for one second. You are doing your own sequences on Animalympics. You're kind of a mini-director. Did you feel that you might eventually end up leaving animation to become a full-time director?

Roger: No. I was too involved with the process and developing my skills. I was rather satisfied. I wasn't thinking of ways to take control of the entire production. I really just fell into directing—sweet talked is more like it. I was an animator. I worked as a story artist for various studios. I even worked at Nelvana in Canada.

Bill: When did that happen?

Roger: I had come back from Europe with my family. Then I learned that *Tron* was at Disney, and that not everyone was going with Steve. I had to find work, wherever it may be. I went up to Canada because that's where Darrell (Rooney) was from. In 1980, I got a job working on *Rock & Rule*.

Bill: Whom did you work with up there?

Roger: That's where I met Tom Sito, Dave Brewster, Anne Marie Bardwell, Charlie Bonifacio, Robin Budd and Chuck Gammage.

Bill: Great crew!

Roger: They were really talented people. But I had a miserable time there! I just didn't get along with the upper management. I loved the talent. But I just didn't fit in.

Bill: Let me guess. No help, no constructive criticism, just pure complaining.

Roger: Yeah! Constantly too. Someone would say, "That's a great scene," Then I would hear, "Well, Patrick doesn't like it." Then I'd come out of the screening and he'd say, "That was *shit*!" As an artist, you're prepared to take criticism. But this guy never had anything good to say. If I'd say hello to him in the hall, he would look the other way. There was nothing I could do to please them. I was miserable.

Bill: How long were you there?

Roger: Two years.

Bill: Even though they hated you that much, they kept you for two years?

Roger: I can't explain it. Anyway, I'm looking for work again. Worse still, my visa was running out. Now, if you remember, I called you and said, "Bill, I need work!" You directed me to *Little Nemo*, which turned out to be my next job. I got hired and was sent to Tokyo to work with Ray Bradbury. He was writing the script, and it was a great experience working with Ray. And, of course, it was Tokyo!

Bill: How long where you there?

Roger: Tokyo was another two years.

Bill: Two years animating?

Roger: No, we couldn't get the story off the ground.

Bill: Did you just do storyboards for two years?

Roger: Yeah, I sure did. I was constantly coming up with new ways of interpreting the story.

Bill: Wow, two years boarding in that Nemo style!

Roger: You mean that comic style? That's what attracted me to the project. I thought that comic strip style was great. But this turned out to be a very difficult venture for Tokyo Movie Shinsha. In terms of living, it was fascinating. And my son was born there! Work, on the other hand, was hard. We couldn't seem to get anything going. Nothing ever got approved. And every so often, the backers of the film, who looked like yakuza, would come on set and cause a stir. You had to look seriously busy because the "bosses" were there.

Bill: Who was in charge?

Roger: Well, Mr. Yataka Fujioka was the head of the project. He had the last word. In fact, he started it as a joint production with Gary Kurtz of *Star Wars* fame. But Gary dropped out after a while. Production was an absolute mess. The method of storytelling was really different in terms of the Western crew versus the Eastern crew. We liked each other, but we didn't share the same vision. Communicating your ideas was difficult, if not impossible, at one point.

Roger Allers. Photo: Leslee Hackenson

Bill: Do you have an example?

Roger: I remember a scene in which Nemo is just standing, and there are all these people around him. Nothing had happened, but something was really troubling the character. At the end of the board, we stopped and said, "So what's Nemo's problem? And I remember all the Japanese saying, "He's feeling very badly because of what everyone else is thinking. And he doesn't know. That's the problem." We were speaking two different languages! Seriously, I love the animators over there. But that was just a hard project.

Bill: How did you decide to leave?

Roger: Well, everyone that had been brought in with me just left. We were done. No progress was being made. It was a creative stalemate. So, we respectfully walked away.

Bill: What year was this?

Roger: The end of '85, and as I was about to leave Tokyo, Dave Stephan called. He said, "Roger you should really come work at Disney." A lot of people from the Lisberger days had gone to work at Disney because of *Tron*. It was always a dream of mine, so when I got back into town I met Dave for dinner. He explained that Disney was in need of a story artist. One of the story artists on *Oliver & Company* had suddenly died. This was a guy that had been working very closely with George Scribner on *Oliver*.

Bill: Pete Young.

Roger: It was a sad way to make an entrance into Disney. But that was the situation. I called Don Hahn and got an interview. However, there was a big problem. I just got back from Japan. Everything was in boxes and in transit. I didn't have my portfolio! Nevertheless, I interviewed with him and George, and we got along great. But I had nothing to show. So they gave me a xerox of some of the characters and said, "Just go and do some drawings." Well, this wasn't so easy. My wife and I were living out of motels. We had a baby. We're trying to find a place to live. It was a challenge just to find time to work. Anyway, during my kid's naptime I managed to pull something together. I took my drawings back and got hired. It was definitely a "by the seat of your pants" kind of thing. They dropped me right into the middle of the story, and I loved it! *Oliver & Company* was my first job at Disney.

Bill: Was Jeffrey there yet?

Roger: Oh yeah, Jeffery Katzenberg was there. I remember everybody on *The Great Mouse Detective* being moved out of the lot at Disney into the warehouses in Glendale. I think they were on probation. Jeffrey and Michael Eisner didn't like or see the value in the division. To them, it wasn't going to bring in money. And there was definitely some conflict. But I remember Roy Disney saying, "No, you've got to give them a chance!"

Bill: How long did you do story work on Oliver?

Roger: About two years. And at some point I was heading up story. My office was next door to Vance Gerry, who is a fantastic artist. I used to go into his office just to talk to him. In a way, he mentored me simply by letting me go in and look at his drawings. I would study how he did his boards, his beautiful dramatic lights and darks. He was just such a fantastic storyteller.

Bill: Did you finish Oliver?

Roger: I actually didn't. Howard Ashman and Alan Menken were working on the music for *Little Mermaid*, which Ron Clements and John Musker were developing. They were writing the songs across from my cubical, and the songs came through the walls.

The place didn't really have ceilings, so you could hear everything. As I was working on my boards, I kept saying to myself, "This is great! I love these songs!" After Ron and John gave me a copy of their screenplay, I just had to work on the movie. I was frantic about it. So I actually left *Oliver & Company* before it was finished, even though I was head of story.

Bill: **You requested to go on Mermaid?**

Roger: Yeah.

Bill: **And George let you go?**

Roger: I kind of said I was going. I was really driven to get on *Mermaid*. When I look back, I didn't handle it the right way. If my head of story did that to me … not finish the movie! I spent almost two years on that movie with George. Fortunately, Mike Gabriel finished it. There were only a few months left on the project. But still … mea culpa! I've apologized to George.

Bill: **Mermaid was a big crew right?**

Roger: Very big. By the time I came on, Kelly Asbury, Joe Ranft, and Ed Gombert were already working on it. Anyway, I moved over to *The Little Mermaid* and just *loved it*! I loved it. It was a musical. To me, this was classic Disney. This is why I dreamed of working at Disney as kid. Howard brought his expertise as a showman of Broadway musicals. I remember the first time I met him. I was working on my boards, the Witch's song 'Poor, Unfortunate Souls' and he suddenly stuck his head into my office. He was looking at my boards and had recognized some recordings that I had made earlier in the day … a German lady called Dagmar Krause. We had this long conversation about music. We talked about what influenced his work and Allen's. The next day, on my desk there was an album of Kurt Weill's *The Threepenny Opera*. It was fantastic getting to know him. That was a real privilege.

Storyboards, Roger Allers, *The Little Mermaid*, 1989 © Disney.

Storyboards, Roger Allers, *The Little Mermaid*, 1989 © Disney.

Storyboards, Roger Allers, *The Little Mermaid*, 1989 © Disney.

Bill: What happened when you were done with Mermaid? How did you transition to another project? At this point, did you want to stay at Disney?

Roger: Oh! I was so happy! I could have had a trailer instead of an office. I wouldn't have cared. I was so happy doing the work. That's also when I started working with Brenda Chapman. I was sort of her mentor. We did sequences together on *Little Mermaid*. It was great fun. We worked really well together.

Bill: And after Mermaid?

Roger: The studio at the time had at least two movies going at once. While one picture was being animated, the story on the other one was being finished. The story guys were always jumping to the next one. It was like a long

Storyboards, Roger Allers, *The Little Mermaid*, 1989 © Disney.

string of trains and the story artists are leaping from car to car. I went on to *Rescuers Down Under*, and that was kind of a hard project. Something just seemed to be wrong. Jeffrey was never happy with it. And development seemed to be moving in circles. Jeffrey would say, "Do it this way. I want to see it next week." Everybody then rushed and put it up. But then he'd come back and say, "No! Who told you to do it that way? I want it done this way." It went on like that for weeks. Unfortunately, no one was in a position to tell him what he was doing. It was a very hard project. I think the movie turned out beautifully. But the process of getting there was tough.

Bill: Were you head of story?

Roger: Nope, I think that was Ed Gombert. After that, I went on to *Beauty and the Beast* with Howard and Allen. Now I was head of story, and that was really the first time that I oversaw everything. *Beauty* had a bit of a rocky beginning too because Linda Woolverton, the writer, wasn't used to working in animation. There was a lot of misunderstanding. She would complain that we were changing her dialogue. But the process of doing animated boards entails one important principle: things change! You're looking for ways to make things visually exciting. But I remember Jeffrey had actually said, "Do her script and don't change a word."

Bill: That was Jeffrey's way. Did she involve Howard?

Roger: No, she didn't work with Howard at all.

Bill: So she does the script all by herself?

Roger: She does the script, and everybody is just expected to board it. I've run into this all over Hollywood. That's generally what some people who get into animation without any experience do. They assume you get a script and then just make a movie. In animation, it's the changing and the molding during the boarding process that makes something truly entertaining.

Roger Allers pitching storyboards to Roy Disney and Jeffery Katzenberg, © Disney.

It's where the best ideas bubble up. It's a constant sculpting process. Anyway, I think I did a good board with her script, especially on the scene where Belle goes to the castle and meets the Beast for the first time. I made a few edits, but everyone, Jeffrey included, loved that board. As a result, everyone started to introduce their own edits without too much trouble. When Linda finally took the matter to Peter Schneider, I actually had to defend the process. Peter finally said, "Linda and Roger, you guys have to work together. You have to work in the same room. This is how we are going to solve the problem." So, Linda would come into my office, which I also shared with Brenda, and we would discuss the scenes that still needed to be written. She also started accompanying me when I'd visit the story guys and review their boards. Suddenly, Linda not only saw the process, but she also felt more included than ever before. The whole dynamic changed. We were writing scenes together, laughing, and having a great time. I have to give credit to Peter. That was all because of him and his wisdom.

Bill:	**How did you run the story crew? How did you oversee them and their interaction with the directors?**
Roger:	With a whip and Iron Glove.
Bill:	**Seriously!**
Roger:	That was really toward the very end.
Bill:	**Well, were the directors telling you to go off, create, and come back to them with a story?**
Roger:	Before Linda and I were put together toward the end, I was pretty much doing things on my own, And that was the norm. We'd get pages from Linda, or story artists could also write their own sequences, then we'd board them and work with the directors along the way. When they were done, we'd gather a large group together. That was the big test. Anyone could come and comment. It was an open room. That's how I was really used to working. I'd been a story artist all that time. It was always a much more creative atmosphere if everyone felt free to say anything, as long it was constructive.
Bill:	**So in the beginning, you were handing out script pages, then meeting with individual artists, and then finishing things up as a whole?**
Roger:	Yes, yes, and yes.
Bill:	**You sound pretty happy.**
Roger:	It was a great bunch of people: Chris Sanders, Brenda Chapman, Vance Gerry, Burny Mattinson. It was a great time. Kirk Wise and Gary Trousdale had just been promoted from story. When everyone gathered in a room, whether you were a director or story guys, we felt like we came from the same trenches.

Bill: After Beauty, was it *Lion King* or *Aladdin* that came next?

Roger: Right after *Beauty and the Beast*, George Scribner and Linda Woolverton started writing what was to become *The Lion King*. At that time, it was called *King of the Jungle*. I sat in on the brainstorming sessions concerning the story line. George's ideas weren't quite in sync with the tone the studio was looking for. Since Linda and I now worked well together, I ended up helping them develop the story. And this is when I got seduced with the idea of directing. If I helped George and it worked out, the possibility of directing with him was dangled in front of me. Moreover, while I was working on *Beauty and the Beast*, people kept saying, "You should be a director." In my mind, however, directors were the first ones in and they never got to leave. When do they see their families? I wasn't sure I wanted to be a director. I liked to go home and see my family at the end of the day. But all that flattery started to work on my brain.

The Lion King, 1994. © 1994 Disney.

Bill: But you did work on Aladdin, right?

Roger: As I was working with George and Linda, the guys from *Aladdin* came and said, "Roger, we could really use your help." They had a big story crisis. Every movie has one, eventually. *Aladdin* sounded like fun, so I couldn't say no. I went off and worked on *Aladdin* for about eight months. At the end of that, I was also developing a story with Dave Stephen to pitch. It was going to be a version of *Swan Lake*. But then Peter called and said, "You're going back to work with George on *King of the Jungle*." I tried to keep working on my pitch with Dave until Jeffrey called. Basically, he explained that my *Swan Lake* idea wasn't going to happen. *King of the Jungle* was top priority, and I had to do it. So I teamed up with George and got Brenda and Chris to come along. Really, George's and my tastes and sensibilities were so different from each other, it was difficult finding a middle ground.

Bill: How did he see it?

Roger: He thought it should be an intense tale of blood and revenge. He was also really attracted to this photographic approach. All the artwork resembled photographs from *National Geographic*. Everyone had to study this documentary film about lions and hyenas, which are mortal enemies. It was all drama, nothing but teeth and claws. This was George's vision. But then I would pitch a concept that looked like *Peter Pan*. It was stylized, large, and simplified. Needless to say, I wanted to find a middle ground. But George won. We put together a presentation based on his concept. The studio, however, hated it. Now around the time of that presentation, I had put in for some vacation days. My wife and I were in Boston when I got the phone call. George was taken off the picture, and Don wanted to give me another shot at it. That's when they teamed me up with Rob Minkoff.

Bill: Did you know Rob?

Roger: Hardly. I think I had lunch with him once in the commissary. But Rob's taste and mine were way more in sync. Even our sense of humor and appreciation of music were similar. To have to start all over again, we were a good mix. The first thing we did was to have a big meeting. Brenda, Kirk, Gary, Don, Rob, and I sat in a room for a couple of days and hashed it out. We plotted out nearly every aspect of the story line. This was now the tale of someone who was going to become king. We talked about how Simba was born, his psychological state after the death of his father, and how he was going to break through these mental and spiritual barriers to take his rightful place as king. It was also during that long meeting that we decided to bring Mufasa back as a ghost, and, based on my idea, to change Rafiki from a court advisor to a crazy, spiritual monk. I got the idea from the Ben Gunn character in *Treasure Island*. "Ah! I have a treasure and I know where it is, hee hee hee!"

Bill: Were both you and Rob first-time directors?

Roger: That's right.

Bill: First-time directors on a major studio picture, that must have been a lot of pressure. The crew on that movie was gigantic.

Roger: Right.

Bill: So what was your approach? How did you divide the responsibilities?

Roger: Of course, neither of us wanted to give up anything. This was our first chance to direct! We wanted to do everything! So, for a while we actually were doing everything together. Finally, we divided the movie into sequences. Each of us had about a half. Still, when it came to story, editorial, and music, we always did that together. The animation was the only thing we did separately. Then during the dailies we reviewed each other's work and gave final approval. And this is where you had to speak up, if you felt something was wrong. Once a scene was approved, you didn't go back and make changes. That was the process.

Bill: Did you view each other's work at any time before that?

Roger: No. It was just during those dailies. It was Rob and me, usually early in the morning on a Monday. We tried to respect each other's territory. Before a scene went up for approval, we had full control over animating our sequences.

Bill: How often did you guys argue over approving a scene?

Roger: A few times. In a codirecting system it's inevitable. And sometimes you have to bite your tongue. As much as we were in sync, we were two different men, with different ideas. Learning how to let go is a tricky lesson.

Bill: How would you contrast your skills and strengths?

Roger: We're both intuitive people, so we tend not to mull things over endlessly, or overanalyze. We work in the moment and go with what feels right. I guess I'm a little more conservative. Once I have a good structure, I'm more willing to stick with it and refine it. Rob's the kind of guy who comes in the next day with an idea, something that came to him in a dream, and wants to tear down the structure you just built. Certainly those kinds of revelations can be good, but that was essentially how our styles were different. I was more likely to say, "No, wait. I think we got something really good here. Let's not throw it out just yet." Rob was more impulsive. But I suppose we balanced each other out.

Ron Diamond: Once you became director, were you able to give up control over story? Head of story was your job. Sometimes it's not so easy to give up something you really love.

Roger: Brenda became our head of story, and we had always worked well together. It was easy for me to turn the reins over to her. It was definitely challenging for her. But I think that had more to do with adjusting to Rob's style. She was used to working with me. Like I said, Rob's a passionate guy. Sometimes, especially during editing, his off-the-cuff comments could be hard to swallow. You needed to have a thick skin. Nevertheless, I was thrilled that she was overseeing story. For one thing, as a first-time director, it is overwhelming! Your day is 12 hours long. Every morning I had a schedule that spelled out what I had to do every hour. I was usually working through lunch. To have a head of story that I honestly trusted, that took a little pressure off, and it made letting go a lot easier. I also felt like she was a full partner whenever we talked about scenes. Brenda was always there when we went over script pages with the writers. It was important for her to be on the same page as Rob and me.

Bill: Was this also your first experience with voice casting?

Roger: Yes.

Bill: Did you find the process difficult?

Roger: Rob and I were very much in agreement. With George, however, and a lot of the voices were cast when I was with George, we would often have big disagreements. We were having trouble casting the hyenas, and I had taken a trip to New York for a casting session that George couldn't attend. I recorded Nathan Lane and Ernie Sabella, and they knocked me out! They were so funny. They were doing *Guys and Dolls* at the time, so they actually came in and recorded together. The way their comedy fed off each other brought tears to my eyes. I was laughing that hard. When I returned, I immediately played the tape for George. I was confidently yelling at the top of my lungs, "These guys are great! Listen to them!" But, for whatever reason, George didn't like it. The tapes got shelved. Then, when Rob and I were struggling to find Timon and Pumba, I remembered Ernie and Nathan. I dug up that recording and played it for him. It may have been Ernie and Nathan as hyenas, but we both knew that we were listening to Timon and Pumba. And it was a perfect fit for them, since they were such good friends. They would come in together and record … it was such a fun time. And I have to give credit to Robert Guillaume, who was hired to play Rafiki early on. He was brought on to do this very grave and sophisticated voice. He was the wise counsel to the king. I told Robert, "Well, he's still wise. But he's a crazy baboon now." Robert really adapted and threw himself into it. He found his way.

Bill: That's rather amazing that you didn't recast after George was taken off the project.

Roger: No recasting.

Bill: Were you and Rob handling the dialogue recording and dialogue direction together as a team?

Roger: Absolutely. The writers were usually there too, and sometimes Brenda came along. Don Hahn was always there.

Bill: How did you guys handle overseeing the design process?

Roger: We had Chris Sanders and Andy Gaskill working on designs. They would show us stuff, and we'd either approve it or send it back. But, honestly, it took us a while to get our sea legs, so to speak. As a director you need to know what you're looking for. You need to give your crew a clear path on which to play and create. I'm sure we were pretty frustrating to work with in the beginning. We had people doing things this way and that way for a long time, too long. As soon as we had that vision and could convey it to everyone, the process got better. Decisions became much easier.

Bill: How did Elton John get involved?

Roger: He got involved through Tim Rice. Tim had been instrumental in providing songs when the studio needed them in a hurry. He had written a song for *Oliver & Company*, and when Howard died he stepped in on *Aladdin*. I don't remember who approached Tim, but he was already a part of the project when I was brought on. Anyway, he was the one who suggested Elton. To me, that wasn't immediately the logical choice. I was rather into the idea of using African music and rhythms. We had gathered tapes from all kinds of contemporary African musicians. We had King Sunny Ade and Ladysmith Black Mambazo. I suggested that Tim take these tapes to Elton for reference and inspiration.

Roger Allers and Chris Sanders—Research trip for *The Lion King* © Disney. (Courtesy of Roger Allers.)

But Tim emphatically explained, "Oh no. Elton writes his songs and then you can arrange them." Fortunately, we got Hans Zimmer to do arrangements and the score. Hans had Lebo M. write all the choral work in Zulu. He's the one who brought the feel of Africa to Elton's tunes. Elton's music was great, but it didn't have anything to do with Africa. It was strange to interweave those threads. But it worked.

Bill: There is also that famous story about how Jeffrey assumed the film wasn't going to be a success. How did you deal with that?

Roger: It was rough in the beginning. I remember Jeffrey saying to us, "I don't know. I don't know what this story is. I don't know what the hook is. Now, *Pocahontas*, I know *Pocahontas*. That's clear to me. You got the girl. You got the guy. There are two worlds. It's *Romeo and Juliet*." Worse still, he actually said, "If this movie can earn 50 million, I'll bow down to both of you." He was giving us one big vote of no confidence! On the other hand, because he felt that way, I think he gave us more room to work. We were somewhat independent and devised our own solutions for key problems.

Bill: How was that opening weekend?

Roger: A little strange, actually. They sent Rob and me to Tokyo to promote the movie, which wasn't going to open there for a few months.

Bill: They sent you out of the country during the opening weekend?

Roger: Yes! And not just during the opening, but we even missed the premier in Hollywood, where they bring in all the stars.

Roger: *You weren't at the premiere of your own movie?*

Roger: No.

Bill: Wait. Wasn't there a premiere in New York?

Roger: That's right. I almost forgot, we went to that one. Maybe that was the premiere. I can't seem to recall the details.

Bill: I think that was the premiere. But that wasn't the Central Park screening, right?

Roger: No, this was at Radio City Music Hall. Anyway, we were off to Japan, which was a great trip. I was able to take my family. We got to see where we used to live and where our son was born. It was fantastic. I'm very grateful to the studio for sending my family with me. But to not be in LA on opening weekend was kind of sad.

Bill: Did you ever find out if there's a story behind that, or a tactic?

Roger: To this day, I still don't know. We were in Kyoto doing press interviews at the time. We were in this traditional hotel that didn't even have phones in the room. The staff had to bring one to you. It was a very traditional Japanese inn. We were sleeping on the floor on tatami mats. I remember getting the call from the studio at two or three in the morning. I can't even remember who was on the other end. But I could hear the popping of champagne corks in the background. I was half asleep, so I don't think I was as excited as I should have been. Rob was able to wake up a little more for it. It wasn't till the next day that it hit me. The movie was a success. It was great. "But why aren't we there?" that's what I kept asking myself. "Why are we not at the El Capitan with all the stars, feeling the energy in the street?" Again, it was kind of sad.

Bill: I remember going to the preview at the El Capitan. When Mufasa died, the theater was dead silent, except for three crying children.

Roger: Oh, no.

Bill: At that point, a lot of people were a little uneasy, I think. It was scaring the children.

Roger: Ha!

Bill: But by the end of the movie, everything had changed. In one screening I felt this metamorphosis, if I can call it that. The movie went from a perceived worry to a megahit. Come Monday morning, you're sitting on this immensely popular movie.

Roger: Yeah.

Bill: Did the studio realize this by the time you got back from Tokyo?

Roger: Yeah, it was an out-of-control hit.

Bill: What was that like, returning? Was there any kind of acknowledgment when you got back to the studio?

Roger: We actually didn't come back right away. Rob and I were in Tokyo for another six days. When we did get back, the studio had a gathering to celebrate the success of the first week. Tony Bancroft even reminded Jeffrey about his promise to bow down before us. And he did. Jeffrey was a good sport. He got down on his knees and bowed. It was a huge celebration. Everybody was thrilled.

Bill: Now it's time to choose your next project. What is the studio saying to you?

Roger: Actually, it was the first time that I could take a sizable vacation. For all the years that I had worked at Disney, which I think was eight, I had only managed to get a week off. My contract only provided two weeks off a year. I used one week at Christmas and then took a day here and there, usually to take my kids someplace for the day. I never had a real vacation, where I wasn't working. Sure, I had been traveling. But that was for the studio. And when one movie was just about wrapped up, they immediately moved on to another one. I just wanted to take an extensive break from the long hours.

Bill: Did you get a vacation?

Roger: I did. I took a nice long summer vacation. It was fantastic. At the end of the summer I was back in the studio, hunting for the next project. That's when Tom Schumacher brought up the idea of a movie set in ancient South America … ancient pre-Colombian culture. Some images utilizing Aztec, Incan, and Mayan culture were displayed for my viewing. There was this fantastic one of Machu Picchu. In fact, my wife's friend had recently traveled there and brought back great photos and stories. I was already charmed and bewitched by that city on the mountain. I was definitely interested in using this in a movie. I immediately wanted to develop a story about the Incas. One aspect of the job I love is the research. As a legitimate part of my job, I got to research and read books about the Incas. I got to look at the art and learn about the culture. It was great.

Bill: Were you developing this by yourself?

Roger: Pretty much. Charles Solomon was helping me. He was calling art exhibits and galleries to schedule visits for me. Eventually, Jeff Ranjo, who was new at the studio, was brought in to help. He helped me do sketches as I was outlining the story. And, of course, the development people at Disney were helping as well. I spent about six months developing it. The initial reception to the pitch seemed pretty good.

Bill: What happened next?

Roger: The next step was getting a writer. I was working with Matthew Jacobs for a while. But then *Lion King* the musical was getting underway, and both I and Irene Mecchi, the writer from *Lion King,* had to work with Julie Taymor. Julie needed help taking the hour-and-a-half-long movie and expanding it into two hours for the stage play. At that point, we had lived these characters for so long, we knew them like old friends. We could even do the voices off the cuff. Julie was so impressed she said, "Do you guys want to write this?" Next thing I know, Irene and I are adapting the screenplay for the stage. We wrote new scenes, edited it down, and worked with the crew. It was very exciting.

Bill: Did you have to go to New York?

Roger: I was going back and forth. I'd be in LA working on the Inca project one day. Then I'd be flying to New York and meeting with Julie the next day. Like I said, very exciting.

Bill: Writing for the stage must have been a completely different experience.

Roger: Absolutely. I had never done anything for the stage before. I'd always enjoyed theater, but never worked in it. In film you cut here, you cut there…. You shape your movie through the cutting and editing process. You don't have that kind of freedom on the stage. You can't just cut. You need set pieces and a clear sense of transition. It's a different rhythm that you're creating. You have to be able to sustain a scene on the stage just through the dynamics of the acting and interplay. You don't have the camera to move around to create a unique rhythm and energy. It's a stationary thing. Julie definitely pushed the boundaries. She came up with novel ways of creating movement and depth in such a small space. Still, it's all about the live dynamics of a scene. At the end of the day, you don't get to cut and shape that visual element. It's got to be there in the script and stage direction.

Bill: Did you stay around after to help with the staging?

Roger: No. We weren't involved in that. We watched rehearsals and made suggestions for either paring a scene down or even creating a new one. One problem area was the to big "Be Prepared" number. It was a huge production; everyone was in hyena costumes. But the next scene was going to be in the canyon, the wildebeest stampede. Well, everybody needed enough time to change costumes. We couldn't just jump from one scene to the next. Irene and I came up with another scene to cover the gap. We built this entire scene around Zazu confronting Simba after he's clearly failed in his duties. Mufasa plays with him and teases him. Then they have this moment where Mufasa is worried about Simba's rashness. But Zazu reminds him that he too was once rash. That was a great moment, to be able to play with characters that you truly knew and loved.

Bill: So you finished this version of *The Lion King*, and now you're back to pitching the Inca project. How does that get going?

Roger: Well, it's been going. We've put stuff on boards. We've got some reels. And since it took a long time to iron out *The Lion King* musical, development had progressed quite nicely. I even had Sting involved with the project. He was writing some great music. When *The Lion King* finally opened on Broadway, it was a big hit. Peter and Tom returned flushed with triumph.

Of course, they loved theater. That's their background, so they were just having a great time. Animation, however, was not Peter's first love. Anyway, when he returned and looked at the reels, he hated it. He loved the idea conceptually when I pitched it, but it wasn't working for him. From that point on, it was a long road. We got a lot of notes from Peter that said, "I hate this. Take that out." After cutting, cutting, and more cutting, we found ourselves gutting the story we had created. Finally, it reached that point where it couldn't go any further.

Bill: **How did that feel?**

Roger: It was horrible. I worked on it for four years.

Bill: **How do you handle those kinds of comments? Where do you find solutions when you're faced with a person who is not responding to your vision?**

Roger: In retrospect, maybe I could've fought more for my ideas. Maybe I should have been more combative. But that generally hasn't been my nature. I want to solve problems. I want to get the machine up and running. And sometimes I've worked too hard to please people. For better or worse, I worked under the assumption that the guys at the top truly do have the last say. Like a good soldier, I kept trying to come up with alternative ways to achieve a good balance, a compromise. Again, I could have been more resistant. But it became clear that there was no way to please Peter. After that long struggle, he came in one day and said, "I know what this movie is. It's a comedy!" It definitely had comedic elements, but I had worked so hard to create a *Lion King* type of film with a mythological and spiritual center. We have a guy who is put in someone else's place. He has to learn how to bring humanity to his role as a leader. He's the llama herder who would become the king. He's the good shepherd. I even brought the Incan gods into the story. Peter just couldn't get behind the whole thing. It was a very painful, painful trip.

Bill: **OK, he says it's a comedy. Is he also saying you're not cut out for it?**

Roger: Pretty much. He had seen a board that Chris Williams had done, which was very tongue in cheek. Chris is a brilliant story artist, and I think Peter was drawn to that. To make matters worse, the studio kept wavering. At one point they blatantly said, "We're not going to do your story." Then Tom Schumacher started to have second thoughts. But he was also on the verge of throwing out all of Sting's music. And Sting had truly written some Oscar-caliber stuff. All that was going to get trashed. In the end, they had a competition of sorts. Mark Dindal and Chris Williams had come up with their own story line, and they wanted us to present our ideas. It was awful. Basically, my entire team was torn in half, and I had to defend and salvage my story line. It was awkward. Peter went with Chris and Mark. That was it. That was the end for all my hard work.

Bill: What did you do then?

Roger: Well, it wasn't my movie anymore. I went off and licked my wounds for a while. It was very painful. But I had to find something else to do. I had to come up with a new idea. While I was doing that, I helped out on a few projects. I even helped on storyboarding for *Lilo & Stitch*. Then I heard that Roy Disney had always wanted to do a story set in Ireland. Considering that's my heritage, I found the idea very attractive. So I basically plundered an old Scottish folk song. It was about this guy who is stolen by the queen of the fairies and the woman who tries to save him. I adapted it into a feature, and Steve Anderson helped me out with the boards. I was very excited when we pitched it to Michael Eisner. But he killed it. He said, "That's really good. But does it have to be in Ireland? And that's really funny. Does he have to be a leprechaun?" As it turned out, he and Roy were in the middle of their biggest conflict. I think Michael knew this was something that Roy wanted. I got caught in the middle. So, I watched that one go down in flames too.

There were a few difficult years for me at Disney, even with the success of *The Lion King*. In this business, you have to be ready to pick yourself up and jump into something new, if you really want to survive. I'm not the only one who has had their project, their passion, killed right in front of them. There's a long line of directors who know this very well; people who have gone in with passion and heart and dedication, only to be taken off the film or to watch their story turned into something else. Those are some of the tough laws of Hollywood. *The Lion King* is a good example. George's *King of the Jungle* became my *The Lion King*. My *Kingdom of the Sun* became Mark's *Emperor's New Groove*.

Bill: I got it on Quest.

Roger: You got it on *Quest*. I guess we've all been there. Those who aren't in the business, or even those just starting out, don't really know about horror stories like that. You really need to stay committed and focused. You need to not only feel but also say, "I'd rather be trying to make movies than not making movies. I'd rather do something new than sit and cry about something that didn't happen."

Bill: Did you do anything else at Disney after that?

Roger: What did I finally manage to do before leaving Disney? Don Hahn and Roy were working on a new *Fantasia* short. They asked me to work on it. Of course, this was being done on the QT, so some executives were unaware. Talk about dysfunctional families! Don asked if I'd like to do a version of Hans Christen Anderson's *The Little Match Girl*. That was a favorite story of mine, so I jumped at it. I worked on that and boarded it with a couple of other artists.

The Little Matchgirl, 2006. © 2006 Disney.

Bill: You were a director from the start?

Roger: Yeah.

Bill: How did you find people to work on this secret project?

Roger: We used people who were waiting for their script changes, or they were in between projects, so the studio had to keep paying them. Basically, if they were experiencing a bit of downtime, we grabbed them. I also had the Paris studio at my disposal. We put it together, and I got the Emerson String Quartet to do the music. I had fun boarding that piece.

Bill: After that, you left, right?

Roger: Yeah. My contract ended and I left. I went to work at Sony.

Bill: Was that a direct transition?

Roger: Yeah. Irene and I had developed some ideas that we were pitching around. But I was soon hired over at Sony. They had lured me over by saying, "Would you like to do a Celtic tale?" I thought, "All right, here's my chance to do another version of that story." While I was developing that story at Sony, poor *Little Match Girl* was languishing at Disney because Michael Eisner had gotten wind of the project. They had to show him everything they had done, and I had to come back in. When he saw *The Little Match Girl*, he said, "It can't end like that. She dies in the end." I said, "Well, she has to die!" Michael didn't like that. He said, "It's too overt. You have to find a way to do it and not show it." The whole time I'm working at Sony, trying to develop *Tam Lin* and then later working on *Open Season*, I'm also communicating with guys back at Disney trying to revamp the ending.

Bill: Did you change the ending?

Roger: Several times. We did about three alternative endings. I hated them. When Don submitted it for Annecy, they actually accepted it. Somebody wrote back and said, "I loved it! And I love that you gave it a happy ending." That's when I knew this was all wrong. I got Don to pull it. I think he knew something was going on at Disney. He shelved it as if he knew it just needed to be hidden for a while. Sure enough, something did happen. A few months later, Michael left, and I put it back the way it was in the beginning. Three years later, it was showing at festivals.

Bill: Wow.

Roger: That little film had a long history.

Bill: That's almost unbelievable.

Roger: It won an award at Zagreb, and got nominated for an Oscar. That was a very exciting time.

Bill: You did outlast the management on that one. That was an achievement.

Roger: Yeah. I did.

Bill: Did the studio make revisions on Open Season?

Roger: Endless revisions. In fact, it wasn't going anywhere and needed help. It was stuck in preproduction and having story problems. If a movie reaches this point, usually everyone will be called in for a screening. It's a brainstorming session, a chance for fresh eyes to offer constructive criticism. Kirk Wise and I came to the screening. Based solely on the suggestions I was making, they asked me if I'd jump in and codirect with Jill Culton and Tony Stacchi. My Celtic story, *Tam Lin*, had ultimately been rejected. It was evidently too passionate. They were really looking for a comedy. The market was just driven by comedies at the time. Audiences were responding very well. They were lining up to buy tickets. Studios weren't thinking in terms of drama and romance. So I went to work on *Open Season*.

Open Season, 2006 © Sony.

Bill: Whose idea was that exactly?

Roger: Steve Moore. He's the newspaper cartoonist who does *In the Bleachers*. He submitted this idea of a bear and a wacky deer that are friends. He had a bunch of crazy, funny drawings. They had to come up with a story to fit around them.

Bill: In what way?

Roger: The entire structure of the story! When I came on, they still didn't know how to make it work. It was all over the place. The story needed emphasis in some areas and cutting back in others. The interaction between the main character and villain still needed to be worked out.

Bill: Was there any discussion pertaining to your role as the third director? Did you have any sense of your authority coming in so late?

Roger: The structure was odd. Jill had a background as a story artist at Pixar, and she was the director. Tony was the codirector, but that really meant sub-codirector. Because he had less story experience than Jill, he had to take a back seat, I think. I'm sure neither Jill nor Tony wanted me on that project. If I were in their position, I would have questioned having another director assigned to the movie. But they were very gracious about it. From my perspective, I was told that the project needed help. In reality, they needed somebody else in there fighting for the story.

Bill: When you looked at it, what was the problem?

Roger: Do you seriously want me to go through the specifics?

Bill: A general overview would be fine.

Roger: It was mainly about the relationship between the deer and the bear. The bear has untied him from the hunter's car, so it's this sense of gratitude. But he's a guy that's just never had friends. Clarifying that relationship was crucial for the story. Essentially, it's, "I'm your buddy. I'm your new best buddy." And we had to play on that as much as possible.

Bill: How do you divide a movie between three directors?

Roger: We literally divided it up into thirds.

Bill: Each takes a sequence?

Roger: Each takes a sequence. We worked individually with story artists and then came together as a group. I have to say, it takes a lot more negotiation when you've got three voices in the room. They're both super talented people, but, like

I said before, we're different people. We have different ideas and approaches. That was tough. The script was constantly being changed.

Bill: **That must have resulted in a lot of notes.**

Roger: A *lot* of notes from the producers. They really wanted to be involved with every word on every page. And they were attending the recording sessions with the actors.

Bill: **Ah, two codirectors and two producers.**

Roger: Exactly. I'd be in the room reading with an actor, and we'd get to this great place. The actor has nailed the scene. But then, in the earphones, I hear this voice from the booth saying, "Uh, Roger, could you do another version that sounds like …" Then the actor is confused because he thought he just nailed it. That's not the way I like to work. It's not very constructive. That was hard.

Bill: **You can't instill any personal vision or rely on instinct in that situation.**

Roger: That's right. And to get a good momentum going, to get that perfect synthesis between the script and the boards, it's nearly impossible. Everything is constantly going backwards to be reviewed.

Bill: **That was Sony's first picture, right? How was their studio structure? Did it work? Or was it nearly a teaching experience for you?**

Roger: It was taking them a while to get their pipeline in order, but, in terms of working with the different departments, it was working fine. Sony has fantastic departments. They were doing incredible work with effects. These guys had worked on the *Spiderman* movies. And this was my first full CG (computer-generated) movie, so it was quite a learning experience, actually. It was quite illuminating to see these crude models being slid around in a scene, as a first pass for animation. I was used to things getting sloppy and sketchy, but the sense of posing was always there from the very beginning. You could see it in the scribbles. This was different. Sometimes the posing was very rudimentary, and it was more about placement. That was really something for me to get used to. I felt like you had to work through this process of the models before you got to the real acting.

Bill: **Did you get used to it?**

Roger: I did. I never liked the early stages of it. I liked it better when it was more complete and I could actually see what the acting was trying to express. It was too hard to judge, looking only at crude poses.

Bill: Do you have a preference? Would you rather work with 2D or 3D?

Roger: I have such a long background in 2D. I just enjoyed that more. I enjoyed seeing the expressiveness of people's drawings right off the bat. That's the exciting part. The CG stuff takes longer before you actually see that. Once you get there, it's fantastic. But it's such a long road.

Bill: Was Open Season successful?

Roger: It did all right. It was successful enough that they decided to do a video. And the video sales went through the roof. So they decided to do sequels and things like that.

Bill: How did a Sony wrap-up compare with a Disney one, in terms of publicity and promotion? What were your press obligations?

Roger: There was press, but not on the same scale as Disney. Of course, I'm comparing Disney during *The Lion King* days. At that point, that studio was building hit after hit, and their publicity outfit was quite a well-oiled machine, which dealt on a global scale. Sony didn't have that much behind them. Honestly, I don't think the people at the top of Sony were ever that excited about animation.

Bill: They had to be into it? Just to be part of it, right?

Roger: I guess. Animation was so successful at the time. If you had the investors, it would seem like a good business to get into. But it wasn't coming from people saying, "I want to make animated films." It was people saying, "We want to make animated films, and we want you to do it." I never felt passion coming down from the top. They're indeed passionate about their live-action films. But that was their first animated film, and my last one for Sony.

Bill: What happened when you finished? Was there a conversation about your next project?

Roger: By that time, I had this idea for a Broadway musical in the back of my head for several years, and I was ready to take a break from the studio system. I really wanted to start working on that idea, actually start writing. So, I finished off my contract. I continued to act as a consultant for Sony, but I started writing my musical.

Bill: Wanting a break is understandable. You weren't just thrown into a 3D movie, you were also in unknown territory. That was one of those classical moments where the management really wanted control, even if that meant disregarding the creative vision and talent of the crew.

Roger: Yeah, it would've worked better if they just had a little more trust in their artists. Sometimes you just have to let them go and do it.

Bill: I wanted to ask you an important question about *Lion King*. How is that movie different, or unique, because you were brought on to direct?

Roger: I think I was instrumental in bringing out the spiritual side of the movie. The themes of finding dignity in life and the connectedness of everything were issues I pressed. Focusing on the circle of life was my idea. In fact, I said, "Oh, when Mufasa is taking Simba out to show him the kingdom, maybe there should be a song and the song can be called 'The Circle of Life.' He's going to teach Simba about how everything is connected in the animal kingdom and in nature." And that included both happiness and sorrow. They are both part of life's beauty. Those are the ideas, the underpinnings of the story, that were important to me. I think I brought that to the picture. The character Rafiki was also largely due to my design.

Bill: The crazy monkey?

Roger: Yeah, the crazy monkey. I can't claim everything. There were a lot of people working on that movie. But I had a part in that crazy sense of humor. In storytelling, I like the contrast between playing a serious moment and then breaking it with something comical, or planting something serious within the comical. There is another short film that I loved as a kid. It was called *Magical Maestro*. This magician is forcing an opera singer to do all these different kinds of musical styles, and everything turns on a dime. This eclectic quick change of styles just seemed so cool to me. My tastes are also eclectic, and I can always find humor in the juxtaposition of unrelated things. That's a large part of my style.

Bill: I always tell students that to be an artist, you really do need a life. Even in your case, it wasn't just the industry. You traveled. You lived abroad. You had other interests before you came to the business. It's not hard to see how you can bring a sense of spirituality to a story. Everything you just described was arguably the most crucial aspect of *The Lion King*.

Roger: I love artists. I love people. It's been great being out of the studio. But I really miss being in a room working with other crazy artists. I love the process. I love the energy of people working together, and I really don't care about who comes up with the idea. It's not about getting credit. All these creative minds conjuring up something beautiful, that's the payoff. And it's so much fun too! I need that fun in my working environment. It really does translate into what you see on the screen. I really believe it comes out in the final product.

Bill: Were you able to get that personal on Open Season?

Roger: A little. The buddy scene where they collapse around the campfire, I took charge of that. Boog the bear asks Elliott the dear to sing the "Teddy Bears Picnic" song to him, so that he can fall asleep. Boog pulls the string on his teddy bear and it starts playing the tune, but Elliott has never heard the song before. He starts making up lyrics, and it's really stupid. But, again, here is this serious moment that's suddenly deflated by some good old-fashioned humor. That's my trademark!

Bill: You've just finished the animated feature film The Prophet. How did you get involved in that?

Roger: [DreamWorks producer] Bonnie Arnold recommended me. When I saw that they were looking for a director for *The Prophet*, I jumped at it. The book *The Prophet* was really meaningful for me. I got it when I was in college. I had had a really intense experience one night while reading this book with a friend. We wound up sitting on the floor reading this book. The farther we went into the book, I just had this incredible experience of a shift in consciousness. I had this intense feeling just being so completely connected to everything in the world and in the universe. A very intense reaction. Someone else might have had it by listening to a gong in a Chinese temple or something. For me, this book was that. I jumped at the chance to work on it. I had no clue how one was to turn this book into a movie. It's a really an unlikely piece, but whatever. I jumped in and started researching Kahlil Gibran.

Bill: What was the state of the project when you came aboard? Was there a screenplay? Were there storyboards?

Roger: Nothing. The concept was Kahlil Gibran's *The Prophet*, various animators doing poems, and somebody's going to do a story that helps connect them. That was it. I don't know how they sold this. It's kind of a minor miracle that they even sold this idea to backers with no script and with no director.

Bill: That is unbelievable.

Roger: Yeah. It is amazing. This whole movie is filled with things like this. So many people for

The Prophet, 2015 © GKids/Participant Media.

some reason jumped onto this movie to make it in ways that totally shouldn't have happened. There's been a very interesting energy about this movie. I came up with a concept for a story and presented it to all the producers. I said, "Let me develop it and see how you feel about it." I spent a few months writing up the screenplay.

Bill: **Were you working alone at this time?**

Roger: Completely. I went off and wrote, mimicking his (Gibran's) style of speech for the characters, which, being written in the 1920s, was not very modern. Even while I was writing, I was thinking, "Is a modern audience going to be able to listen to this?" It was very much of another time, very much old-fashioned. The producers felt it needed to be more contemporary and easier for people, more entertaining.

(Producer) Salma Hayek came up with the idea of introducing a child character. One of the things she really wanted was to have this appeal to a broad audience. She was hoping for very young kids all the way to old people. That was the challenge: to make a movie that would appear to a broad audience age-wise and yet try to stay true to Gibran's intentions and the sense of philosophy. It was challenging.

Bill: **Where did you start?**

Roger: I started at the beginning. The beginning starts off in the book where this guy, who's wise and beloved, has been stuck in this place called Orphalese for something like 12 years—they don't say why—and one day he sees his ship arrive. He knows that that ship has come for him and he's going to return home. As he starts walking down the hill, he meets people and they say, "Don't leave us," or, "Before you do, speak to us of …," and then each one is a different chapter. The baker says, "Speak to us of food." It's that kind of thing. That was as much of a story as there was.

At the end of the book, he gets on the ship and sails away. That was the story. A guy has been somewhere, thinks he's going to leave because he sees a ship, he talks to a bunch of people, gets on the ship, and leaves. I was thinking, "All right. Why has he stayed here in Orphalese? Gibran had written some poems critical of the government. So I came up with this story of a guy who'd been arrested for a political poem, had all this time of contemplation up on the mountain, and we find him on the day that he's released by this sergeant who comes up from the town. Basically, the story takes place with him being escorted down to the harbor to be put on a ship to be exiled back to his home country. But then, there are some complications at the end. I won't spill all the beans.

Bill: So you finally get the script to them, and they're wildly enthused …

Roger: No, no. It was really constant rewrites, basically. The script is being adjusted the whole time you're working, because you go to storyboarding and then the script changes.

Bill: Where did you board the film?

Roger: In a couple different places. I was able to ask the Brizzi brothers to help me board this film. They're two really talented twin brothers from France who had a studio in France but sold it to Disney and came to Burbank and worked at Disney. They were hugely instrumental in creating *The Hunchback of Notre Dame*. They also did the *Firebird* sequence for *Fantasia/2000*.

I had always wanted to work together on a film because they're just such beautiful artists. Incredible. They happened to be considering coming out to LA that summer, and I asked them if they could storyboard for me. They said, "Sure." They could do three months. So they came out. They helped with design elements at that point as the story was coming together. Then we moved into boarding, and they boarded for three months. In October, they had to go back to France, but they continued boarding from there, so then we did it long distance from Paris.

Bill: So it was pretty much just you and the Brizzi brothers?

Roger: Pretty much. I wasn't doing any boarding. I was just doing a sketch here or there. But they almost single-handedly boarded this whole movie. I did have some help from Will Finn. He did a sequence. I had some help from Ralph Zondag, and also Ben Gluck did a sequence as well. Three sequences from those three, but the Brizzis did everything else.

Bill: At what point did you decide on production design? Who was doing the production design of these sequences?

Roger: The Brizzis.

Bill: They were literally boarding and designing.

Roger: They were boarding and designing. As I said, when they first started, I was still working up the story, but they started with design concepts for the main characters, for the look of the town, the setting, the house, and the island. Then as they started boarding, basically, their boards were so beautifully conceived that it was also designing the scenes in a way. They're such cinematographers in their own right in terms of visualization. Certainly, we worked closely together. It was a great collaboration. We were so much on the same wavelength. We boarded this movie so quickly—unbelievably, I think.

Bill: How did you get it up on reels? Did they send the boards to you and you had an editorial team here?

Roger: Yeah. We had a little office set up in Santa Monica. It was like a three-room place. My room had a big screen so I could have Skype meetings with them. So much of this movie was done over Skype. I had a character designer in Berlin I worked with completely over Skype. Our Danish art director was living in Berlin, so I was mostly working with him this way, although he made a few trips out and we did get to work face-to-face a little bit. Also, all the chapter directors—the poem directors … I whittled down the poems to eight poems. They were thinking more like 12 at the beginning.

Bill: When did you decide that structure? You ended up having individual sequence directors for each of the individual poems, right?

Roger: Right.

Bill: Was that a plan from the beginning when you first conceived it?

Roger: Yes. That was where this started. They were looking to find different animators, different artists around the world to do their version of chapters. The idea was to let those artists work in their own styles, finding ways of making transitions in and out of these things visually and story-wise. So I'd make suggestions to them, but more in relation to how their chapter related to the overall movie. I pretty much gave each director a free hand to do their vision, which I think was really exciting because, frankly, that's one of the interesting things about the project: there are all these different people with their different styles, different mediums, and different techniques. We have Bill Plympton doing his scribbling in colored pencil. We have Tomm Moore with his studio in Kilkenny doing their refined, elegant graphic style.

Bill: How did you cast them?

Roger: The producers had a big list of people they had compiled. I think they had approached some and others had not been approached, so I went over the list with them and selected who I thought would be really good for these different chapters and enlisted them. There were some who came later who had not been on the original list.

Bill: Did you let the individual directors redesign and re-art-direct the sequences as they wanted to?

Roger: They did not re-design. They came up with their original approaches to their poems from the beginning. And that was true of everyone even in two instances where I asked the artists to come up with a completely new approach, in those instances that was driven by story needs and clarity of the over-all structure and intent.

Bill: How did you handle sound? I assume there's dialogue and voice tracks?

Roger: *Yeah, tons of dialogue, actually.*

Bill: That was what you wrote in your script, right?

Roger: I was writing all the character dialogue.

Bill: Were you recording here in LA and supplying those tracks to your directors?

Roger: No. I don't mean to minimize this at all, but what they were dealing with was interpreting the poem. Sometimes, I would have edited down the poem if the length was too long, so I would give them an edited version of the poem. Some were done in their entirety, but others were edited down. They came up with their visuals, but basically, the soundtracks would be … In our case, we got Liam Neeson to do the voice of Mustafa, so they would get the recording of Liam Neeson narrating the poem. But in three situations, we opted to turn the poems into song. In those situations, it was not Liam singing but other people. One song—the one about children—was written by Damien Rice, an Irish musician. He sang it and gathered his musicians to support him. The other one was Glen Hansard, who wrote the music for the movie and the musical *Once*.

Bill: How long did this process go on? You were basically juggling eight directors at once?

Roger: That's right.

Bill: So they're all sending in dailies, and you're looking at stuff and you're reacting to this?

Roger: I'm writing the script. I'm supervising the storyboarding. I'm working with the chapter directors. So I'm building my piece. I was hired to do a 20-minute story just around these poems, which, as things developed, grew into about a 55-minute story. It turned into much more than I thought it was going to be. I was constructing the 55-minute framing story while the directors of the poems were doing their pieces. Those poems ranged from about three to five minutes long each. But as I said, they were pretty largely autonomous. Mostly any notes I would give would be trying to integrate it into the overall structure, if I felt like anything was going to interrupt the overall structure in any sort of way.

Bill: Was Salma Hayek just one of the producers looking at everything you were reviewing? Were you having to go through two sets of reviews? You'd review things with all of your production people, and then you'd have to turn around and you would show it to all your producers? Is that how it worked?

Roger: Basically, yeah.

Bill: Did you have a lot of changes, a lot of notes from your producers?

Roger: On everything. Nothing went through the first time through.

Bill: That had to be very tough.

Roger: It was. Working with such a short schedule is like having this giant clock ticking away in front of you, but you're being asked to redo things. It was intense.

Bill: Did directors actually complete the finished films?

Roger: Yes, they did.

Bill: So they were subcontracting companies in a way?

Roger: Yes.

Bill: You didn't have to go to India to make the movie. You just went to Bill Plympton and the different companies, and they made the movies?

Roger: Right. And they send us the digital files.

Bill: You said you wrote all this connector material. Who made that?

Roger: Starting off, they asked me how I'd like to do it, and I said I would love to do it traditionally and contracted a studio in Canada, which basically had hired people around the world to work for them because they didn't have a staff. So again, it was another far-flung operation, but this time it proved to be more than they could handle. After about six months of them being in production, they became quite behind schedule and over budget, and big red flags went up and we had to change course. The investors would not allow any new money to be put into this thing, so we had to figure out what we could do with what we had left. Basically, the decision was made to turn it into a CG animated film. That was economically probably the only way we could get this film made.

Bill: And that's when you went to Bardel in Vancouver. Wow, that is a huge left turn.

Roger: It was ghastly, because at the point where all the red flags went up, there was a question of whether we were even going to be able complete this movie. It was really stressful. I broke out completely in a full-body rash that never left me until a week after the Cannes festival was over.

Bill: So you go to Bardel, and they're working off the Brizzi storyboards?

Roger: Yeah. Bjarne Hansen is our art director, and everybody loved all of his work and the style of picture as we'd been doing it. So the technique we did was to do it CG but run it through a program called toon shading, which flattens it out, defining line work to edges, so that we could maintain the look of that flat graphic style. Basically, the style of the backgrounds was like a watercolor pen-and-ink style.

We also had a 2D crew who then worked on top of the CG work and embellished the animation and cleaned up faces and all sorts of things, to really flesh it out and bring the look up to what we were striving for. The ghastly thing was it was a huge cast of characters, because we were thinking, "Well, if it's 2D, you can design as many characters as you want!" And we did. Uwe Heidschötter, our German character designer, did beautiful design. I was determined to preserve these designs because I just loved them, but then we had to have these characters built as CG models and have them built in order to still look like the 2D graphic characters, which was a nightmare, quite honestly. We had a company in China that did the building, and then a lot of repair work had to be done at Bardel. It was such a challenging picture.

Do you know Nik Ranieri from Disney?

Bill: I do.

Roger: He came up and headed the 2D animation embellishment and cleanup of the characters, and the final product is really interesting. It's a blend of CG and 2D.

It took a couple of months just to build our cast of characters—more than that, really. Animation started in October. Pixar basically closed down. All of a sudden, there were all these animators—really great animators—available and we were able to snatch them up.

Bill: Where did you finish the film?

Roger: It was up in Vancouver. Bardel did all the animation of the framing story—everything: the color and all that. Then our sound studio was up in Vancouver as well as our DI (digital intermediate) house.

Bill: I guess I'm not putting words in your mouth if I guess that this is like no other directing experience you've had before.

Roger: No. Every movie is difficult in its own way, but this one was crazy tough. I just have to say that I was so lucky because I had so many incredibly talented people working on this thing, and it was just miraculous that we got it done, quite honestly.

Bill: Did you learn any lessons from this that you can carry forward?

Roger: I'll tell you one lesson I learned. When I first called back, responding to this job, they said, "This is going to be short schedule and small budget. There won't be any executive interference. You'll just take this thing and you'll run with it." But of course, that doesn't happen. It's never that way. But I fell for it. I'm a little bit wiser now. When you're promised autonomy, you're really going to have to be pleasing people.

Bill: Inevitable.

Roger: That's right. But then there was the music. Gabriel Yared wrote the score and did an incredible, diverse, fantastic score—very emotional, really beautiful. And I got to record Yo-Yo Ma doing two cello pieces. That was really a cherry on top, getting to record Yo-Yo Ma and then recording with Gabriel at Abbey Road Studios in London. That was a big treat.

Bill: Do you feel you have grown as a director? Has it changed your feelings or your style in any way?

Roger: The hardest thing is addressing notes, quite honestly. I think that's always actually the toughest thing in some ways for me: pleasing producers and executives and maintaining your own vision and all that at the same time and just trying to keep up with the hours and the grueling pressure of production. That's the tough part. But working with the artists, coming up with ideas, going over animation, and making it work well—is fun.

10
Chris Buck Interview

Chris Buck was not just a terrific character animator; he was a terrific animation designer. That rare combination of artistic skill, animation craft, good taste, and a flair for entertainment made him the go-to guy for many productions before he was asked to direct. When he became a director, all of those gifts enriched his projects.

To me, a hallmark of Chris's personality was revealed in the cross-country bicycle trip he took with this future wife just as his career was taking off. It wasn't just that he set business aside for an enriching personal experience. He did it in such an animator way, drawing original cartoon silhouettes around the road kill they found on the highway. Pete Docter may have had his flipbooks, but Chris had his chalk!

Chris is another of those deceptively mild-mannered, polite animators that mysteriously guide productions with remarkable strength. His style is to listen, to collaborate, and to inspire, but he is as firm as any director when he believes in a creative idea.

Having worked in studios big and small, in many areas of production, he has a better hands-on understanding of the production process than many, with the result that his productions, although often complex and demanding, flow smoothly.

We interviewed Chris at The Walt Disney Studios in Burbank.

Bill Kroyer

Bill: Let's start at the beginning. When did you first become aware of animation?

Chris: I grew up watching cartoons on TV: Hanna Barbera cartoons, *Jetsons*, *Flintstones*, Warner Brothers. My whole family watched cartoons together.

Bill: What was your favorite short?

Chris: Besides the Warner Brothers' shorts, which I absolutely loved, the one that stands out is *Bambi Meets Godzilla* (Marv Newland, 1969). I think it was in black and white. It was so different. In fact, if they're going to show it, I'm not going to give anything away. It's hilariously fantastic!

Bill: Do you recall where you saw that originally?

Chris: PBS (*The International Festival of Animation* with Jean Marsh 1977). I'm not sure what show it was, and I think they showed international shorts … Anyway, I loved it! It's just so quirky and weird. It has a great sense of humor.

Bill: When did you start thinking about making animation, or even making it your career?

Chris: I was always drawing. I loved it. But when I saw the rerelease of *Pinocchio*, probably in the mid-sixties, that's when I fell in love with animation. I was at a local theater in Kansas City. I loved the humor, the drawing, and the songs. I even loved being a little scared at times. That film just had everything for me, both the dark and the light elements. But I didn't know I wanted to do animation until high school. I had a book called *The Art of Animation* by Bob Thomas. It was basically a book promotion for *Sleeping Beauty*. I think this was during my sophomore year in high school. It also talked about plans for building an art school in Valencia, California, California Institute of the Arts. I had no idea if it even existed, but I decided to look it up. Long story short, I was eventually put in contact with Eric Larson at Disney and got an interview. I had moved to Orange County, California, and had a friend that was in charge of music at Disneyland. He was responsible for introducing me to Eric, even though he didn't know him personally. So I met Eric and showed him my portfolio. Eric was very encouraging.

Bill: **What was your portfolio?**

Chris: I had life drawings from my Saturday morning classes at Art Center in LA. I mostly went to the zoo and sketched the animals. Eric said that everything looked very promising and that I should go to CalArts. He firmly believed it was the place I needed to be. So I applied and got in. To be honest, I didn't know if I was going to stick with it. If I didn't like it after the first semester, I planned to move on.

Bill: **What did your parents think?**

Chris: My mom was always very supportive. I think my dad was fine with it. The first time he ever complimented my work was when he sat down and watched some of my videos one day. I would always bring stuff home to review, and my dad would mostly go in and out of the living room. But one day he just sat and actually watched. And then there was an article in the *LA Times* about my work on the original *Family Dog* episode for *Amazing Stories* with Brad Bird, which for some odd reason wasn't eligible for an Emmy that year. That type of recognition was pure validation in the eyes of my father. He kept saying over and over again, "You guys got robbed!" He really wasn't into animation or the arts, but this level of recognition changed things just a bit.

Bill: **When you attended CalArts, who were your classmates?**

Chris: There were a lot of really great people there. John Musker, John Lasseter, Brad Bird, and Tim Burton. Tim and I got to know each other very well. We kind of grew up together in the CalArts days. And even though the art form was starting to fade a little bit, all these guys were intent on keeping it alive. There was this pervasive enthusiasm about animation, and everyone wanted to do something great with animation. We wanted to experiment and see where we could take it. There was a unique energy and excitement at CalArts in the seventies.

Bill: When did you realize that animation was going to be your focus?

Chris: My first love was really character animation, not necessarily the layouts or even the story. I simply loved bringing the characters to life. I loved drawing them, moving them around, and getting inside them. I remember having to wait till second year to add sound and dialogue to my work. First year was all about drawing. The first time I heard one of my characters speak was pure magic. Here is this character I created, and now it suddenly had its own life! It had a voice that wasn't mine anymore. Of course I loved animation, but at that point I was hooked.

Bill: How long were you at CalArts?

Chris: I was there for two years. After my second-year film, Disney Studios invited me to their summer internship program, which was overseen by Eric Larson. Basically, you had to do a number of tests over three months. At that time, they were just starting the film *Fox and the Hound*. It was the summer of '78. Fortunately, I made it through the testing process and was hired at the end of the summer. I could've gone back to school, but I knew I was going to learn a lot more at Disney.

Bill: So you started as an in-betweener?

Chris: Yeah. A rough in-betweener. It was great. We had done a lot of in-betweening at CalArts on our own projects, so it was fairly easy. I first started rough in-betweening with Brad Bird, and then a little bit with John Musker. Brad left the studio, and I ended up working with Glen Keane, mostly on *Fox and the Hound*. At that point, I was also working on my own personal test during off hours. I was trying to become an assistant animator. That went on for a while, but I eventually got promoted while working on that film. And after that, I worked my way up to animator.

Bill: That was rather fast, right? Just a few years?

Chris: Yeah. Timing was also a key factor. The studio needed somebody to do the opening scenes of *Fox and the Hound*. And Brad and Glen were also responsible, in a way. I learned so much from them. They were such different animators, everything from their drawing to their sense of timing. I got a lot out of that.

Bill: Did you feel like you had your own style?

Chris: You definitely have to find your own style. But in the beginning, it was this tricky negotiation between emulating the Disney style and trying to find your own voice. It was hard. I could draw like Brad a little bit. And then I started to draw like Glen when I was with him. But it was hard to find your own style. I don't know. Maybe at school you have your own style, and then you start at Disney and lose it a little, because you must draw in that distinct style. Some people can do it very easily.

They can turn it on and off. That wasn't me. I had to wait till I went off on my own and did other things. Then I found my own style.

Bill: **How long did you stay with the next Disney feature, *The Black Cauldron*?**

Chris: I was on *Black Cauldron* for one whole week! Well, I was working on a lot of projects at that time. I worked on *Fun with Mr. Future*, which was a short; *Mickey's Christmas Carol*; and then a lot of experimental animation for *Roger Rabbit*. This was before Richard Williams, when Darrell Van Citters was in charge. But then Robert Zemeckis stepped in as the director and everything went into this strange transition. Certain animators were chosen to work on the movie, and the rest of us went onto *Cauldron*, where I was basically stuck doing cleanup in-betweens.

Animation drawing, Chris Buck, *Fun with Mr. Future*, 1982 © Disney.

So, I had come full circle. I did my assistant work, worked my way up from animation assistant to animator, and then all the way back down to cleanup in-betweens.

Bill: **Were they punishing you?**

Chris: Well, there was a little of that. But I came in around the middle of the picture, so everybody was already cast. Glen and a lot of the top guys weren't on that picture. I think they challenged the crew and the directors too much, so they weren't invited to participate. Anyway, I was on it for about a week, doing cleanup drawings. Honestly, the drawings weren't very good, so I technically had to draw poorly. I actually had to make in-betweens look bad! It was frustrating. Eventually, I just walked in one day and knew it was time to go. I had to leave. At first, I said, "I'll take a sabbatical. I just needed a break." But it didn't take long for me to find interesting projects. I did some commercials with Sam Cornell at FilmFair. Tim Burton was working on this live-action short, a side project called *Frankenweenie*. He asked me to do some storyboarding. So, I left the studio and immediately had two gigs. The weird thing was, the commercial Sam and I were making was a Fanta commercial with Disney characters. I was drawing Mickey, Donald, and Goofy. How's that for irony? I had to quit Disney to actually get to draw Mickey, Donald, and Goofy! Anyway, that was why I finally left. I couldn't take *Cauldron*. One week of *Cauldron* and that was it.

Bill: **Did you start work on *Little Mermaid* while you were doing these commercials?**

Chris: I did a lot of commercials over at FilmFair. And I loved working with Bob Kurtz. He used all these unique and quirky styles. It was a lot of fun. I wasn't ready to go back to the (Disney) studio full-time. But then John Musker and Ron Clements asked me to do some character designs on *Little Mermaid*. They gave me a copy of the music, and one day I went for a bike ride down at the beach.

Character sketches, Chris Buck, *The Little Mermaid*, 1989 © Disney.

After listening to the songs on my Walkman, I was just blown away. They were so good! At that moment, I knew the movie had potential. I accepted their offer, but I still wasn't ready to work full-time at the studio. Basically, I did character designs for several months and then moved on. Then John and Ron came back and asked if I would animate Ursula. Since I had worked on some early designs of that character, I was definitely interested. But Shelley, my soon-to-be wife, and I were going on this cross-country bicycle trip. That was the summer of '88, and we planned it well in advance. I asked if they could wait till September, but that just wasn't possible. So I had to pass on that, but I loved my summer off, exploring the United States on bicycle. But there is a little regret …

Character sketches, Ursula, Chris Buck, *The Little Mermaid*, 1989 © Disney.

Character sketches, Ursula, Chris Buck, *The Little Mermaid*, 1989 © Disney.

Bill: **You cycled across the U.S. Was that fun?**

Chris: Yes, it was fun. You're cycling 60 miles a day and going pretty slow, so you do have to amuse yourself. Any road kill that we came across we would chalk an outline, like a crime scene. We thought motorists might get a kick out of that. I can only imagine what people thought when they saw them. There was a little mouse at the very end of the trip. We drew this giant Mickey Mouse around it, of course!

Bill: **What happened when you got back?**

Chris: At that point, I was teaching character animation at CalArts and continuing with freelance work. Then Brad Bird's show *Family Dog* came up. It was a TV episode of *Amazing Stories*. Steven Spielberg loved the idea from the first time Brad pitched it, and Tim Burton had done the original storyboards. I had helped fill out and expand on what Tim had done. I truly enjoyed working with Brad. His enthusiasm and creativity is inspiring. He has passion for what he does.

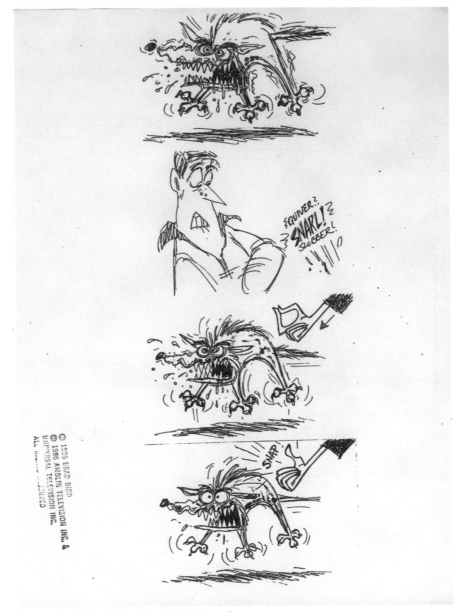

Storyboards, Chris Buck, *Family Dog,* 1993 © Universal.

Bill: So far, you've only animated. When did you start thinking about directing?

Chris: While I was animating, I was always watching and learning. Guys like Brad Bird, John Musker, Ron Clements, and Darrel Van Citters are responsible for teaching me so much. And it wasn't just about animating and drawing. Simply being in the same room allowed me to observe them as directors. I got to see and experience their different styles. But even when I had to go back and do cleanup at Disney, learning that skill makes it easier for you to direct someone responsible for that job. Only then can you get into their shoes and understand their mind-set. All my experiences were making me a better filmmaker, even if I hadn't thought about directing. That came later. After *Family Dog*, TV animation was starting to pick up again. *The Simpsons* were just starting on the Tracey Ullman Show.

Animation drawing, Chris Buck, *Family Dog*, 1993 © Universal.

That's when I worked at Hyperion Studios for a while. We were working on something called *The Backyard Gang*, which was like *Honey, I Shrunk the Kids*, but they were a bunch of insects.

Bill: Didn't a *Family Dog* series come out?

Chris: Yeah. But before that I worked at Warner Brothers, with Darrel Van Citters again. At first, I worked on reviving some of the classic characters, like Bugs and Daffy. We did one short called *Box Office Bunny*, but this was more about merchandizing and helping out the stores. That's when I was given the opportunity to work on the *Family Dog Show*. Brad wasn't involved, so it was bit of a sticky situation. But Tim Burton was involved as an executive producer and he really wanted me on board. This was the first time I thought I could try directing. But it was a tough road. I didn't know if these characters were a good fit for a TV schedule. The main character doesn't even talk!

Bill: This was your first directing job?

Chris: Yeah. *Family Dog* was my first directing gig.

Bill: Did you direct every episode?

Chris: Well, I was the overall director. I oversaw and guided everything, but the episodes themselves had individual directors. Directing that show was one tough year. It's all about this quirky family and their dog that doesn't talk. As it turned out, our head writer, also an executive producer, hated dogs and kids. So this guy despised most of the characters he was writing. It wasn't a shock that it only lasted a few episodes. Unfortunately, I think the best episodes were those that never made it on TV. Of course, those were the later episodes, after we started to figure out what we were doing. It was tough, and I even got fired in the end. I did all this stuff you're not supposed to do with the voice actors. I gave them line readings, for example. I did everything wrong. I had no training at all. I was just thrown into it. Tim was there once in a while, but not a lot. He was too busy directing his movies. It was just too much. They let me fly, and sometimes I would just fall on my ass! It was a real learning experience. Most of it was bad. But there was enough good in it that I wanted to direct again. After that, I did some work back at Hyperion. I directed *Wooly Bully*, a little short based on the song (Sam the Sham and the Pharaohs, 1965). Due to legal reasons, however, it never saw the light of day.

Bill: Is this when you went back to Disney?

Chris: Mike Gabriel asked if I would come back to the studio to animate on *Pocahontas,* so I came back. I wanted to give it another shot. I started animating the little pug dog, Percy, who had actually had lines and an actor already cast in the role. But then Jeffrey Katzenberg just happened to watch *Snow White* and noticed that none of the animals talked. He came back to the studio and removed that from the story. Once Percy lost his lines, I didn't have much to do. There just wasn't that much footage anymore. They offered me the Indian chief (Powhatan), but I didn't know if I wanted to do that. He was a pretty sober character. Then they offered me the villain's sidekick, Wiggins. Now that looked fun. I took that. But I still didn't have enough footage, so they also offered me Grandmother Willow. At first, I didn't know who or what Grandmother Willow was. I came out of the office feeling like Charlie Brown on Halloween, when he gets the rock. I got a tree! Anyway, it turned out to be a really interesting character, because she was a blend of hand-drawn and computer animation.

Bill: Who was her voice?

Chris: Linda Hunt. She was terrific.

Bill: Did you attend her recording sessions?

Chris: I did. I got to meet her too. She was great.

Bill: What happened next?

Chris: While I was finishing up *Pocahontas*, Kevin Lima was finishing up *A Goofy Movie* for the TV division and the studio wanted him to direct a feature version of *Tarzan*. But he had to have a codirector. Kevin called me, since we'd been friends for a long time. But it wasn't an easy decision. First, I thought Tarzan has been done a million times over. Second, I didn't know if I wanted to direct for Disney. I just saw all my friends go through the wringer. It's a tough, tough road. You watch your friends age about ten years in three. It's a lot to take on. I didn't know if I really wanted it. I took a break after *Pocahontas*. I went skiing up at Mammoth. In the condo there was this *Reader's Digest*, which always has these little blurbs on the bottom of the pages, sort of little proverbs or words of wisdom. One said, "People regret more of what they haven't done than what they have done." That made me think. What if *Tarzan* comes out and it's a big success? What if … Obviously I said yes.

Bill: Wait. We have *Reader's Digest* to thank for your decision?

Chris: Yeah. Thanks to *Reader's Digest*. That's why I did *Tarzan*. And I knew it would be tough. But I had to do it. I don't regret it at all. I'm thrilled I did it. I learned a lot too. This was when we added a process called deep canvas, where you could use computer backgrounds that actually move. Tarzan could really swing through the trees. Came up with sort of this "surfing through the trees" thing that really gave life and energy to Tarzan.

Bill: How did you guys divide up your duties?

Chris: At first, we stayed together through the story phase and the recording sessions. I learned a lot in the recording sessions too. That's where I didn't give actors line readings! Overall, I just learned how to work with various kinds of actors.

Animation drawing, Glenn Keane, *Tarzan*, 1999. © Burroughs and Disney. Tarzan®.

Rosie O' Donnell, for example, was great. She had a lot of jokes and punch lines, so she was in the room doing her thing, as a comedian. But we're on the other side of the glass going back and forth, trying to decide whether to scrap these lines or rewrite them. Poor Rosie is giving her all, and we keep saying, "Can you try that again?" This went on for about 15 minutes, and we just watched her performance start to go down. Then we realized what was going on. I stepped aside and let Kevin fly. Rosie was being pulled in too many directions. I just sat back and laughed as they continued. Through the glass, she could see me laughing and her performance got better. I wasn't an actor myself. I didn't grow up doing drama. I had to learn what they were going through. I had to try to get into their skin.

Bill: **What was your method of developing the picture through the story process?**

Chris: The first script wasn't exactly what we wanted. It was a little too dramatic. The writer had already been attached to the project by the time we arrived. We looked at the script and worked with the writer for a little bit, but it wasn't quite what we wanted. We were still trying to find the tone. We weren't sure if the characters were going to sing or if we were just going to use background music. Both Kevin and I did not want to see *Tarzan* out on a tree limb in the jungle singing. An "I want" song was the last thing we wanted. We had a flash-forward, about six years later, and Kevin and I are in New York on Broadway watching *Tarzan* on Broadway singing. Anyway, we were still trying to find the movie … where it fit between drama and comedy. We eventually had to bring other writers in to help. Unfortunately, we just didn't have a script that we could immediately pass around. Only parts of it were good. At that point, we also had a lot of people waiting in the wings to work. This was a big studio, and we needed to "feed the beast." The initial process was very piecemeal. Sometimes sequences had to go into animation before we had the movie up on reels, which I find really horrible.

Bill: **How did you and Kevin divide up the movie?**

Chris: We split up about halfway through production, when things got really crazy. Kevin did layout, while I did animation. Usually on Friday nights everyone would gather for approvals. Kevin and I would then review and discuss what we both had done and just kept each other in the loop. Like most codirectors, we went back and forth on stuff. That was to be expected.

Bill: **What about art direction and color?**

Chris: We didn't split that up. We felt like we had a pretty emotional story. We were concerned that if we went too cartoony, the audience wouldn't connect as much with it. *Tarzan* is more of a dramedy. It's a blend of comedy and drama.

Tarzan, 1999. © 1999 Burroughs and Disney.
Tarzan®.

Bill: **Didn't you actually go to Africa?**

Chris: Yeah, we went. It was amazing to walk through the jungle. It's all hills and vines, which have probably been growing for thousands of years. It's a dense landscape that seems to easily consume you. Being there allowed us to bring a distinct feel and tone to the movie, something we might have missed, if we didn't go. And seeing the mountain gorillas in their natural habitat was truly a unique experience.

Bill: **Is that dangerous, getting so close?**

Chris: Well, you can't look them in the eyes, because that's a threat. You also have to crouch down and pretend to eat leaves, just act like you're part of the group. The little babies didn't have any fear. They would come right up and grab your backpack or camera. It was a little scary, because they're tugging and playing with your stuff, and the silverback is just watching from a distance. One time, we accidently walked right between a silverback and his whole family. He didn't like that. He got up and started to beat his chest! And they're not the sensitive, pristine creatures that the Discovery Channel makes them out to be. The entire time you're watching them, they're making a very distinct noise. At first, I didn't know what it was. As it turns out, all of them were constantly farting! Seeing them in their natural habitat is not like going to the zoo. At the zoo, you look at them and they look back at you, kind of a sad look in their eyes. In the wild, their eyes are still bright. There's a distinct energy surrounding them. That's the *wow* moment. And we wanted to bring that quality to our characters.

Bill: **Did you do preview screenings?**

Chris: Yeah, and we thought we had a pretty good movie. The first preview was rather well received. I was scared, though. I learned on the spot that the audience was made up of teenagers. I thought they were going to kill us! But they got it. And we were sitting anonymously in the theater, right in the middle of the crowd. It was fun to watch them respond and just enjoy the movie. But I wasn't too familiar with teenage lingo, which made for interesting reading when it came to the note cards they left behind. One said, "This is the bomb!" and I actually thought that was a negative comment. Someone had to inform me that in teen slang "bomb" meant good. Anyway, it previewed well. It was definitely hitting the right buttons. The only problem with the release wasn't the movie itself, but the highly anticipated George Lucas's resumption of the *Star Wars* series, *The Phantom Menace*, which also came out that same summer.

Bill: **But in the end, *Tarzan* was pretty successful, right?**

Chris: Yeah, it was very successful, including its overseas release. I think Phil Collins also contributed to that success. People love Phil's music, and his songs became the voice of *Tarzan*. Phil's name had been brought up a few times. We were going for something similar to *Toy Story*, where the characters don't sing. This wasn't going to be like a Broadway musical. We only wanted background music and songs. Phil's stuff was just great. And, being a fantastic drummer, he added a unique beat to the whole soundtrack. It gave us a different sound from *Lion King*, which had that great African chorus. We tried to stay away from that, and Phil's drumbeats were perfect.

Bill: **After *Tarzan*, did you decide to stay at The Walt Disney Studios?**

Chris: I decided to stay. Kevin wanted to go off and do live action, but at that point I wasn't sure what I wanted to do. I honestly thought about going back to drawing, much like actors who want to act after directing a movie. I missed the animation. I missed the drawings. So Mike Gabriel and Mike Giaimo, who were directing a movie called *Sweating Bullets*, brought me in to work on the villain, this ghost cowboy. It was going to be really cool, but then the whole story changed. The directors were changed, and I got assigned another character and a cow. The studio was going through a tough period. They were also moving away from hand-drawn animation. *Sweating Bullets* became *Home on the Range*, and that was the last hand-drawn movie for a while. It created a bad atmosphere at the studio. Morale was horrible. As soon as people were done with their animation, they were let go. They had nothing to do anymore. Needless to say, notes were not that welcome, or even acknowledged. They would call you in the office and say, "I thought you were a team player."

Bill: **What was the transition to computer animation like for you?**

Chris: Initially, I just went with it. I started training on Maya. But then I soon realized that I missed directing. I really missed it. There are times on a movie where you just don't understand the decisions being made. You know it's all wrong, but you can't do anything about it. I wanted to get back in a position where I could do something. That's when an opportunity came up at Sony. They had a movie about surfing penguins that sounded great. Who doesn't like a cute penguin? And although I had never surfed, I had always loved body surfing. Besides, doing surfing research sounded fun. On top of that, it was going to be done in the style of a documentary. That had been done before in shorts, but not—I don't think—as a feature. The whole project seemed like something I could really sink my teeth into. So, I left and went over to Sony to direct *Surf's Up*.

Bill: **There was another director on it, right?**

Chris: Right, Ash Brannon, who was one of the directors on *Toy Story 2*. It was great. We did a lot of great research. Sony, however, was different. We had executives who were all over us. They would open up the oven before the cake was done. You wouldn't have a sequence done, let alone the whole movie up on reels, and they would ask, "Where is it? Can we see it? Can we see it?" They would essentially distribute comments before anything was finished. That was really frustrating. They also didn't quite understand what we were trying to do with the documentary approach. We also wanted to have all the characters, three or four, together during a recording, and that would scare the hell out of the executives. The sound guy didn't mind. He was great. There were three or four different mics and the actors would play off each other, like on a live-action set. We didn't mind if they stepped on each other's lines. That actually added to the documentary feel of the movie. We got great stuff. We had everything transcribed so we could go back through it later. It was just great working with actors like Jeff Bridges. Jeff was used to the live-action way of working, and he wanted us to send him the scripts ahead of time; his manager was rather insistent about that. We didn't even have the whole script. It was just pages. When we recorded, the execs wanted to be there. They sat in the room with the sound engineer. I learned that I wanted to be in the room with the actors. I wanted to play off of them too and feel the energy. I didn't want that wall between us. So, Jeff, Shia LeBeouf, Zoey Deschanel, and myself are in the room trying to work out this scene. After about four hours, the execs were freaking out. I'm just letting Jeff and the others play. We didn't care about staying on schedule as much as the execs did. It was a better fit for the documentary style of the movie.

Surf's Up, 2007 © Sony.

Bill: How did the audience feel about that approach?

Chris: It was interesting for the audience because they didn't expect it. A lot of people said, "This is happening in the moment." Well, that was the idea!

Bill: What about your surfing research? How did that go?

Chris: We studied the different kinds of waves. And we actually got all of our guys in the water at Zuma. There were about 50 of us! Artists gone surfing. There were instructors, of course, but Zuma isn't an easy break to learn on. It's a shore break surf, which means you don't have much time; you have to get up and immediately find your balance. It's not a long Hawaiian break that slowly pushes along. Seriously, if you're not up and working it, forget it. It was quite a sight to see 50 guys trying to get up and then wiping out! But people loved it. And everyone got a feel for being in the water and the basic power of the waves. And these were only two or three feet. This wasn't a 50-foot swell, the kind we put in our movie. But the guys did study those big breaks too, the famous waves of Pipeline, Jaws, Teahupo'o, and Mavericks up in northern California. We also had pro surfers like Kelly Slater and Rob Machado do voices in the movie. They also acted as surfing consultants. They helped ensure the surfing was as realistic as possible.

Bill: Did they get to preview the finished product?

Chris: Oh yeah, and they invited all their surfer friends, the top guys in Hawaii. I just thought they were going to either love it or hate it. Fortunately, we did our job. They quickly recognized their waves. Guys were saying, "That's Pipeline! That's Jaws!" They picked up on all the subtle details and just loved it. It was a great feeling to have these famous surfers explain that you got it right. We didn't capture the sport or the competition. We captured the feel of surfing.

Bill: Do you have a favorite scene or moment during production?

Chris: When Jeff's character, Big Z, is teaching Cody how to make a surfboard, our story artist, Ed Gombert, played off that series *American Chopper*. As a show about a father and son building motorcycles, it was perfect. And although we had a script, we also let Jeff Bridges and Shia Laboeuf ad lib and help create the scene. It was amazing to watch them work together. We put an object in front of them, something to focus on, and they just mentally transformed it into a surfboard. Suddenly, they were shaping and talking about this board. It was great. It added a unique interpretation of the scene. We did that a lot.

Bill: Couldn't you have given the executives a script that reflected that process?

Chris: They hated that too! Eventually they got on board. One day they finally said, "I get what you guys are doing." I still think they were worried about falling behind schedule. But on the other hand, that created one of the strengths of the movie. The relationship between the characters and the believability of the documentary style came from this creative freedom. And not everybody got it or liked it. I know that. People that are used to a traditional animated movie thought it was slow. There wasn't enough "bing bang boom." It was a risk. But, for me, it was worth it. We got a lot of really cool things in there.

Bill: Was this your first CG (computer-generated) film?

Chris: Yeah, that was my first time directing a CG movie.

Bill: What did you think?

Chris: In terms of story, going from hand-drawn to CG isn't any different.

Bill: What about the performances?

Chris: No, it still wasn't that different. Thinking back, I had been working with computer animation for a long time. We had computer-generated backgrounds in *Tarzan,* and even Grandmother Willow in *Pocahontas* had a computerized part of her. I was already used to it. The real difference is the time it takes to get to a colored test with hand-drawn animation. You start with rough animation and the numerous stages of clean up before it's done. In CG, you start with a very rough gray model of character that can be fully rendered right away. You get this immediate, complete view of what your character may look like.

In the end, the performance is the main thing. I was always talking about the performance with the guys. We can visually create beautiful characters, whether it's hand-drawn or in CG, but if it's not believable, if that character doesn't have life and personality, then you don't have much. So it wasn't that much different for me. I know there are people who would disagree, but I'm just more concerned with how we're breathing life into these animated figures.

Bill: How did you guys script the movie? Did you divide that up per sequence?

Chris: No, we stayed together on that. Sometimes one of us would be in editorial while the other was overseeing the animation on a sequence. So you would have to go back and look at what had been done. But we basically stuck together on the script. It was a lot of creating in the editorial room because of our recording style. After a recording session, we often interviewed the actors about what just happened. They had to adlib about everything. We didn't know if we were going to use any of it. But for a documentary-style film, this gave us a lot of creative material to work with in editing. It gave us an opportunity to seek out unexpected ways of making the audience laugh, things that went beyond the storyboards. Since we were basically creating a lot on the fly, we had to stick together. It was a miracle we finished that movie! We barely made it to the finish line! We had a release date, and it wasn't so good. We were going up against big anticipated movies: *Pirates of the Caribbean 3*, *Shrek 3*, *Ocean's 13*. We got clobbered!

Bill: Even on opening weekend?

Chris: We got decimated at the box office! I also think people thought we (*Surf's Up*) were a copy or sequel of *Happy Feet* (George Miller, 2006). It takes a movie three or four years to get to the screen, so you don't really know what other studios are doing till about a year prior to release. *Happy Feet* had already come out and hit video stores by the time of our release date. That didn't help us at the box office.

Bill: Having worked in both 2D and CG, which process, overall, do you find more difficult?

Chris: You suffer more with 2D. It's the individual frames. You really are looking at the drawings. You have more agility with CG. You can maintain the essential model while simultaneously deviating here and there. The finite details of a character's physical motion are right there from the beginning. You're not a slave to the drawings like you are with 2D.

Bill: CG is primarily motion. But you can cheat with 2D. You can create greater facial expressions.

Chris: True. You've got a lot of guys in CG that started out with hand-drawn animation. They're used to squashing and stretching their characters. And they've been pushing the shapes in CG to find that same kind of expressiveness.

Bill: How did it feel, losing momentum at the box office because of the competition?

Chris: Everyone put so much of themselves into the movie. It wasn't easy. I couldn't say anything to make them feel better. To put your heart and soul into a project only to watch it die, that's the worst thing imaginable. But when the Oscars and the Annies announced our nomination, we knew we won in the end. We didn't expect to win. We were up against *Ratatouille* (Brad Bird, Pixar) and *Persepolis* (Marjane Satrapi). We were definitely the underdog. Regardless of the box office, we knew that people noticed what we had accomplished.

Bill: So what happened after *Surf's Up*? Did you stay at Sony?

Chris: Yeah, we were working on something else at Sony with Chris Jenkins, the producer of *Surf's Up*. But that died out. Sony was also going through a management change. So, I started to put the feelers out. And that's when John Lasseter and I reconnected. I'd known John for years at CalArts, but we had never worked together. He did approach me for *Toy Story*, but I had just bought a new house, my first house. I wanted to stay put, unless he was going to buy me out of my house! Flash-forward a few years, and finally the opportunity was there. Since the merger of Walt Disney and Pixar in 2006, John was heading up Walt Disney Animation and he wanted me to try something with him. Of course, I couldn't say no. John wants directors to take ownership of what they're doing. The film has to mean something to them. If you're going to spend three to four years of your life on a movie, you better love it! You must want to come in every day and tell that story. And that's why I came back. This time it's been more of a solo thing so far. That's been great. I love working with somebody, but sometimes it's a little easier as a solo director. Whether it's a good or bad decision, in the end it's all yours.

Bill: Working and developing a project on your own, what's that process like? Where do you start?

Chris: That's a good question. Everyone's different. And I've had a different team each time. I rely on both the people around me and my gut instinct for what I think is entertaining. It has to be something I would want to work on for three to four years. Then I have to surround myself with a writer, a head of story, and a production designer that I really connect with. This entire project is your responsibility. You need to delegate, and you need guys that can do the job. I don't want to be the guy that moves someone to the side and says, "Let me do this." I did a little of that on *Tarzan*. I was actually retiming some of Glen's stuff.

Bill: And he was OK with it?

Chris: Well, he was in Paris [*laughs*]. I could retime it and send it back. He was a gentleman about it. So, I had to learn to back off and let everyone do their job. I'm the director, the guy with the big picture in mind. I have to make sure the movie is going in the direction I want it to go. Your team needs creative freedom. They should feel like they're leaving their creative mark on the project. Only then are you getting their best work. Then they're putting their heart and soul into the project. To a certain extent, they need to take ownership of the movie too. It's not just my movie. It's not just Disney's movie.

Bill: *Frozen* was based on the Hans Christian Andersen fairy tale "The Snow Queen." They've been trying to make a film of it since Walt Disney optioned the story in 1943.

Chris: I looked up the 1943 stuff in the (Disney) Archives and saw notes for a musical number. But it was never made. I also saw Marc Davis did some beautiful designs for an attraction at Disneyland in the 1970s.

Bill: So why did it succeed this time, and so spectacularly?

Chris: I always thought there was something we could do with it. I wanted to do something with a Scandinavian setting, and I knew John Lasseter and Ed Catmull wanted a musical. So we pitched it as a musical. I didn't look much at the earlier treatments, but instead went back to the original book. That inspired me. The original Snow Queen was much more evil, and in the beginning Elsa was a villain. But as we went along, the big breakthrough was making Anna her sister. The original story had two little children, Gerda and Kai. So we aged them up and made Anna out to save her sister instead of Gerda out to save her friend. Sisters who were once very close, then separated. It made the journey much richer. Audiences wanted to see them get together again. Love conquers all. But it is love of sister for sister.

When we discussed with Bobby and Kristin the song Elsa sings at the top of the mountain, it became clear that Elsa was not a villain, but misunderstood and hurting from her personal shame. So that's where the song "Let It Go" came from. Elsa became more sympathetic and the relationship stronger. When we saw how that song connected with people, with all the YouTube imitations and sing-alongs, that's when we realized we succeeded in making people feel Elsa was more than a villain.

Bill: **The music has been an integral part of this movie, more so than in previous films. Why do you think so?**

Chris: I hadn't done a full-blown musical yet. *Tarzan* had musical numbers, but we didn't have Tarzan and Jane singing the songs on camera like we do in *Frozen*. The team of Kristen Anderson-Lopez and Robert Lopez had been brought up as potential song-writers. They had just finished up the songs for the new *Winnie the Pooh* and done a terrific job. I also went to New York and saw Bobby's work in *The Book of Mormon* and *Ave Q*. As adult as the themes are, I could tell that his shows were classic musical theater at its best. And that Bobby and Kristen would be perfect for *Frozen*. Around the same time, Jennifer Lee, who was still a screenwriter on Wreck-It-Ralph, was giving fantastic notes to me on our early screenings. I sensed that we both had the same vision for the film. So when she finished up Ralph, I was lucky enough to have her jump on as *Frozen's* screenwriter. We all worked very closely together, spending two hours every morning, video-conferencing with Kristen and Bobby in New York and Jenn and I in Los Angeles. We all challenged each other, making sure that the songs were intrinsically woven into the plot.

Bill: **Jennifer Lee, who is not an animator, became your codirector.**

Chris: I was working to a level of exhaustion, and dealing with personal issues (illness of a child). So when John and Ed approached me tentatively with "What do you think about Jennifer as your codirector?" I was like, "Great! I could use the help [*laughs*]."

Peter Del Vecho, Chris Buck, Jennifer Lee © Disney.

She brought her instincts for story, and I showed her the day to day of working with the animation pipeline. Animation and color model approvals, etc.

Bill: **After over a decade of no animated musicals, *Frozen* has been one of the biggest Disney musical hits in years. People are calling it the best musical since *The Lion King*. Why do you think so?**

Chris: I don't know. I'm still processing it all. The music is terrific, and maybe it hit at a right time, with what's happening in the world. Much of the eastern seaboard was struggling with a pretty rough winter (2013–2014). Maybe we made all that snow and ice seem magical. Also, so many girls identified with Elsa. She was engaging, her story of hiding something special that made her feel like an outcast connected with a lot of people. It became a story of hope.

Frozen, 2013. © 2013 Disney.

Bill: Did you ever study cinema at school?

Chris: I don't think I was a real student of cinema when I first started. I was more into cartoons. Only as I progressed as a director did I begin to appreciate different filmmakers. Then I found myself noticing how certain shots were created. Even if I don't necessarily like a movie, I can look at it in new ways now. I can appreciate a film as art. In the beginning, I was entirely focused on finding an interesting story and interesting characters. That was it. But now I can step back and look at my weaknesses. I can see how I can make my movies better. And that comes from watching movies. That includes independent films, not just the greats like Spielberg and Scorsese. Even if I don't know who the director is, a movie can just leave me thinking, "If only I could do that!"

Bill: Do you draw much anymore?

Chris: Except for my annual Christmas card, not really. My wife still makes me draw. And sometimes when I start a movie I'll draw a bit. I did that on *Surf's Up*. But, as a director, that's not my job. I'm delegating and overseeing the animators on my team. I definitely miss it. But there just isn't enough time for that.

Bill: What advice would you give a young filmmaker?

Chris: I've always told people, especially those that have been in the studio for years and years and years, that it's ok to go some place else. It's OK to try a different studio. I think that invigorates and energizes you. It opens you up to so many different styles and ways of working. You meet people with whom you might otherwise never work. For me, it was good thing. During my first stint at Disney, I had good times and bad times. But I had to go away for while and learn other things before I could come back. And it's still good for me to move around and try different things. If I were to give a young filmmaker any advice, I would say stay flexible and keep learning. Don't just do the same thing over and over. You can become great at one thing, but you need to stay fresh.

I also tell students at CalArts that they can't just watch animation. And a lot of them are guilty of that. They need to watch live action and other forms of storytelling. For me, a pivotal moment, of all places, was at the zoo. I was there with my sketchbook. I was diligently drawing the animals until I just got bored. So I stopped. I started listening to the conversations around me, which were both fascinating and hilarious. I started writing down what people were saying. Then it hit me. I'm not just interested in drawing, but actual characters. Maybe that's when the director in me emerged. I don't know. I just knew drawing and animating weren't enough. I wanted to bring some of this humor to the screen.

11

Tim Johnson Interview

Tim Johnson.

Tim Johnson and I have known each other since 1996, when I worked with him and his team on DreamWorks' first feature film, *Antz*.

A tall midwesterner with a soft voice, Johnson is one of those rare breeds of traditional animators who early on saw the potential of computer animation. While many of his peers were intimidated by the technology, he embraced the challenge. He became one of the first hires by the Silicon Valley–based CG (computer-generated) powerhouse Pacific Data Images (PDI). Through the 1980s, he honed his skills on a number of commercial projects, including some of the first motion capture, Waldo C. Graphic for the Jim Henson TV show. In 1995, when PDI was acquired by DreamWorks to be their CG arm, Tim went on to lead their entrance into the theatrical film format. He codirected the films *Antz*, *Sinbad*, and *Over the Hedge*, and was executive producer of *How to Train Your Dragon* and Director of *Home*.

He is a man of refined tastes, a musician who plays his guitar in his office while he thinks. He is perpetually curious about those around him. You would expect someone of his skills and status to be garrulous, perpetually holding court with his opinions to all around. But on the contrary, Tim is a very good listener. And you'd think he is storing away the details of your conversation for use in some future project.

We sat down in his office at DreamWorks Glendale Studio to talk.

Tom Sito

Tom: So, you know about the nature of this book, right? I think I explained it earlier.

Tim: Yeah, your e-mail was pretty articulate. Frankly, it's really exciting just to document this strange club of people who have made animated features. I'm really flattered to be asked to join the group.

Tom: Now, we don't have to delve into every detail of your back story, but you originally started out at a computer graphics company, right? That wasn't necessarily the typical animation starting point.

Tim: Well, not really. I started with drawn animation.

Tom: Really? When?

Tim: I came out of Northwestern in '83 with a literature degree and two student films that I shopped around to the animation community in Chicago, which was very small at the time. There was, however, a huge advertising community. So I quickly found myself stuck between the two. I was animating and directing hand-drawn spots on a *Captain Crunch* commercial, for example. From about '83 to '87, I was a part of countless 30-second spots. I was even one of the very first people to work with the Alias computer animation system.

I stumbled into that because I wasn't the typical art and literature guy. Before I graduated with the literature degree, I was a physics major, so I knew a little bit about computers and programming. And in those days, programming was required, if you were interested in computer animation. It was not the artist-friendly piece of gear it is now. When a company in Chicago called Post Effects bought the very first Alias computer animation system, complete with a Ridge computer and an SGI workstation, I was the guy they hired to use it. And that was before Alias had a user interface, so you were programming everything. You made a cube and you shouted, "Hooray!"

Basically, we were all logo pilots in those days, just trying to get call letters from TV stations to animate. My love of hand-drawn animation was definitely what got me into the profession. But I quickly became excited about computer animation. In those days,

Tim Johnson, Pacific Data Images. (Courtesy of Tim Johnson.)

there was a lot of work to be done. There was this exciting challenge to see if you could take this logo-making machine and use it to tell a story. Could you use this thing to make a character come alive? And that challenge was exceedingly hard back in '86 and '87. Yet, as we know, in a few short years the creative breakthroughs began.

Tom: What was your first experience with directing? Was it on a short or a commercial?

Tim: I started with directing commercials. And it was a good place to start. Commercials are like go-carts. They only have to hold together for one ride down the hill. After that, who cares if the wheels fall off? Feature films, on the other hand, are like monstrous battle ships. They have to sail across the seas and engage in tough combat. You know, I kind of miss directing commercials. It was all chewing gum and sealing wax. And the kind of experimentation you could indulge in was fantastic. Commercials, in fact, were very much the proving ground for a lot of brand new technology and creative exploration. As a director, you had to storyboard the spot and then go back and forth with the agency about the creative content and core idea of the commercial. I was overseeing a small team, about a half a dozen people, just to pull off one spot.

Tom:	What was it like to transition from running a small crew to directing a large feature crew?
Tim:	Directing a TV spot is like being the leader of a jazz trio. You're expected to play well as you lead the trio in song. Moving from that to directing a feature film is like going from a quartet to conducting an orchestra. You are no longer expected to play any of the instruments. You might, but the odds are you can't play them nearly as well as anybody out there. Your job becomes ensuring that all the players play the same song.
Tom:	That's a good way to put it.
Tim:	One of the primary tasks that a director has is to help 300-plus artists make the same product. You're the central communicator. You really are a conductor keeping the tempo, reminding everybody of the common goal, while simultaneously being a sounding board for all the different ideas that arise. But you are no longer hands on, and it can be intensely frustrating. Although I think my wife loves that, because there are days where I come home and nothing makes me happier than doing the dishes. There is a mess, and 15 minutes later I can point to something I've accomplished.
	As a director, your job is often to help people by pointing out what they've accomplished. But you go home after a 12-hour day and don't feel like you finished anything. All artists have that motivating fire to create something, to finish something. So it can be very frustrating that you have to wait three years until the day of the big release to get a sense of satisfaction. Day-to-day gratification can be very hard to find.
Tom:	Do you ever get exhausted from making decisions? At the end of the day, when my wife says, "What do you want for dinner?" I can only mutter weakly, "I don't know."
Tim:	[*Laughs*] No kidding! After my last decision on set, whatever she puts in front of me I'll eat. I think there's a scene in Terry Gilliam's *Brazil* where the main character is trying to talk to his boss, but he can't make headway because the man is racing down a cold, sterile hallway, surrounded by people asking questions. That's what you feel like as a director. You're just the answer machine. You're there to make sure that everybody has the next piece of information they need so that they're all playing the same tune.
Tom:	So how did the idea for your current film originate?
Tim:	I'm in the middle of development right now on numerous projects. I'm the executive producer on *Home,* like I was on *How to Train Your Dragon.* We loved the original books, and in both cases, my role as producer was to help the story make the transition from book to film. It was an exciting process. But the last film I directed was *Over the Hedge,* which came out in '06. That was originally

a comic strip written by Mike Fry and drawn by T. Lewis that I just adored. It was classic: four panels, a setup, the development joke, joke.

Tom: What was the origin of Home?

Tim: In 2007, my boys were aged five and seven. At bedtime, I liked to read to them aloud. I finished one and didn't have another, so I got online and typed "Books Read Aloud—Ages 5–7," and this great review from the *New York Times* for something called *The True Meaning of Smekday* popped up. I ordered it and it arrived on a Friday. That night, I read the first two chapters to my kids. I was so intrigued that after they had gone to sleep, I stayed up and read on ahead and finished the book. I was just blown away. By 2:00 a.m., I was e-mailing everyone at DreamWorks development. "Guys! This is such an astonishing story for animation! We have to get it!" By Monday morning, we were deep into securing the rights.

Tom: And how did that original idea change as the project progressed?

Tim: We wanted to honor the spirit of the book, but make the project larger, as befits a motion picture. So where the books had Tip and Oh racing around the United States, we made them go around the world, ending up in Australia. Adam (Rex, the author) was totally behind the idea.

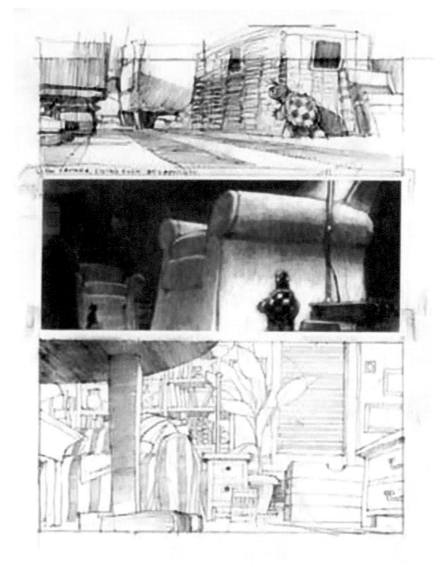

Storyboards, *Over The Hedge*, 2006 © DreamWorks Animation LLC. All Rights Reserved.

Tom: Many feature-animated films begin as a children's book. Shrek was a little six-page ...

Tim: Practically a little poem more than a book!

Tom: **So it was essentially a one-note joke. And *Over the Hedge* was a series of comic strips. How do you begin to expand such source material into a three-act, 90-minute story?**

Tim: *Shrek* is a good example. I was a part of that team, and it was actually a painful journey to go from book to film. But whenever things went astray, we just had to go back to that little book. It was the simple irony of an ogre that was proud and owned his ugliness. Every time we got lost, we just had to go back to that, no matter how many plot points we invented or how much we expanded the story to flesh it out. If you read that book, I think you'd say, "Oh yeah! That's Shrek! That's the same guy that DreamWorks brought to life on the screen."

With *Over the Hedge*, we had learned from that experience. RJ and Verne are great characters. They're Felix and Oscar. They're the odd couple (*The Odd Couple*, Neal Simon Play and film, 1965); they seem like complete opposites, and yet somehow complete each other. I knew that if we stayed true to that, then we would preserve the core of that great comic strip. And after looking at all the strips, all the stories, we decided to tell a genesis story. The comic had never explored how RJ and Verne met.

Tom: **When you're working with such identifiable material, there's always the fear that you'll stray too far away from the original source. How much input did the original comic strip artists have? Did they give you notes?**

Tim: Absolutely! There's no greater accomplishment than the original idea. And it's something I think Hollywood forgets sometimes; certainly, screenwriters are known to complain about this all the time. The person that stares at a blank piece of paper with either a drawing pen or a writing pen in hand is somebody you need to respect. I was profoundly honored that these guys were letting us play with their characters. It was like they built this beautiful sandbox and said, "Sure, it's OK if you guys come and play." It was important to me right from the start to get a conversation going with them and keep that conversation throughout the process.

So Mike and T were definitely involved. T. Lewis, who does the drawings, did lots of character drawings for us, as well as inspirational drawings for other animals and characters, many of which really influenced the characters that we brought to the screen. And Mike Fry is the guy who writes the strip. He was absolutely the core of that relationship between RJ and Verne. So we were always asking, "What would RJ or Verne do in this situation?" At DreamWorks, we would put up a screening every six to ten weeks, and we'd probably invited Mike and T to every other one to get their feedback. Even in the very beginning, when we just had the script, we'd send them pages for comments.

Tom: **On *Home*, I noticed you stayed faithful to the book's illustration style.**

Tim: We're aware that when you develop something for animation, you are taking someone's baby and taking it to a new art form. In a way, we're taking them hostage, then rebirthing them for a new medium. Adam Rex is this great illustrator who wrote the story as his first novel. He remained spiritually the voice of the story. When we adapted his characters, the Boov, our lead designer, Takao Noguchi, and I shared a passion for little Japanese vinyl character toys. It's a parting from the same old space aliens based on 1950s' sci-fi or UPA (United Productions of America)-type styles.

Tom: **And your main protagonist, Tip, was an African American girl?**

Tim: Not only African American, but Afro-Caribbean. Being an immigrant herself, her story more closely parallels the alien's journey as immigrants. It lets us honor the book. She's a great character.

Tom: **How do you handle the task of giving these characters a voice? They're comic strip characters, after all. They've never had an actual voice before. Was there a lot of trial and error?**

Tim: Yeah, there was a lot of trial and error. I had worked with Gary Shandling before on a movie

Home, © 2015 DreamWorks Animation LLC. All Rights Reserved.

called *Tusker* that we developed for a long time and then ultimately didn't make it. I think Gary's a genius. He brought something really special to the microphone. So Verne was actually cast before RJ. And then we looked around for an RJ, and we actually got Jim Carrey involved in the project. We worked with Jim for several recording sessions, but he just didn't enjoy the process. In an animation studio, the actor doesn't have the full script. They only have the scenes that we are far enough along to record, and there is no makeup, hair, sets, or other actors.

Jim is a physically spontaneous guy who wants to react and improvise. We just looked at each other after several sessions and said, "You're not really happy, are you Jim?" So, it was an amicable parting. Jeffrey Katzenberg then asked for a list of names by the following morning, and Bruce Willis was on the top of that list. We actually didn't think he would do it. But we called Bruce's people anyway and said that we had an animated film to show him.

The very next morning, he came into DreamWorks and said, "I'm curious. Show me what you got." After watching the film, Bruce just liked the character. He could see what we were trying to do. He could see the story. So, without even a job offer, he volunteered to record something, so that he could play around and experiment. Literally, the first time he got on the mic he nailed it. Karey Kirkpatrick, my codirector, and I immediately said, "There's RJ!" Looking back, I think it was pure fun for Bruce. That was 2004, and he had just ended a string of serious drama and action movies. I don't think he had been that lighthearted or comedic in a while.

Tom: **What else have you learned from actors, in terms of working with them, that's made you a better director?**

Tim: Every part of directing an animated film is cool. But one of my favorite parts is walking into a studio with an actor. So much of what we do in animation is like building a skyscraper. It's engineered. It's meticulously planned and storyboarded obsessively. Then it's obsessively edited. Animation is the ultimate anal-retentive art form, right down to the frames. So, when you walk into a studio with an actor, you're in a completely different world. It's a world of discovery and spontaneity, which doesn't really exist in the animation process, except for the preplanning and brainstorming stages. As a director, when you're on that stage with an actor, you not only need to know what you want, but also know it in a way that allows an actor to experiment and play with his or her craft.

If you go in with a voice already in your head, you're doing a great disservice to the actor in front of you. You need to be a good audience, a good listener. You have to help this actor craft the performance, so that you can ultimately learn something about your character. I learn something from every actor I work with, and I'm constantly amazed by the courage of great actors. The way they can instantly put themselves into the most vulnerable emotional place, in a cold room with a microphone and no costumes or other people to act with. One of the joys of working at DreamWorks is we get to work with insanely talented people. It's actually quite exciting to work with very famous people and realize that they're famous for a reason. Because they're really damn good!

Actors are great communicators. They compel you to listen to them, and they communicate on a level that's more than just words. Christopher Walken on *Antz*, for example, was an amazing guy to learn from. He's very articulate and meticulous about his process. He approaches the script and its text in a Stanislavski way. And he prepares more than anybody I've ever worked with.

Chris voiced the character Colonel Cutter, who in the original script was a bad ass, a real hard guy. But the thing you learn about Chris right away is that he brings a certain nobility to his characters. His characters have an instant history as soon as he reads the line; it doesn't feel like it's an isolated written moment. It's funny, as soon as we'd recorded Chris and put him in, you suddenly did not want Colonel Cutter to be a bad guy. He was too noble. He had a real vision. He had real pride. And so we changed the story. It was based on what Walken brought to it. We said, "No, this guy has to turn on his boss in the last act. He has to redeem himself and become the guy that we can hear in Chris's voice." So that's the task in front of you. Unlike live action, where you have about 60 days for your shoot, in animation you have two years. You can record and rerecord. You have to listen to these voices, because they might inspire you to adapt and craft your movie in an unexpectedly cool way.

Tom: **Isn't fun to have an open process, as opposed to a TV script that's been approved and comes with an implied "don't mess with it" label? It's like Humphrey Bogart and the Claude Rains characters in *Casablanca*, where the two men got along so well that Rains's character, Captain Renault, evolved into something entirely different from the original script. And who can imagine that iconic character now in any other shape or form?**

Tim: It's exactly that. It's that discovery process. I mean, over the two or four years it takes to make a film, on some days it's your friend, on others your enemy. You do need some flexibility. Basically, with that amount of time, there's never an excuse to make a bad animated film. You have too much time and talent in your hands. If it fails, you have no one to blame but yourself.

Tom: **Ha! Very true!**

Tim: That's the terrifying truth about it. That being said, time can also be your enemy. You need to test your film, and not in some weird Hollywood marketing way. As a creative person, you need to get your film up on its feet in story reels. Invite friends and family to see it first, and then go out in the world with it. One of the biggest reasons you need to test it is that you need to remember what was funny. You forget it was funny! You sit with storyboard artists and crack up in the brainstorming room, and then you board it and you laugh 80 percent as hard as you did before. And then you cut it into a story reel and now your laughing at about 60 percent. It doesn't mean the joke is any less funny. It's just wearing out its welcome. Seriously, you've now heard the same joke hundreds of times.

Tom: **You are also a musician. When you're making a movie, how important is music? Do you actually think about the music when you're developing an idea?**

Tim: For me, music and the art of animation are completely inseparable. My favorite, obscure Walt Disney quote is that he supposedly said, "All animators are frustrated musicians."

And I don't think there's a better truth than Walt's observation. The art of animation is surprisingly mathematical; only an animator knows how to divide 24 by every number conceivable. Twenty-four is a good number. It's divisible by 12, 8, 6, 4, 2, and 1. Whoever decided the frame rate of film did a really good job for us animators, because we can break down walk cycles and footsteps and rhythms into these frames, and that's exactly what a musician does. They're breaking sound into discrete frames, discrete notes, and elements. They're painting a picture of a whole, but concentrating on one moment. One of my favorite musicians is a guitarist named Michael Hedges. Passed away about 17 years ago, phenomenally gifted acoustic guitarist. He said that the joy of playing music is that you're in three time zones simultaneously.

You're listening to the note you just played and appreciating it as a listener. You're plucking the string and trying to execute perfectly, and you're anticipating the reach that your fingers are going to have to stretch to hit the next note. You're listening, playing, and anticipating. That's exactly what an animator does! I remember how often I would skip lunch because I was in those three time zones. I would have a character's foot falling to the ground put in, but I wouldn't have the entire fabric yet. I would have to simultaneously start anticipating the arm rising up to shoot a basketball. So I'm following through on motion I created in the past, but I'm also drawing the present moment. I'm doing and I'm thinking ahead to anticipate and set up the weight of the basketball being thrown. It's the same exact process.

Now, the problem with animation is you're working all that out in your head visually, you're in the zone, and then somebody comes in and shouts, "Lunch!" And it's all gone. You're out of the zone. Then you come back from lunch and it takes an hour and a half to get back into the zone. So many an animator has crossed their legs because they can't go to the bathroom or skipped lunch and ignored their stomachs because they're juggling those three time zones. It's exactly the same as a musician.

Tom: **Was it Dick Williams who used to call it the "flow?"**

Tim: Yeah!

Tom: He said you're in this pure state of concentration. And then you suddenly look up and the sun has gone down.

Tim: And I think only a musician can talk about that same thing, when you're playing music and it just becomes a process of channeling something through yourself. And it's really true in animation. There are times when you're so inspired by the voice or the film or just the art of the animation that the world is seen through this lovely tunnel vision. That's how we all get carpel tunnel and bad posture! And, of course, we now animate with soap on a rope; that damn mouse is giving us all problems. But that's only one part of your question about music. The other part is how much music plays a role in a feature film, and its actually mortifying how important its role is.

It's absolutely terrifying. I mean, I don't think I'm exaggerating when I say that 30 percent of the emotional impact of the experience of watching a feature film comes from the music. Music is the balm that heals awkward moments. It's the story-telling tool that tells you how to feel about a scene, to anticipate an emotion or to follow through on it. One of my favorite moments in *Over the Hedge* is a chase scene in which we have RJ and Verne with a big wagon full of stuff that they've stolen from the suburbs. During this comic chase, they ignite a backyard propane tank that rockets the wagon straight up in the air. Of course, it promptly comes crashing back down to earth.

When we did the original score for that scene, the music was big action adventure. We all watched it and kind of rubbed our chins. Then Jeffrey Katzenberg, my boss, said it best, something that Jeffrey consistently does. He said, "You haven't told the audience that it's OK to have fun. You've told the audience that somebody could die at any moment, and you've told them that with the music." So we went back to the composer, Rupert Gregson Williams, and he immediately got it. Suddenly you thought, "This is a fun ride and I get to laugh at this outrageous circumstance. They're not going to die." It's the same images and the same voices, but altering the music completely changed the feel of the scene.

You've had 300 people working for years, and then one guy comes in at the very end and changes your movie. But he did it in a good way. It's terrifying when you realize just how much as a director you need to know about music, you need to trust and communicate with your composer. Do you want the strings to indicate tension before the character walks into the dark room, or do you want them to walk into the dark room and then only after something goes wrong those strings come in and start to sizzle? That's a major narrative choice that changes the audience's experience of a scene. From moment to moment, there are thousands of these choices in every film.

Ron: At what point in your career did you realize the connection between the picture and the music? Was there an epiphany?

Tim: It's often said that novels tell the story of the inner life of a character, and films tell the story of the external life. Films are about action and movement, and novels are about thought. Except where music enters film. Music combined with the visual can tell you about the inner life of a character in ways that rival, I think, what a novel can do. So for me, my appreciation and discovery of what music can do first came as an audience member, long before I was tasked with ever making a film or a commercial. I can think of two films that profoundly did that for me. One was *Never Cry Wolf*. It's one of my favorite books, and there's a moment at the end of the film—this is a spoiler—where this man who passionately cares about these wolves has seen them scatter and go off hopefully to safety.

He then begins narrating, reflecting on these wolves and his life in the wilderness. In the background, the music by Mark Isham, who is a great composer, is a set of tones that are in a minor key. As the narration is playing and the character is staring off into the wilderness, he picks up a bassoon and plays one note. This note completes the cord to make a major cord. He basically did something you're not supposed to do in film. He interacts with the score in a very subtle way and its profoundly spiritual. You break a rule, and suddenly the music gives you this hair on your arms standing up experience, and you are now in the inner life of the character, magically transported into his mood of wistfulness and concern.

The other one is *Days of Heaven*, Terrance Malik's great movie. As a guitarist, I'm a real fan of Leo Kottke, who is a phenomenal acoustic guitarist. There's a moment where the trains pull into the plantation and all the migrant workers are getting off. There's this guitar music playing, it's beautifully indescribable. It's a marriage of music and picture with neither narration nor dialogue that transcends what anybody could write in a script. As an audience member, I learned that music could be a part of the narrative in storytelling that was way beyond what an actor's face or a writer's words or even some beautiful framing could do.

Ron: **When did you start playing guitar? Was that the first instrument you learned?**

Tim: My father was a very capable musician. He played clarinet and banjo, both from a love of jazz and jazz-inspired folk music. So I grew up in a house that always listened to Pete Seeger, Pete Fountain, and the kind of eclectic stuff that my dad was into. I inherited a clarinet and played that in marching band in grade school. Then somewhere around sixth or seventh grade, I didn't want to play clarinet anymore. And my dad very wisely said that I could, but that I would have to choose another instrument. He wouldn't let me off the hook. I didn't get to just sit around and watch TV.

I picked guitar, and it was somewhat of a profound decision. There's nothing more magical than a simple box with some strings that can play jazz, rock, pop, and classical. It's portable, relatively quiet, and the fact that your fingertips can create music is just profoundly moving to me. So I've played guitar since I was 14 or 15 years old. I play every day. I'm not a great musician, but it means a lot to me. And the kind of music I play is solo guitar stuff. It's a great release, a great creative escape for me. I often say that I make movies with 300 people, but I play guitar alone. It's the time I don't have to compromise or do anything I don't want to!

Ron: Would it be different if you had picked up an accordion?

Tim: Ha! Exactly! Play an accordion, go to jail. It's the law.

Tom: Getting back to the movie soundtrack concept, what do you think about source music? On Shrek there was a decision at an early point to use classic or golden oldies kind of rock and roll.

Tim: Look at Cameron Crow's movies. They are so beautifully scored with pop and rock music. If you use something recognizable, you get the instant benefit of all the emotions associated with that song. So I've always been jealous of how Cameron Crow, with his incredible ear for music, was able to bring in a pop song and flood his movie with a very precisely chosen, extra seasoning.

On *Over the Hedge*, we actually had Ben Folds, a great singer-songwriter and piano player. He wrote several original songs that are featured throughout the film, and that process was really exciting. Ben's task as a lyricist was to write the voice of RJ, what he was thinking, feeling, and experiencing. It added a great layer to the film. I can't imagine *Over the Hedge* without Ben's songs. They really elevate the film and invite the audience into the head of this character. As I said earlier, RJ is a scoundrel and he's hard for the audience to bond with. One of the reasons you do bond with him is that Ben's songs make him vulnerable.

But the business of music and film has changed. For a long time, the soundtrack album would be a significant source of revenue in the whole enterprise of releasing a film. The music business now, the entire way music is sold, has changed. Yes, your soundtrack can still generate revenue. But the drive to have a marketable youth appeal, in terms of the music, is very different now.

With *Over the Hedge*, Ben Folds is great and he's got a huge fan base. But you don't invite Ben Folds in because he's going to bring in an extra million moviegoers or sell a multiplatinum album. We brought Ben in because he had a wry ironic sensibility and a tunefulness that we wanted for the film. Sometimes it is a marketing consideration. You want to appeal to younger people in both the film and the soundtrack. And other times, it's just about the voice of this movie and who is the best singer-songwriter for the job.

Tim Johnson and Ben Folds, Music session, *Over the Hedge*, 2006 © DreamWorks Animation LLC. All Rights Reserved.

Tom: When you're cutting your rough reels, do you drop in a rough score before the composers come in?

Tim: Yeah, we always work with a pretty elaborate temp score. But there's a danger to that too. It's like I was saying earlier. Music is a powerful tool in storytelling. You can take music from the soundtracks of other films and create a very customized, emotionally temporary score. But you often fall in love with it too much, and it's heartbreaking to have to change it. We call it temp love. You can get temp love.

Tom: How about codirectors? Have you always worked with a collaborator or a codirector?

Tim: Yeah, on three of the films I've directed. I directed *Antz* with Eric Darnel, *Sinbad* with Patrick Gilmore, and *Over the Hedge* with Karey Kirkpatrick. In each case, the partnership was indispensable to me professionally and personally. Making a film is like a long-drawn-out battle siege. When I watched the last *Lord of the Rings* movie, I thought it was just a documentary about animated filmmaking. It's great to have a partner by your side, somebody to cross-check your own instincts and to battle and argue with over some of the creative decisions. There's nothing better than testing your ideas on someone with a strong, creative opinion. I look for that in my head of story, in my producer, and in a directing partner.

Tom: **How do you break down the duties that you share with your collaborators? Some directing teams split up sequences, while others divide their responsibilities handling different departments, like Art direction and animation.**

Tim: It's different with each partner. Eric and I divided up *Antz* into scenes. Then we'd develop those scenes with a separate team over a couple weeks before showing them to each other. With Patrick and Karey, we sort of shared the directing duties equally. It just came down to the day-to-day operation.

Sinbad Legend of the Seas, 2003 © DreamWorks Animation LLC. All Rights Reserved.

It's funny; a scene would require someone's attention before being recut and going to editorial. I would have expected more debate over such problems. But so many scenes needed attention that we were split up constantly in order to feed the beast of animation. It was always a moment-to-moment decision about who would cover this or that.

Tom: **It's easy for a director to bury yourself in editorial. You just sit there with the editor and eight hours can fly by.**

Tim: Yeah, give me a catheter and an IV and I would never leave.

That is because editorial is the hub of animation; everything flows in and out of editorial. It's where the film is made. It's a bit of a cliché, but in animation you make the film before you make the film. The reason that oxymoron works is because you're working with story panels, a temporary score, and voice recordings. Then you cut it together and explore until you find the movie.

Tom: **How closely do you work with your editor?**

Tim: There really is no bigger partner to a director than the editor. If the Academy ever realized how important animation editors were to storytelling, let alone how hard they worked, they would never give another Academy Award for editing to a live-action film.

The creative impact of editing in animation is tremendous. Editors are literally the fourth or fifth person to be hired for a film. And from the very start, an editor is often a person that's on the film as long as the director, whether that's three or four years. You work side by side with that person on both the moment-to-moment decisions and the global ones concerning how to craft a story. An editor in animation isn't stuck with what was shot. An editor in animation can turn to the director and say that we need a close-up here or a tracking shot there.

It's another relationship that can help you create a better film, help you further define and refine that film's voice. It's like I said before, there is no excuse to make a bad animated film. On every film I've made, I can point to the second it happened, the moment your film tells you what it needs rather than you shoving things down its throat. And it's just a place where your toddler suddenly gets to walk on their own and point at what they want to eat that day. Suddenly, your baby is not just something you control. It has a life of its own and has its own opinions and wishes.

Tom: **Well what about a film like _Tusker_? You created and developed this concept, but ultimately it never made it to full production.**

Tim: The path to green light is a strangely shared experience among creative types in Hollywood. The phrase itself even sounds wrong. It's like the start of a drag race. You just slam on the engine and go! Actually, that light is vaguely green, so you walk in that direction and eventually a film develops. There's enough momentum to get going. But there are so many ways that you can lose a tire. _Tusker_ was a dramatic film about a herd of elephants in Southeast Asia. We had the screening up and we were trying to find a comic tone for the movie. But we got to this place where it started to talk to us and said, "I'm a drama. Don't try to force comedy down my throat!"

We had just released *Shrek*, which had been our first certifiably huge hit. Jeffrey Katzenberg sat me down and said that the audience just voted for comedy. Like I said, we had been trying to make *Tusker* funny, but it just wasn't happening. There was so much success with this outrageous comedy that he didn't feel it was the right time to make a drama. So, *Tusker* got shelved. Now *Tusker* is out there in the world, and it may still get made. More recently, I was working on a film with Dave Reynolds, a great writer that worked on *Finding Nemo*. Dave and I worked for a year on a film we called *It Came from Earth*. It was about Martians on the planet Mars that treat the arrival of the first human astronaut as an alien invasion. We were basing it a little bit on the Norman Jewison 1966 Cold War spoof *The Russians Are Coming*. And we were a year into this thing when a European company announced *Planet 51* (Sony, 2009).

I think we were looking at a 2010 release date. But then we learned that they were getting their film financed and made for a 2009 release. Are you going to spend 100 million dollars on a movie that's going to come out second? No, you're not. And so that was insanely painful! I made the analogy already that these are your children; you're raising them from infancy, spoon feeding them, and caring for them when they are weak and might not survive to the next screening. You get to that place where they become toddlers and begin to talk to you. Then somebody comes along and says that we are not going to continue to raise that child. You literally mourn.

Going back to *Tusker*, it didn't die because it was a bad story. *Tusker* died because the zeitgeist had spoken, and Jeffrey Katzenberg made a decision that I still respect. I think it was the right one at the time. And *It Came from Earth* didn't die because it was a bad idea. In fact, it was a great idea, so good that somebody else had a real similar one and was pursuing it. That's just the way it works sometimes. And there's no one to blame, no matter how heartbreaking decisions like that can be.

Tom: **Looking back at all your films, what's your favorite part of the process?**

Tim: It's so nice that you're asking me to look at my children and pick a favorite! That being said, I think because I started as an animator, working with animators remains an incredible experience for me. I was an animator. I shared that world. And it's always amazing to witness artistic talent, especially at a place like DreamWorks. Although, sometimes I feel like Salieri to Mozart around here; I'm just not in their league.

Tom: **Really?**

Tim: As a fellow artist and fan, I just appreciate what animators bring. I think I've literally shed a tear on every motion picture when animation wraps. Your job every morning at 9:00 a.m. is to walk into a room with 45 of the most talented people in the world in animation. And every one of those 45 people is there at 9:00 a.m. to show you their work, stuff nobody else has seen. You're an audience of one for phenomenally creative work by 45 phenomenally talented artists. It's a privileged place to be. And it happens every day.

Tom: **On that note, I wanted your opinion about the importance of casting your artists.**

Richard Williams told me that sometimes what is almost as satisfying as being able to create work that goes beyond what you thought you were capable of is providing an opportunity for other artists to go beyond what they thought they were capable of.

Tim: I think that's often the source of a director's joy. Walking away from a group of artists, who are talented beyond expectation, and feeling like you helped them achieve something that is now special to them, something that made everybody better artists and truly helped your film, that's when you just know you're telling a good story. It's a great feeling when a bunch of artists not only understand and see your story, but also want to help you tell it.

Steve Hickner, who is a great director and storyboard artist and producer in animation, said something very important to me on *Antz*. He said, "Always remember, as a director, that the people that work for you will go home at the end of the day and sit down with their spouse or friend. And that person will ask them how their day was. The answer to that question is entirely dependent on the 30 seconds they spent with you." I really think that's the responsibility of a director. I've been there with my boss, those 30 seconds I get with Jeffry Katzenberg where he looks at my scene and simply says that it doesn't work and then leaves the room. And it doesn't. It's missing something. In 30 seconds my day, my week, feels ruined!

So, you have to go back and figure it out. On the other hand, if he says, "Wow! Great job!" I'm opening a bottle of wine that night. It was a good day! So, I just try to remember that these are people whose only goal every day is to knock your socks off, to make you happy, and to contribute to the film in a way that elevates it. And when you reach that moment when you have something negative to say, when you have to lay down some hard criticism, just make sure to treat that with respect. Make sure you explain why something isn't working. You need to help them find the path to success. And when you see something you like, praise the heck out of it! Let them know you recognize the accomplishment. Good moment or bad moment, share the process of creating a film.

Tom: **I've seen very good artists struggle when they get their first shot at directing. Those who find themselves inarticulate at explaining the reasons something should be done a certain way, would end up pulling rank and dismissing all further discussion with "Just do it because I said so."**

Tim: I have two rules for directing, which I break all the time; I'm only human. Never say, "Do it because I said so." And never give an actor a line reading. You're basically confessing that you don't know what you're doing. If you give an actor a line reading and say, "Say it like this," then why did you hire the actor? Really, are you that good of an actor? Same thing with an animator, if you tell him to move an arm like this and then two frames later snap it down … really? You're that good of an animator? I was good in my day, but I'm not in the same league as these people.

What you want to say is, "I don't feel the aggression of what they're experiencing. I don't feel their frustration. I think you could be more forceful with what the character is doing." That allows an animator to focus his creative instincts in a better direction. It allows the artist and the film to develop in a good way.

Tom: **With the codirector system, do you ever run into the situation of artists trying to play you against your partner?**

Tim: I have. And that's a pretty easy thing to shut down. The way you shut it down is say, "Don't try to play me against my partner!"

Of course, try to be respectful about it. But you have to directly call them on it. Whether it's Karey or Eric, we may have a difference of opinion, but I'm the guy they need to please at that moment. So we need to address the issue and move on. Animators are just like the rest of us. They've got a deadline and they'd like to get home for dinner. They're going to do what it takes to get their shot finalized.

Tom: What's your least favorite part of the process?

Tim: Well, there comes a time in every animated film where it has to become the phoenix. It has to burn itself down to cinders and emerge from the ashes. It's sort of a cliché to say that. But it has to happen. Essentially you build the tower too high and it begins to sway and topples. Then you look at the mistakes and learn from them. You rebuild it better the second time. Is there any better way to do it? Nope. Do I anticipate that happening and, in a weird way, look forward to it? Yep. Is it fun? Oh no, it's not fun.

That's a sleepless two weeks where you had a screening and it just didn't work. All the good intentions were up there. A couple of scenes were really funny. People liked that character. But in terms of making an emotionally compelling truth happen, it didn't work. And so you gather your best people around you and figure it out. And this is where directors often make a big mistake. They go hide in this hole that their ego and misplaced confidence built. You have to recognize that you don't have all the answers at your fingertips. But you can look and see what's good and locate exactly where the film is falling apart. Then you rebuild and make it stronger.

Tom: **You finish a movie, and now you have three or four years of experience. As you get ready for your next project you tell yourself you're not going to make those same mistakes again.**

Tim: Right. You say that to yourself. Then you make those same mistakes all over again.

What's fascinating to me about storytelling is how right Joseph Campbell was in the *Hero's Journey*. Stories do share a huge amount of DNA, the way human and fruit fly DNA is like 80 percent the same. There are just more similarities than differences. So you'd think it would be really easy to take these familiar building blocks and put it together. But if you do too much by the book, there's a problem. How do you give an audience what they expect in an unexpected way? And that's so frustratingly hard. As an audience, you want the hero to triumph. You want the guy and the girl to fall in love. So you don't want to be surprised when they don't. That's not what you paid your ten bucks for. But you do want to be surprised by how they get there.

It does get easier with each film. You do build upon your experience. You do end up trusting your instincts. But when you hit those inevitable problems, you will beat yourself up. After your third film, why are you experiencing this freshman error? The truth is, 150 films come out every year. If this was easy to do, all of them would be riveting, memorable, and just great. But they're not. So, in spite of the fact that we have 10,000 creative professionals all over Hollywood, who have worked on some great films, it is still possible to throw a bunch of these guys together and make a bad film.

Tom: **Do you feel that your style has evolved since your first time directing?**

Tim: Evolving, I think, is a weird combination of learning to trust those instincts that drew you to your first projects, which means digging deeper into why those first projects were interesting to you, and the natural artistic and personal growth that makes you want to reach for new things. I've learned that the stories that have a social satire woven into them, a fundamental irony, are the ones that get my blood going. They're the ones where I know I'll be creatively able to dig deeper faster. And so I'm not going to do the outrageous physical comedy. That's just not the film that I'm going to bring something special too. But if the film has a smart contemporary and ironic sensibility, that's what makes me laugh.

Over the Hedge was a really great experience for me. It was an irreverent take on consumer culture and the expanding world of avaricious humans into this innocent world of animals. And that juxtaposition of animals getting addicted to soda and things like that was really a look at our own culture. I really had a good time on that. This will sound a little preachy, but if you're making a film for a large family audience, much like any piece of art, something that's going to potentially have a global release, you're actually fashioning culture. There's a responsibility that comes with that. I don't mean you have to be preachy and dogmatic with some problematic lesson. But with a family audience, you have an opportunity to talk about something that matters to you.

So in *Antz*, at what point do the conformist rules deserve and need to be broken? At what point do you have to stand up for yourself? That's a very fundamental and often scary question that everybody faces, especially people in their teens. I was very proud that *Antz* played to an older and more sophisticated audience than other animated films did at the time. And *Over the Hedge* brought an irreverent tone to just typical suburban living. It was fun to poke a few sharp needles into some basic things we take for granted. On the other hand, I struggled with *Sinbad*. It's a film I'm incredibly proud of, especially since it's a 2D movie and the last gasp of big-budget 2D movies from DreamWorks. Making it was a joy. But it was a dramatic action adventure, and honestly, that's not where my instincts, sense of humor, and strengths are. *Sinbad* was a personal struggle for me.

Tom: What first inspired you to get into illustration and animation? I'm talking about that time before college. What made you realize that this is what you wanted to do?

Tim: For the longest time, my ambition was to be a cartoonist

Antz, 1998 © DreamWorks Animation LLC. All Rights Reserved.

and to have a cartoon strip. And my father had a hand in sending me down this path. At night, he would read us Walt Kelly's *Pogo* from these beautifully worn anthologies, which I still have. As he read aloud, he would perform all the voices, but eventually we would take on the roles of certain characters. I would always be the porcupine and my sister would be *Pogo*. I just thought it was amazing that with a few drawings and a few words you can create humor and emotion in the physically tiniest of spaces.

A four-panel script is a great lesson in what's at stake in the scenic nature of filmmaking. The great strips usually have a punch line on the third panel, and then a comment on the punch line that's often funnier on the fourth. It's a creatively narrow target.

I was very motivated by the storytelling that accompanies the art of drawing. So I learned to draw by tracing comics. I would trace *Charlie Brown* and *Pogo*. To this day, if I'm giving a young person an art gift, I give them a pad of tracing paper. But I think that was more prominent when I was younger. I can't tell you how many times I've given a pad of tracing paper to a kid these days that just looks at me oddly, because you can see straight through it. But I learned to draw tracing those comics, and I even did a

Sketches. (Courtesy of Tim Johnson.)

comic strip at the *Daily Northwestern*. When I left college, I had these two animated films because I found animation was a way to make my comic strip come alive.

Tom: **Back then, before the Internet and self-publishing, it was very difficult to get a comic strip syndicated. It was easier to become a movie star.**

Tim: Absolutely! It's easier to win the lottery. I flailed at it for a little bit. But I had some illustration gigs while I was trying to get a comic strip going. And I loved animation. I wanted to learn more about it. But in the beginning, it was more about paying the bills until that comic strip took off. After a short few months of animation, actually getting paid for a living to animate, I just never wanted to go back to the comic strip.

It was that extra layer of performance, discovery, and narrative that hooked me.

Ron: **And what about your stories? If you were to look back on your career 20 years from now, how would you define your contribution?**

Tim: I take a great deal of pride in being a filmmaker for families. I think that we've reached a place for real family storytelling. And when I say family, I mean mom and dad laugh, the teenager laughs, and the five-year-old laughs. Then Mom

Sketches. (Courtesy of Tim Johnson.)

and dad tear up, the teenager tears up, and the five-year-old is moved. I mean family movies. Seriously, they are a dying breed. I think one of the reasons that animation at DreamWorks, Pixar, Blue Sky, and at any number of these studios has been so successful at the box office is it's the last bastion of family movies, where the whole family can go and nobody feels any condescending tone. And if I could wish anything for my career, for what I have done and what I hope to do in the future, is that I want families to laugh a little, cry a little, and have something to talk about on the way home. That's the goal when I make a movie.

I get very much on the soapbox about it. It's a chance to make culture and communicate to families and provide a family with a shared experience that can be something that they quote to each other in weeks and years to come. I remember growing up and the community experience of sharing a movie with my family was really profound. I remember watching *What's Up Doc* with my mom and dad, which I just shared recently with my kids and holds up beautifully. I remember how fun it was to laugh out loud with my dad. I got the joke! I was a big kid!

Tom: **One thing animation has done better than a lot of live action over the last two decades is musicals. It's true we reached a point of saturation in the late nineties, but being a musician, do you see yourself making a type of musical film?**

Tim: I'm actually very interested in doing musicals. And in some ways, *Over the Hedge* had a little bit of a musical in it. There were songs written by Ben Folds that helped tell our story. And though a character didn't open up and sing on-screen, it was RJ's voice in the opening credits as he walks away under the threat that this bear is going to pursue him.

Those songs are a big part of the storytelling. I'm developing three different films now; one of them is a musical. The trick, I think, to keeping a musical fresh is to make sure that it doesn't feel retro or old fashioned. *Happy Feet* is a great example. They said penguins sing because of an actual story point. They have a heart song. I think that it's hard to do what *Princess and the Frog* did. And if we're honest about *Princess and the Frog*, we can see it struggled because it was perceived as being a little bit old fashioned in that people sang the "I want" song.

Tom: **It was a bit of a throwback.**

Tim: It's a throwback. Now I'm a huge music fan. We make a pilgrimage to New York a couple times a year to try to catch up on some Broadway musicals, and we are at the Ahmanson for the full series. I just think musicals are an elevated way to tell stories. But I think film audiences consistently, now more than ever, are paying their dollars to have an experience that can't be duplicated anywhere else. They are paying their dollars for 3D now, which can't be duplicated anywhere else. And in general, whether it's *Avatar* or *How to Train Your Dragon*, one of the things you're buying at the door of a theater is a door to another fantastic universe.

For better or worse, I think some people would argue that it's the death of the small film. Audiences are looking to the movie theater to amaze them visually as much as move them emotionally. So for a musical, it must have that newness about it, something that feels relevant and appropriate to the story. And it's frustrating as a fan of musicals. *Nine* came out as live action and struggled creatively and at the box office. I think it's a genre that people would embrace and would thrive as soon as we come up with those creative new ways to make it feel fresh and relevant.

Tom: **What was the most insanely bizarre or absurd moment you had in the world of directing?**

Tim: Oh gosh. That is a fun one. I've had a lot of them. Most of them happen when you're trying to help an actor or an animator perform. We have this beautiful campus here at DreamWorks. It's extraordinary landscaping, and there's a river that flows through the building. It's like a park. It's like an amazing campus. I can't count how many times an animator was hunched over in animation posture, fidgeting with the soap on a rope and the keyboard. They are trying to animate something, but it's not working. So I'd say, "Do a lap! Do a lap!"

We actually did a lap. We ran around the campus once. Everyone's blood got pumping again, and we all had a good laugh at how absurd it was. And it worked. They just acted it out and got their forward momentum back. There was also a scene in *Antz* that was eventually cut where Sharon Stone's character, Princess Bala, was supposed to sing a song. Sharon blatantly said that she couldn't sing. I tried to tell her that that was the essential comedy of the scene. She tried to do it, but choked on every take. So I went in and we both tunelessly belted out something that resembled a song! It was a great little directing moment for me, because I had to completely make a fool of myself in order to give her the courage to complete the task. Sure, the scene was eventually cut, but we got the job done, together!

Tom: **Do you ever choose an actor for their voice and immediately they want to "do" a voice? They think you want a cartoon falsetto, like Pinto Colvig, who created the voice of Disney's Goofy.**

Tim: Very seldom have I let an actor do a voice. Steve Carell doing Hammy was about the only guy that I ever let do a voice. For everybody else, I've said, "No, we want you to be you." That's surprisingly hard for some of them, because they looked forward to playing around and being vocally creative on the mic. Taking on a lead role in animated film is a revelation for most actors. We'll often record somebody over 16 or 20 sessions. The first session can last three to four hours based on how hard an actor wants to work that day. And those three to four hours are hard work. When an actor goes to a live-action set, they'll do two or three pages of dialogue that day. Most of the time, they'll be sitting in a chair waiting for costume and makeup and the lights and camera to be set up. Then they'll do a line and that'll be it for the day.

When they come in for an animated film, they're going to do 35 pages. There are going to do scenes where they're being chased, where they're pleading for their life, and when they need to cry. They have to run an emotional obstacle course. Even for me at the end of the day, I'm exhausted. I have to take a nap after those hard sessions. Gene Hackman at the end of *Antz* said, "This is what I thought acting was going to be like when I started. I didn't think acting was sitting in my trailer waiting for lights. I thought it was going to be play, experimentation, improv, going from scene to scene to scene, and really embracing this character and owning it." He had a great time. It was fun. And no matter how hard that experience can be, actors usually love it. After all, the animation process ironically gives them a chance to really challenge themselves as actors.

Tom: **Do you ever use actors that formerly did stand-up? When I worked with Chris Rock, he mentioned how those with stand-up experience have an easier time jumping into this process. He said that they're just used to standing in front of an audience for three hours talking.**

Tim: Comic actors that have stand-up and improv experience are gold. They just know how to do it right away. When you tell Steve Carell, Gary Shandling, or Wanda Sykes to just play and improv, their talent and experience just kick in. Steve Martin was a terrific on *Home*. It's natural to their skill set and creative energy. Those that are used to the camera and the close-up, they often struggle at first with the cold sterility of an animation recording booth.

Ron: **Have you ever brought multiple actors into the studio and just let them bounce off one another?**

Tim: Sometimes. One thing I do like, which doesn't happen enough, is a table read, where you bring in actors and you read through a script start to finish. You can learn a ton from that. Actually, I've tended to not bring actors into the studio to work together very often, mostly because it frankly doesn't work. That's always surprising to people, I know. But on a live-action set, you have something called rehearsal. If you've got Gary Shandling and Bruce Willis, they'll rehearse and figure out their rhythm, how they work together, before the weeks of shooting begin. In animation, you're going to record these guys every eight weeks for two hours. You don't have two hours to give them to figure out that rhythm. Worse still, if you do, they're more likely to now respond to each other rather than listen to you, the director. It's just easier to work one on one. You have iterative chances to record an actor. So even if Gary does something cool and unexpected, something that no longer works with Bruce's recording, you can go back and let Bruce play and respond. In many ways, this allows you to ultimately control what you need from these performances and how they reflect the physicality of the scene.

Ron: How much of the footage or imagery do you feel is important to share with the actors?

Tim: It's a case-by-case basis. Some of the actors absolutely love it, and their energy level soars when you show them production art. Some ask for it; they need to see the physical space of the scene. Chris Walken, though, was different. He said that he just wanted the lights off and a little reading light. Literally, Chris wearing all black would be in this pitch-black recording room with a tiny dim reading light, and we would turn off all the lights in the engineering booth so that it was just an empty world that Chris could perform in. In fact, some of his performances were so intense that you couldn't use them. They were too powerful and terrifying. He's the guy who just goes to his internal tools to make it happen. Others need the lights, costumes, and any input you can give them to perform.

Tom: I've had some actors like that, who actually don't want to look at anything.

Tim: I love working with actors because every one of them has their own individual process. Part of the fun of animation is that you can accommodate it, whatever that is. If they want a body in the room to act at, we'll put someone in there. And sometimes you need to take the experience you gain from seeing all these individual processes and help an actor along. Gary Shandling's character had a real dark and lonely scene, and Gary was having a rough time nailing it. Finally, I decided to try the Walken route. I turned off all the lights and gave him just a tiny reading light. He nailed it instantly. He needed dramatic space, and that was how we found it for him. As a director, being able to help another creative person achieve success is just a great feeling. That's a good day. You go home and you feel like you did something.

Tom: A question about short films. Take a minute and tell us about a short film that just stands out in your mind, something that people should see.

Tim: Cool! Well, I'm a huge fan of short films and animation. I think it's where we discover new talent and new techniques. The unique way animation can tell a story is often best celebrated in shorts. And I'd have to say one of my favorite animated shorts is *Monk and the Fish* (Michael Dudok deWit, 1994). When I first saw it, I was so taken with the animation, the sort of joyous, energetic, and sharp movements. I sat there with a smile on my face the whole time, and I raced back to see it again. I think that was at the Ottawa Animation Festival.

Actually, the second time I was moved to tears. It was like I was seeing a totally different movie. The first time was joyous, but the second time was profoundly moving. This was about a monk chasing a fish that he was never going to catch. If there is a better metaphor for life as an artist than the pursuit of the unattainable, I haven't seen it.

Ron: Do you have a mentor, or maybe just somebody you look to for inspiration?

Tim: My mentors come from music as much as narrative and film. I talked already about two guitarists that are profoundly influential. Michael Hedges is this guitarist that talked about being in three time zones at once as an artist. Listening to the note you've played, playing and executing the note perfectly, anticipating where you're going to go; I find that really profound. I think that's a very interesting way to approach the artistic process. Leo Kottoke's music also inspires me. I've always been somebody who is more the jack-of-all-trades type. I'm always jealous and fascinated by people who are unbelievably gifted at one thing. I think I'm too ADD for that. But my heroes are that way.

In terms of a filmmaking mentor, this will sound like brown nosing but its utterly true: Jeffrey Katzenberg. He's my boss, but very much my mentor. He taught me all about the craft and tool set that is unique to animation. He really took me under his wing and guided me. He was constantly telling me to try different things. And when he thought a certain technique really worked for me, he told me. Better yet, he explained how editorial could be my best friend, that I didn't have to fight it. Step-by-step through *Antz*, this incredibly busy guy, who was starting DreamWorks animation, was a partner not in terms of telling me what to do creatively, but providing me with the tools that now are the bedrock that I stand on every day. He openly shared with me the knowledge he acquired over his entire career, especially how all those great films during his tenure at Disney were made. He's a real inspiration.

Tom: All right, say you went down to the cafeteria and there was another person who had just been promoted to director for the first time. He or she is sitting with a cup of coffee, stunned at what just happened and unsure of what to do. What would you tell this person?

Tim: I would first of all tell him or her to trust the process. It's almost like a religious faith. Trust the process! As a first-time director, the hardest thing to know is when you really should panic and when you really don't have to panic. It all comes at you at the same time, so it's hard to distinguish between the two. But the process, the fact that these things do take four years to make, means that at any given time you only have to spin two of those plates really fast. Others can wobble and it's OK, because six months from now they'll be the priority and you'll get them up to speed.

Trust the process. The other thing I'd mention is the usual mistake freshman directors make. Don't try to do it all yourself. As a director, you feel like you're supposed to have all the answers. Well, you have to have direction, and direction is not the same thing as answers. It's OK to say, "I know on the horizon where I want us to be, because I know my film and I know my characters. But I don't know the next step to get to that horizon. I don't know how to fix this scene to get there. Help me."

You don't have to have all the answers. You really need to have the questions as a director. And it's very hard as a freshman director to have the security to not have the answers all the time.

Tom: **On my first few films, I would wind up redoing scenes myself. Then at eight o'clock at night I'm thinking, "Wait a minute, I have animators! Why am I killing myself?"**

Tim: I don't know who said it first, but I think it was a filmmaker. Basically, hire people better than you and let them do their job! It's really true. Trusting the process means getting those creative people in a room and let them go. One of the most damaging things a director can do is to stop a brainstorming session when it feels like it's going off track. I swear, you only find out what you really need by going way off the path. Only then do you have the distance to look back and make those key choices. Ben Folds said something that was a genuine epiphany in the moment. We were struggling with a song and someone on the team told Ben that there was just something wrong with the sound. Ben said, "No. That song has exactly the right amount of wrong in it."

I thought there's no better description for what we're looking for as artists. We're all looking for exactly the right amount of wrong. If it doesn't have the right amount of wrong, it's predictable. It doesn't surprise you, and that's what we want when we buy that ticket. We want to be surprised. Having the right amount of wrong is something a director has to constantly allow space for. Again, you have to trust that process. Let this thing go off its rails, you know. You may be looking at a scene that's overly crazy and doesn't seem to belong in your film, but if you let it go crazy, you just might find the two biggest laughs in your movie. I can actually talk about working with you, Tom, on *Antz*. You were a storyboard artist, and it was a nonstop stream of single-panel gags from you!

Ron: **Are there any other artists, in terms of fine artists or motion picture filmmakers, that you look to for inspiration?**

Tim: Thinking about my early days of exploring animation, I would say John Musker at Disney and Bill Kroyer, both graduated with literature degrees by the way.

We have three animation directors with literature degrees from a small liberal arts college. I first met John when he visited Northwestern. I showed him the animated short I had been working on, and surprisingly, he told me to come by Disney if I ever made it out to California. So, on Easter break of my senior year of college, I flew out to California. John gave me a tour of Disney and he was profoundly encouraging. It was amazing that a man of his accomplishment would take the time to show me around.

At the time, I thought I might go to CalArts for a master's degree. John even offered to write a letter of recommendation. I will always be thankful to John for taking a face in the crowd and giving them a few precious hours of his busy life. It was unbelievably motivating. But I'm constantly inspired by other artists and from other media, whether it's going to the symphony every Sunday, finding that new pop tune that's a three-minute gem of emotional release, or a painter working with Mars-1, a painter from San Francisco that I want to work with on developing animated films.

Lately, I've been intrigued by the world of vinyl design, toys made in vinyl. Some of these artists are doing the best character design I've ever seen. Reaching out to other artists and allowing yourself to be influenced, excited, and motivated by what's out there is one of the things that keeps you alive. It makes you wake up in the morning and keeps your game up.

Ron: **This was wonderful. Thanks, Tim.**

Tim: Cool. It's flattering to just chat about this stuff.

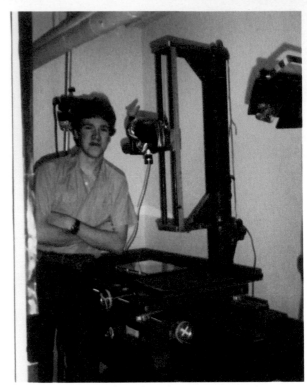

Tim Johnson. (Courtesy of Tim Johnson.)

12
Bill Plympton Interview

Bill Plympton.

Bill Plympton's breezy, casual nature belies the fact that he is one of the hardest-working artists in contemporary independent filmmaking. Almost a one-man studio, he draws, writes, and designs most of his films. Even feature-length ones. His films *Your Face*, *25 Ways to Quit Smoking*, *The Tune*, *Hair High*, *Idiots and Angels*, and *Cheatin'* have garnered him kudos worldwide. And he usually would be there to receive them. No matter where you are in the world, odds are if you attend an animation festival, Bill Plympton will be there. I got to know Bill well from encounters in LA, Annecy, New York, Majorca, Ottawa, London, and all points between. He does the festival circuit like a rock star. In a business populated in the main with reticent, behind-the-scenes types, Bill Plympton is indeed one of contemporary animation's more colorful characters. We got Bill to stand still for a moment to talk with us at the offices of Acme Filmworks in Hollywood.

Tom Sito

Ron Diamond: Let's talk about your inspirations. How did you get started? When did you first think that you wanted to make animation?

Bill: Like most people, I was a Disney freak. I grew up in Oregon, which is a pretty wet environment, so instead of going outdoors to play, I would stay in and amuse myself. I was drawing all the time. In fact, my mom remembers that even when I was in the crib, I was drawing on the wall. But it was entirely indecipherable. She would turn her head upside down just to figure it out. So, I always had a facility for drawing. I always loved drawing. When I saw my first cartoon on TV, I flipped out. I don't know what it was. It could have been Bugs Bunny or Daffy Duck or something, but I thought it was the funniest thing I had ever seen. That's when I knew that I wanted to do it, because the drawings really became magical. They talked, they sang, they moved, the color, the music: it was just a much richer experience than the little drawings I did on paper or comic strips. I was never much into comic strips. I liked comic books. But for me, animation was really the magical art form. And I remember the *Wonderful World of Disney* on Sunday. That was really my Bible. I remember when they would go behind the scenes and interview the animators. I said, "That's what I want to be. That's who I want to be, one of those guys! That's the coolest thing in the world!"

I remember going to Disneyland when I was about 12 years old. My aunt lived in Long Beach, so I went with her. And I think my folks gave me 20 bucks or something to go on the rides. This was a long time ago, so 20 bucks actually bought you a lot of rides. I stopped in the Disney shop and there was this book, *The Disney Story* by Bob Thomas—you probably have that book. And I said, "Oh my God, this is it! This is my Bible!" So I spent my 20 bucks on the book. My aunt said, "Are you crazy? Don't you want to do the Mad Hatter ride or the monorail?" I said, "No, I just want to get this animation book."

Clearly, at a very early age I was obsessed with animation; I always wanted to do it. But the problem was that I lived in the woods, so I had no real access to movie theaters, art studios, or art museums. The culture was very far away. So a lot of my early influences came from television, mostly movies on television. I think the first movie, first animated movie, that I saw on the big screen was *Sleeping Beauty*, which came out in 1959. That was the first time I'd seen an animated film on the big screen. It was really awesome. From that point on, I just knew that's what I wanted to do.

Tom: Some people get interested in animation and they just want to become a cog in the system. They just want to be a staff animator or a staff artist. But at what point did you think you could direct an animated film? And more importantly, make it by yourself?

Bill: That was around 1983. I had tried in college. I went to the School of Visual Arts for two semesters and they had an animation class. But they didn't really deal with how to make a film. They talked philosophy and this kind of stuff, so I left school and became an illustrator. At that point, we're talking the early seventies, animation was dead. There was no real way to get into it. I didn't know who to talk to. I didn't know how to get in the business. And, of course, in New York City there was very little animation going on. So, I worked as an illustrator. Then in 1983 a woman by the name of Connie D'Antuono, who had worked in the industry, showed me how to make a film. At this point, I was making this film called *Boomtown*, which was produced by Valeria Vasilevski and written by Jules Feiffer. They knew that I wanted to get into animation, to learn how to actually make an animated film. And so they brought me in. They paid me nothing. Seriously, I didn't get a dime. But I thought, "Wow, I finally get to make an animated film!" I was just so excited. Again, Connie D'Antuono was instru-

mental, and she was just someone I fortunately met by chance through an acquain-
tance. She ran me through the process, you
know, "These are your exposure sheets. This
is your field guide. Choose a field guide you
like. These are your acetate cells." That was
what I needed. I just needed to know the
technology of making a film. I had a lot of
story ideas, character designs, and jokes.
I just didn't know how to put them together.
As it turned out, *Boomtown* was kind of a
hit. After that, in '85, I went to Annecy and
started to interact with an entire group of
animators. Marv Newland, in particular, said,
"You know, you should do your own film."
I said, "Wow, that'd be great, you know,
make my own movie." After Annecy and
Boomtown, I finally had enough momentum where I was excited about being in the
business. That's when I did *Your Face*. Now
this wasn't really much of a film. There's no
real plot to it. There's only one shot. It's just
one character and a really bad song. But the

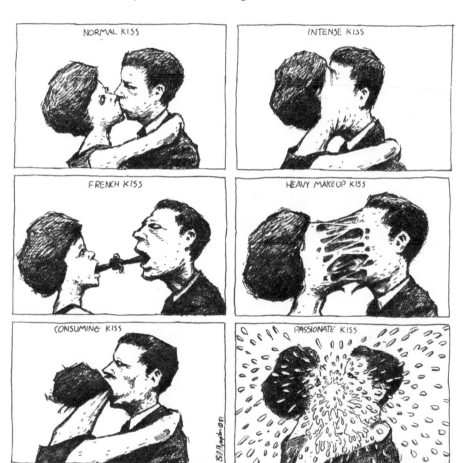

How to Kiss, 1988. (Courtesy of Bill Plympton.)

drawings are so strange, they're so compelling, that people liked it. I think it's a conflict between the surrealism of the imagery and the boringness of the song that gets people excited. That was the first time that I realized I could direct my own film. But there's another story I should probably tell you about.

At an ASIFA meeting, someone suggested that I enter *Your Face* into the competition. So I entered it. Some real heavyweights were there; Bob Blechman, Michael Sporn, Howard Beckerman, Candy Kugel, and John Canemaker were judging. I was pretty shy at the time too. When *Your Face* came on, I was hiding in the back row. I thought they were surely going to boot me out of the screening room. After about three seconds, people started laughing. I thought, "Holy shit, this is what I've waited my whole life for." Whenever I did comic strips, political cartoons, or illustrations, I could never hear anybody laugh. It all went out on print. Suddenly, I was in the room, listening to people laugh at my artwork. That was such an amazing experience. My whole body kind of glowed, you know. It was like nirvana. It was like the first time you have sex! Then people came up to me and said, "What's your name again, Bill Plympton? Wow! *Your Face*, we like *Your Face*." I was just so high. Even Howard Beckerman came over and talked to me. It was such a success that I called up all my print media the next day, every magazine and newspaper, and said, "I'm leaving print. I'm going into animation." They all laughed at me and said, "Are you nuts? Nobody makes money in animation. It's a dead-end job." But it didn't matter. I just thought I could make money doing these short films. And, sure enough, I did: *How to Kiss*, *25 Ways to Quit Smoking*, *One of Those Days*. Then MTV started buying them and I never looked back. I never did print again.

Tom: Who influenced you as an artist?

Bill: OK, first of all, there's Disney. Walt Disney and Preston Blair were the big influences early on. I got that Preston Blair book when I was 12 or 15. Again, that was my Bible. That was such an amazing book: the mouth positions, the running and the walking cycles, the emotions. That line of action was so important to me. In fact, I still use the line of action today. I think it's such an important concept. And I see a lot of student films that don't use the line of action. These people don't understand it. They don't get it. Uh, let's see: Tex Avery, of course, Bob Clampett, R. Crumb, Milton Glaser, Charles Addams.

Charles Addams was one of the first guys to make fun of death, pain, and evil. You have to realize that this was America in the thirties. The emerging media was very "innocent." And he was a popular cartoonist expressing a very dark sense of humor. That was a big influence on me. It's something that I still use today, a lot of death, pain, and injury. I find it very funny. Then there's Virgil Partch. There was a lot of sex in his stuff, so I liked Virgil Partch, otherwise known as VIP. Then I went through a Blechman phase. I ripped off Blechman a lot! Brad Holland was a big influence too. And in college I found a little Roland Topor book that blew my mind, since I love cross-hatching. Then there's David Levine, Jacques Tati,

Oscar Grillo, N. C. Wyeth, Thomas Hart Benton, Richard Lester's film, *Petulia* is one of my favorite movies. Of course, I can't forget Stanley Kubrick. *Dr. Strangelove* was a huge influence. And as I started to move in the world of animators, there were Marv Newland, Joanna Quinn, and Tomi Ungerer.

Tom: Is that it?

Bill: Oh, let's not forget Goya. Look at an ink drawing by Goya and you can see where Brad Holland got his style. Goya's work is just so powerful and raw. I try to use a lot of his stuff in my drawings. And certainly Quentin Tarantino and Frank Capra. I love Frank Capra. I don't know how he does it. Even his minor characters are so alive and vibrant. Then there's Carlos Nine and Peter de Sève. There's just too many! I can't think of everyone right now.

Ron: In the context of that amazing list, is there any particular film that profoundly moved you, something you just keep going back to?

Bill: For me, the early fifties' Disney stuff was really good. The people behind the scenes at that time were probably the catalyst that sent me down this path. Guys like Milt Kahl, Winsor McCay, A. B. Frost, Tex Avery, and Heinrich Kley. In terms of films, the *Song of the South* was the real highlight. It was so dynamic and full of character. I like the darker and edgy stuff. It's what prevented me from getting into Chuck Jones. I liked some of the Road Runner stuff. But it was all too cute for my tastes. Who was Bob Clampet's animator?

Tom: Rod Scribner.

Bill: Scribner. Yeah, Rod Scribner. The guy blew my mind! He was so good! Rod Scribner. Next!

Ron: Was there a particular short film that influenced you?

Bill: I remember when I was in college at Portland State University. I was getting involved in film then. I hadn't done animation, didn't know much about animation. All I knew was TV, you know: Bugs Bunny and Daffy Duck. But they had this animation program. I forget who put it together, but there was this film called *The Do-It-Yourself Cartoon Kit*. And I had never seen anything like it. I was used to Hollywood films, Warner Brothers, Fleischer Brothers, and Disney, of course. This thing comes on and it gets crazier and crazier and crazier. I said, "What the hell is this film?" Then I find out it's Bob Godfrey's independent film, and I had never heard of independent animation. It just blew my mind, the freedom, the craziness, and the surrealism. It showed me that I could make animated films without going to the big guys. And that's why it was a big influence on me. Every year when I'd see Bob Godfrey, I'd tell him this story and he'd laugh. He was one of my best friends. I love Bob Godfrey.

Tom: So what's your process like? When you have an idea for a film, do you just grab a pencil and start drawing? You are sort of unique in the industry, and approached more as an individual, since you don't have an army of people and producers under you.

Bill: OK, let's take, for example, *Idiots and Angels*, which is one of my recent feature films. I don't really know where that idea came from. I was at a festival in France, and this kid asked what my next project would be. I suppose it was just percolating somewhere in the back of my head, because it just came to me. Anyway, the idea is that this asshole guy wakes up one morning and he's got wings on his back. The kid says, "That could be fun." It then occurred to me that is was an interesting idea, the concept of a guy that wants to be bad, but the wings force him to be good. He's basically fighting for his soul. I was so inspired that night that I lay in bed sketching and outlining the possible details of the story. I didn't want to lose that instant passion. I didn't want to forget any ideas that came to me. I hear a lot of interviews with writers that become so obsessed with their novel that they forget to eat and sleep. It's this burning passion to get this thing down on paper, and that's how it was with *Idiots and Angels*.

Once I got the storyboard and the character design done, I was just a man on fire. I would get up at six in the morning and I would work it till eight or nine at night. I had no social life. I wasn't married, of course (Bill got married on December 23, 2011). I had no kids at the time, so that helped. But I was drawing night and day, trying to do 30 seconds of animation a day. I was obsessed with this film for a year. I'd become so involved with the characters, the story, and the art that I couldn't think of anything else. At that point, you have no choice but to push ahead until you fantasize this film on a big screen with everybody in the audience giving you a standing ovation. And then you are up there getting your Oscar, you know. After a year had passed,

Rough Animation, *Idiots and Angels*, 2008. (Courtesy of Bill Plympton.)

I finished it and just collapsed. I think I slept for a week. I didn't even go to work; I was just so burned out. Not all my films are like that. *Idiots and Angels* was peculiar in that regard. But it's that certain drive, that passion, to finish the film and to get these ideas down on paper that is very powerful. One of the reasons that I'm different from other studio people is that they have to go through a lot of meetings. They have to go through a lot of executive notes, background changes, and story changes. I don't have to deal with that. I'm my own producer, so whatever my decision is, I have to follow it! Well, there are changes. But they are my changes, and that makes it a lot easier to do.

Tom: **Where do your films come from? How do you come up with these ideas?**

Bill: Well, first of all, I live in New York, and that's such a cartoon city anyway. There are a lot of crazy characters there. I think you have to be a child. I think you have to be innocent. I think you have to be looking at life like you've never seen it before. And that's where a lot of my ideas come from. For example, with the first *Guard Dog* film, I was walking in a park and I saw this dog barking at a bird. I knew that dogs like to bark at birds, but I never realized why they do it. Why do dogs bark? And so, like a child, I instantly went inside the dog's brain to discover

Animation, *Idiots and Angels*, 2008. (Courtesy of Bill Plympton.)

Final Animation, *Idiots and Angels*, 2008. (Courtesy of Bill Plympton.)

the reason why dogs bark. And I made up this crazy theory that the dog was afraid that the bird would attack his master and he would lose his meal ticket, which is obviously absurd. I was so excited about the idea, I thought, "Yeah, that's got a lot of potential. All these little innocent flora and fauna in a park are ultimately dangerous attackers and killers." So I went home that night and started drawing the film. And it turned out to be a very successful film. I also carry a notebook around with me, so whenever I get an idea, I write it down immediately. Often, I'll think, "Oh that's a great idea. I'll remember that." Then five minutes later it's gone, and that's an idea that I could have made a million dollars with. Who knows? I think it's really important to carry around a notebook, and I also have lots of pens because I'm always afraid that one will go dry and I won't be able to write down the idea. I have my primary pen, my backup pen, and my third backup pen. I really do not want to miss the idea. The idea is so important to any successful film. I also like to lie in bed in the morning and just daydream. I think daydreaming is a very important talent to have. I remember when I was in school, I daydreamed a lot. Teachers would get mad at me and say, "Mr. Plympton, please pay attention." But I find that daydreaming, letting your mind take a walk, letting your mind wander and make up these fantasies, dramas, and stories, is crucial. I get a lot of ideas that way. You just have to explore your ideas and fantasies. You have to see where it goes.

Guard Dog, 2006. (Courtesy of Bill Plympton.)

Tom: I heard your film Cheatin' had an interesting origin.

Bill: The inspiration for *Cheatin'* was a love affair I had 15 years ago. It was all passion, and then it went very bad. Sometimes I wanted to strangle her, and other times I wanted to have sex with her. The mood reminded me of a dark Hollywood film noir. So, when I did *Cheatin'*, I made it look kinda thirties to fifties. Lots of shadows and cars and clothing looking 1950s.

Cheatin, 2013. (Courtesy of Bill Plympton.)

Cheatin, 2013. (Courtesy of Bill Plympton.)

Cheatin, 2013. (Courtesy of Bill Plympton.)

Tom: During the development of a story, how much do you allow it to deviate from the original concept? Do you just let it go, let the trajectory surprise you?

Bill: Going back to *Idiots and Angels*, there was a lot more action and adventure I envisioned in the original storyboard. Then I realized that this was a different kind of film. It was more about the drama of interior emotions. I threw away, I think, 40 pages of storyboard. I just threw it away. It wasn't working for me. And so I went back to that central premise, this idiot's internal conflict and how he relates to the wings. But there was some pretty cool stuff that we animated. At one point, I had him cut off the wings with a chainsaw. And when he went back to this bar to find his girlfriend, his entire chemistry changed and he started to trip out. It got really crazy. We created this psychedelic trip in which the bar filled up with water, his girlfriend started to drown, and he had to grow his wings back to save her. It was very surreal. After I screened it a few times, I just felt like it was too much. It had gone too far. That was about five minutes of animation that I cut out. Anyway, I think the answer to your question is that about 10 percent of the original storyboard is changed in the end. So, I guess I just stuck with my original, visual concept.

Tom: How about feedback and criticism? Who do you show your stuff to? Friends? I mean, this is a difficult thing for everyone, regardless of what they do.

Bill: It's always been the same actually. I'll show it to friends first. And these are close friends, people I trust, people who will be honest with me and say it's not funny or they don't understand. Then I'll show it to strangers. I do sneak previews. I'll show it at film festivals. I even hand out cards just like the big studios. And I'll often get up at the end and blatantly ask them what worked and what didn't work. Mostly, I want to know what didn't work, whether the characters were engaging or they simply need to be thrown out! If I spend two or three years on a feature and it lays a big goose egg on the screen, since I didn't test it, that's the worst feeling in the world. Even now I look at some of my films and find scenes that I wish I could change. But there's nothing you can do. It's stuck up there, and you're just going to cringe every time you see it! I really believe in testing. I want to make sure that it's the best film that I can make.

Tom: Have you ever had a joke you felt strongly about? That you worked hard on, but then when it was in front of an audience …

Bill: It dies? Of course. On *Guard Dog*, the premise was this dog in the park that sees every innocent animal as a potential threat to his master. So I envisioned this little snail, in the dog's eyes, holding a sanding machine that was sharpening the blades of grass. And the snail had the welding goggles on, the whole shot. As he's walking on the blades, he's leaves behind a trail of snail slime. Well, the dog imagines his master slipping on the slime and being impaled on the grass. I thought it was hilarious. That's gonna knock 'em dead. But no one in the audience liked it. To this day, I don't know why. So I had to cut it out. It was my favorite joke. But if the audience doesn't like it … The audience is God. The audience decides.

Tom: You've done both short and feature-length films. How do you know when an idea is feature-length material?

Bill: Oh boy, that's a tough one. I don't know. The dog films were just a one-note kind of issue, five-minute shorts. I just don't think the dog could carry a feature film. It's mostly humans that carry a feature film. There's more complexity, personality, and detail available. I mean, you can see a lot more with a human. They have all those great adult topics to talk about: sex, violence, love, romance, revenge, etc. That'll carry a feature film. My short films are mostly about jokes, about humor. And they do very well because they're humorous, whereas the features contain more serious topics. I've honestly never thought about it much before. But I guess that would be the criteria. My feature ideas have more serious subject matter.

Tom: How do you work with your editor? In some cases, the relationship between directors and editors is very close. Some editors do their own cuts and have a lot of input on the film.

Bill: Well, I show him the storyboards, and that's essentially his first cut. It's all about the storyboards. After working on it and testing it, if some parts don't work, or if I have another idea, I will redraw it or suggest he recut it. If that fails, then there are still problems with the story, and I'll send him off to recut everything. My editor is much better at tempo than I am. I'm trying to learn, but tempo is such an important part of filmmaking, especially animation. The editor, I think, understands timing, understands pauses, and when to speed it up and when to slow it down. That, I think, is my editor's contribution.

Tom: How do you approach the soundtrack? Do you go through the track first, or do you think about it after?

Bill: My working operations are a lot different than big studios'. For me, it's the storyboard. The storyboard is the primal source of the film. If I get a good storyboard, I know it's going to be a great film. It obviously has no dialogue. But everything is there: your story, your character design, the camera angles, the lighting and backgrounds, the emotions. I don't deal with scripts. I tried to write a script once. Nobody liked it. The dialogue probably sucked. I don't know. So, for me it's the storyboard. That's the magic. After the storyboard is done, then I'll bring in the sound, the music and the dialogue. I find that telling stories visually is more powerful than telling stories with dialogue. After all, we're humans. There was a time when we had no language. Think about it, a life without language. It must have been a very primal experience to tell a story without words. Besides, focusing on the visual also makes it easier to translate all over the world.

Storyboards, *Mutant Aliens*, 2001. (Courtesy of Bill Plympton.)

Storyboards, *Mutant Aliens*, 2001. (Courtesy of Bill Plympton.)

Tom: What other creative artists do you collaborate with on your films?

Bill: Musicians, mostly. The musicians are a very important part. I have two musicians that I work with now. Nicole Renaud, who is a French chanteuse living in New York. She does all the very romantic, very mystical kind of stuff. Then I have Corey Jackson, who actually lives out here in LA. He does more of the John Williams orchestral, heavy stuff. The deeper, darker stuff.

Then of course there's my producer, like Biljana Labovic, who worked on several productions. She worked in the studio with me every day. And she is a genius at the technology side of it. She's a genius at design, coloring, and art. Any time I had a problem, I'd go to Biljana Labovic. She's from Serbia. She studied graphic design in school and has made a bunch of films. So she really understands the process. She was also good at updating and working with new technology. She's very good. I'm still old school. I just do pencil on paper. I rub 'em. I do the details. I create a whole stack of drawings. Then I'd put it on Biljana's desk and she made sure that the film got made. Yeah, I'm lucky.

Tom: **What would your ideal contract be? Unlimited money? Unlimited resources? And what would you do with it?**

Bill: That's a great question. I have a bunch of those! I'd like to make a *Fantasia* with Beatles music. I think it would be great. Now, I wouldn't do every sequence. I'd do maybe one or two sequences. Then I would love to use different famous animators with different Beatles songs for the rest. As you know, the rights to the music are so expensive. And some of the music you can't get anyway, but I think that would be a fantastic project. I know a couple of people have tried it. For some reason, it hit a stone wall. It'd be such a big, big, big, popular film.

Ron: **Could you ever imagine working at a big studio: Disney, DreamWorks, Pixar, Sony, places like that?**

Bill: Well, it's funny you should ask this, because at your dinner the other night I was sitting next to *********** and they were telling me these horror stories. They were saying, "Oh God, Bill. You're so lucky! You don't have to deal with studio politics." And then they started talking about how they're having trouble getting their next project off the ground. I said, "You just did *******. You can't get another project off the ground? Are you kidding me?" It's a world that I'm not aware of. I really don't understand it. I am very jealous of their success. They show in 3000 cinemas across the U.S. I'm lucky to get in 50. So, I would like to, at some point, change from a cult status to something a bit higher in terms of budgets, distribution, and marketing costs. I would be interested.

If a studio called me and wanted me to direct a film, I would be very excited. I'd be very interested. I think I could do a good job. I've made seven animated feature films. I think I know how it works. And I understand that you have to make changes at the whim of the executives. I know that there are a lot of meetings and story sessions; it's a lot of drudgery. Still, I'd be willing to make that sacrifice to have one of my films reach such a large audience. In fact, it might be better, since I'm not completely happy with some of my storytelling. I know it needs work. I know my films aren't perfect. And I think it would be nice to have somebody that's really professional, really slick, someone who can bring in a truly talented team to work with me on a feature. At the end of the day, I still love animation. So I'd like to see what I could do with a bigger budget. The budget for *Idiots and Angels* is about 125,000 dollars. Theoretically, I could make 1000 of those films with the budget of just one Pixar film.

Tom: You've worked with a lot of mature and adult themes, topics that have become more commonplace these days. Do you ever worry about staying current?

Bill: Yes, certainly. I've always worried about someone surpassing me. And many people do surpass me. That's the nature of the business. But, honestly, I'm still one of the few out there fighting to make adult animation a popular art form. It's very difficult to change the entire mind-set of the industry, let alone convince the population of the States that animation isn't just for children. Maybe you'll get an occasional Japanese film in here, or a French film, or something like that. It might even make 10 million. But it's still not a big popular hit. And I think the world, the U.S. especially, is waiting for an adult film, a Quentin Tarantino film, but in animation! I mean, that's all it is. It's just a Quentin Tarantino film, but with cartoons. And for some reason, this country feels that cartoons are sacred, since they are only for children. You can't have sex or violence in them! In that respect, I am the avant-garde. I'm not behind the times. But in terms of technology, I'm definitely behind the times. Like I said, I'm very old school. I don't think I ever will go digital. It's too slow. It's too expensive. The budgets for a CG (computer-generated) film are so high. You have to hire so many computer operators, all that machinery, software, and hardware. It's just way beyond my budget. If I want to remain independent, I'll probably never do a CG film.

Tom: Some believe that the problem directors at the big studios have is that Hollywood is addicted to making tentpole blockbusters. Walt Disney can make a movie like *Pocahontas* and be disappointed with its 175 million gross. But a *Slumdog Millionaire* can make 35 million and be considered a gigantic hit. Do you think there's room in animation for pictures that aren't monster hits?

Bill: Well, that's what I'm trying to do! I go to Sundance almost every year that I have a feature, or maybe Slamdance. I do the deal, but very rarely do I get picked up. I think the only film that was ever picked up for major distribution was *I Married a Strange Person*. That was with Lionsgate. And they did a pretty decent job. I don't think they made 35 million. They may have made a couple of million. But that's the market that I'm going for. I'm definitely not mass market. It's a niche market. I know there are people out there that come to my screenings. They're packed! So I know there's an audience for the kind of film I make. I just don't have the distribution setup that you find at the big studios. What we need in this country is a national distributor that's set up strictly for animated films, independent animated films. I think there's a market for it. *Sita Sings the Blues* and *Book of Kells* are good examples of great films that never got major distribution.

Tom: To make *Cheatin'*, you launched a Kickstarter campaign.

Bill: It helped complete it. *Cheatin'* was more expensive that some of my earlier movies. We did the film in a digital watercolor technique in Photoshop. I drew the film myself, all 40,000 pencil drawings. The technique gave it a color-etching feel that harkened back to the kind of illustrations I used to do in the 1970s. But to render these drawings in this technique, I needed to bring in an additional ten artists to help me. Four months before the end of production, we ran out of money from our original production's budget. So we went to Kickstarter to raise the 80,000 dollars to finish the project. We got 100,000 dollars. Adam Rackoff handled the campaign, and he did a wonderful job. It seems like Kickstarter is the wave of the future. Not having to get turned down by the same Hollywood execs. My fans who believe in me supported the film. It is a very liberating feeling.

Tom: You may not be with a major studio, but you're still responsible for a lot of executive producing work on your own films. You take meetings. You go to festivals. You work on distribution deals. How do you divide your time between that and actual artistic creation, drawing out the next idea?

Bill: That's a tough one. For most animators, myself included, your love is in the drawing and in the making of a film. But you do have to sell it. The same goes for live action. No matter how much you love the process, there's that unavoidable and very difficult business aspect. It's amusing how many people think, "Wow! Let's just make a film and we'll get rich!" There are basically three parts to making a film. One is getting the money to make the film. And that kills a lot of ideas right there; it kills a lot of projects. Two, you're making the film. That's the fun part; everybody wants to be involved in that. And finally, there's selling the film and getting your money back! Getting the money from the film when it's done is the hardest part. Like I said, I have to go to a lot of festivals. I have to aggressively meet distributors, aggressively promote, aggressively do press. Which I don't mind. I like doing press, actually. And I like going to festivals. Festivals are a lot of fun. I always enjoy myself. I just don't think people realize how much footwork is involved in making a movie profitable. It's not winning the lottery. You're not instantly rich just because you made a movie.

Tom: And in the last few years you are now married with a family.

Bill: Yeah, I need to carve out three hours a day to be a daddy for my son, Lucas.

Tom: As a director, what do you think is your greatest strength?

Bill: I think I know how to tell a joke. I know how to make people laugh with my drawings. And I think I'm a fairly good artist. I'm not the best. Guys like Joanna Quinn, Alexander Petrov, and Glen Keane are probably better draftsmen than me. But I'm good.

Tom: How about the development of that skill set? Are you satisfied with how you've progressed as an artist?

Bill: No. I try to get funnier. I'm trying to improve my humor, and certainly to improve my draftsmanship. In fact, I go to life-drawing lessons. And I still draw in front of the TV. If I see something interesting on television, I do drawings. And my style is still evolving. In *Cheatin'*, I'm sort of stretching the look. It's more exaggerated. It's a lot more stylized. So, I always want to evolve. But you have to work at it.

Tom: How do you deal with creative gridlock? You know, the animator's version of writer's block.

Bill: Sorry, but I never get it. My biggest problem is that I have too many ideas! I just don't have time to work on all of them. Sometimes I do get stuck on a joke. But eventually, I will come up with a solution for a gag. The cow film is a good example. I had a different ending for that film. But after I showed it to my class—I'm teaching an animation class—I had to go back and rework it. They didn't like the ending. It's just a matter of trying different variations, of looking at all the possible directions it could go. These are essentially the same problems I had when I did comic strips.

Tom: Do you have to come up with ways to pace yourself as you're going through the process? Do you wake up and say, "I need to do 30 seconds today!"—something like that?

Bill: Yeah, I like to set goals. But they usually pertain to the storyboard. You're looking at six panels per page on a storyboard, and each panel is basically a shot. Sometimes three panels are a shot. But mostly each panel is a different, and each shot is maybe three seconds. I'd like to do a page per day, about 20 seconds. Sometimes I can. Sometimes I can't. It depends on how busy I am with other projects. And I don't have a set time frame in which I feel like I have to finish a movie. There's no release date set. When it's done, it's done. But self-motivation is a good thing. I'll even get up at six in the morning and start drawing.

Tom: Do you ever have to force yourself to get moving? Or is there a certain trick that you use?

Bill: I don't know how to work a computer. So there's no Facebook, let alone e-mail. Actually, when the animation is done, and I have to start the shadowing, texture, and the highlights, that I can do in front of the TV. I find that very relaxing. On a Saturday or a Sunday, with no phone calls or schedule, I just sit down and watch some old movies on TMC (Turner Classic Movies) or a video. I can get a lot of work done like that. I don't really have a hard time getting motivated.

Tom: So what's your favorite part of the job?

Bill: I have three favorite parts. One is the storyboard, which is basically taking the idea and visualizing it. Number two is the animation. I just love making these drawings, making these people come alive. That's so much fun. And then number three is the music. The music adds a whole other dimension to a scene or sequence. It can really bring it to life. And the music is such a magical part of movies. All the great animated films seem to have that perfect music: *Yellow Submarine*, *Fantasia*.

Tom: Quite a few directors have said that their favorite part is the mixing session. You have everything together, and now it's going from individual ingredients to a ...

Bill: ... a stew. The flavors get blended together. Yeah, that's not for me.

Tom: Really?

Bill: Well, I like the mixing session. But it's the drawing, the storyboarding, and the music that excite me. I also like character design. That's fun.

Tom: On that note, what's like your least favorite part of the job?

Bill: The contracts. The business side. That's a nightmare. I find it funny, though, cause my dad's a banker. He's a businessman. You think I would've picked up something from that, but no. I'm terrible with contracts. My eyes just suddenly go shut when I read a contract!

Ron: As we've already mentioned, your shorts and your feature films have serious themes: sex, violence, and dark humor.

Bill: In my master class show, I do a demonstration of this Marilyn Monroe poster I did back in high school. A buddy of mine, Mike McCullaugh, was running for student body president. So he says, "Oh Bill, I know you're an artist. Why don't you do a poster for my campaign?" So I did this very sexy drawing of Marilyn Monroe with a bikini on. It said, "Vote for MM!" And then on the bottom, "No, not Marilyn Monroe, Mike McCullaugh!" The next day I heard over the intercom, "Will Bill Plympton, the pornographer, please come to the principal's office!?" I thought, "Oh my God, my life is over. I'm going to get kicked out of school. I'll never go to college. I'll be a bum on the streets." When I came back from the principal's office, everybody in the class said, "There's Bill Plympton, the radical provocateur!" I was the "maverick artist!" So I suddenly had this status. I was the guy breaking barriers and boundaries. And I think that's what I'm doing now. I want to make films that make people think differently, that make people see life in a different way. And if I did a kids' film, I'd just be like, "Oh you know, look at this. Isn't this cute?" I want to create humor through crazy and wild ideas. It's like Quentin Tarantino. He's really my hero. That's the kind of stuff I want to do in animation. I think there's a market for it.

Vote for MM, 1964. (Courtesy of Bill Plympton.)

Ron: But do you think you could ever make something strictly for kids?

Bill: I've done children's stuff. *Fan and the Flower* was very good for children. I've done this before. You just don't use sex. And the violence would be more of the innocent type. I know how to tone it down. *Gary Guitar* and *Guard Dog* don't have any brutal sex or violence. I could certainly do it. Honestly, I don't understand why people spend all this time making films about children when they're adults. I don't think about bouncing the ball or having a make-believe tea party. That's not my mind-set. My mind-set is geared toward adult themes: love, jealousy, hatred, etc.

Tom: Have you ever felt overwhelmed by the sheer number of decisions you have to make as a director? How do you deal with the burden of decision making?

Bill: There are a lot of decisions. And a lot of them for me are not artistic decisions, they're business decisions. And that's the real crisis. Whether to go Blu-ray or not is a good example. Blu-ray is really expensive, and I don't know if I can afford it. It's like 3000 to 4000 dollars. Do I get a famous band to play or a less popular band? Those kinds of business decisions are very difficult, and they burn my brain out. I really don't like it. But that's part of the responsibility. If you're going to be an independent filmmaker, you have to make these decisions. And hopefully you get better and better at making them. But that's not always the case.

Tom: You've used celebrity voices in the past. What are the pros and cons of using big Hollywood names?

Bill: Well, I've been very lucky. I used Paul Giamatti and Matthew Modine. Those are the only two guys I've ever been associated with. And they were great! Oh, I'm sorry! No, no, no. *Hair High* had …

Tom: *Hair High* had a ton of people!

Bill: I know: David Carradine, Keith Carradine, Sarah Silverman. We had some good voices for that.

Tom: Craig Bierko …

Bill: Yeah, Craig Bierko. But that wasn't my doing, though. That was Martha Plimpton, a distant relative of mine. She wanted to get involved as a producer for *Hair High*. So, she called up all her friends and got 'em to do voices. It was great! It was expensive, though. It wasn't cheap. But it was exciting working with big name voices. They were very professional. But they didn't really help in selling the film. I thought they would. I thought, "Wow, David Carradine and Sarah Silverman would really add marquee value to the film." I don't know why. In the end it just didn't help.

Hair High, 2003. (Courtesy of Bill Plympton.)

Tom: Is there any difference in the quality of performance at all?

Bill: Certainly! Professional actors are *so* much better than amateur actors. Paul Giamatti was brilliant. Matthew Modine was great. David Carradine was phenomenal! Can I tell a funny story about David Carradine? He's gone now, but I think it's OK.

Tom: Yeah, go ahead.

Bill: We were shooting at this studio in Hollywood and I didn't have a big budget. I think each actor got a thousand or two for one hour's work. They did it mostly as a favor for Martha Plimpton. So anyway, they were all lined up for one-hour segments. David comes in!

Now I'm a big fan of David Carradine, as well as Keith and his father. John Carradine is one of my heroes. So, after he comes in, I give him the contracts to sign. As he's sitting down, he suddenly falls over on his head, almost hits the table as he falls to the floor. Of course, I help him get up and get him back into the chair. David then says, "Well, I need to use the bathroom." After 20 minutes, I'm starting to get worried. The clock is ticking away. We're running out of time. So I said, "David, we need you pretty soon. Can you come out here?" He comes out and gets behind the chair with his script. He then starts to light up a cigarette. The engineer freaks out and yells, "Whoa, whoa, whoa! You can't do that! The fire marshal will shut down our studio!" They hastily escort him outside so he can smoke his cigarette. Now we're down to like … like ten minutes left. The next guy is already in there, ready to go. And David's telling me these stories about John Ford and John Wayne. At this point, I carefully say, "Yeah, those are neat, David. Can we get back in and finish up your lines?" So he comes in with about four minutes left. He nails it! It's the best reading all day! He is so good. He was so professional. I don't know what he was doing with the falling down or the bathroom stuff. Whatever it was … it worked. He actually left a minute early.

Tom: **What's the most insane, bizarre, or absurd moment that you've had as a director?**

Bill: Oh God … I remember once I was at a screening in Seattle. They were showing *Hair High*. I don't know if you've ever been to Film Forum in Seattle. It's a great cinema. But anyway, they were showing it, and I was sitting outside talking to one of the ticket takers. Suddenly, people start running out of the cinema. And there's screaming. I thought, "Geez! I didn't know the film was that powerful!"

Tom: **What happened?**

Bill: Oh it gets better. I finally ask, "What the hell? What's going on in there?" Finally someone said, "Well some guy stood up, unzipped his pants, urinating all over the seats and the audience."

Tom: **What the f…?**

Bill: I know! Apparently he was drunk. They escorted him out and had to clean up the mess. I think maybe four people came back in to watch the film. I should've asked him why he didn't use the bathroom. It was right there. That's the most surreal moment, I think, of my film career. Wait, what about the transvestite sequence? Did you hear about that Ron?

Ron: **No, please tell.**

Bill: Oh, this was a live-action film I was making called *J. Lyle*, and this is why I don't do live-action anymore. Anyway, we're shooting on the streets of New York, a little west of 12th Street, on a beautiful Sunday morning. We had a crew of about ten people, very small. Out of nowhere, this naked transvestite, with the exception of a see-through blouse and a pair of spiked heels, comes up to us. He says, "You're shooting on my turf! You shouldn't be here! You're ruining my business! Get out of here! Go away!"

He then tips over the craft services table, starts throwing donuts and coffee at the actors, and then jumps into the van and pulls out a pair of long scissors. As he's lunging at the actors, I'm completely freaking out. So I grab a big C-stand and lunge at the guy, who is definitely cracked out. I miss him and he swirls around and pokes me in the elbow with the scissors.

Ron: **I can't believe I've never heard this story.**

Bill: So it's a transvestite and me "sword fighting" on the streets of New York! Finally, the paramedics and the cops show up and they wrestle the guy to the ground. And I think he even stabbed one of the cops in the knee. As the paramedics are trying to take me to the hospital, I say, "I can't! I'm trying to make a film here. We're on a tight schedule to finish this thing!" So they all left. Then I realized that you don't have these kinds of episodes when you're making animation. You don't have naked transvestites trying to stab you. That's why I went back to animation.

Tom: **Do you ever see yourself working on somebody else's project? Maybe even a remake of something you liked?**

Bill: I would love to do it! There are so many people that are doing great stuff out there. I would love to do character design for someone. Seriously, I don't know why nobody has asked me to do character design or story jokes. I would love to do that, if the price is right, of course. I'm a whore. I'm a real whore for animation.

Ron: **Was there a recent movie that you would have just loved to work on?**

Bill: Well, I remember seeing the animation in *Kill Bill*. It would have been cool if Quentin called me to do that. It was brilliant. Don't get me wrong. But I would have loved to do that. Other than that, I can't think of anything else at the moment.

Tom: **So what's next for you? If you can't be specific about the project, just discuss what new or creative challenge you'd like to try.**

Bill: I've done three couch gags for *The Simpson's* TV show intro, a section of the film *The Prophet* based on Khalil Gibran that Selma Hayek is producing, and something called *The ABCs of Death*. I'm starting a new feature written by Jim Lujan about the underbelly of Los Angeles in Los Angeles. It's a pretty raw story. This film will be more flash oriented with manipulation of characters arms and legs.

I'm pretty happy with the way my life is going right now. I do one or two shorts a year, and then a feature every two or three years. I see myself working until 90 at that pace. I'm certainly not going to be rich. I'm not going to be a rock star animator guy. But it's a nice life. You get to travel, go to a lot of screenings, and see a lot of people and places. I'm happy. And I've been fortunate enough to retain ownership of my films. Over the years, things get more valuable, so it's an income provider. I'm able to make more films. I don't really have any more goals. I like my life. I would certainly love to get an Oscar nomination for one of my features. That would be nice. But my films are too cheap. They're too raw. They're not Oscar-type films. There's too much sex and violence. But a few nominations would be really nice. I'm a simple man with simple needs.

Tom: You've been successful in an endeavor most of the animation industry finds challenging: making successful shorts. A number of studios have tried, but they flounder. Why do you think you've succeeded while the others haven't?

Bill: I have this thing called Plympton's dogma. It's my formula for success in short films. And I love short films. I think short films are a great medium. I know a lot of people in Hollywood look at short films as a ticket to a three-picture deal. But I look at them as an end in and of themselves. It's just a great art from. So I've worked out this formula called Plympton's dogma. Rule number one: Make the film short. And when I mean short, I mean five minutes or less. If you want to make a 10-minute film, or a 15-minute film, or even a 20-minute film, go ahead. But no one's going to buy it. No one's going to put it on television or DVD compilations, cause it's too long! Number two: Make it cheap, like a thousand dollars per minute. It's pretty easy to make that money back. I remember talking to Chris Wedge at some gathering after he had just finished *Bunny*. He was complaining how impossible it is to make money on shorts. I said,

Bill Plympton, Master Class.

"Chris, how much money did you spend on *Bunny*? A million bucks?" He said, "Yeah, something like a million." Well of course no one can make money on a short with that kind of overhead. Finally, number three: Make it funny. If it's a funny film, everybody's going to show it: television, theaters, DVD collections, the Internet. It's automatically going to be a popular film. Look a Don Hertzfeldt. He just draws stick figures and he's the perfect Plympton's dogma animator. It's short, cheap, and funny.

Ron: What advice would you offer someone who wants to be a director, someone who's maybe made some short films?

Bill: I think the Shane Acker model is a really good one. He did a short film called 9, and it got nominated for an Oscar. That guaranteed that he would have an opportunity to make a feature film. If you have a good short film, that's a wonderful calling card. That's all you need, even if it's just two minutes. So that's what I would recommend, just make a short little clip. Show people what you can do. But make it a complete story. It needs to have a beginning, middle, and end.

Ron: You may not think of yourself as a superstar, but you can fill an auditorium with thousands of people.

Bill: It still shocks me, that time Tom took me to that Disney party in San Diego. People said, "Oh my God! There's Bill Plympton!" Wait. Ron, didn't you want to ask me why I make films?

Ron: I don't think so. But go ahead. Why do you make films, Bill?

Bill: That's right. Tom and I were talking about this before you got here. And I think it's one of the most important questions that should be asked. But no one ever asks me that question. Because a lot of filmmakers out there make films for so many different reasons, I guess it's avoided. Some want to get rich. Some want to be a rock star. Maybe some have personal, psychological problems to get out of their system. It's a very important question.

Ron: Uh, let's hear it!

Bill: Why didn't you ask!

Ron: OK, let me ask again. Why do you make films?

Bill: For me, it's the glory. The real emotional payback is sitting in an audience and hearing people laugh. And there's something refreshing and healthy about that. It just feels like I'm an important part of their life, the audience's life. At a cocktail party, I can't tell jokes. I can't make people laugh. But I know in a dark room, on a movie screen, I can make people laugh. And to me, that is the most fulfilling thing. Certainly, it's nice to win prizes. It's nice to make money and pay my bills. But that's not why I make films. It's to hear the audience laugh. I think that's the ultimate reward. In fact, it's almost as important as sex. That would be the perfect evening for me, having sex in a movie theater where everybody's laughing at my film!

Ron: You know, I think we should leave it right there, "Oh my God! It's Bill Plympton!"

Bill: Yeah, yeah, that's me. Wild Bill Plympton, the provocateur.

Bill Plympton, Artist.

INDEX